UNDERSTANDING INEQUALITY, POVERTY AND WEALTH

Also available in the series

Understanding global social policy
Nicola Yeates, The Open University

"Nicola Yeates has brought together an impressive, coherent collection of contributors providing comprehensive coverage of developments in global social policy across a wide range of policy areas. The relationship between globalisation and social policy is one that is rapidly evolving and differentiated. This collection successfully captures these dynamics whilst at the same time providing empirical substance to developments at a particular point in time."
Patricia Kennett, Department of Applied Social Sciences, The Hong Kong Polytechnic University
PB £19.99 (US$32.50) ISBN 978-1-86134-943-9
HB £60.00 (US$80.00) ISBN 978-1-86134-944-6
240 x 172mm 352 pages June 2008

Understanding immigration and refugee policy
Contradictions and continuities
Rosemary Sales, Middlesex University

"This book provides a much needed overview to the key concepts and issues in global migration and the development of immigration and asylum policy. The book is thought provoking and deserves to be read widely."
Alice Bloch, City University London
PB £19.99 (US$34.95) ISBN 978-1-86134-451-9
HB £60.00 (US$80.00) ISBN 978-1-86134-452-6
240 x 172mm 296 pages June 2007

Understanding health policy
Rob Baggott, De Montfort University

"This book by a leading commentator on health policy breaks new ground in understanding how health policy is made and implemented."
Martin Powell, University of Birmingham
PB £18.99 (US$34.95) ISBN 978-1-86134-630-8
HB £60.00 (US$80.00) ISBN 978-1-86134-631-5
240 x 172mm 292 pages June 2007

Understanding health and social care
Jon Glasby, University of Birmingham

"This is an ambitious and wide ranging book which provides a valuable historical perspective, as well as a forward looking analysis, based on real experience. It will be a valuable tool for leaders, policy makers and students." **Nigel Edwards, Policy Director, The NHS Confederation.**
PB £18.99 (US$34.95) ISBN 978-1-86134-910-1
HB £60.00 (US$80.00) ISBN 978-1-86134-911-8
240 x 172mm 216 pages June 2007

Understanding the mixed economy of welfare
Martin Powell, University of Birmingham

"This book provides an up-to-date account of welfare pluralism that is both accessible to students and likely to revitalise an important debate within Social Policy. A must-read for academics and students alike."
Kirk Mann, University of Leeds
PB £22.99 (US$39.95) ISBN 978-1-86134-759-6
HB £60.00 (US$80.00) ISBN 978-1-86134-760-2
240 x 172mm 272 pages February 2007

For a full listing of all titles in the series visit www.policypress.org.uk

www.policypress.org.uk

INSPECTION COPIES AND ORDERS AVAILABLE FROM:
Marston Book Services • PO Box 269 • Abingdon • Oxon OX14 4YN UK
INSPECTION COPIES
Tel: +44 (0) 1235 465500 • Fax: +44 (0) 1235 465556 • Email: inspections@marston.co.uk
ORDERS
Tel: +44 (0) 1235 465500 • Fax: +44 (0) 1235 465556 • Email: direct.orders@marston.co.uk

UNDERSTANDING INEQUALITY, POVERTY AND WEALTH

Policies and prospects

Edited by Tess Ridge and Sharon Wright

First published in Great Britain in 2008 by

The Policy Press
University of Bristol
Fourth Floor, Beacon House
Queen's Road
Bristol BS8 1QU
UK

Tel +44 (0)117 331 4054
Fax +44 (0)117 331 4093
e-mail tpp-info@bristol.ac.uk
www.policypress.org.uk

British Library Cataloguing in Publication Data
A catalogue record for this book is available from the British Library

Library of Congress Cataloging-in-Publication Data
A catalog record for this book has been requested

ISBN 978 1 86134 914 9   paperback
ISBN 978 1 86134 915 6 hardcover

The right of Tess Ridge and Sharon Wright to be identified as editors of this work has been asserted by them in accordance with the 1988 Copyright, Designs and Patents Act.

The statements and opinions contained within this publication are solely those of the editors and contributors and not of The University of Bristol, The Policy Press or the Social Policy Association. The University of Bristol, The Policy Press and the Social Policy Association disclaim responsibility for any injury to persons or property resulting from any material published in this publication.

The Policy Press works to counter discrimination on grounds of gender, race, disability, age and sexuality.

Cover design by Qube Design Associates, Bristol.
Front cover: photograph kindly supplied by www.gettyimages.com
Printed and bound in Great Britain by Hobbs the Printers, Southampton.

Contents

Detailed contents

List of tables, figures and boxes

Tables

Figures

Boxes

Acknowledgements

We are grateful to everyone who helped with the production of this book. In particular, we would like to thank: Angus Erskine, for inspirational early discussions; the anonymous reviewers, for careful and helpful comments; the team at The Policy Press, who have been a delight to work with; and last, but certainly not least, Ember and Kris, for their love and support.

Glossary

Actuary A person who uses research and statistics to calculate risks and premiums for insurance companies, for example, the life expectancy of different groups of people.

After housing costs (AHC) The amount of household income available once the actual costs of housing, such as rent, have been taken out.

Annuities A fixed sum paid to a person, often for the rest of their life.

Asset wealthy Estimated using the relationship between housing wealth and the contemporary Inheritance Tax threshold, ie, households that would be liable for inheritance tax if all adult memebers were to die today.

Before housing costs (BHC) The amount of household income available before taking account of the cost of housing, such as rent.

Budget standards What is needed in terms of food, services and activities in order to achieve a certain standard of living and how much this costs in a given place at a given time, for example, how much would it cost in Britain in 2008 to have access to a certain amount of food, services and activities.

Centre for the Analysis of Social Exclusion (CASE) An academic research centre funded by the Economic and Social Research Council (ESRC) and based at the London School of Economics and Political Science (LSE) from 1997 until 2007, which carried out a wide range of empirical research on social exclusion.

Child Poverty Action Group (CPAG) A national voluntary organisation formed in the 1960s, which campaigns on the issue of child poverty. It also provides extensive advice and guidance on rights to welfare benefits and tax credits.

Core poor People who are simultaneously income poor, materially deprived and subjectively poor.

Cycle of deprivation The controversial idea that poverty and deprivation experienced by parents may be 'passed on' to their children who are therefore more likely themselves to experience poverty as adults.

Decile Any of the 10 equal-sized groups into which a given population has been divided; *see* quintile.

Deprivation The lack of material benefits, that is, goods and services, which are considered to be necessities.

Diversity and difference An emerging term used when studying minority ethnic experiences; it signals the importance of recognising contrasting and perhaps contradictory outcomes for different minority ethnic groups in the UK.

Ethnic penalty The disadvantage minority ethnic groups experience in the labour market in comparison to their white counterparts.

Exclusively wealthy People with sufficient wealth to exclude themselves from the norms of society. A subset of those who are asset wealthy. Those able to access private health and education and to have multiple foreign holidays a year; those able and showing evidence of also purchasing new luxury cars outright. Defined more precisely at the monetary wealth threshold where such behaviour becomes normal.

Gender pay gap The difference in hourly earnings between men and women.

Gini coefficient A statistic, ranging from 0–1.00, that indicates the degree of income inequality in a society or social group; higher values indicate greater inequality.

Globalists There are two main uses of this term. The first refers to entities (for example, governments, corporations) and individuals who use the increase in trade links and other opportunities linked with capitalism to increase their profits. A much wider use of the term refers to those who adopt a global perspective on social questions.

Global social policy This field of studies focuses on the impacts of diverse 'globalisation' processes on social policy and social development and vice versa. It particularly privileges the global and transnational dimensions of social policy formation and provision.

Households below average income (HBAI) UK government statistics produced annually on the numbers and percentage of the population with incomes below certain proportions of average incomes.

Inequality Differences in the distribution of resources or outcomes, for example, in income among the population.

Inequity A lack of justice or fairness.

Internationalists A global movement of people who want to improve the connections between countries and people for the benefit of all.

Lifecourse The totality of the transitions occurring during an individual's whole life, in terms of employment, partnering, parenthood, informal caring, health and illness.

Limiting long-term illness (LLTI) Includes any chronic illness, health condition or disability that limits daily activities or work.

Mean The average of a set of numbers.

Median The middle value in a set of numbers, for example, if five workers were earning respectively £100, £200, £400, £800 and £1,500 per week, the median would be £400 (whereas the mean is £600).

Mis-selling To sell something to a customer based on misleading or false information.

Morbidity Illness or disease (whereas mortality refers to death).

Othering A way of defining one's own identity by stigmatising somebody else, that is, 'the other'.

Pensions A regular payment received by people above retirement age as well as by some disabled people and widows. Most workers contribute to a state pension and some also to an occupational pension operated by their employer or to a personal pension, arranged individually.

Pensions privatisation This refers to the policy of promoting private pensions while reducing the role of state pensions.

Percentile Percentiles are used in a similar manner to quintiles and deciles, that is, they divide a population into groups of equal size according to a variable, such as their salary.

Poverty rate This refers to the proportion of a particular population living in poverty.

Poverty and Social Exclusion (PSE) Survey A major survey carried out by researchers based at the University of Bristol at the end of the 1990s to develop a measure of poverty and social exclusion based on indicators of deprivation which a majority of respondents identified as essential. This measure is now widely used in research in the UK and in other European countries.

Psychosocial The interaction of psychological factors with the social environment.

Purchasing power parity (PPP) This concept is used to indicate how much different currencies will buy, using a standard set of goods and services. For example, the PPP compares the number of pounds the goods and services would cost in the UK with the number of dollars they would cost in the US.

Quintile A fifth of any population that has been ranked according to a variable. For example in a set of examination marks, the bottom quintile are the 20% of students with the lowest marks.

Replacement level The difference between income in work and the level of benefits when out of work.

Social Exclusion Unit A small cross-departmental unit established by the UK government in 1998 to improve the coordination of policy and practice on social exclusion; transformed into a taskforce (based in the Cabinet Office) in 2007.

State pension age The earliest age from which a person can claim their state pension. Currently, the state pension age is 65 for men and 60 for women, although this is set to change.

Upper earnings limit The upper earnings limit refers to the amount of annual earnings up to which you have to pay National Insurance contributions.

Winter fuel payment The winter fuel payment is an annual payment for people over the age of 60 to help them with the cost of heating their home in winter.

Notes on contributors

Pete Alcock is Professor of Social Policy and Administration and Head of the School of Social Sciences at the University of Birmingham. He is the author and editor of a number of books on social policy. His research interests include poverty and social exclusion and the role of the voluntary and community sector in welfare. He was Chair of the Social Policy Association 1995–98.
www.iass.bham.ac.uk/staff/alcock.pdf

Dimitris Ballas is Senior Lecturer in the Department of Geography, University of Sheffield. He is an economist by training (1996, University of Macedonia, Thessaloniki, Greece) and also has a Master of Arts (with distinction) in Geographical Information Systems (GIS) (1997, University of Leeds) and a PhD in Human Geography (2001, University of Leeds). His research interests include economic geography, social and spatial inequalities, social justice, exploring geography of happiness and well-being and the socioeconomic applications of GIS.
www.shef.ac.uk/geography/staff/ballas_dimitris

Danny Dorling is Professor of Human Geography at the University of Sheffield, working with the social and spatial inequalities group. He is also Adjunct Professor in the Department of Geography, University of Canterbury, New Zealand, and Visiting Professor in the Department of Social Medicine, University of Bristol. He studied and first worked at Newcastle University, Newcastle upon Tyne, England, living there for 10 years before moving to work in Bristol, Leeds and then Sheffield – again all in England. To try to counter his myopic worldview, in 2006 Danny began work with a group of researchers on a project to re-map the world (www.worldmapper.org). His research tries to show how far understanding the patterns to people's lives can be enhanced using cartography and bringing to life statistics about the population. He is an academician of the Academy of Social Sciences.
www.shef.ac.uk/geography/staff/dorling_danny/

Akwugo Emejulu is Lecturer in Social Justice and Community Development and is the Director of the Centre for Equality and Discrimination at the University of Strathclyde. Her research interests are in minority ethnic women's labour market outcomes and in discourse analysis and identity construction. She is currently working on two research projects: one focused on minority ethnic labour market expreriences in Scotland and one focused on the changing discourses and identities of British and American community development.
www.strath.ac.uk/eps/staff/emejuluakwugoms

Jay Ginn was employed as Senior Research Fellow, Sociology Department, University of Surrey and was Co-director of the Centre for Research on Ageing and Gender until her retirement in November 2004. She is now a Visiting Professor of the university. Research interests include gender, class and ethnic differences in the economic resources of older people, and the impact on women of pension system reforms, cross-nationally, especially the shift from state to private pensions. Recent books include *Women, work and pensions: International issues and prospects* (2001, Open University Press, co-edited with D. Street and S. Arber) and *Gender, pensions and the lifecourse: How pensions need to adapt to changing family forms* (2003, The Policy Press).
www.soc.surrey.ac.uk/staff/jginn/index.html

Petra Hölscher is working as a social policy officer in the UNICEF Regional Office for Central and Eastern Europe and the Commonwealth of Independent States (CEE/CIS). Before joining UNICEF in 2006 she was Research Fellow at the University of Stirling (2004–06) and at the University of Dortmund in Germany (1997–2003).
www.unicef.org

Richard Mitchell is Reader in Health Inequalities at the University of Glasgow. Originally trained as a geographer, he subsequently specialised in public health. In recent years he has worked with Danny Dorling and Mary Shaw, among others, on a variety of projects that explore how social and environmental characteristics can combine to increase or decrease the chances of poor health.
www.gla.ac.uk/departments/publichealthpolicy/ourstaff/richardmitchell/

Gerry Mooney is Senior Lecturer in Social Policy and Staff Tutor, Faculty of Social Sciences, The Open University. He is co-author of *Rethinking welfare* (2002, Sage Publications); co-editor with Gill Scott of *Exploring social policy in the 'new' Scotland* (2005, The Policy Press) and co-editor with Alex Law of *New Labour/hard labour?* (2007, The Policy Press). He is currently researching

neoliberalism and urban policy in the Scottish context and the impact of New Labour's welfare reforms on public sector workers.
www.open.ac.uk/socialsciences/staff/people-profile.php?staff_id=66526102

Michael Orton worked for over 15 years in the voluntary sector and local government prior to joining the University of Warwick, and is currently Senior Research Fellow in the Warwick Institute for Employment Research. His principal interest is in issues of economic inequality, wealth and poverty. His recent research has included work on debt, tax and social policy, European public policy and citizenship in relation to 'better-off' citizens.
www2.warwick.ac.uk/fac/soc/ier/people/morton/

Tess Ridge is Lecturer in Social Policy at the University of Bath. Her main research and teaching interests are poverty and social exclusion – especially childhood poverty and social exclusion – children and family policy, social security policy and comparative social security, in particular support for children and families. Tess is a trustee of the Child Poverty Action Group and Honorary Secretary of the Social Policy Association. Publications include *Childhood poverty and social exclusion* (2002, The Policy Press).
www.bath.ac.uk/soc-pol/staff/profiles/tess-ridge.html

Karen Rowlingson is Professor of Social Policy and Director of Research in the Institute of Applied Social Studies, University of Birmingham. Her research interests include: credit and debt, money management, asset accumulation and use, asset-based welfare, inheritance, wealth inequality, the rich, social security and taxation policy.
www.iass.bham.ac.uk/staff/rowlingson.pdf

Gill Scott is Emeritus Professor of Social Inclusion and recently retired as Director of the Scottish Poverty Information Unit at Glasgow Caledonian University. She acted as an external adviser to the Scottish Executive's Cabinet Delivery Group on Closing the Opportunity Gap 2003–06 and chaired the working group examining client needs for the Workforce Plus Strategy in 2005. Her academic interests focus on developing a critically informed analysis of the social relations that inform social policy. She has published widely around poverty and devolution, childcare and gendered poverty, and welfare change and labour activation strategies in Europe. Her publications include, co-edited with Gerry Mooney, *Exploring social policy in the 'new' Scotland* (2005, The Policy Press) and, co-authored with S. Innes, 'Gender, care, poverty and transitions', in L. McKie and S. Cunningham-Burley (eds) *Families in society: Boundaries and relationships* (2006, The Policy Press).

Mary Shaw is Reader in Medical Sociology in the Department of Social Medicine at the University of Bristol. She has published extensively in the field of health inequalities and is an active proponent of the use of photography in social science.
www.epi.bris.ac.uk/staff/mshaw.htm

Ben Wheeler is Research Fellow in the Department of Social Medicine at the University of Bristol and also works with the South West Public Health Observatory. Previous research posts have been with the Social and Spatial Inequalities Research Group at the University of Sheffield, and at Victoria University, Wellington, New Zealand. His research interests include health, social and spatial inequalities, environment and health, and health geography, and the application of GIS and spatial data analysis in these fields.
www.worldmapper.org/about_us.html

Sharon Wright is Lecturer in Social Policy at the University of Stirling. Her research interests are in poverty, social security, welfare-to-work reforms, quasi-markets in employment and benefits advice, and the processes of making and implementing social policy. Her teaching interests are in: understanding social policy, poverty, income and wealth, gender, work and welfare and qualitative research methods. She is Managing Co-editor of the journal *Social Policy and Society* and Co-convenor of the Scottish Social Policy Network.
www.dass.stir.ac.uk/staff/showstaff.php?id=61

Nicola Yeates is Senior Lecturer in Social Policy at The Open University. She has published widely on issues of globalisation, migration, gender and care as they intersect with social policy. She is author of *Globalisation and social policy* (2001, Sage Publications) and *Globalising care economies and migrant workers: Explorations in global care* (2009: forthcoming, Palgrave), and editor of *Understanding global social policy* (2008: forthcoming, The Policy Press). She is an editor of *Global Social Policy: Journal of Public Policy and Social Development*.
www.open.ac.uk/socialsciences/staff/people-profile. php?name=Nicola_Yeates

Introduction

Tess Ridge and Sharon Wright

> What thoughtful rich people call the problem of poverty, thoughtful poor people call with equal justice the problem of riches. (Tawney, 1913, p 10)

Introduction

R.H. Tawney's quote is as apt today as it has always been. This book follows Tawney's injunction to provide a critical understanding of poverty in the context of inequality and in relation to wealth. The fundamental principle that underpins the book and runs throughout each section is that poverty and inequality cannot be understood or adequately addressed without an equally clear critical understanding of richness and wealth and its role in society.

Why look at poverty, inequality and wealth together?

Poverty is inextricably linked to inequality and wealth. It is not just about material, social and economic resources, it is also about social relationships, social processes and the control and exercise of power. Therefore the study of poverty, inequality and wealth raises fundamental questions about the organisation of society, social structures, relationships and social justice.

Previous approaches to understanding poverty have tended not to include an analysis of wealth in relation to poverty and inequality (for important exceptions see Townsend, 1979; Scott, 1994). Indeed the study of wealth and assets is a relatively new field of empirical research. Poverty has therefore tended to be studied mainly in isolation, as a situation of extreme disadvantage experienced at the 'bottom' of the social and economic scale. The primary focus has been on definitions, measurement and explanations, and as a result we know a considerable amount about durations of poverty, poverty dynamics – movement in and out of poverty, how many people are living in poverty, who they are, and why they are experiencing poverty (for example, unemployment) – although we know far less about the experience of poverty and the meaning of poverty in people's lives (see Beresford et al, 1999). However, while poverty lies under the social and political microscope and the lives and experiences of people who are living in poverty are defined, explained and addressed according to different social and political dispositions, we know considerably less about the generation of advantage and privilege, and the lives and practices of the wealthy.[1] The dynamics of wealth are largely hidden from view.

By focusing on wealth as well as poverty this book provides a more relational understanding of issues of socioeconomic inequality in the UK. It draws on both national and international research and uses theoretical insight, empirical data and social policy analysis to explore the patterns, explanations, structures, complexities and interrelationships of poverty, inequality and wealth. It also examines the role of state action (and inaction) in the UK in the mediation of poverty, inequality and wealth, through its social and fiscal policies.

What do we mean by poverty, inequality and wealth?

Poverty

> Poverty is best understood as a function of social, economic and political structures and processes which create and perpetuate an unequal distribution of resources both within and, in a global context, between societies. (Lister, 2004, p 51)

By poverty, we mean the experience of lacking 'resources to obtain the types of diet, participate in the activities and have the living conditions and amenities which are customary, or are at least widely encouraged or approved' in a particular society (Townsend, 1979, p 31). Poverty researchers generally accept this type of relative definition of poverty because it acknowledges that human life is not just about sparse physical survival. Understanding what poverty means involves understanding the implications of not being able to afford to have simple things (like a hot dinner) when almost everyone around you can. While small things like being able to eat fresh fruit, having a washing machine or being able to go out for a drink with friends are not technically necessary for survival, in the UK they are considered as ordinary parts of daily life. Defining poverty is, therefore, closely linked to measuring it since it involves making judgements about what people *need*. However, such debates can quickly slip into considering what 'other' people *deserve to have* and this is why the issue of poverty continues to be contested. Thus, defining poverty is not just a scientific measure but also a political act, and it is the more dominant and powerful groups in society that have tended to construct discourses of poverty, rather than those who have experienced it (Lister, 2004).

Despite the robustness of this approach to understanding poverty and the volume of well-publicised scientific evidence readily available, public attitudes continue to resist the acceptance of poverty as a problem within the UK (Bamfield and Brooks, 2006). The practice of defining, conceptualising and measuring poverty continues to present challenges because recognising poverty implies that something should be done about it. This process involves moral judgements that are related to political ideologies. Discourses of poverty and exclusion are culturally and historically specific; they change over time and reflect different political and social conditions and dispositions. Therefore, how poverty is defined and by whom is an important issue that affects the ways in which wider society understands poverty and disadvantage.

Furthermore, different conceptions of poverty generate different explanations of poverty, and these in turn reflect different value positions. People who are experiencing poverty do so within an established, if fluid, framework of social relations and public and policy discourses about poverty which can impose shape and meaning on that experience. Explanations for poverty and disadvantage are contested and range from the structural and social (including social class, gender, citizenship and social rights) to the cultural and individualised (underclass and intergenerational transmission of poverty; see Chapter Four). Different explanations of poverty also tend to generate different policy responses, therefore welfare provision, such as the adequacy of social security benefits, and the flexibility and sufficiency of support for people who are experiencing poverty, for example, lone parents, unemployed people and sick and disabled people, vary over time and according to the dominant conceptions, measurements and meanings of poverty held by the government in power. Indeed, supranational policy actors and institutions also influence these national and regional approaches to poverty through international institutions (such as the World Bank, the Organisation for Economic Co-operation and Development [OECD] and the European Union [EU]). These international influences create orthodoxies of social and economic action that shape and constrain resources and priorities for poorer nations and for poorer people within rich nations. In this book, we focus on what this means for the UK (for a greater in-depth discussion of world poverty and international policy influences, see Townsend and Gordon, 2002).

Throughout this book we will be using a structural analysis of poverty and inequality that is located in a framework of social relationships, social justice and citizenship rights. This structural approach draws on wider social processes, including gender, age and labour market inequalities to explain the causes and consequences of poverty.

Inequality

Inequality refers to disparities between individuals, groups and nations in access to resources, opportunities, assets and income. Economic inequality is particularly significant for people's capacity to have access to and command of resources. Inequality has an impact right across society. It is evident in people's life chances, their health and life expectancy, and their education and employment opportunities. It maps on to social cleavages such as class, gender, ethnicity and age, and it runs like a fault line through social processes and societal relationships. Inequality is not synonymous with poverty, although it is closely linked; it refers to comparisons between individuals and groups, whereas poverty adds a further dimension of disadvantage through a severe lack of resources to meet essential social, material and economic needs. Inequality is a strong link between poverty and wealth – as inequality increases in society the gap between rich and poor also increases. For example, in 2001, EU countries with higher levels of income inequality also had higher rates of poverty (Hills, 2004). Inequality in the UK is also rising. In his analysis of inequality and the role of the state in the distribution of resources in the last quarter of the 20th century in the UK and US, Hills found that there had been 'dramatic growth in income inequality – the gap between rich and poor – and in earnings disposition – that between low and high pay', and this was not, he argued, a result of global trends but, rather, specific to the UK and US (Hills, 2004, p 261). Blanden et al (2005) also found that over the same period intergenerational mobility had fallen markedly, due in part to the greater advantages gained from the education system by the better-off. As Blanden et al contend, 'the level of intergenerational mobility in society is seen by many as a measure of the extent of equality of economic and social opportunity' (2005, p 2).

Wealth

To be wealthy is to enjoy a standard of living that is greater than that normal for members of a particular society. If deprivation is the condition of life of the poor, 'privilege' is the condition of life of the wealthy. (Scott, 1994, p 17)

Linkages between poverty and wealth are rarely explored, theorised or articulated. Yet poverty cannot be separated from wealth; they are interconnected and each represents a polarised social condition, which together are inextricably bound one to the other on a continuum of social and economic relationships. At one end of the scale poverty represents a severe and damaging exclusion from economic and social resources while at the other end wealth and richness buy economic, social and political power and advantage in abundance. As Scott (1994, p 17) argues:

> Deprivation and privilege should be seen as complementary terms and as indicating contrasting departures from the normal lifestyle of the citizen. If it is possible to recognize a 'poverty line' it may also be possible to recognise a 'wealth line'. The 'poverty line' defines the level at which deprivation begins, and the wealth line defines the level at which privilege begins. From this point of view, deprivation and privilege are polarised conditions of life that reflect the polarisation of wealth and poverty. A recognition of this fact forces us to recognise the causes of poverty cannot be separated from the causes of wealth: indeed, the one may be a necessary condition of the other.

What Scott draws our attention to is that poverty and wealth are not merely different ends of a status hierarchy, the 'bottom' and the 'top', but rather 'distinct conditions and social statuses, defined, in many situations, by "catastrophic" boundaries in the distribution of resources' (Scott, 1994, p 173). Scott argues that a fundamental link between poverty and privilege is the nature of exclusion – those experiencing poverty endure exclusion from resources while those who enjoy wealth are able to exclude others from their special privileges. As inequality in the UK rises, the richest draw even further away from the poorest. Lansley (2006), in his study of wealth in modern Britain, points to the rise of a new 'super-wealthy' class, with the number of billionaires growing threefold since 1990, and the number of people worth over £100 million rising fivefold.

What is it like to experience poverty or wealth in the UK?

Poverty and wealth are polarised experiences, and it can be hard to get an insight into what it is like to experience a life organised around the constraints of poverty or the freedoms and privileges of wealth without some examples drawn from real-life experiences. *Boxes 1.1* and *1.2* contain accounts of two very different lives. *Box 1.1*, Bella's life, is drawn from research carried out with children experiencing poverty in the UK. This research drew on the children's own accounts of their everyday lives to illustrate, through Bella's story, some of the challenges facing disadvantaged children on a regular basis.

Box 1.1: Bella's life

Bella is 12 years old; she lives with her mother, sister and brother on an inner-city housing estate. There is little in her neighbourhood for her to do except play out on the street. Although there are some after-school clubs and activities she cannot afford them. She is unhappy at school and is being bullied. She is particularly apprehensive about her clothes and trainers believing that other children are bullying her because she cannot afford better things. Bella feels excluded *within* her school, she misses out on school trips and is concerned about being seen as 'different' and this undermines her social confidence. She was especially upset when most of her tutor group went to Germany and she was left behind. "I wanted to go to Germany and it was about a hundred-odd quid and mum goes 'No'. It's like we go on a ferry, a coach, really posh ferry, hotel, we get to meet friends there. And mum she said 'No'. So I missed that ... I just had to continue with my lessons while everyone else were out in Germany.... I always miss out on the school trips and everything."

Source: Drawn from Ridge (2005)

Bella's experiences shaped her life in particular ways – she lacked confidence and her self- and social identity was fragile. Her accounts of her home and school life are layered with uncertainties and anxieties about her life; she is preoccupied with her future, her friends, her social relationships and her anxieties about fitting in at school. In contrast, ***Box 1.2*** gives us some insight into the lives of the very rich, and reveals some of the benefits that wealth and privilege can buy.

Box 1.2: Philip's life

Philip Green is one of the richest men in Britain; he pays himself around £3 million a day and can earn that in a couple of hours from his retail empire. He is no stranger to extravagant spending. In 2002 he spent £5 million on his 50th birthday. Presents included a special edition of 'This is Your Life' presented by Michael Aspel, and a solid gold monopoly set with diamond studded dice, on which the properties represented his high street assets. In 2005 he spent £4 million on his son's bar mitzvah. Stonemasons and craftsmen were flown out to a private peninsular where they built a synagogue to seat 300 people. The guests stayed at the £1,000 a night Grand-Hotel du Cap-Ferrat. Music was provided by Beyoncé and Destiny's Child.

Source: Drawn from Lansley (2006)

The UK profile of rising poverty, inequality and wealth

The UK is one of the richest countries in the world, but its phenomenal wealth is accompanied by widespread poverty. This profile is exceptional, even among countries of comparable size and economic performance. The UK has:

- the highest level of inequality of any European country (ESRC, 2007);
- one of the worst records for child poverty of all rich nations (UNICEF, 2007).

Figure 1.1 below illustrates the differences between median incomes and the incomes of those in the richest 10% (the 90th percentile) compared with those in the group with the lowest 10% of income (the 10th percentile). This shows that during the 30-year period from 1971–2002 incomes have risen overall. Those with the highest incomes have increased more rapidly and to a much greater extent than average (median) incomes, that is, the rich have got richer. Median incomes have risen at a relatively stable rate. Those in the bottom income group have seen the smallest gains.

Figure 1.1: Distribution of real household disposable income, UK (1971–2002)

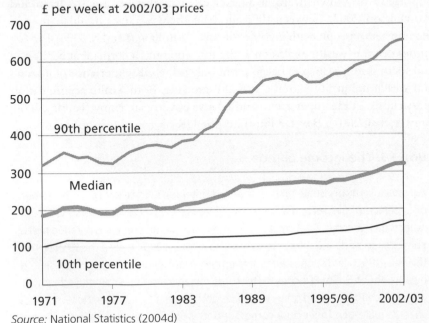

Source: National Statistics (2004d)

Figure 1.2 uses the Gini coefficient measure to illustrate rising income inequality.

Figure 1.2: *Income inequality in Great Britain (1979–2005), measured using the Gini coefficient*

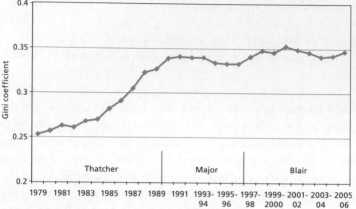

Note: The Gini coefficient has been calculated using incomes before housing costs have been deducted.

Source: Brewer et al (2007) calculations using Family Resources Survey and Family Expenditure Survey, various years

Income inequality in the UK is at an all-time high and the top 1% of the population now own nearly a quarter of all marketable assets (Orton and Rowlingson, 2007). Between 1995 and 2005, there was an eightfold increase in the number of people with incomes of over £1 million (Lansley, 2006). Lansley argues that the 'wealth explosion at the top represents a permanent economic and social shift' (2006, p x) because not only is the UK experience of income and wealth inequality extreme, it is also growing. Both wealth accumulation (particularly of the 'super-rich') and relative poverty are rising (Lansley, 2006; Brewer et al, 2007). *Box 1.3* illustrates the UK's income distribution.

Box 1.3: The income parade

A powerful way of visualising the income distribution in the UK is through the idea of a 'parade of dwarfs and a few giants' (Pen, 1971) where each person's height reflects their income. The population is lined up in height order and paraded past a particular point during the course of one hour. Hills (1995) applied this to the UK in the early 1990s and suggested that average (mean) income could be represented by a height of 5 foot 8 inches. After three minutes a single unemployed mother with two children would go by with a height of 1 foot 10 inches. After 9 minutes a single male pensioner on Income Support would go by at a height of 2 feet

6 inches. People with average (mean) incomes do not arrive until 37 minutes into the parade. After 50 minutes, the heights begin to rise considerably and we see the first giants at 8 feet 7 inches tall. After 59 minutes, a chief executive and his wife walk by and are both 60 feet tall. In the last seconds, the tallest would go by with their heads lost in the clouds: Britain's richest man and his partner would both be four miles high. According to Wakefield (2003), if such a parade were organised today, then the person of mean height (and income) would be taller (and richer) than two thirds of the population and so would pass by after 40 minutes had elapsed.

Karen Rowlingson

Inequalities in income and wealth are significant in and of themselves, but this is not the full story; such inequalities have severe consequences. Differences in income and wealth create divisions that are deeply embedded in society. The situation into which an individual is born remains a very strong determinant of life chances and life expectancy:

- Wealthier citizens live substantially longer than those with lower incomes:
  - professionals live (on average) for eight years more than unskilled manual workers (National Statistics, 2004a).
- Income group has a significant impact on access to goods and services that can affect well-being:
  - in 2002, 59% of households in the lowest (quintile) income group had no access to a car, compared with 8% of the top group (National Statistics, 2004b);
  - in 2002, only 15% of people from the lowest (quintile) income group had access to a home computer, compared with 86% of people from the highest income group (National Statistics, 2004b).
- Educational opportunities and attainment vary according to income group:
  - in 2002, 77% of children in Year 11 in England and Wales with parents in higher professional occupations gained five or more A*–C grade GCSEs. This was more than double the proportion for children with parents in routine occupations (32%) (National Statistics, 2004c);
  - the likelihood of participating in further or higher education is influenced by socioeconomic group. Young people with parents in professional occupations are more likely than those with parents from routine or lower supervisory occupations to be in full-time education (National Statistics, 2004c);

- higher qualifications are clearly related to higher earnings (National Statistics, 2004c).

Excessive inequality by accident or design?

There is nothing inevitable about this situation and when we compare the UK with other industrialised nations, we can see that extreme income and wealth inequality is not a necessary precondition for economic success (ESRC, 2007). There is also evidence that for 20 years a consistent majority of people in the UK have viewed the gap between low and high incomes to be unacceptably large (Orton and Rowlingson, 2007). So why have successive UK governments tolerated or exacerbated excesses of wealth and the proliferation of poverty?

This is fundamentally a question of values and ideology. It is no accident that extreme levels of inequality in poverty and wealth exist in the UK. The economic, tax and social policies of consecutive governments have served to push a wedge between the incomes of those at the bottom end of the distribution and those at the top of it. Throughout the 20th century, governments have consciously failed to make arrangements for adequate minimum wages and have persisted in paying benefits at rates below the level necessary to cover basic essentials. This has meant that neither social security nor earnings have provided the necessary protection from poverty for millions of people at the lower end of the income distribution. At the top end of the income distribution, the organisation of taxation, including tax breaks and tax loopholes, has allowed wealthier people to accumulate wealth through high incomes and the amassment of assets. This has been influenced, particularly since the late 1970s, by neoliberal ideology and monetarist economic doctrines. Since the Thatcher era, UK governments have prioritised controlling inflation over social spending. Tax and benefit reforms between 1979 and 1997 had the direct result of increasing inequality by cutting taxes for the better-off and developing taxes that impact disproportionately on people with lower incomes, removing wage protections (by weakening unions and abolishing wage councils) and lowering benefits (by changing the system for annual up-rating from being in line with average earnings to being in line with average prices, setting in place a year-on-year devaluation of benefits in relation to earnings). (These policies and processes are examined in greater depth in Chapters Twelve and Thirteen.)

Structure of the book

The book is divided into four parts, each addressing key issues in the study of poverty, inequality and wealth. The contributing authors present a range of distinctive approaches to these issues. Part One, 'Key concepts and issues', establishes the key concepts used in the study of poverty, inequality and wealth. In Chapter Two Karen Rowlingson introduces the concept of wealth and explores the distribution of wealth and income in the UK. Pete Alcock introduces poverty in Chapter Three and highlights key dilemmas in examining poverty and social exclusion in relation to wealth. In Chapter Four Gerry Mooney provides a critical account of the main explanations of the causes of poverty, inequality and wealth. Part Two, 'People and place: divisions of poverty and wealth', examines divisions in the experience of inequalities in poverty and wealth. In Chapter Five Nicola Yeates examines inequalities in poverty and wealth as transnational and global processes; in Chapter Six Danny Dorling and Dimitris Ballas focus on the geography of poverty and wealth; and in Chapter Seven Gill Scott analyses gender as a category when examining inequalities of income and wealth or poverty. In Chapter Eight Akwugo Emejulu highlights inequalities in wealth and income among different ethnic groups in the UK. The following two chapters then highlight inequalities in wealth and poverty that are related to age: Petra Hölscher (Chapter Nine) explores the impact of poverty in childhood, and Jay Ginn (Chapter Ten) examines experiences of poverty and wealth in older age. In Chapter Eleven Mary Shaw, Ben Wheeler, Richard Mitchell and Danny Dorling conclude this part by examining the relationship between ill-health and inequalities in income and wealth. Part Three, 'The role of the state', focuses on the ways in which the state mediates inequalities in income, poverty and wealth. In Chapter Twelve Michael Orton discusses state approaches to wealth at the individual and collective level, and Tess Ridge and Sharon Wright, in Chapter Thirteen, consider state approaches to dealing with poverty, social exclusion and inequalities. Part Four, 'Prospects', containing Chapter Fourteen by Tess Ridge and Sharon Wright, draws together the three main parts of the book to highlight key arguments and debates in the study of poverty, inequality and wealth and to reflect on some important issues for the future.

Note
[1] The Luxembourg Wealth Study provides the first cross-national database of household assets and liabilities (see Siermanska et al, 2006).

References

Bamfield, L. and Brooks, R. (2006) *Narrowing the gap: Final report of The Fabian Commission on Life Chances and Child Poverty*, London: The Fabian Society.

Beresford, P., Green, D., Lister, R. and Woodard, K. (1999) *Poverty first hand: Poor people speak for themselves*, London: Child Poverty Action Group.

Blanden, J., Gregg, P. and Machin, S. (2005) *Intergenerational mobility in Europe and North America*, A report supported by the Sutton Trust, London: London: Centre for Economic Performance, London School of Economics and Political Science.

Brewer, M., Goodman, A., Muriel, A. and Sibieta, L. (2007) *Poverty and inequality in the UK: 2007*, Briefing Note No 73, London: Institute for Fiscal Studies.

ESRC (Economic and Social Research Council) (2007) *Inequality in the UK*, London: ESRC.

Hills, J. (1995) *Income and wealth: The latest evidence*, York: Joseph Rowntree Foundation.

Hills, J. (2004) *Inequality and the state*, Oxford: Oxford University Press.

Lansley, S. (2006) *Rich Britain: The rise and rise of the new super wealthy*, London: Politico's.

Lister, R. (2004) *Poverty*, Cambridge: Polity Press.

National Statistics (2004a) 'Health' (www.statistics.gov.uk/cci/nugget. asp?id=1007, accessed 8/11/07).

National Statistics (2004b) 'Living standards' (www.statistics.gov.uk/cci/nugget. asp?id=1006, accessed 8/11/07).

National Statistics (2004c) 'Education' (www.statistics.gov.uk/cci/nugget. asp?id=1003, accessed 8/11/07).

National Statistics (2004d) 'Income' (www.statistics.gov.uk/cci/nugget. asp?id=1005, accessed 8/11/07).

Orton, M. and Rowlingson, K. (2007) *Public attitudes to economic inequality*, York: Joseph Rowntree Foundation.

Pen, J. (1971) *Income distribution*, London: Penguin.

Ridge, T. (2005) 'Feeling under pressure: low-income girls negotiating school life', in G. Lloyd (ed) *Problem girls*, London: RoutledgeFalmer, pp 23-36.

Scott, J. (1994) *Poverty and wealth*, Harlow: Longman.

Sierminska, E., Brandolini, A. and Smeeding, T.M. (2006) 'Comparing wealth distribution across rich countries: first results from the Luxembourg Wealth Study', August (http://ssrn.com/abstract=927402).

Tawney, R. (1913) 'Poverty as an industrial problem', Inaugural lecture, reproduced in R. Tawney, *Memoranda on the problems of poverty*, London: William Morris Press.

Townsend, P. (1979) *Poverty in the United Kingdom*, Harmondsworth: Penguin Books.

Townsend, P. and Gordon, D. (eds) (2002) *World poverty: New policies to defeat an old enemy*, Bristol: The Policy Press.

UNICEF (2007) *Child poverty in perspective: An overview of child well-being in rich countries*, Report Card 7, Florence: UNICEF Innocenti Research Centre.

Wakefield, M. (2003) *Is middle Britain middle-income Britain?*, IFS Briefing Note 38, London: Institute for Fiscal Studies.

Part One

Key concepts and issues

Wealth

Karen Rowlingson

Overview

- This chapter makes a fundamental distinction between 'wealth as assets' and 'wealth as riches'.
- It discusses these concepts and ways of defining and measuring them.
- Data on the current distribution of income and assets in the UK is reviewed to show high, and increasing, levels of wealth inequality.
- A spotlight is shone on the very richest individuals in the UK.

Key concepts

wealth; assets; riches; the rich; income; inequality

Introduction

'Poverty' has been the subject of academic inquiry for many decades (see Chapter Three in this volume). By contrast, there has been very little theoretical debate or empirical investigation about 'wealth' (see Orton and Rowlingson, 2007). As a consequence, this term is often used very loosely.

Sometimes 'wealth' is used as a synonym for personal assets (such as financial savings, housing assets and so on). Using this definition, it is possible to have zero 'wealth'. At other times, 'wealth' is used to mean the opposite (in some vague way) of poverty. Using this definition, 'wealth' means having a high level of economic resources. These two uses of the term are conceptually distinct but they are related, as people at the top of the economic distribution (the 'wealthy') usually have very high levels of assets ('wealth') as well as high incomes. Those in poverty usually have no assets ('wealth') at all as well as low incomes. But the distinction between these two meanings is an important one as there are some people with high incomes but few assets (sometimes referred to as 'income-rich, asset-poor') as well as some with low incomes but substantial assets ('income-poor, asset-rich'). It is therefore possible to be 'wealthy' (through high levels of income) while at the same time having low levels of assets ('wealth').

It is important to be very clear about terminology, and in this chapter the term 'wealth' is avoided, with the following terms used instead:

- *assets:* this term refers to a stock of money (in contrast to income as a flow of money);
- *riches:* this term refers to the 'opposite' of poverty;
- *the rich:* this term refers to those towards the top of the economic distribution (on either income, assets or a combination of these measures).

All of these terms will be discussed in further detail in this chapter.

Differences between income and assets

The Royal Commission on the Distribution of Income and Wealth (1977) conceptualised assets as money that is fixed at a point in time (a stock of economic resources), whereas income was conceptualised as an amount that is received over a particular time period (a flow of economic resources). This seems a reasonably clear distinction as we can see the difference, for example, between the flow of money from a monthly wage payment and a stock of money held in a savings account. However, there are some complexities here. For example, people can receive income from assets (for example, from interest on a savings account or rental income from a buy-to-let property). Furthermore, 'capital gains', for example from inheriting a house, fall somewhere between income and assets and are treated separately in the tax system. In more theoretical terms, economists often talk of the flow of expected future earnings as representing a stock of human capital and the benefits of owner-occupation may be said to constitute a stream of imputed income or rent. So, both conceptually and in practice, a flow of income can be converted into a stock of assets, and vice versa (McKay, 1992).

Conceptualising and defining income

There has been considerable *measurement* of incomes in the UK and much discussion of some of the technical issues surrounding income measurement (see below). However, the *conceptualisation and definition* of income has received less attention. If income is considered to be a flow of money over time, what time period is considered appropriate? Incomes tend to vary over time, even from week to week (Hills et al, 2006), so the period chosen will make a difference, whether it is weekly, monthly or annual income.

There is also an important distinction to be made between earned and unearned income: income that requires some form of labour (for example, from employment or self-employment) is considered earned income as opposed to income that does not require labour (for example, income from investments). Once again, however, the distinction may not be entirely clear. If someone has worked hard to renovate a property and then rents it out, the income is usually considered unearned income despite the labour that has gone into the property. Other forms of income include income from social security benefits which do not easily fit into either 'earned' or 'unearned' categories and so normally form their own category.

Another important distinction is between gross and net incomes. Gross income refers to income before tax and National Insurance payments have been made. The difference between gross and net incomes gives us information about the role of the state in redistributing income (see Chapter Twelve, this volume).

Conceptualising and defining assets

Assets have received much less attention from researchers compared with income. Perhaps the most important classifying criterion for assets is 'liquidity', also referred to as 'marketability'. Assets that provide an income stream but which cannot be 'cashed in' or 'realised' are known as illiquid or non-marketable (for example, occupational pensions and trust funds). Assets that can be realised are known as liquid or marketable assets (for example, savings and property net of mortgages). But levels of marketability vary depending not only on the type of investment but also on factors such as the nature of the market and the divisibility of the asset. For example, a house counts as a marketable asset but a less liquid form than money held in an open-access savings account. And the liquidity of property depends on the nature of the housing market at any particular point in time.

Jenkins (1990) has argued that, as is the case with income, it is important to distinguish between 'gross' assets and 'net' assets. For example, there may be two people with £50,000 in net assets. One may own a house outright worth

£50,000. The other may have just taken out a mortgage on a house worth £500,000 (using £50,000 as a deposit). Analysis of assets usually focuses on net assets but gross assets may also say something important about the lifestyles and expectations of different groups.

As well as considering different aspects or dimensions of assets it is also common to divide assets into three particular types: financial, pension and housing. Financial assets (usually) represent very liquid forms of money; pension assets are (very largely) non-marketable; and housing assets sit somewhere between these two. These different types of assets also play different roles in people's lives. Housing assets provide a commodity that contributes to someone's current standard of living. Pension assets provide a current or future income stream and financial assets provide a flexible resource that may be used in diverse ways.

Another important dimension of assets is how they have been accumulated. A broad distinction can be made between assets that have been inherited by, or given to, someone from a family member or generous friend and assets that have been accumulated through one's own personal income. Rowlingson and McKay (2005) found that almost half of the population (46%) had received some kind of inheritance at some point during their lives. One in twenty (5%) had inherited £50,000 or more.

This chapter focuses on assets in their positive form but they also have a negative form: debt. Debt is usually divided into 'problem debt' and 'credit'. People have 'problem debt' where they owe money on household bills or are struggling to repay credit commitments. 'Problem debt' is most widespread among people on low incomes. Those on middle or high incomes are more likely than other groups to use credit to spread expenditure over time (for example, a mortgage is a form of credit enabling people to buy property). Debt is a complex issue in its own right and so is not considered in detail here (see Kempson, 2002; Kempson et al, 2004; Department of Trade and Industry, 2005).

Conceptualising and defining 'riches' and 'the rich'

'Poverty' may be a highly contested term but there is at least a framework for debate in terms of definition (for example, absolute and relative conceptions of poverty) and measurement (see Chapter Three in this volume). Debates about poverty often involve the use of other terms such as 'hardship', 'deprivation', 'low income', 'disadvantage', 'social exclusion' and so on. Once again there is a literature on each of these and their definition (see also Lister, 2004), but there is much less of an agreed framework for talking about other groups. Scott

(1994) provides one of the few discussions on riches using the term 'wealthy' to describe people in a state of privilege. He states that:

> To be wealthy is to enjoy a standard of living that is greater than that normal for members of a particular society. If deprivation is the condition of life of the poor, 'privilege' is the condition of life of the wealthy. (Scott, 1994, p 17)

This, of course, begs the question about what is 'normal' for members of a particular society. Scott goes on to say that it is possible to identify a 'wealth line' above which people 'enjoy special benefits and advantages of a private sort' (1994, p 152). Scott (1994) and Giddens (1998) both consider those at the 'top' of the distribution to be a particularly privileged group and they define them as those who have the ability to exclude themselves from society. This appears to mirror the 'forced' exclusion experienced by those at the 'bottom' of the economic distribution.

Dean with Melrose (1999) carried out one of the very few empirical studies on the conceptualisation of riches. Their in-depth interviews identified two groups of people beyond poverty: those who lived in 'comfort' and another group that were able to have 'fun' without any economic worries. Other terms used by the public, media, policy makers and politicians for 'non-poor' groups include those on 'modest' income, 'moderate or middle' incomes, 'middle England', 'better-off' groups, 'affluent' groups, 'the rich' or 'wealthy'. But these terms carry little precise meaning and have received little attention from academics (for a discussion of 'middle-income' Britain see Wakefield, 2003). Lansley (2006) focuses on a group he labels 'the super-rich', and it may be useful to divide 'the rich' into further sub-groups, depending on their level of riches.

It is clear that there has been little *conceptualisation* of 'riches'. There has been even less academic attention on issues around its *definition*. Unfortunately, neither Scott (1994) nor Dean with Melrose (1999) provide a more detailed framework for defining and then measuring 'privilege', 'wealth', 'comfort' or 'fun'. However, there are a number of possible definitions that could be used, mirroring the ways in which poverty is defined. The choice of definition should be made in relation to our conceptualisation of riches otherwise the choice seems quite arbitrary. But it may also be useful, as with poverty, to draw on a range of different definitions (see *Table 2.1*).

The main official definition of poverty takes a *relative income* approach: 60% of median income. A similar approach could be taken in relation to riches. For example, we could look at those with twice or three times median income. Or we could use other statistical techniques, for example, to look at those with

Table 2.1: *Summary of possible ways of defining riches with examples*

Ways of defining 'riches'	Examples
Relative income	Three times median income Two standard deviations above mean income
Absolute income	Those with income above £40,000 Those with income above £100,000
Threshold for eliminating poverty	The point at which poverty would be eradicated if income were redistributed to people in poverty from rich people above this point
Relative assets	Three times median assets Two standard deviations above mean assets
Absolute assets	Those with liquid assets over £1,000,000 Those with liquid assets over £5,000,000

Costing a basket of luxuries	Incomes at a level to be able to afford a range of luxuries such as:
	    substantial residence
	    new top-range car every three years
	    private education for children

Social indicators	Possession of luxuries such as:
	    substantial residence
	    new top-range car every three years
	    private education for children

two standard deviations above the mean. Or we could look at the top decile (10%) of income or the top percentile (top 1%).

A further approach could be to use *absolute income* definitions. For example, riches might be defined as having an individual income of (say) £40,000 (around the point at which earners pay top-rate income tax) or £100,000. Once again, the exact choice of threshold would need to relate back to our conceptualisation of riches.

Given the importance of assets for rich people, some kind of relative or absolute definition of *asset levels* might also be appropriate (for example, three times median assets as a relative measure or liquid assets over £1,000,000 as an absolute measure).

Medeiros (2006) has proposed a different income-based approach to the construction of a riches line. His riches line is linked directly to the level of resources needed to eradicate poverty in a country. He asks us to imagine the richest individual in a society giving some of their income to the poorest individual until the poorest individual has as much income as the next poorest. At that point, the two poorest individuals both start receiving resources from the richest and so on until the richest person 'only' has as much income as the next richest, at which point the two richest people both start giving some of their income to the poorest individuals. This process continues until all those under the poverty line are raised just above it. When this happens, the resulting level of income of the richest individuals is calculated and this is considered the riches line. Medeiros does not necessarily suggest that this redistributive device should be used in practice but it is an interesting theoretical device for understanding and measuring riches.

An alternative approach would be to identify a 'basket of luxuries' that rich people would need to sustain their lifestyle. This would mirror the 'basket of necessities' approach to poverty (see Chapter Three, this volume) used by researchers from Rowntree (1901) through to Bernstein et al (2000). The basket of goods would be identified by members of the public (or 'experts') and so would change over time according to social expectations. It might currently include: private healthcare, private education, a substantial and secure residence, a top-of-the-range new car every few years, two overseas holidays per year and so on. Once the items have been identified, the next step would be to work out how much the basket would cost. Anyone with an income above that amount would be considered rich.

The social indicator approach would be another possibility, as first developed in relation to poverty by Townsend (1979) and then modified by Mack and Lansley (1985), Gordon and Pantazis (1998) and Gordon et al (2000). With this approach members of the public (or 'experts') could be asked to draw up *indicators* of riches referring to specific possessions (for example, an MP3 player through to a plasma screen television); the quality of goods (for example, type of car owned); activities (such as the number and destination of holidays); or perhaps ability to afford private healthcare, absence of debts or lack of money worries. People would be considered 'rich' if they possessed a certain number of luxuries. If someone lacked a particular luxury, it would be possible to ask them whether this was because they did not want it or they could not afford it. Those that could afford a luxury could be included in the measure even if they chose not to have it.

Combining income and assets

When conceptualising and defining riches, an important issue is how to combine income and assets. Typically, those at the top of the income distribution are also those at the top of the asset distribution, but some people may have high levels of assets, especially housing wealth, but a low income. This is what is often referred to as being 'asset-rich but income-poor', particularly in relation to older people (Rowlingson et al, 1999; Orton, 2006). Similarly, some people may have high levels of income but low levels of assets (particularly young professionals). There has been very little thinking about this issue but the hypothetical examples in *Box 2.1* cause us to consider the importance of different combinations of income and assets.

Box 2.1: Discussion point: Who is 'better off'? Why do you think that?

Case study 1

- A single woman in her mid-20s with an income of £22,000. She has no private pension or financial savings and is making £100 per month in debt repayments (which will take another year to pay off). She is renting a flat.
- A single man in his mid-20s with an income of £15,000. He has no private pension or financial savings or debts. He has just put a £10,000 deposit down on a flat worth £80,000.

Case study 2

- A couple in their mid-50s with a joint income of £30,000. They own a house outright worth £250,000 and have savings of £10,000. They have no private pension savings.
- A couple in their mid-50s with an income of £40,000. They live in a house worth £150,000 and have no savings. They have pension savings that will give them a joint private pension income of £15,000 when they retire at the age of 65.

Measurement issues

Once a particular conceptualisation has been agreed and definitions chosen, the next issue would be how to measure income, assets and riches using empirical data. Most empirical data on income and assets come from large-scale representative surveys of the general public (see, for example, DWP, 2007). But some data on assets also come from analysis of assets left when people die (see HMRC, 2003). The measurement of income, assets and riches raises a number of important challenges, as detailed below.

Should income be measured before or after housing costs (BHC or AHC)?

The case for using a BHC or AHC income measure is discussed in some detail in Brewer et al (2006). Analysts tend to focus on BHC incomes when considering the overall income distribution because housing costs can generally be thought of as a consumption item like any other (for example, food, utility bills and so on). There is therefore no apparent reason for treating housing costs differently from other costs. But, when focusing on poverty and low incomes, AHC income tends to be seen as a better measure of living standards among social renters and pensioners who are owner-occupiers, who are particularly prevalent at the lower end of the income scale. Levels of poverty are typically higher using AHC income compared with BHC income.

What is the appropriate unit of analysis for income and assets?

Should income and assets be measured at the level of the individual, the 'family' or the household? This depends on the degree of sharing within families and households. If we measure income or assets at the household level we will be assuming that all individuals within the household share these resources (or at least the benefits of these resources) and therefore occupy the same position in the income/asset distribution. This may or may not be appropriate.

How do we compare households of different sizes?

The official income statistics take household size into account by adjusting household incomes for the different needs that different households face, using equivalence scales (see Brewer et al, 2006). This is important because a weekly income of £300 will provide a much higher standard of living to an individual living alone than to a family of five.

Can people report their assets accurately?

It is relatively straightforward to ask people about how much money they have in savings and other forms of financial accounts but it is difficult to estimate net housing wealth as some owner-occupiers have endowment mortgages which make it difficult to assess the amount of equity owned outright. Even where there is no mortgage, homeowners may not know the value of their house or may estimate it incorrectly. Council Tax band can give some idea of the relative value of a property but it is not particularly accurate. So there are some difficulties gaining an accurate measure of housing assets from surveys.

There are even greater problems measuring pension assets as these cannot be realised. Rowlingson et al (1999) analysed survey data on pension contributions to measure what a person would have been entitled to if the pension provision ceased further operations immediately but honoured obligations already entered into.

Can we measure riches accurately?

There are particular problems measuring *high* incomes and assets. We know from comparisons with the Survey of Personal Incomes (which is based on tax returns) that general public sample surveys under-report the number of people with very high incomes and also understate the amount of their incomes. This is likely to be for a number of reasons:

- rich people seem to be less likely than other people to take part in surveys;
- rich people who do take part in surveys may be more likely to refuse to answer particular questions about income and assets;
- rich people who do take part in surveys may, wittingly or unwittingly, underestimate the extent of their income and assets.

Distribution of income

Having reviewed the conceptualisation, definition and measurement of income, assets and riches, this section moves on to provide a picture of the distribution of income before focusing on the distribution of assets, and then shining a spotlight on the rich.

From 1961 to 1979, incomes grew throughout the income distribution, with those at the bottom experiencing the fastest income growth. From 1979 to 1994/95, however, incomes rose fastest for the richest (the richest tenth saw their real incomes rise by 60% while the poorest tenth saw only a 10% rise). Hills (2004, pp 25-6) summarises the trends during this time as 'the poor fell behind the middle; the middle fell behind the top; and the top fell behind the very top'. Due to this, income inequality soared along with relative poverty.

Since 1994/95, the picture has been quite mixed but most groups have shared in fairly rapid income growth. Hills (2004, p 26) summarises the trends during this time as: 'the poor catching up on the middle to some extent, but the top moving away from the middle'. The very top has therefore 'stretched' away from the rest. For example, research by Income Data Services has shown that the average earnings of the chief executives of the country's 100 largest listed companies rose from an average of £2 million in 2004/05 to £2.9 million in 2005/06, a rise of 43% (BBC, 2006). The typical boss (chief executive) of a top 100 company therefore earns 86 times more than a typical employee in one of these companies.

Overall, income inequality was higher at the start of the 21st century than at any time in the previous 50 years (Hills, 2004), with the top tenth of the population receiving a greater share of total income than the whole of the bottom half in 2002/03.

Hills (2004, p 37) states that 'Britain's inequality growth was exceptional internationally', with income inequality in Britain becoming second highest (to the US) when compared with 15 OECD (Organisation for Economic Co-operation and Development) countries by the mid–1990s.

Distribution of assets

As with income inequality, asset inequality decreased over much of the 20th century (Atkinson and Harrison, 1978; Atkinson et al, 1986), but the 1980s witnessed a stabilisation in the levels of asset inequality that then began to rise in the late 1990s (see *Table 2.2*). For example, the share of marketable assets of the top 5% fell from 74% in 1950 in Great Britain to 46% in 1986. This group's share in the UK stabilised in the 1980s at around 36% before rising to 43% in 2001. *Table 2.2* also shows that the Gini coefficient, a measure of overall inequality (see *Box 2.2*), rose from 64% in 1991 to 70% in 2001 (Inland Revenue, 2003). And between 1988 and 1999, the top 1% of the population increased its share of personal assets from 17% to 23% (Paxton and Taylor, 2002). The cause of this rise in asset inequality is unclear but it is probably a result of the increases in income inequality that took place in the 1980s, which then filtered through into wealth inequality in the 1990s (Hills, 2004). The stock market boom and rise in property prices in the late 1990s are also likely to have had an effect.

Box 2.2: The Gini coefficient

The Gini coefficient is a commonly used measure of inequality. A Gini coefficient of zero represents complete equality, where income is shared equally among all households. A Gini coefficient of 100 represents complete inequality, where only one household has all the income and the rest have none. For further information see www.statistics.gov.uk/about/methodology_by_theme/gini/default.asp

The distribution of assets is far more unequal than the distribution of income. For example, the Gini coefficient for the distribution of assets in 2001 was 70%, twice the figure for income (Hills, 2004). This is at least partly due to life cycle effects in the distribution of assets (see *Box 2.3*).

Table 2.2: *Changing distribution of personal assets*

	Share of marketable assets of			Gini coefficient (%)
	Top 1%	Top 5%	Top 10%	
(a) England and Wales				–
1923	61	82	89	–
1930	58	79	87	–
1938	55	77	85	
(b) Great Britain				
1950	47	74	–	–
1955	44	71	–	–
1961	37	61	72	–
1966	31	56	70	–
1971	29	53	68	–
1976	25	49	65	–
1986	23	46	63	–
(c) United Kingdom				
1976	21	38	50	66
1981	18	36	50	65
1986	18	36	50	64
1991	17	35	47	64
1996	20	40	52	68
2001	23	43	56	70

Notes: (a) Atkinson and Harrison (1978, Table 6.5)
(b) Atkinson et al (1986, Table 1)
(c) Inland Revenue (2003a, Table 13.5)

Source: Table from Hills (2004)

Box 2.3: Life cycle model of asset accumulation

When considering the distribution of assets it is important to note that asset accumulation is a dynamic process associated with the life cycle (Modigliani and Brumberg, 1954; Friedman, 1957; Atkinson, 1971). According to general life cycle theory, young people are typically on low incomes and have not had time to accumulate assets. At this stage in life, it makes economically rational sense to borrow money, given the likelihood of income increases in future. Later on, in middle age, incomes are higher and so debts can be repaid and money saved for later life when incomes will fall. In retirement, any savings will be drawn on. Life cycle theory therefore predicts an 'inverted U' or 'hump' shape to the distribution of assets across someone's lifetime. This means that even if people have the same level of lifetime assets, we would expect some inequality in assets with people in late middle age having higher levels of assets than other groups.

Figure 2.1 compares the distribution of income and personal assets and shows very clearly the inequality of both income and assets as well as the higher degree of asset inequality compared with income inequality. For example, the bottom three deciles (the equivalent to 30% of the population) had no personal assets at all while the top decile (the top 10%) owned half of all personal assets.

Distribution of different kinds of assets

So far, we have considered the overall distribution of personal assets. If we look separately at housing, financial and pension assets, we see slightly different pictures. For example, housing assets are more equally distributed among the population than other kinds of assets. This is due to the increases in home ownership over the past 50 years. According to the Office for National Statistics (2004), home ownership increased from 49% to 69% between 1971 and 2002, with most of the increase occurring in the 1980s. The increase has levelled off since then. The 'Right to Buy' scheme introduced in the early 1980s has contributed to the increase in home ownership, as it allowed local authority tenants, typically people on lower incomes, to buy their own home. Although

Figure 2.1: Distribution of income and personal assets, by deciles

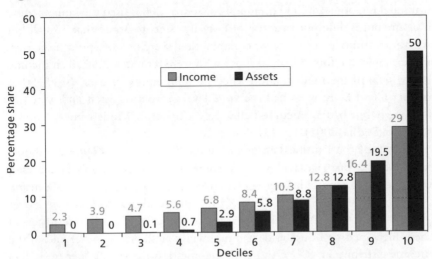

Source: Family Resources Survey 1994/95, cited in Rowlingson et al (1999)

home ownership has increased overall, there is concern that a division may now exist between homeowners and renters in terms of living standards and life chances. There is also considerable difference in the value of housing assets across the population.

As far as financial savings go, the proportion of people with no savings is around a third. This proportion is far higher for those with lower incomes (Paxton, 2002). As far as pension assets are concerned, there is substantial inequality in their distribution among people aged 50 to state pension age: the 10% of individuals in these families with the greatest family pension assets (state and private) had, on average, £874,000 in 2002/03, whereas the 10% of individuals in families with the least family pension assets had just £50,000 (Banks et al, 2005). Private pension assets were much more unevenly distributed than state pension assets. Banks et al (2005) also found that holdings of different assets did not offset each other. For example, older people with low pension assets also tended to have low levels of housing wealth. As a result, total assets were very unequally distributed. The 10% of older individuals in the richest families had at least £1,000,000 of family wealth, whereas the poorest 10% had less than £110,000.

Combining income and assets

Orton (2006) has analysed data on income and housing assets to argue that low-income households in high value properties are 'exceptional' (2006, p 9). He defined low income as income below the poverty line (less than 60% of median income) and found that households with poverty level incomes in the three highest Council Tax bands (F, G and H) represented only 0.7% of all households (about 180,000 households). Sodha (2005) used the same income measure but a different measure of housing assets to argue that a small but significant minority of those who were retired were income-poor, asset-rich. For example, she found that, of those who were retired, 4.2% had an income below 60% of the median and owned housing equity of over £100,000. A further 6% of pensioners had the same level of housing assets and were not in poverty but had an income below Age Concern's 'Modest but Adequate' standard (Sodha, 2005).

Analysis of the Family Resources Survey (2003/04) in *Figure 2.2* shows, in relation to financial savings, that income and assets are closely linked with those on high incomes having higher levels of saving also (for example, nearly a third of those with incomes over £1,000 per week also had savings of over £20,000 in 2003/04), but the analysis also shows that nearly one in ten of these high-income households had no savings at all. At the other end of the income distribution, 8% of those on incomes less than £100 per week had savings of £20,000 or more.

Figure 2.2: *Distribution of savings by total household income*

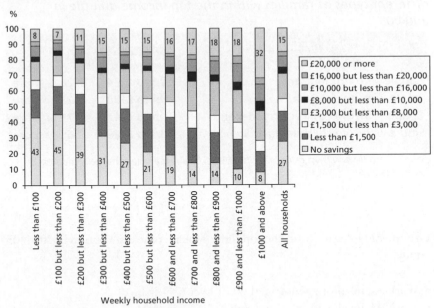

Weekly household income

Source: Family Resources Survey 2003/04

The rich and their riches

As has already been argued in this chapter, there is no clear conceptualisation or definition of 'the rich' or 'riches' and so this section will provide a variety of statistics based on available data (which is scarce relative to data on poverty). To start with, we take a fairly broad definition of riches as the top quintile (or fifth) of the population in terms of income. As we can see from ***Table 2.3***, the net income of this group varied in 2004/05 from at least £323 per week for a single person with no children to £771 per week for a couple with two children aged 5 and 11, about two-and-a-half times more than the incomes of similar families in the bottom quintile.

Further data from the households below average income (HBAI; see DWP, 2005a) show that the groups *most* likely to be in the top quintile of the income distribution in 2004/05 were:

- single/couple both in full-time employment (38% chance)
- single/couple with one or more full-time self-employed (28% chance)
- couple without children (37% chance).

Table 2.3: *Net household income before housing costs for different types of families within the top income quintile in 2004/05*

	Bottom quintile	Top quintile
Couple with no children	Up to £214	£528 or more
Single with no children	Up to £130	£323 or more
Couple with two children aged 5 and 11	Up to £312	£771 or more
Single with two children aged 5 and 11	Up to £229	£565 or more

Source: http://www.dwp.gov.uk/asd/hbai/hbai2004/excel_files/chapters/chapter_2_excel_hbai05.xls

Groups *least* likely to be in the top fifth of the income distribution in 2004/05 were:

- workless, head or spouse aged 60 or over (7% chance)
- workless, head or spouse unemployed (2% chance)
- workless, other inactive (4% chance)
- single female pensioner (7% chance)
- single with children (4% chance).

As far as assets are concerned, the Family Resources Survey 2004/05 (DWP, 2005b) shows that 15% of families had financial savings of £20,000 or more. Pensioner couple families were twice as likely as average to have at least £20,000 in financial savings (31%) so while the income data show that workless families aged 60 or over had little chance of being in the top fifth of the *income* distribution, these families had a higher chance than average of being in the top fifth of the *asset* distribution. This is linked to life cycle dynamics (see above).

The top 15%–20% is a fairly broad definition of riches. A slightly narrower measure is the top 10% (the top decile) of the population who owned about half (50%) of all personal assets and received 29% of all income in the mid-1990s (Rowlingson et al, 1999).

A particularly narrow focus on what might be called the 'super-rich' has been the subject of study for Atkinson and Salverda (2003), who used tax records to investigate the changing share of income held by the very top. They show that the share of income of the top 0.05% (sometimes known as the 'top ten thousand') fell between the mid-1920s and mid-1970s but then grew rapidly such that by 1999, their share of income was higher than it had been in 1937.

An alternative source of data on the super-rich comes from *The Sunday Times* (2007) Rich List, which identifies the top 1,000 richest people living and working in the UK through publicly available information on assets, whether land, property, racehorses, art or significant shares in publicly quoted companies. Bank accounts and small shareholdings in private equity portfolios are excluded because there is no publicly available information on these.

In 1997, the combined assets of the then top 1,000 amounted to £98.99 billion. In 2007, the total assets of this group had risen to nearly £360 billion. *The Sunday Times* notes that the rich got much richer under Labour (since 1997) than they ever did, in percentage terms, under the Conservatives from 1989 to 1997. In particular, the assets of the top 1,000 grew by £60 billion in 2006/07, representing a near 20% increase, one of the highest rises in a year recorded since the list was first produced in 1989. This is attributed to increases in the stock market and property values as well as money made through takeover deals and big City bonuses. It is surprising that recent shocks over oil price rises, continuing tensions in the Middle East and concerns about property markets overheating seem to have made no dent in levels of assets. In 2007 individuals in the top 1,000 had at least £70 million each.

The very top of the heap in terms of wealth are the billionaires (see **Table 2.4**). In 1997, there were 'just' 16 billionaires in Britain (*The Sunday Times*, 2007). By 2007 there were 68. Of the top 10, three have come to live in Britain from overseas. Many Indian, Russian, Scandinavian and Icelandic multi-millionaires moved to the London area.

Table 2.4 shows the top 10 in the Rich List, starting with Lakshmi Mittal, who is based in London but retains his Indian passport. According to *The Sunday Times*, he paid £70 million to Bernie Ecclestone, the Formula One

Table 2.4 *Richest People in Britain, 2007 (*Sunday Times *Rich List)*

Rank	Name	Total assets	Source of wealth
1	Lakshmi Mittal	£19,250m	Steel
2	Roman Abramovich	£10,800m	Oil, industry, football
3	Duke of Westminster	£7,000m	Property
4	Sri and Gopi Hinduja	£6,200m	Industry and finance
5	David Khalili	£5,800m	Art and Property
6	Hans Rausing and family	£5,400m	Food packaging
7	Philip and Tina Green	£4,900m	Retailing
8	John Fredriksen	£3,500m	Shipping
9	David and Simon Reuben	£3,490m	Property
10	Jim Ratcliffe	£3,300m	Chemicals

Source: http://business.timesonline.co.uk/tol/business/specials/rich_list/rich_list_search/

supremo, for a house in Kensington Palace Gardens and spent £30 million on his daughter's wedding. Roman Abramovich made his fortune from the privatisation of the Russian oil industry, buying the Sibneft oil business in 1995 for about £120 million with his partner, Boris Berezovsky. Ten years later, the company was sold and the stake held by Abramovich and his partners was worth about £7.5 billion. Number three in the list, the Duke of Westminster, owes much of his riches to inheritance. He owns vast estates in Lancashire, Cheshire, Scotland and Canada as well as prime real estate in central London's Mayfair and Belgravia. His assets include substantial art treasures. The only woman in the top 10 is Tina Green, who is the legal owner of most of her family's assets for tax reasons.

In August 2006, *The Guardian* (2006) reported bonuses of £19 billion paid out mostly to high-flying City financiers and dealers in the early months of 2006, the time when such bonuses are typically paid. This amount is the equivalent to Britain's entire annual transport budget. *The Guardian* quotes Frances O'Grady, Trades Union Congress (TUC) Deputy General Secretary, as saying, 'the huge amounts being paid out in City bonuses continue to beggar belief. Many working people helping to deliver vital services can only dream of earning what a small number of City high-flyers receive each year in their annual bonus'.

Conclusion

The gap between rich and poor in the UK is very large by international standards and has increased in recent years. Income inequality is now higher than at any time in the previous 50 years and asset inequality grew in the 1990s for the first time in a century.

This chapter argues that a distinction needs to be made between 'wealth as assets' and 'wealth as riches'. Greater thought needs to be given to how we conceptualise and then operationalise assets and riches. There is a lack of data on assets and riches but two new datasets are emerging: the Luxembourg Wealth Study (Sierminska et al, 2006) and the British-based Wealth and Assets Survey. These should enable much-needed further research in this field.

Summary

- There have been far fewer studies of assets and riches than of income and poverty.
- 'Assets' refers to a stock of money which it may be possible to cash in (such as financial savings or property) or which may provide a future income (such as pension assets).
- 'Income' represents a flow of money such as from salaries or social security benefits.
- 'The rich' are those at the top of the economic distribution, typically with both very high incomes and large amounts of assets.
- There is very little agreement about how to conceptualise and define 'riches'.
- Income inequality grew rapidly during the 1980s and then stabilised.
- Asset inequality grew rapidly during the 1990s for the first time, it seems, in the 20th century.
- The distribution of assets is twice as unequal as the distribution of income.

Questions for discussion

- Why do we have much less information on assets and riches than we do on income and poverty?
- What is a luxury? Make a list of some luxuries.
- To what extent, and how, did the rich get richer in the 1990s?

Further reading

Compared with all the numerous textbooks and empirical reports on poverty there is very little on assets and riches. Scott (1994) is probably the best place to start, with a broadly sociological overview of wealth in relation to poverty. Rowlingson et al (1999) provide quantitative and qualitative data on wealth inequality from a life cycle perspective and Hills (2004) summarises more recent statistics on inequality. Lansley (2006) provides a highly readable account of the rise of the super-wealthy in the past 20 years.

Electronic resources

www.dwp.gov.uk/asd/frs/2004_05/index.asp – Family Resources Survey
www.forbes.com/billionaires/ – Forbes 'the world's billionaires' website

www.ifs.org.uk – Institute for Fiscal Studies
www.dwp.gov.uk/asd/hbai.asp – HBAI website
www.hmrc.gov.uk/stats/personal_wealth/menu.htm – HM Revenue and Customs information on the distribution of personal wealth
www.statistics.gov.uk –Office for National Statistics
http://business.timesonline.co.uk/section/0,,20589,00.html – *The Sunday Times* Rich List 2007

References

Atkinson, A. (1971) 'The distribution of wealth and the individual lifecycle', *Oxford Economic Papers*, vol 23, Oxford: Oxford University Press.

Atkinson, A. and Harrison, G. (1978) *The distribution of personal wealth in Britain*, Cambridge: Cambridge University Press.

Atkinson, A. and Salverda, W. (2003) 'Top incomes in the Netherlands and the United Kingdom over the twentieth century' (mimeo), Oxford: Nuffield College [cited in Hills (2004)].

Atkinson, A., Gordon, J. and Harrison, J. (1986) *Trends in the distribution of wealth in Britain 1923-1981*, STICERD Discussion Paper 70, London: London School of Economics and Political Science.

Banks, J., Emmerson, C., Oldfield, G. and Tetlow, G. (2005) *Prepared for retirement? The adequacy and distribution of retirement resources in England*, London: Institute for Fiscal Studies.

BBC (British Broadcasting Corporation) (2006) 'Massive rise in top bosses' pay', 17 October (http://news.bbc.co.uk/1/hi/business/6060392.stm).

Bernstein, J., Brocht, C. and Spade-Aguilar, M. (2000) *How much is enough? Basic family budgets for working families*, Washington: Economic Policy Institute.

Brewer, M., Goodman, A., Shaw, J. and Sibieta, L. (2006) *Poverty and inequality in Britain: 2006*, London: Institute for Fiscal Studies.

Dean, H. with Melrose, M. (1999) *Poverty, riches and social citizenship*, Basingstoke: Macmillan.

Department of Trade and Industry (2005) *Tackling over-indebtedness*, London: Department of Trade and Industry.

DWP (Department for Work and Pensions) (2004) 'Households below average income', Chapter 2, Table 2.3 (www.dwp.gov.uk/asd/hbai/hbai2004/excel_files/chapters/chapter_2_excel_hbai05.xls).

DWP (2005a) 'Households below average income' (www.dwp.gov.uk/asd/hbai/hbai2005/supp_tabs.asp).

DWP (2005b) *Family Resources Survey 2004-5* (www.dwp.gov.uk/asd/frs/2004_05/pdfonly/frs_2004_05_report.pdf).

DWP (2007) 'Households below average income' (www.dwp.gov.uk/asd/hbai. asp).

Friedman, M. (1957) *A theory of the consumption function*, Princeton, NJ: Princeton University Press.

Giddens, A. (1998) *The third way*, Cambridge: Cambridge University Press.

Gordon, D. and Pantazis, C. (eds) (1998) *Breadline Britain in the 1990s*, Aldershot: Ashgate.

Gordon, D., Adelman, L., Ashworth, K., Bradshaw, J., Levitas, R., Middleton, S., Pantazis, C., Patsios, D., Payne, S., Townsend, P. and Williams, J. (2000) *Poverty and social exclusion in Britain*, York: Joseph Rowntree Foundation.

Guardian, The (2006) 'City bonuses reach record £19bn', 17 August (www. guardian.co.uk/executivepay/story/0,,1851785,00.html#article_continue).

Hills, J. (2004) *Inequality and the state*, Oxford: Oxford University Press.

Hills, J., Smithies, R. and McKnight, A. (2006) *Tracking income: How working families' incomes vary through the year*, CASEReport 32, London: Centre for the Analysis of Social Exclusion, London School of Economics and Political Science.

HMRC (Her Majesty's Revenue & Customs) (2003) *Distribution of personal wealth: An introductory note* (www.hmrc.gov.uk/stats/personal_wealth/ wealth_oct03.pdf).

Inland Revenue (2003) *Inland Revenue statistics 2003*, London: Inland Revenue.

Jenkins, S. (1990) 'The distribution of wealth: measurement and models', *Journal of Economic Surveys*, vol 4, no 4, December, pp 329-60.

Kempson, E. (2002) *Over-indebtedness in Britain: A report to the Department of Trade and Industry*, London: DTI.

Kempson, E., McKay, S. and Willitts, M. (2004) *Characteristics of families in debt and the nature of indebtedness*, Department for Work and Pensions Research Report No 211, London: The Stationery Office.

Lansley, S. (2006) *Rich Britain: The rise and rise of the new super-wealthy*, London: Politico's.

Lister, R. (2004) *Poverty*, Cambridge: Polity Press.

McKay, S. (1992) *Pensioners' assets*, London: Policy Studies Institute.

Mack, J. and Lansley, S. (1985) *Poor Britain*, London: Allen and Unwin.

Medeiros, M. (2006) 'The rich and the poor: the construction of an affluence line from the poverty line', *Social Indicators Research*, vol 78, pp 1-18.

Modigliani, F. and Brumberg, R. (1954) 'Utility analysis and the consumption function: an interpretation of cross-section data', in K. Kurihara (ed) *Post-Keynesian economics*, New Brunswick, NJ: Rutgers University Press.

National Statistics (2004) 'A summary of changes over time' (www.statistics. gov.uk/cci/nugget.asp?id=821).

Orton, M. (2006) 'Wealth rich but income poor?', Paper presented at the Social Policy Association Conference, Birmingham, July.

Orton, M. and Rowlingson, K. (2007) 'A problem of riches: towards a new social policy research agenda on the distribution of economic resources', *Journal of Social Policy*, vol 36, no 1, pp 59-78.

Paxton, W. (2002) *Wealth distribution: The evidence*, London: Institute for Public Policy Research.

Paxton, W. and Taylor, M. (2002) 'Bridging the wealth gap', *New Statesman*, 12 July.

Rowlingson, K. and McKay, S. (2005) *Attitudes to inheritance in Britain*, Bristol: The Policy Press.

Rowlingson, K., Whyley, C. and Warren, T. (1999) *Wealth in Britain: A lifecycle perspective*, London: Policy Studies Institute.

Rowntree, S. (1901) *Poverty: A study of town life*, London: Macmillan (reissued in 2001 by The Policy Press).

Royal Commission on the Distribution of Income and Wealth (1977) *Report Number 1*, Cmnd 6999, London: HMSO.

Scott, J. (1994) *Poverty and wealth: Citizenship, deprivation and privilege*, Harlow: Longman.

Sierminska, E., Brandolini, A. and Smeeding, T. (2006) 'Comparing wealth distribution across rich countries: first results from the Luxembourg Wealth Study', Luxembourg Wealth Study Working Paper Series 1 (http://ssrn.com/abstract=927402).

Sodha, S. (2005) *Housing-rich, income-poor*, London: Institute for Public Policy Research.

Sunday Times, The (2007) '*Sunday Times* Rich List 2007' (http://business.timesonline.co.uk/tol/business/specials/rich_list/).

Townsend, P. (1979) *Poverty in the United Kingdom*, Harmondsworth: Penguin Books.

Wakefield, M. (2003) *Is middle Britain middle-income Britain?*, IFS Briefing Note 38, London: Institute for Fiscal Studies.

three

Poverty and social exclusion

Pete Alcock

Overview

- Poverty has been the focus of academic research and policy concern for over a century in the UK.
- Social exclusion has only recently come on to the research agenda.
- In practice both are complex and interrelated problems, which require coordinated policy responses.

Key concepts

expenditure; income; deprivation; participation; poverty; social exclusion

Introduction

Academic research on poverty has a long history in the UK, usually traced back to the pioneering work by Booth (1889) and Rowntree (1901) at the end of the 19th century. Their work was the first to use social science methods to seek to define and measure poverty, and to use the findings of this to seek to influence policy debate – both Booth and Rowntree expected that their discovery of high levels of poverty in Britain would lead to policy initiatives to combat this. Since then many other academic researchers have followed their lead, most notably Townsend (1979; see also Abel Smith and Townsend, 1965). The Townsend Centre for International Poverty Research at the University of Bristol now carries on the tradition through new empirical research on poverty and social exclusion in the UK (Pantazis et al, 2006), and through the promotion of international and comparative studies (Gordon and Townsend, 2000; Townsend and Gordon, 2002). Poverty and social exclusion are now better understood and more widely debated than ever before, and, as the other chapters in this book demonstrate, they are part of ever more increasing disparities of income and wealth – despite this, however, they remain significant social problems both within the UK and across the rest of the globe.

Defining and measuring poverty

The definition and measurement of poverty are, however, a contested terrain. There is no simple and agreed definition of poverty, nor any single measure that can determine the scale of the problem. In part this is because poverty itself is a political term. Poverty is an unacceptable state of affairs, and use of the term implies that something should be done about it (see Alcock, 2006, pp 4-6) – a contrast with inequality, and wealth, which are seen as inevitable or even desirable. The definitions adopted by academics have sometimes therefore contrasted with those employed by politicians. Townsend famously adopted a new notion of relative poverty in the 1960s, linked to social security benefit rates, in research that found unexpectedly high levels of such relative poverty in the UK (Abel Smith and Townsend, 1965). Yet the Conservative politician John Moore openly challenged this notion in the 1980s. In challenging the evidence of these higher levels of poverty, he dismissed such a relative approach:

> When the pressure groups say that one-third of the population is living in poverty, they cannot be saying that one-third of people are living below the draconian subsistence levels used by Booth and Rowntree. (Moore, 1985, p 5)

Moore was dismissing the relative approach in part, of course, because the government did not then want to commit significant resources to combating poverty in the country. Townsend has always argued that his evidence of higher levels of poverty should lead to policy initiatives to reduce these. Policy and definition are always interlinked. More recently the Labour government under Tony Blair identified child poverty as a key policy issue and committed themselves to removing this within 20 years (Blair, 1999). This then led to official debate about how such poverty should be defined and measured (DWP, 2003), with a new, three-dimensional measure being introduced (see *Box 3.2* below).

For most academics, however, and for most politicians and policy makers too, it is the contested nature of poverty that makes it such an important and challenging topic to study. It is *because* something must be done about it that we argue about the definition and measurement of poverty. In this sense poverty is therefore different to inequality. All societies are unequal to some extent, and arguably it would be impossible to remove all such differences, even if we could agree that this was a desirable policy goal. The extent of inequality varies, of course, both across different societies and over time, and studying changes in these trends can tell us much about the nature of social order in society and the political and policy responses to that.

Absolute and relative poverty

The existence of inequalities within societies is not itself a problem, however (see Chapters Six and Eleven, this volume). The existence of poverty is. No one would argue that poverty was an acceptable outcome of the social order – although, of course, there would be debate about how much of a problem this was, as we saw above. In an extended discussion of the concept of poverty (in the introduction to the major report on the most recent Poverty and Social Exclusion [PSE] Survey on poverty in the UK), Gordon contrasted different approaches but argued that there were underlying similarities in the notion that poverty implies being without key indicators of acceptable social functioning (Gordon, 2006). This draws on Sen's famous argument that there is an absolute core to the concept of poverty, based on the human need to 'live without shame' (1983, p 163), although, as mentioned in Chapter Six (this volume), it was Adam Smith writing in the 18th century who first suggested that the shame associated with the lack of a linen shirt for a labourer would make this a necessity for social life then (Smith, 1776, p 691).

This raises the much-discussed distinction between absolute and relative approaches to the definition and measurement of poverty. *Absolute* poverty is usually associated with the idea that those who are experiencing poverty do not have enough to survive, and is sometimes also referred to as subsistence poverty. *Relative* poverty is based on the idea that the nature of poverty will be different in different social circumstances and therefore will change as society itself changes. The absolute approach has sometimes been associated with the early work of Rowntree, and the relative approach is often associated with Townsend, who has openly championed it (see *Box 3.1*).

Box 3.1: Absolute and relative poverty

A family living on the scale allowed for must never spend a penny on railway fare or omnibus. They must never go into the country unless they walk. They must never purchase a halfpenny newspaper or spend a penny to buy a ticket for a popular concert ... and what is bought must be of the plainest and most economical description. (Rowntree, 1901, p 167)

Individuals, families and groups in the population can be said to be in poverty when they lack the resources to obtain the types of diet, participate in the activities and have the living conditions and amenities which are customary ... in the societies to which they belong. (Townsend, 1979, p 31)

However, in reality neither Rowntree nor Townsend adopted exclusively absolute or relative approaches in their research (see Alcock, 2006, pp 66–70). And, as Gordon (2006) discusses, in practice both absolute and relative approaches overlap when they are operationalised in research on poverty, with researchers generally seeking to identify those things that are regarded as essential in the society being studied and then to find ways of measuring the number of people experiencing deprivation from these as a result of low incomes and inadequate resources.

In practice, therefore, all definitions and measures of poverty depend on the social circumstances in which they arise. For the most part poverty is therefore contrasted with the standards of living that most people enjoy or take for granted in society, often seeking to identify those falling below some average measure, as we shall return to discuss shortly. Of course this takes no account of the much higher standards of living enjoyed by the wealthy, who at the upper end of the scale of resources have incomes and assets much higher above the average than those who experience poverty are below it, as discussed in Chapter Two, this volume. Our views of poverty, and what it means to be without sufficient resources in society, might well change if we compared this with the extreme wealth enjoyed by some, and this might also change our views about what could, or should, be done about the problem.

This raises the more general question of perceptions of poverty. Most academic research and political debate about poverty has been conducted using *objective* definitions of the problem, based on evidence of income or living standards. This generally leads to a proportion of the population being defined as poor. However, this perception of the condition of poverty may not be shared by those who are experiencing it themselves, or indeed by others in society. *Subjective* perceptions of poverty may not map on to the objective definitions of the researchers. Indeed there is growing evidence that, when people with limited resources are asked about their experience of poverty, many do not readily identify themselves as having such a problem (see Beresford et al, 1999). In part, of course, this is because those who are experiencing poverty may not feel that they have the power to define their situation, and indeed this powerlessness is itself a feature of poverty. It is others who define and determine the fate of those who are in poverty, through processes that act to both label and isolate them. This issue is discussed more generally by Lister (2004) in her book on *Poverty*, where she explored the contradictory implications of 'discourses of poverty' and the importance of extending understanding beyond academic definition and measurement, to the experiences, and the agency, of those who are in poverty.

Key dilemmas

Nevertheless, most academic research on poverty does operate with objective definitions, not the least because it is much easier to measure these and to compare trends over time and place. Even here, however, the situation is a complex one. Different measures can be employed, and they will provide different pictures of the poverty problem. Alcock (2006, chapter 6) and Lister (2004, chapter 2) explore the implications of these different measures in more detail. However, it is worth mentioning some key dilemmas here.

First there is the question of whether to measure income or expenditure. Income is much easier to identify, or at least find information about. But it is really expenditure that determines whether someone is experiencing poverty, and this may not be the same as income. For instance, those with savings and assets can enjoy a higher standard of living than their weekly income would suggest and conversely those repaying debts may be living much below their weekly income level. Ringen (1988) has argued that it is expenditure that should be adopted as the most accurate measure of poverty, and this can be done using data from the Expenditure and Food Survey (EFS) or the Family Resources Survey (FRS) carried out by the Department for Work and Pensions. However, it is more common to use income measures, as indeed the government does in its major research on poverty, discussed below.

Second there is the question of whether to measure resources available or deprivation experienced. Income measures do not necessarily tell us about standard of living. In part this is because of the distinction that Rowntree (1901) made between primary and secondary poverty. *Primary* poverty is when people do not have enough resources to buy what they need. *Secondary* poverty is when people do have enough resources but still go without necessities because income is spent on other activities. Of course, this begs the more general question – what are necessities? This has prompted a range of researchers to seek to develop measures of poverty which focus on attempts to identify a list of socially approved necessities, and then to count the number of people who are going without significant numbers of them. This approach was pioneered by Townsend (1979) and has most recently been developed in the 2000 PSE Survey led by Gordon (Gordon et al, 2000; Pantazis et al, 2006). It has also now been recognised by the government and incorporated into their threefold measure of child poverty (see *Box 3.2*).

Box 3.2: Three measures of child poverty

- Absolute low income – 60% of median average income in 1998/99 in real terms, to compare whether there were improvements against a fixed benchmark.
- Relative low income – 60% of contemporary median income, to compare poor families against general rises in incomes.
- Material deprivation and low income combined – including a measure of lack of material necessities, to compare living standards more broadly.

Source: DWP (2003)

This leads on to the more general question of whether it is possible, or desirable, to operate with only one measure of poverty. Given the complex nature of the problem, incorporating aspects of income and expenditure, and resources and living standards, it may be that we are better accepting that we will need multidimensional measures of poverty to capture the multidimensional nature of the problem. Analysis by Finch and Bradshaw (2003) has revealed that different measures do indeed lead to different people being defined as living in poverty. This led them to speculate whether different measures should be the basis for measurement, but could then be combined into an overlapping, or overall, poverty concept. This *overall poverty* approach has been taken up by the United Nations (1995) in an attempt to capture the different dimensions of poverty internationally, and by Gordon and Townsend (2000), who have argued that the PSE approach could be used to measure overall poverty across the European Union (EU).

Despite this variety and complexity, simple measures of poverty are sometimes needed, and in practice are widely employed. The most important, and most widely used, are those based on the numbers below fixed points on the income scale, usually a proportion of average wages. This is the approach used by the government in their annual survey of poverty and income inequalities, the households below average income (HBAI) report (DWP, 2006a), and it is also now employed by the EU in the collection and comparison of poverty rates across member states. The most commonly used poverty measure used to be 50% of mean average income, but the mean can be distorted by small numbers of very high incomes, and so the more popular measure now is 60% of median income (the mid–point in the scale). In practice, however, both give largely similar measures of poverty.

For 2004/05 this 60% median measure gave 9.2 million (16%) of the population living in poverty before taking account of housing costs (BHC) and 11.4 million (20%) after taking housing into account (AHC) (DWP, 2006a, Table 3.5). *Figure 3.1* compares the distribution across social groups using the AHC measure and reveals the high risk of poverty for lone parents.

Figure 3.1: *Percentage risk of poverty by social group (2004/05)* *(60% median income AHC)*

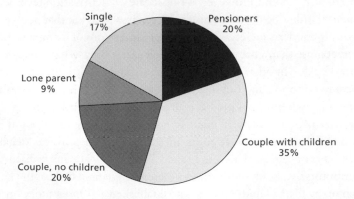

Source: Adapted from DWP (2006a, Table 3.5)

It is this 60% of median income figure that the government included within its new measures of child poverty (see *Box 3.2*). Here it is using it to track changes in levels of poverty over time in order to assess whether the target of removing child poverty in 20 years from 1998/99 is being achieved. It distinguishes here between income levels at current values and when compared to 1998/99 values. This reveals a major problem with this average income measure of poverty. In a growing economy average incomes are always rising. This has certainly been the case in the UK since 1998 and thus the proportion of people experiencing poverty by the current measure will be greater than that using 1998 income levels. Anti-poverty policy is shooting at a moving target here, and the 1998 measure has been included to reveal how many fewer children are in poverty in these 'absolute' terms than was the case in 1998.

The government child poverty measure also includes a measure of material deprivation, drawing on the PSE research on lack of necessities, which identified a list of indicators of deprivation deemed as essential by a representative sample of the population and counted those lacking significant numbers of these. As discussed above, these different measures will give differing numbers and proportions of people in poverty. This can be confusing, but it is also an explicit and official recognition of the differing approaches to definition and measurement that have always characterised academic and political debate on poverty. More recently, however, this debate has been extended to also encompass the concept of social exclusion, and this has added further, and broader, dimensions to our understanding of the social problems that are faced here.

Social exclusion

Definition and measurement of poverty has traditionally focused on resources, and in particular, income. However, as the debate on deprivation reveals, access to resources is only one dimension of the standards of living that people enjoy (or do not!) in modern society. These broader dimensions of living standards, or lifestyle, recognise that what matters to people is not only 'what they have', but also 'what they do'. In other words social activity, and in particular the ability to participate in common and popular social groups and pastimes, can be critical in determining whether people have an acceptable standard of living.

Failure or inability to participate is now generally referred to as social exclusion. The concept has it roots in academic and political debates in continental Europe, in particular in France (Paugam, 1991), and is discussed by the contributors to a book on European dimensions edited by Room (1995). It was taken up by the EU in the 1990s who established an Observatory on Social Exclusion to monitor the progress of national policy activity (Robbins et al,

1994).The EU clearly saw social exclusion as a broader, and more intractable, problem than poverty (see *Box 3.3*).The Observatory is now closed, but in 2000 all member states committed themselves to monitoring their own national action plans to combat social exclusion.

> **Box 3.3:** Defining social exclusion (European Commission definition)
>
> Today, the concept of social exclusion is taking over from poverty, which is more static than dynamic and seen far more often as exclusively monetary poverty.... Social exclusion does not only mean insufficient income, and it even goes beyond participation in working life.... More generally, in stressing the rupture of the social link, it suggests something more than social inequality and therefore carries with it the risk of a two tier society, or the relegation to the status of a welfare dependent. (J.-P. Tricart, European Commission official, cited in Robbins et al, 1994, p 12)

What the EC definition in *Box 3.3* also reveals is that social exclusion is both an individual and a collective problem. Social exclusion is a problem for those who are not able to participate in social activities and so live with a deprived lifestyle. But it is also a problem for society more generally if there are those who are not able to take part in social relations, including, of course in a democracy, political participation and involvement. In a seminal study of some of the differing dimensions of social exclusion published by the Child Poverty Action Group (CPAG) in 1986,Ward argued that the lack of political participation was often associated with other aspects of poverty and social exclusion (Golding, 1986, chapter 3). In such a context social exclusion may become a problem for society more generally, if some sections are excluded from the processes and relations on which the functioning of society depends – a problem that is also sometimes referred to as 'social polarisation'.

These broader dimensions of social exclusion are now the subject of more widespread academic enquiry in the UK.A major Centre for the Analysis of Social Exclusion (CASE) was established at the London School of Economics and Political Science (LSE) from 1997 to 2007.They engaged in wide-ranging research on the problem and published some key findings (see Hills et al, 2002), arguing, for instance, that social exclusion could be defined in terms of participation in key activities in society such as:

- *Consumption* – purchasing of goods and services,
- *Production* – participating in economically or socially valuable activity,

- *Political engagement* – involvement in local or national decision making,
- *Social interaction* – with family, friends and communities. (Burchardt et al, 2002, p 31)

In 1998, the government recognised the importance of social exclusion and the need to combat it with the establishment of the Social Exclusion Unit (SEU). This was a small new cross-departmental unit with a brief to focus on specific issues of social exclusion identified by government (early priorities were rough sleepers, truancy and teenage pregnancy), and to coordinate responses to this from government and other public agencies, referred to by the Prime Minister as promoting 'joined-up solutions'. The SEU initially reported direct to the Cabinet Office, although in 2006 it was restructured to become a Task Force and some of its activities were transferred to the new Department for Communities and Local Government. The SEU and Task Force also only operate in England. However, both the Scottish Parliament and Welsh Assembly have developed similar government initiatives to tackle social exclusion. In 1999 the devolved government in Scotland launched a social justice strategy, and there is now a Social Inclusion Division within the Executive, promoting partnership work in particular at community level. In Wales the Assembly has a Social Justice and Regeneration Committee with a wide range of responsibilities for supporting social inclusion.

The SEU was clear evidence of a new-found commitment to combat the problem of social exclusion, and it has been responsible for a number of major policy initiatives, including the Neighbourhood Renewal Strategy (SEU, 1998, 2001) and the action plan on promoting inclusion in childhood (Cabinet Office, 2006a). It has also played a key role in developing analysis of social exclusion and promoting research. Its website contains a definition of social exclusion which now informs both academic debate and policy development (see www.cabinetoffice.gov.uk/social_exclusion_task_force, and also *Box 3.4*).

Box 3.4: What is social exclusion?

Social exclusion is about more than income poverty. It is a shorthand term for what can happen when people or areas have a combination of linked problems such as unemployment, discrimination, poor skills, low incomes, poor housing, high crime and family breakdown. These problems are linked and mutually reinforcing. Social exclusion is an extreme consequence of what happens when people don't get a fair deal throughout their lives, often because of disadvantage they face at birth, and thus disadvantage can be transmitted from one generation to the next.

Source: www.cabinetoffice.gov.uk/social_exclusion_task_force/context.aspx

As mentioned above, the UK government is also now committed to producing and monitoring a national action plan on social inclusion, as agreed by all EU members in Lisbon in 2000, outlining activity being undertaken across the UK by all of the devolved administrations (Cabinet Office, 2006b). Monitoring of social inclusion policy is also carried out in an annual report from the Department for Work and Pensions called *Opportunity for All*. This lists a total of 59 indicators of exclusion and measures progress in reducing the prevalence of these, with the most recent report identifying positive progress in 40, with only seven getting worse (DWP, 2006b).

These indicators provide a good summary of the kinds of activities which the government identifies as constituting social exclusion, and they extend much beyond more traditional measures of income poverty and lack of resources (see *Box 3.5*). A similar annual monitoring exercise is also carried out by an independent research agency, the New Policy Institute (NPI), also using a long list of indicators. The NPI also now carries out parallel assessments in Scotland and Wales, and summaries of all the reports are available on its website (www.npi.org.uk).

Box 3.5: Selected indicators of social exclusion

Government measures (DWP, 2006b):
- School attendance
- Infant mortality
- Fear of crime
- Households in fuel poverty

Independent measures (NPI; see Palmer et al, 2005):
- Insecure at work
- Mental health
- Help to live at home
- Without a bank account

Indicators of exclusion can provide a wide-ranging picture of the extent and depth of the problem within society. However, as Berthoud (2006) has pointed out, they cannot provide us with a definition of either poverty or social exclusion – they are just indicators of the circumstances which could lead to this. However, there is evidence that the experience of lack of indicators of exclusion or deprivation is closely associated with other dimensions of poverty, as suggested by Townsend in his 1960s' research (Townsend, 1979). Levitas (2006) discusses this, utilising data from the PSE Survey, and concludes that non-participation in the kind of activities identified as essential is closely linked to poverty and lack of resources.

The relationship between social exclusion and poverty is a complex one, however. Participation, or non-participation, depends crucially on individual agency – the decisions taken by those who are excluded and those who exclude them. Social exclusion is about the *process* of social relations rather than the *outcome* of them. As Barry (2002) points out in his contribution to the CASE analysis of the problem, wealthy people too can exclude themselves from social relations, for instance, in exclusive gated communities with private security guards, or in expensive private schools outside local communities. This may be 'voluntary' exclusion, but it can have dangerous social consequences in accentuating differentiation and polarisation in society. Conversely, for those who have the least financially, exclusion is frequently something which is to a large extent determined by others – the public services that are too remote to access, the social clubs that they cannot afford to join, or in some cases the discrimination that keeps them out of certain areas or activities. Social exclusion is a product of social relations and of the actions of those who exclude, as well as those who are excluded. It may be closely linked to poverty, therefore, but it is not always and for everyone the same problem. It also impacts differently over time.

Dynamics of poverty and social exclusion

Definition and measurement of poverty and social exclusion can provide us with pictures of the problem. Most of the research mentioned above is quantitative and provides statistical pictures, but there has also been a growing tradition of qualitative work that provides detailed description of the struggles that many people have to endure to survive in modern society. Some of this research was usefully summarised by Kempson in 1996. However, much of this quantitative and qualitative research has focused on those currently experiencing poverty at the time of the investigation. It therefore provides 'snapshots' rather than 'moving pictures'.

However, we live our lives over time, and over time people's risks and experiences of poverty may change. Poverty is a dynamic problem and research and analysis of the problem needs to recognise this. In fact, one of the earliest poverty researchers, Rowntree, did recognise this dynamic dimension when he identified the changing risk of poverty over the life cycle with 'five alternating periods of want and comparative plenty' (1901, pp 136-7). This life cycle approach has been much developed recently in research on the changing risk of poverty over people's lives (see Chapter Two, this volume; and Leisering and Leibfried, 1999; Dewilde, 2003), and more recent work has focused on the lifecourse (the changes which different individuals experience) rather than the life cycle (a standardised pattern affecting all).

Of course, research to track people's changing experience of poverty and exclusion needs to be able to draw on data about lifecourse changes. This has not always been readily available (apart from the decennial Census) and can be very expensive to collect. However, in the past decade or so such longitudinal data have been developed through the maintenance of panel surveys. These are quantitative surveys of a representative sample of the population that are updated regularly to take account of changes in people's circumstances. In the UK this includes the British Household Panel Survey (BHPS), and there are similar panel surveys in a number of other European countries, coordinated through the EU.

There are a number of problems in gathering and maintaining such datasets, not the least the attrition (or loss) of respondents over time, which are discussed by Leisering and Walker (1998). Nevertheless the BHPS has been used to provide analysis of the dynamics of poverty and social exclusion in the UK, in particular by researchers in CASE (Hills et al, 2002). What this reveals is that for most people who are living in poverty the experience is a temporary one. People move into and out of poverty over time. This pattern of change can be a varied and complex one, however, resulting in different kinds of 'income trajectories'. Rigg and Sefton (2006) identified a number of these in research employing 10 years' of BHPS data, including rising and falling trajectories, 'blips' (short periods in or out of poverty) and fluctuating trajectories (movement both in and out) (see **Table 3.1**).

Periods of poverty therefore vary in intensity and extent. This is partly good news, for it means that those who are experiencing poverty will not always do so. However, it also means that for some the experience of poverty over time

Table 3.1: *Income trajectories by type*

Trajectory type	Ten waves of BHPS data (% of cases)
Flat	24.3
Flat with blip(s)	23.8
Rising	12.6
Falling	14.3
Fluctuating	12.6
Other	12.5

Source: Adapted from Rigg and Sefton (2006, Table 1)

can lead to an accumulation of deprivation, which is more extensive than that experienced by those who are only briefly going without. One dimension of this is the so-called 'revolving door' phenomenon of people leaving poverty for a short period of time, but only moving a short way up the income scale and returning later to the bottom. This sort of recurring deprivation is not captured in snapshot research on poverty.

Furthermore, long-term experience of poverty and exclusion can significantly accentuate the problems associated with it. Over long periods of poverty savings are expended and perhaps debts accrued, household items begin to fail and have to be replaced (or not!), and the ability of individuals and households to escape, in particular into well-paid employment, may gradually reduce. The effects of this were captured well in qualitative work by Kempson et al (1994), which described the increasing desperation felt by those experiencing long periods of poverty, and summarised this using a swimming analogy as 'sinking', 'drowning' or 'struggling to the surface' (1994, p 128).

Some commentators have suggested that long-term experience of poverty and deprivation can lead to those who experience it becoming increasingly cut off from the rest of society, so much so that they are unable – or unwilling – to rejoin it and become a separate *underclass*. This has been popularised in particular in the work of the US academic Murray (see Lister, 1996), but has been much criticised for suggesting that such people are really the authors of their own misfortune in refusing to participate in society or in taking responsibility for their own improvement. Longitudinal analysis using panel data at CASE (Burchardt et al, 2002) and across the EU (Whelan et al, 2002) has challenged such a construction and revealed that persistent poverty and exclusion do not interact to create a social cleavage between a minority of excluded people and the rest of society.

Most of the research on the experience of poverty over time has focused on the experience of individuals or households over a period of years, perhaps utilising panel data. However, the dynamics of poverty and exclusion may also have a longer-term impact, extending even over generations. There was concern expressed in the UK in the 1970s about the possibility that there might be a 'cycle of deprivation' through which the poverty and deprivation of parents was passed on to their children who would grow up to experience higher risks of poverty as a result (Joseph, 1972; and see Denham and Garnett, 2001). Extensive research into this at the time did not establish such clear links between generational experiences of poverty (Rutter and Madge, 1976; Brown and Madge, 1982). However, the notion of intergenerational transfer of deprivation has returned to the policy agenda in the early 21st century, and the concern to combat the effects of deprivation on children was a major feature of the government's 2006 action plan on social exclusion (Cabinet Office, 2006a).

The CASE researchers have also recently explored this intergenerational dimension on poverty dynamics. For instance, Sigle-Rushton (2004) has done research using the British Cohort Study, which concludes that there is evidence of intergenerational transfer of some outcomes, such as social housing, manual employment and low income. However, the researchers are at pains to point out that although there are identifiable links between deprivation in early years and later social inequalities, the correlations discovered here are not as strong as some policy makers assume (Hobcraft, 2002).

Distribution of poverty

Study of the changing nature and risk of poverty and social exclusion over time does not only reveal differences in the individual dynamics of poverty. Tracking levels of poverty over time also reveals significant variations in the extent of the problem in the UK. Of course there are all sorts of methodological problems in comparing levels of poverty over time, in particular when the sources of data or the definitions or measures of poverty employed have changed.

Much recent official analysis has been confined to the period since the introduction of the HBAI reports in the 1980s, since these do provide a

Figure 3.2: *Population with below average income (BHC) (1961–2002/03)*

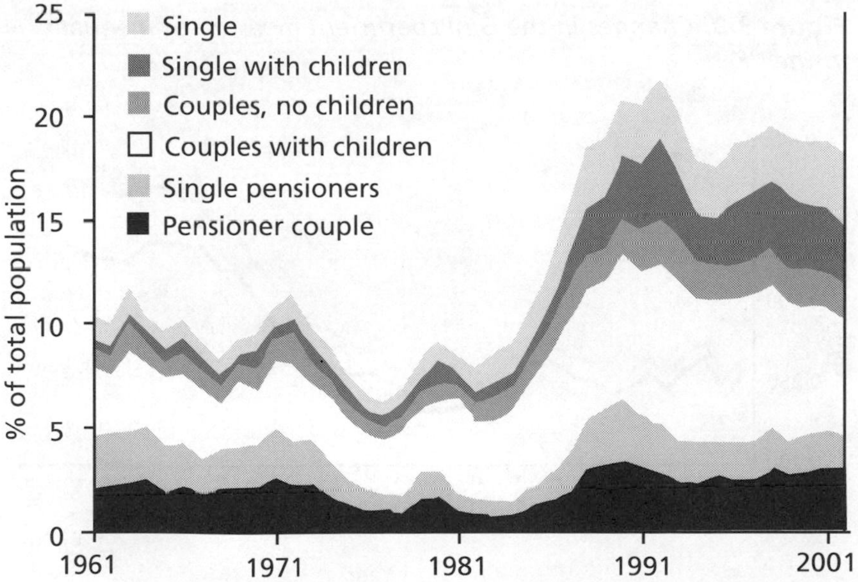

Source: Hills (2004, Figure 3.1, p 48)

consistent annual data source for the UK. Although Glennerster et al (2004) have provided an excellent guide to trends in poverty and policy over the whole of the past century, Hills in particular has sought to track changes over the past 40 years or so, with the support of the Joseph Rowntree Foundation (JRF), who sponsored a wide-ranging *Inquiry into income and wealth* in the 1990s (Hills, 1996). More recently he has extended and updated this work, and, as can be seen from *Figure 3.2*, it reveals dramatic changes in the levels of poverty in the UK, with a major rise in the 1980s, which has only reduced to a limited extent since then.

This figure employs the 50% of mean average income figure mentioned earlier, which was widely used as a simple measure of poverty, although it is now usually replaced with the 60% of median income figure. Both, however, give a broadly similar picture. *Figure 3.3* tracks changes in inequality over a similar period, using the Gini coefficient measure – where the extent of inequality in society is expressed as a decimal place, with higher figures revealing greater inequality. This figure includes both BHC and AHC trends, and reveals that these have become more accentuated in recent years, as the relative costs of housing have increased. What it reveals, however, is a very similar pattern of increase in inequality in the 1980s and some flattening out since then. Therefore, although poverty and inequality are not the same thing, both were effected by similar social and economic changes in the 1980s, when the UK became a much more unequal country with higher levels of poverty – and since then has not returned to pre-1980 levels.

Figure 3.3: *Changes in the Gini coefficient measure of inequality in the UK*

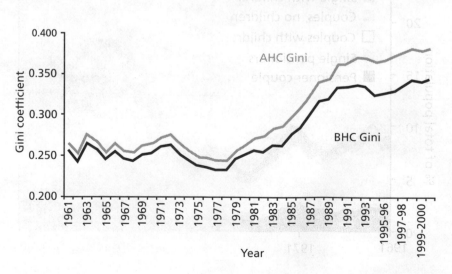

Source: Goodman and Shephard (2002, Figure 5)

Statistical data on poverty and social exclusion are always changing as new information is collected, in many cases on an annual basis by the government. However, published material inevitably lags behind these latest sources. Hills has done further work to bring together data on the changes in poverty and inequality under the Labour governments across a range of dimensions (Hills and Stewart, 2005). CPAG publish a regular guide to recent trends called *Poverty: The facts*, the most recent being Flaherty et al (2004; also available online, see Electronic sources). But readers who wish to study the latest figures are best advised to search electronic sources that can be updated almost instantly. The government's HBAI report is made available annually on the Department for Work and Pensions website (DWP, 2006a), but the best source of new data is probably an independent website on poverty maintained by the NPI with support from the JRF (see Electronic resources).

This website includes a summary of key facts, which reveals that 11.4 million people were living in poverty in the UK in 2004/05, based on the 60% of median income measure, a drop of 2.5 million since 1996/97, when the current Labour government came to power. This includes 3.4 million children living in low income families, a drop of 0.8 million since 1996/97 (NPI, 2006). This is an important figure because of the government's commitment to removing child poverty in 20 years from 1998, which included a promise to reduce it by a quarter by 2004/05. The evidence reveals that it did not quite meet this target, and that new policy initiatives will be needed if it is are to meet the further target of reducing it by a half by 2010 (Hirsch, 2006a). Child poverty levels in the UK also compare poorly with those in most other industrialised countries, with 15.4% living in poverty in the UK compared to 10.2% in Germany, 7.5% in France and 2.4% in Denmark, according to UNICEF (2005, p 4), although the improvements in the figures in the UK over recent years are better than those in all the other countries studied (UNICEF, 2005, p 15).

The risk of poverty also varies for other groups within UK society. As we saw in *Figure 3.1*, lone parents are at particular risk. They constitute a fifth of those in poverty and yet less than a tenth of households. People from particular minority ethnic groups also experience greater levels of poverty. More than half of Pakistani and Bangladeshi households are low-income households, while less than a fifth of the overall population are in low-income households (NPI, 2006). People with disabilities are also at higher risk, with average incomes 20% lower than non-disabled people (Burchardt, 2000) and higher levels of unemployment (only 51% of disabled men are working compared with 85% of non-disabled men: Flaherty et al, 2004, p 92). These aspects of the distribution of poverty and exclusion are discussed in more detail in other chapters in this book, and for an extended discussion of the impact of poverty and social exclusion on a number of key social groups see Alcock (2006, Part III). In addition to this, poverty and social exclusion are also differentially distributed spatially – a 'geography of poverty' (Philo, 1995), as discussed in Chapter Six, this volume.

Poverty or social exclusion?

The new data now provided by the government, such as the Index of Deprivation 2004 (ID2004) and the HBAI figures, and the annual monitoring of indicators in *Opportunity for All*, are evidence that poverty and social exclusion are taken seriously by UK policy makers, and this is revealed most clearly in the pledge to eradicate child poverty by 2020. This latter commitment is also important, of course, because it in effect commits future governments to continue the policy measures needed to achieve this, or admit that they are formally abandoning it.

Furthermore, the concern with the uneven spatial distribution of poverty and social exclusion has spawned a whole range of policy programmes and new initiatives that seek to combat different aspects of local deprivation. These include *Sure Start* for pre-school children, *Action Zones* on health, education and employment, the *New Deal for Communities* (NDC) and *Neighbourhood Renewal*. These new programmes are generally referred to as 'area-based initiatives' (ABIs). They are coordinated by a unit now based within the Department for Communities and Local Government, the Regional Co-ordination Unit, which lists over 50 different policy programmes on its ABI website (www.reu.gov. uk/abi; see Chapter Thirteen, this volume, and Alcock, 2006, chapter 16).

This is in stark contrast with the policy climate of the 1980s, when the Conservative government refused to recognise that poverty was a significant problem in the country and argued that specific policy initiatives to combat it were unnecessary in a modern affluent economy, as evidenced by the quotation from John Moore earlier. In the 21st century the government has reclaimed the problem of poverty. It has also become an issue of popular and international concern, as the 2005 Make Poverty History campaign on global poverty revealed.

However, as we have seen, there is far from agreement among both academics and policy makers about what poverty is and how it should be defined and measured. Indeed, much of the more recent political and policy concern has tended to focus on social exclusion rather than poverty as the major issue to be addressed in a modern economy – hence the SEU (now Task Force) and the ABI agenda. What is more, the increasing tendency towards a multidimensional approach to poverty measurement, based on access to various indicators of exclusion and deprivation, has tended to reinforce this broader approach.

Is there a danger here that poverty has not really been reclaimed as a policy issue in the UK, and that it is social exclusion that is now driving academic debate and policy action? This may be particularly worrying if the wide-ranging notion of social exclusion exemplified in the indicators used in *Opportunity for All* and the NPI monitoring (see **Box 3.5**) is adopted, as this could make almost any and every social problem an aspect of social exclusion. Combating poverty and promoting social inclusion may therefore become a catch-all for everything and anything that the government does to improve society.

One response to this concern is simply to turn it on its head. It is only by wide-ranging and multidimensional policy measures that we will be able to combat poverty and social exclusion, and one of the limitations of past academic research and policy action was its narrow focus on income protection (mainly through social security) which could never tackle the wider problems of inequality and wealth discussed in the rest of this book. We really do need 'joined-up solutions' because the problems are themselves joined up.

This is an important point, but it is not the only defence of current research and policy. In a recent review for the JRF entitled *Where poverty intersects with social exclusion*, Hirsch (2006b) examines some of the evidence discussed in this chapter and concludes that the various measures do overlap and that poverty and social exclusion need to be understood and tackled together. This confirms the findings of the PSE Survey, which sought to develop indicators of exclusion, based on representative survey evidence, which could be used to arrive at a measure of poverty, and found that these overlapped closely with more traditional measures (Pantazis et al, 2006).

Conclusion

So social exclusion has not superseded poverty as the focus of academic and policy concern. Understanding of poverty needs to embrace the contested nature of definition and measurement and the importance of the need for multidimensional approaches, within a dynamic time frame. And social exclusion is an important concern for research and policy, extending analysis beyond the issues of access to income and resources to include the many ways in which participation in society may be reduced, or prevented. Furthermore, the problems of poverty and social exclusion are closely linked to growing inequalities in the UK and the rise of excessive wealth. Research evidence continues to demonstrate that social participation and access to resources are closely related. Understanding poverty and social exclusion is therefore a joint challenge for academics and policy makers.

Summary

- There is now a wide range of research aiming to define and measure poverty in the UK and internationally. Within this, poverty is generally distinguished from wider inequality as the problem of 'being without'.
- There is no agreed definition or measure of poverty and academics and policy makers are increasingly employing multidimensional approaches.
- Social exclusion is usually distinguished from poverty as a broader focus on restrictions in activity and participation within society.
- Dynamic analyses of poverty and social exclusion reveal how both of these change over time, and over the lifecourse.
- The extent of poverty in the UK increased dramatically in the 1980s. Since then it has stabilised. However, risk of poverty is not distributed evenly across society with children and families, people with disabilities and some minority ethnic groups experiencing higher levels.
- Combating poverty and social exclusion are key policy issues for the UK government in the new century.

Questions for discussion

- Why can we not agree on how to define poverty?
- Why has the UK government adopted a threefold measure of child poverty?
- Why is agency important to our understanding of social exclusion?
- Why do 'moving pictures' tell us more about the problem of poverty?
- What have been the major trends in distribution of poverty in the UK over the past 30 years?

Further reading

Alcock (2006) provides the most comprehensive general introduction to research and policy on poverty and social exclusion. Lister (2004) provides a convincing explanation of why poverty is a problem and how we should respond to it. The CPAG publication, *Poverty: The facts*, provides regularly updated summaries of the major statistical information on poverty, the most recent being by Flaherty et al (2004). A useful summary of research and academic debate on social exclusion from CASE at the LSE can be found in Hills et al (2002). The report on the findings of the 2000 PSE Survey (Pantazis et al, 2006) contains both excellent theoretical discussion of the measurement of poverty and exclusion and detailed analysis of the findings from the research.

Electronic resources

Government websites
www.dwp.gov.uk – The Department for Work and Pensions website lists most government documents and statistics relating to social security and anti-poverty policy
www.rcu.gov.uk/abi – A specific section of the Department for Communities and Local Government website (the Regional Co-ordination Unit) focuses on ABIs
www.cabinetoffice.gov.uk/social_exclusion_task_force – The Social Exclusion Task Force website contains summaries of the work of the former SEU and policy documents and government research reports carried out within its remit

Independent research and policy agencies
www.cpag.org.uk – CPAG reports on campaigning and welfare rights activity and its website contains poverty research, policy briefings and summaries of new statistics
www.jrf.org.uk – JRF's website has copies of research findings from the extensive range of research projects funded, including many on poverty and anti-poverty policy
www.npi.org.uk – NPI's website has copies of recent research and briefing papers on topical policy issues including annual monitoring of poverty and social exclusion indicators
www.poverty.org.uk – The Poverty Site is the most up-to-date general website for statistics on poverty and social exclusion. It is maintained by the NPI and supported by the JRF

References

Abel Smith, B. and Townsend, P. (1965) *The poor and the poorest*, London: G. Bell and Sons.

Alcock, P. (2006) *Understanding poverty* (3rd edn), Basingstoke: Palgrave.

Barry, B. (2002) 'Social exclusion, social isolation, and the distribution of income', in J. Hills, J. Le Grand and D. Piachaud (eds) *Understanding social exclusion*, Oxford: Oxford University Press.

Beresford, P., Green, D., Lister, R. and Woodard, K. (1999) *Poverty first hand: Poor people speak for themselves*, London: CPAG.

Berthoud, R. (2006) 'How can deprivation indicators help us to understand poverty?', *Benefits*, vol 14, no 2, pp 103-14.

Blair, T. (1999) 'Beveridge revisited: a welfare state for the 21st century', in R. Walker (ed) *Ending child poverty: Popular welfare for the 21st century*, Bristol: The Policy Press.

Booth, C. (1889) *The life and labour of the people*, London: Williams and Northgate.

Brown, M. and Madge, N. (1982) *Despite the welfare state*, London: Heinemann EB.

Burchardt, T. (2000) *Enduring economic exclusion: Disabled people, income and work*, York: Joseph Rowntree Foundation.

Burchardt, T., Le Grand, J. and Piachaud, D. (2002) 'Degrees of exclusion: developing a dynamic multidimensional measure', in J. Hills, J. Le Grand, and D. Piachaud (eds) *Understanding social exclusion*, Oxford: Oxford University Press.

Cabinet Office (2006a) *Reaching out: An action plan on social exclusion*, London: Cabinet Office.

Cabinet Office (2006b) *UK report on strategies for social protection and social inclusion 2006-08*, London: Cabinet Office.

Denham, A. and Garnett, M. (2001) *Keith Joseph*, Stocksfield: Acumen Publishing.

Dewilde, C. (2003) 'A life-course perspective on social exclusion and poverty', *British Journal of Sociology*, vol 54, no 1, pp 109-28.

DWP (Department for Work and Pensions) (2003) *Measuring child poverty*, London: DWP.

DWP (2006a) *Households below average income 2004/05*, London: DWP.

DWP (2006b) *Opportunity for All, Eighth Annual report*, London: DWP.

Finch, N. and Bradshaw, J. (2003) 'Overlaps in dimensions of poverty', *Journal of Social Policy*, vol 32, no 4, pp 513-25.

Flaherty, J., Veit-Wilson, J. and Dornan, P. (2004) *Poverty: The facts* (5th edn), London: CPAG.

Glennerster, H., Hills, J., Piachaud, D. and Webb, J. (2004) *One hundred years of poverty and policy*, York: Joseph Rowntree Foundation.

Golding, P. (ed) (1986) *Excluding the poor*, London: CPAG.

Goodman, A. and Shephard, A. (2002) *Inequality and living standards in Great Britain: Some facts*, Briefing Note No 19, London: Institute for Fiscal Studies.

Gordon, D. (2006) 'The concept and measurement of poverty', in C. Pantazis, D. Gordon and R. Levitas (eds) *Poverty and social exclusion in Britain: The millennium survey*, Bristol: The Policy Press.

Gordon, D. and Townsend, P. (eds) (2000) *Breadline Europe: The measurement of poverty*, Bristol: The Policy Press.

Gordon, D., Adelman, L., Ashworth, K., Bradshaw, J., Levitas, R., Middleton, S., Pantazis, C., Patsios, D., Payne, S., Townsend, P. and Williams, J. (2000) *Poverty and social exclusion in Britain*, York: Joseph Rowntree Foundation.

Hills, J. (ed) (1996) *New inequalities: The changing distribution of income and wealth in the United Kingdom*, Cambridge: Cambridge University Press.

Hills, J. (2004) *Inequality and the state*, Oxford: Oxford University Press.

Hills, J. and Stewart, K. (eds) (2005) *A more equal society? New Labour, poverty, inequality and exclusion*, Bristol: The Policy Press.

Hills, J., Le Grand, J. and Piachaud, D. (eds) (2002) *Understanding social exclusion*, Oxford: Oxford University Press.

Hirsch, D. (2006a) *What will it take to end child poverty? Firing on all cylinders*, York: Joseph Rowntree Foundation.

Hirsch, D. (2006b) *Where poverty intersects with social exclusion: Evidence and features of solutions*, York: Joseph Rowntree Foundation.

Hobcraft, J. (2002) 'Social exclusion and the generations', in J. Hills, J. Le Grand and D. Piachaud (eds) *Understanding social exclusion*, Oxford: Oxford University Press.

Joseph, K. (1972) 'The cycle of deprivation', Speech to the Pre-School Playgroups Association, 29 June.

Kempson, E. (1996) *Life on a low income*, York: Joseph Rowntree Foundation.

Kempson, E., Bryson, A. and Rowlingson, K. (1994) *Hard times? How poor families make ends meet*, London: Policy Studies Institute.

Leisering, L. and Leibfried, S. (1999) *Time and poverty in Western welfare states. United Germany in perspective*, Cambridge: Cambridge University Press.

Leisering, L. and Walker, R. (eds) (1998) *The dynamics of modern society: Poverty, policy and welfare*, Bristol: The Policy Press.

Levitas, R. (2006) 'The concept and measurement of social exclusion', in C. Pantazis, D. Gordon and R. Levitas (eds) *Poverty and social exclusion in Britain: The millennium survey*, Bristol: The Policy Press.

Lister, R. (ed) (1996) *Charles Murray and the underclass: The developing debate*, London: Institute of Economic Affairs.

Lister, R. (2004) *Poverty*, Cambridge: Polity Press.

Moore, J. (1989) 'The end of the line for poverty', Speech to Greater London Area CPC, 11 May.

NPI (New Policy Institute) (2006) *Key facts: Summary*, London: NPI.

Palmer, G., Carr, J. and Kenway, P. (2005) *Monitoring poverty and social exclusion 2005*, York: Joseph Rowntree Foundation.

Pantazis, C., Gordon, D. and Levitas, R. (eds) (2006) *Poverty and social exclusion in Britain: The millennium survey*, Bristol: The Policy Press.

Paugam, S. (1991) *La disqualification sociale: Essai sur la nouvelle pauvreté*, Paris: Presses Universitaires de France, coll 'sociologies'.

Philo, C. (ed) (1995) *Off the map: The social geography of poverty in the UK*, London: CPAG.

Ringen, S. (1988) 'Direct and indirect measures of poverty', *Journal of Social Policy*, vol 17, no 3, pp 351-65.

Robbins, D. et al (1994) *Observatory on national policies to combat social exclusion*, Third Annual Report, Brussels: European Commission.

Room, G. (ed) (1995) *Beyond the threshold: The measurement and analysis of social exclusion*, Bristol: The Policy Press.

Rowntree, B.S. (1901) *Poverty: A study of town life*, Basingstoke: Macmillan (reissued in 2000 by The Policy Press).

Rutter, M. and Madge, N. (1976) *Cycles of disadvantage*, London: Heinemann.

Sen, A. (1983) 'Poor, relatively speaking', *Oxford Economic Papers*, vol 35, no 1, pp 153-69.

SEU (Social Exclusion Unit) (1998) *Bringing Britain together: A national strategy for neighbourhood renewal*, London: The Stationery Office.

SEU (2001) *A new commitment to neighbourhood renewal: National strategy action plan*, London: The Stationery Office.

Sigle-Rushton, W. (2004) *Intergenerational and life course transmission of social exclusion in the 1970 British Cohort Study*, CASEPaper 78, London: STICERD, London School of Economics and Political Science.

Smith, A. (1776) *An inquiry into the nature and causes of the wealth of nations* (1892 edn), London: Routledge.

Townsend, P. (1979) *Poverty in the United Kingdom: A survey of household resources and standards of living*, Harmondsworth: Penguin.

Townsend, P. and Gordon, D. (eds) (2002) *World poverty: New policies to defeat and old enemy*, Bristol: The Policy Press.

UN (United Nations) (1995) *The Copenhagen declaration and programme of action: World summit for social development 6-12 March 1995*, New York: UN Department of Publications.

UNICEF (United Nations Children's Fund) (2005) *Child poverty in rich countries*, UN Department of Publications, Florence: Innocenti Research Centre.

Whelan, C., Layte, R. and Maitre, B. (2002) 'Multiple deprivation and persistent poverty in the European Union', *Journal of European Social Policy*, vol 12, no 2, pp 137-58.

four

Explaining poverty, social exclusion and inequality: towards a structural approach

Gerry Mooney

Overview

- This chapter provides an introduction to structural approaches to poverty and inequality.
- It discusses some of the ways in which structural approaches can be applied.
- It outlines and considers how Marxist class analysis approaches the questions of poverty, wealth and inequality.
- It is argued that there is a need for 'upstream' analysis to focus on the activities of the rich.

Key concepts

inequality; poverty; wealth; structural approaches; social polarisation; class; class analysis; upstream analysis

Introduction

Few would dispute that in the early years of the 21st century much of the thrust of anti-poverty policy in the UK, together with poverty policies developed at a transnational level by the United Nations (UN), the World Bank and other organisations (see Chapter Five, this volume), has at its core a concern to transform people's behaviour – that is, of course, the behaviour of people experiencing poverty, not the rich nor multinational corporations! This both reflects and reproduces the view of 'the poor' as 'other', as beyond 'normal', 'mainstream' society. The ability of powerful groups to generate and present particular representations of people experiencing poverty as, for example, an 'underclass', or as in some way responsible for their own position, is a recurring feature in debates around poverty and its causes and accompanies the growth in poverty and inequality that have characterised the last few decades of the 20th century and early years of the new millennium.

Following from the discussions in Chapters Two and Three, the focus here shifts to the key question of how we should approach the issue of poverty and inequality, why they remain such prevalent features of society today. The main explanations of poverty are distinguishable primarily by whether they offer an individualistic-based analysis or are driven by a more structural understanding of social relations. There are contrasting theories and perspectives within these two broad ways of thinking, but nonetheless the division between individual and structural accounts represents the main fault line that characterises explanations in this field of social scientific study. Arguably, in recent times, at government and policy-making levels, there has been a shift (albeit an uneven and at times tentative one) towards more individualistic and behavioural explanations, for example in many 'underclass' and/or 'cultures' of poverty discourses. In this chapter a structural approach is centred as offering a particularly comprehensive and powerful way of making sense of inequalities in society and of 'social problems' such as poverty.

It is clear from the previous chapters that poverty, wealth and inequality are highly contested areas of study and analysis. That there are multiple and competing definitions, measurements and methodologies surrounding the study of poverty and wealth has long been a feature of social scientific investigations in these fields. Such contestations reflect different political traditions and theoretical controversies, not only about the questions of poverty, wealth and inequality themselves, but of social justice, of equality and, indeed, of how society itself should be organised and structured. Further, and linking directly with the overall themes and concerns of this book, the analysis of poverty and inequality is directly related to and entangled with the study of cross-cutting social divisions and questions of class, gender, ethnicity, 'race' and sexuality. It also connects with other long-term concerns of social policy analysis with the social relations of welfare, *the who gets what and who gets naught* of welfare provision.

Not surprisingly, then, when we begin to turn our attention to the question of how we should analyse and explain such questions, the explanations that are offered immediately bring into focus more fundamental social and political questions. It is therefore impossible to offer a 'balanced' or 'objective' discussion and from the outset this chapter is explicit in favouring, as it does, a structural explanation of poverty and inequality, underpinned by Marxist class analysis.

What is meant by a 'structural' perspective or approach to poverty and inequality? At its most basic structural explanations seek to locate the analysis and explanation of issues from poverty and social exclusion through to inequality, wealth and power in the context of the wider social relations that structure society. Social factors and forces, for instance the organisation of an economy, unemployment, working conditions, educational provision, health, housing, environmental factors and so on, all play significant roles in shaping what the sociologist Max Weber termed 'life chances' (Weber, 1978), the interplay of personal and social factors that shape the opportunities and life that individuals will experience (see also Bendix, 1977, p 2; Hughes et al, 2003, p 107).

Structural approaches are built around the social contexts in which we live and which work to shape our lives in different ways. Most social scientists will argue, many of whom follow Weber's approach, that it is the complex interrelationship between these social contexts and structures and individual agency that shape the lifecourse and the opportunities that may come our way. In the discussion that follows, an introduction to the focus and approach of structural perspectives is outlined and explored.

Introducing structural approaches

One-fifth of humanity lives in countries where many people think nothing of spending $2 a day on a cappuccino. Another fifth of humanity survive on less than $1 a day and live in countries where children die for want of a simple anti-mosquito bed net. (UN, 2005, Summary, p 17).

Massive poverty and obscene inequality are such terrible scourges of our times – times in which the world boasts breathtaking advances in science, technology, industry and wealth accumulation – that they have to rank alongside slavery and apartheid as social evils. (Nelson Mandela, quoted in UN, 2005, Summary, p 17)

In the early years of the 21st century we live in a world that is divided and highly unequal as rarely before. In 2005, the 500 richest individuals in the world, the capacity of a large lecture theatre in a UK university today or of an Airbus A380 passenger jet, had a combined income greater than the poorest 416 million people. And 2.5 billion people, around 40% of the world's population, share 5% of global income. By contrast, the richest 10%, the 'super-rich' who live overwhelmingly in the high-income countries, enjoy 54% of the world's income (UN, 2005, Summary, p 18).

On a global scale as well as in UK society, the early years of the 21st century are characterised by massive inequalities in wealth and income, inequalities which have grown enormously since the 1970s. The scale of this inequality is almost beyond comprehension, perhaps not surprisingly as much of it remains hidden from view. How do we understand such inequalities? What issues and questions should be at the core of our explanations? By using the term 'inequality' there is a strong hint as to the direction of our gaze or focus – and to the kinds of explanation that we would wish to offer. Structural approaches of different kinds would share a starting point that there is little that is 'natural' or inevitable about the inequalities that so scar the world today. Instead inequalities are attributed to the unequal social relations between rich and poor. Poverty and wealth, in other words, are related through unequal social and economic relations.

The relationship between poverty and wealth, between rich and poor, is a dynamic one. We can understand that in the 1960s and 1970s in the UK, for instance, the gap between rich and poor narrowed somewhat, although by no means as much as is often argued. We can also find considerable evidence that highlights that since the late 1970s the gulf between rich and poor has increased dramatically (see, for instance, Westergaard, 1995; Walker, 1997). How might a structural approach make sense of this?

Thatcherism and the strategy of inequality

The general story of trends in the distribution of income and wealth in postwar Britain is one in which the gradual trend towards a narrowing of inequality between the late 1940s and 1970s is thrown into sharp reverse in the late 1970s (see Chapter Two, this volume, for data on the distribution of personal assets). Between 1979 and 1993 the richest 10% of the population saw their incomes increase on average by around 63% (Novak, 2001, pp 4-5). But this is only part of the story. Seventy per cent of the population saw their incomes increase by less than average while for the poorest 10% their incomes actually declined in real terms by 16%. In terms of poverty (measured here as less than 50% of average income; see Chapter Three, this volume, for a critical discussion of the measurement of poverty), the numbers living in poverty increased from 5 million in 1979 to 14 million in 1993/94, from 9% to 25% of the population (Walker, 1997, p 3). Therefore, when we compare the end of the 1970s with the early to mid-1990s, the gap or gulf between rich and poor increased dramatically. This is often referred to by social scientists as 'social polarisation' (see Walker, 1997).

There is considerable evidence to back up the claims made here, but how do we explain this rising inequality? The growth of inequality during the 1980s and 1990s (continuing into the early 2000s) was no accident, no simple unfortunate and unforeseen 'by-product' of longer-term economic change, but for Alan Walker (1990, 1997), part and parcel of what he terms *a strategy of inequality*. Prior to 1979 there was a general political consensus that a key task for government was to address poverty and to try to reduce inequalities. The provision of 'social security', full employment and the expansion of a welfare state were widely (although not universally) supported and reflected to varying degrees in government policy making. All this was to change with the election of the Conservative government in 1979. Instead of a commitment to a broad social democratic agenda, which in any case was under severe threat under the previous Labour administration, Prime Minister Margaret Thatcher and the Conservative government embarked on a radically different policy-making project that prioritised different objectives from those of post-Second World War governments.

In place of a concern to tackle poverty and to reduce inequality, 'Thatcherism' celebrated low taxation, the free market, personal freedoms and responsibilities, reductions in state welfare, denationalisation, privatisation and so on. These are key components of what we have subsequently come to term a 'neoliberal' agenda. As Walker argues, 'rather than seeing inequality as potentially damaging to the social fabric, the Thatcher governments saw it as an engine of enterprise, providing incentives for those at the bottom as well as those at the top' (Walker, 1997, p 5).

During the years of Conservative government, between 1979 and 1997, and thereafter under New Labour, an expansive welfare state was viewed as 'a drain' on the economy, undermining national economic competitiveness but also as contributing to 'welfare dependency' among people experiencing poverty, undermining incentives to work. The idea that an underclass of unemployed, feckless 'poor people', 'scroungers', were only too willing to take advantage of hard-working taxpayers became a recurring theme of the 1980s and 1990s, with echoes of this still evident today in New Labour's oft-repeated references to the problems of 'worklessness' and the assorted and multiple moral problems created through welfare dependency (see Levitas, 2005). In place of universal benefits there has, as a result, been a shift towards means-tested benefits, more in-work forms of support such as through tax credits and more targeting of benefits towards those most in need. However, it was not only in relation to welfare spending that the government worked to reshape policy. Reducing, tightening and controlling benefits was accompanied by a new tax regime that was highly regressive, with most taxpayers now paying the same basic rate of taxation. Some capital taxes were abolished while in-work taxation increased along with a hike in National Insurance contributions. The overall effect of this was to shift the tax burden from those with high incomes to those with low incomes. Between 1979 and 1989, for instance, £91,000 million was cut from income taxation, 29% of which went to the top 1% of taxpayers with the bottom 50% receiving only 12% of the cuts (Walker, 1990, pp 41-2).

Reforming the 'morally damaging' welfare state, putting responsibility in place of dependency, was only one dimension of Thatcherite social policies, however. There was also a strong commitment to the belief that any form of welfare provision that was non-state generated and managed was necessarily superior to state welfare. This was reflected in a marked shift towards policies that spoke of the role of the family and of community as well as the non-statutory and voluntary sectors in providing welfare. 'Rolling back the state' to enable such sectors to 'flourish' became an important principle of government policy.

Promoting enterprise and attacking 'dependency' were central to this strategy of inequality. State intervention was damaging in that it undermined the former and worked to increase the latter. This represented a sharp break with the policy-making consensus of the post-1945 era, which tended to support the principles of interventionism and egalitarianism. Economic growth, entrepreneurship and enterprise were to replace reducing inequality and tackling poverty as the main objectives of government policy making. By this route, it was argued, in terms that have come to be infamous, that the fruits of economic growth and increasing wealth would 'trickle down' to benefit the rest of society, including among people experiencing poverty who, freed from the constraints of 'dependency' and 'generous' welfare benefits, would feel empowered to take up new jobs that were being created.

There are other dimensions of this strategy of inequality that we are only able to mention in passing here. Rising unemployment in the 1980s, for instance, was also an important element of this strategy, working as it did to reduce wage costs by acting as a brake on wage levels and demands, and this also had the additional effect of eroding the bargaining position of trades unions and their members, which was also under attack from other government policies, and a series of acts which sought to control and reduce the effectiveness of trades unions.

Promoting inequality, therefore, was a central strategy of the Conservatives during the 1980s and 1990s. Inequality and the growth of poverty were viewed as beneficial for society, or at least for the promotion of enterprise and for enhancing economic growth. Walker's (1990) thesis represents an interesting example of a structural approach, with the focus of the analysis on governments, policy making and on the interrelationship between poverty and wealth. In turn, poverty is understood in relation to wider social and economic goals, in particular providing the right conditions for profitability and prosperity and national economic growth and competitiveness. In other ways this strategy of inequality has worked to increase inequalities in other areas of social life, and here again we are reminded of the idea of life chances introduced above.

The impact of inequality

What emerges strongly from the discussion thus far is the importance of understanding poverty, wealth and inequalities as social relations. By this we mean that while material resources are central to this, social relations are also economic, political, cultural, geographical, environmental and psychological. Questions of security, insecurity, of risk and uncertainty, vulnerability, harm and well-being, are all fundamentally social and political issues, issues of social justice that go to the heart of what kind of society we would like to live in and how we are going to achieve this. In this regard structural approaches tend to view inequality and poverty not as marginal features of society, some brief aberrations, but long-term social processes and relations that permeate the fabric of society and which are reflected in the way in which society is organised and structured. For Richard Wilkinson, the degree of inequality in the social environment is reflected in society in different ways, including in the levels of trust, involvement in community life, morbidity and mortality, in anti-social behaviour, drug and alcohol addiction, anxiety, stress, depression, insecurity and so on (Wilkinson, 2005, p 23). He argues that 'the quality of social relations in societies is related to the scale of income inequality – how big the gap is between rich and poor' (2005, p 24). In claiming that there is a close relationship between inequality and the quality of social relations, Wilkinson offers a structural approach that seeks to locate the causes of 'social problems', for instance drug addiction or ill-health, as well as problems that are often presented as being more 'personal', such as depression and stress, in the unequal relations and structures of society. This approach begins and ends at the social level, locating individuals and groups in their social contexts and understanding supposedly 'individual' issues as inextricably linked to the organisation and structure of society.

One of the clearest ways of understanding such connections and relations is to focus on the links between inequality and health. Wilkinson shows that ill-health and premature death are linked to levels of inequality in society with the US performing worse than most other industrialised countries in this respect. Life expectancy in the UK also declined during the last two decades of the 20th century when, as we have seen, the income gap between rich and poor was also increasing dramatically.

Wilkinson's approach is outlined here to illustrate how a structural account can offer explanations of issues that are all too often regarded as solely individual-centred. His psychosocial emphasis attributes physiological and psychological illnesses to income levels. The more hierarchical a society, the more people experience insecurity about their position within it as well as fears of 'falling' from a particular social position (see Young, 2007). Inequality matters, therefore, in many different direct and indirect ways and works to shape the myriad of day-to-day interactions and social relations in which we are located.

Poverty and inequality are understood in this approach as social relations, yet Wilkinson tends to underplay the role that material factors play in the generation of ill-health. Inequality is much more than a psychosocial state, however, and for some theorists it can only be understood as a dimension of the exploitative and unequal economic and social relations that characterise contemporary capitalist societies.

Class and class analysis: 'an embarrassing and unsettling subject'

Despite the persistence of marked class divisions and structured inequalities across the world today, arguably class has become the social condition that dare not speak its name. The general marginalisation of class in much of the social sciences literature is astonishing. With relatively few exceptions, when class is introduced or mentioned it tends to be as a form of what we might term 'classism', but one of the many discriminations ('-isms') that characterise society. Even where the degree of poverty and deepening inequality is registered, class may be reduced to a descriptive variable, as only one among other equally significant variables in complex systems of stratification, and thereby, in the argument advanced here, minimised as an explanatory concept. As Marxist theorist John Westergaard claimed in 1995, 'class has now been re-declared dead, or dying in all social significance, at a time now when its economic configuration has become even sharper' (Westergaard, 1995, p 114).

Class remains the primary determinant of social life. Intellectually and ideologically, class represented a central point of reference that helped to explain everything from voting patterns and attitudinal differences, political mobilisation, social conflict, to lifestyle and consumption patterns, and even personality traits (see Crompton, 1998; Savage, 2000). Yet, the concept of class no longer occupies centre stage in the analysis of UK society today. Academic, policy and journalistic discourses about modern society have been largely de-classed.

To highlight this eradication of class from the policy lexicon is hardly to make a controversial claim. Class, as Sayer (2005, p 1) put it, has become 'an embarrassing and unsettling subject'. There is something approaching a consensus that class has declined as a significant factor in the routine structuring of social and economic relations in contemporary society. While such claims have been criticised from widely different perspectives (see, for example, Marshall, 1997; Mooney, 2000; Savage, 2000; Ferguson et al, 2002; Skeggs, 2004; Sayer, 2005), they retain significant potency.

In this part of the chapter the main aim is to highlight some of the different ways in which class analysis offers us a powerful and rich form of structural analysis. It makes no apology for arguing that poverty, wealth and inequality are best analysed and explained from the vantage point of Marxist class analysis that seeks to understand these in relation to the structures and organising principles of capitalist society.

Marxist explanations of poverty

Marxism represents the best known of structural explanations of social inequality in capitalist societies. This is not to claim that it is the only structural explanation, but that the entire Marxist tradition is one that readily distinguishes it from all other explanations. In particular, what stands out in Marxist approaches is that the explanation of whatever social issue is taken for investigation always starts from the prioritisation of class and class conflict (see Mooney, 2000). Again constraints of space mean that we are unable to do full justice to the Marxist approach here and instead can only highlight some of the key ways in which Marxists endeavour to analyse and explain poverty and inequality (see also Lavalette, 2006).

As might be expected, the entire thrust of the Marxist approach is to locate the discussion and analysis of poverty within the wider context of class relations and inequalities within capitalist society (see Novak, 1988; Ferguson et al, 2002). In this respect, Marxists make no attempt to isolate people experiencing poverty from the rest of society, but see poverty as part of a relationship of inequality, economically, materially and politically. Thus, poverty is related to inequalities of wealth and income: it cannot be understood outside of the relationship to inequalities of wealth. At the centre of this and underpinning all inequalities is the exploitation and oppressions that are integral to the production of material wealth in capitalist society. For Marxists, the production and accumulation of profit, of wealth, is also simultaneously the production and accumulation of poverty, want and misery. From this position Tony Novak argues that:

> It is the economic and social relationships of capitalist society – the division between a minority who own and control the world's

wealth and those who have no choice but to work for them – that is at one and the same time both the root cause of poverty and the motor of capitalist growth and development.... Poverty thus needs to be understood not just as the end-product of a particular system of distribution – which is how most studies of poverty approach it – but as an essential precondition for the process of production itself. Poverty is not simply about the way that society's resources are distributed, but also about the way these resources are produced. (1995, p 70)

In making such an argument, a Marxist perspective immediately stands out from the other approaches that seek to define, measure and examine people experiencing poverty in isolation from wider society. They also stand apart from the social exclusion approaches (see Chapter Three) which, while recognising that social exclusion results from wider social processes, ignore the class-based inequalities of capitalist society. Both the social exclusion and Marxist approaches see poverty as a relationship, but they understand and analyse this in very different ways. Through the Marxist approach, poverty is viewed as the product of the normal operations of capitalist society, not an abnormal state of affairs. The threat of poverty is an ever-present fear for many working-class people, although the fact that the overwhelming majority of people experiencing poverty are also working class is something that is generally obscured and overlooked in many accounts. Its study and analysis, therefore, must be located within those very relations by understanding it as a relationship of inequality between a highly powerful and affluent minority and the mass of ordinary workers. Like social exclusion, therefore, Marxist explanations see poverty and inequality as relational, but they offer very different ways of analysing this.

In this respect we need to reflect on the idea of poverty and inequalities as mere 'social problems'. Following the structural approach offered here, poverty and wealth represent very different forms of social problem for people experiencing poverty on the one hand, and for people with high incomes on the other: the task of the latter to maximise income and wealth at the expense of the former; the goal of people experiencing poverty to increase their share of income at the expense of the rich and powerful.

For Marxist theorists, there has been too much concern with counting people experiencing poverty in order to regulate and discipline them and to force them into work (see Jones and Novak, 1999; Gough et al, 2006). This is also accompanied by the recurring representation of people experiencing poverty as a problem to be managed, addressed or, failing that, controlled. Jones and Novak argue that:

punitive and negative images of the poor are deeply sedimented, historically, within British society. These images reflect not only the periodic reconstruction of the poor as morally degenerate and culpable, but also a more widespread, deep-rooted and long standing antagonism that has characterised social and class relationships in Britain. (Jones and Novak, 1999, p 5)

Therefore we need to be aware that the history of the study of poverty is characterised by a language and approach that has tended to describe 'the poor' often in the most condemning and derogatory of terms. From a concern with the 'dangerous' and disreputable poor in the 19th century (see Mann, 1992; Morris, 1994) through to 'problem families', 'dysfunctional families/communities' and the 'underclass' and 'socially excluded' of the late 20th and early 21st centuries (Macnicol, 1987; Welshman, 2002; Cook, 2006), how we talk about people experiencing poverty says much about our understanding of the underlying *causes* of poverty and shapes how explanations are then constructed. Labels such as 'underclass', 'hard-to-reach', 'welfare-dependent' (as well as some uses of the notion of 'the socially excluded') are stigmatising and mobilise normative ways of thinking of poverty and inequality that construct 'the poor' and disadvantaged almost as a distinctive group of people living 'on' or 'beyond' the 'margins' of society. In the process this language works to distance 'them' from 'us', the 'mainstream' of society, 'normal', 'hard-working', 'responsible' citizens (see Lister, 2004, chapter 5).

From the 19th century, and reflecting the power of individual-centred explanations, the study and investigation of poverty (and of inequality in general) is highly susceptible to moral condemnation and to blaming people experiencing poverty for their own position. People experiencing poverty are frequently constructed as 'a problem' to be managed and controlled. Poverty itself is often understood and presented as a 'social problem' (although it is not a social problem for everyone). Wealth and the question of 'the rich' are, in stark contrast, rarely viewed in such ways:

what thoughtful rich people call the problem of poverty, thoughtful poor people call with equal justice a problem of riches. (Tawney, 1913, p 10)

In this oft-quoted comment, social critic and historian Richard H. Tawney immediately draws our attention to the power relations that underpin wider social and political discourses and explanations of, and approaches to, poverty and inequality, throwing into the melting pot that how we approach the study and analysis of poverty and inequality betrays our values and our politics.

So, the othering of many people experiencing poverty is by no means a new development even if it has reached new heights with the Conservatives and New Labour over the past two to three decades. Such othering, however, extends to the ways in which the working class and in particular working-class people experiencing poverty are constructed and represented in many social and political discourses today. Jock Young (2007) makes an important distinction between a conservative form of othering, which attributes negative characteristics to the other, and a liberal form of othering, where the other is deemed to lack the qualities, values and virtues that 'we' hold. In this liberal othering, deficits or a lacking are often seen as a consequence of material and cultural factors that prevent others becoming 'just like us'. Young illustrates some of the many ways in which liberal othering works both to *diminish* others – they are less than us – and to *distance* others from us. As Ruth Lister has shown, this is often central to the many discourses that surround the discussion of poverty and of people experiencing poverty in the contemporary UK. For Young (2007) this binary thinking, 'us' and 'them', permeates public thinking and official discourses and is utilised and extended in constructions of other cultures, countries, nationalities and religions. Young rightly argues that such binary thinking is also evident in social sciences discourses and this might be extended to include the othering of the working class, especially of the white working class.

Haylett (2001) and Skeggs (2005) argue that when the working class features in policy making and in social sciences (as well as in journalistic) commentary, it does so primarily as 'a problem to be solved'. Being working class is often constructed as a 'social condition' in desperate need of remedy. Despite the persistence of marked class divisions and structured inequalities within British society today, there is a recurring identification of that part of the working class suffering most from the effects of long-term economic change and of the strategy of inequality as pathological, as beyond the mainstream, in other words as 'a problem'. Such 'problem' groups occupy a highly precarious relationship in relation to the labour market. The most vulnerable sections of the working class frequently become the focus of overlapping pathologisation processes – in relation to social inclusion policies, in debates around educational attainment, in relation to patterns of ill-health and morbidity, and, most publicly, in the mass media, in relation to questions of criminal justice, especially around urban youth crime.

Such otherings can be understood as part of the wider class antagonisms and hatreds that permeate society today. How we approach the questions of poverty, inequality and wealth reflects such antagonisms. The construction of people experiencing poverty as an underclass or dysfunctional group, as a problem, reflects such antagonisms and works both to produce and reproduce what Jones and Novak (1999, p 73) refer to as the 'abuse of the poor'. As John Macnicol

(1987) has forcefully argued, the demonisation of an underclass and of other groups of people experiencing poverty says more about the preoccupations and fears of the rich and powerful and their concerns for a decline in respect for authority and a fragmenting social order. Such discourses carry with them a focus on individual failings or a lacking, sidelining in the process those structural processes that underpin the production and reproduction of poverty and inequality across the world today as in the past. As such they are part and parcel of neoliberalising worldviews that return us time and time again to a focus on the individual (for further detail on individual/behavioural understandings of the causes of poverty, see Alcock, 2006).

Conclusion

This chapter has been primarily concerned to outline some of the key aspects of structural explanations of poverty, wealth and inequality. Structural explanations offer powerful ways of making sense of social issues such as poverty. Against those perspectives, which are largely focused on individual behaviours and 'problem cultures', structural arguments seek to locate the causes of poverty and inequality in the structural organisation of society. These are not approached as some kind of malfunctioning or short-term aberrations in how society is organised. Instead they are made sense of as part of a wider system of oppression, exploitation and inequality that characterises contemporary societies. There is a growing interest among some sections of academic social policy with material inequalities, both at the level of UK society and globally, and how these work to generate and structure disadvantage and poverty. While it is important to maintain a conceptual distinction between poverty and inequality, there is increasing recognition that unless inequality is tackled, then poverty and disadvantage will continue as a pervasive feature of contemporary societies. Inequality matters immensely for our understanding of poverty and social exclusion (see Callinicos, 2000; Jackson and Segal, 2004; Byrne, 2005; Harvey, 2005; Wilkinson, 2005; Orton and Rowlingson, 2007). Through an approach which seeks to centre the unequal social relations of poverty and inequality, we can build a more comprehensive understanding of a wide range of social issues, from ill-health and insecurity through to much more significant concerns with social justice and 'well-being', and to how the wealthy continue to be privileged through economic, social and fiscal policies.

This ties in with growing calls from social policy academics that social policy analysis itself should 'move upstream' (for example, Sinfield, 2004). Sinfield argues that there is an urgent need for social policy researchers to study and explain the underlying structural factors that shape poverty, disadvantage and inequality, an approach which focuses more on the 'root causes' of poverty but which also entails more critical examination of the privileging of the rich through social and economic policies.

Marxism has always offered such an approach. It begins not with poverty, but with the totality of social relations in society, arguing that it is only a totalising explanation that can provide an adequate account of poverty and inequality, relating such issues to questions of class, exploitation and oppression. This has led theorists such as Westergaard (1995) to argue that more emphasis needs to be given to the reproduction of wealth and privilege among the upper class of the rich. Here there is an explicit attack on the preoccupation among politicians, policy makers and in the academy with 'the poor', and we might extend this to include the liberal othering identified by Young.

In many discussions of poverty and of anti-poverty policy, people experiencing poverty exist only as victims or as passive recipients of policies developed by 'us' for 'them'. They are generally denied any sense of 'agency' save attributing to them responsibility for their poverty (see Lister, 2004, pp 124-5). That people experiencing poverty have a 'voice' and can organise to resist attempts to other them as well as to defend the kinds of state services on which they depend has, with some notable exceptions, generally been neglected (cf Piven and Cloward, 1977; Lavalette and Mooney, 2000; Ferguson et al, 2002). As Ruth Lister has argued, there has been a tendency to deny voice and agency to people experiencing poverty, even in some of those structural accounts that dominated UK social policy analysis in the postwar period (Lister, 2004, pp 126-7).

Not all structural approaches are guilty in this respect, however. Let us return to Marxist class theory. This perspective not only recognises and explains that capitalist society is built on and structured around an exploitative set of social relations which work to oppress the overwhelming majority in society, but that working-class people have the capacity, the agency, to resist and to struggle against such exploitations. Poverty and inequality are seen as the inevitable consequence of the exploitative social relations that lie at the heart of capitalist society, not some aberration that can be fully addressed, diluted or managed through social policy alone.

Here is one fruitful way in which we can see that class as structure and class as agency interrelate, and through which the material inequalities that characterise contemporary society can begin to be challenged. What this also reminds us, importantly, is that poverty and inequality are not some naturally occurring or inevitable feature of human society but the product of human relations, that is, of human action and agency. In turn this means that the building of another society is possible in which poverty and inequality are overcome and the pursuit of real social justice becomes the building block of social life.

Summary

- Structural explanations foreground social, economic, political and cultural relations and processes as key factors that generate and reproduce poverty and inequality.
- The idea of a strategy of inequality refers in particular here to the policies and objectives of the Conservative governments during the 1980s and 1990s that sought to increase inequality as a way of disciplining labour, growing the economy and affecting a restructuring of the welfare state.
- Marxist explanations of poverty start from the perspective of exploitative class relations and see poverty and inequality as inevitable features of class society.
- The othering of people experiencing poverty and disadvantaged sections of the working classes has long been central to debates over poverty and its causes.
- People experiencing poverty have generally been denied agency or voice although there is now more recognition that this serves to construct 'the poor' as other.
- 'Upstream analysis' means focusing more on the ways in which the rich are privileged through state policies as well as on the behaviour and activities of the rich.

Questions for discussion

- What are the basic starting points of structural explanations?
- In what ways might inequalities in wealth and income shape other inequalities in society?
- Why does Marxist theory see poverty, wealth and inequality as part and parcel of the structure of capitalist society?
- In what ways might it be better to relate structure and agency in explanations of poverty and its causes?
- What do you understand by the term 'moving upstream'? What would be the focus of an upstream analysis of poverty, wealth and inequality?

Further reading

There are many different books, studies and reports which explore different aspects of explaining poverty and some of these have been highlighted by Alcock (see Chapter Three, this volume). Perhaps one of the most accessible overviews is provided by Lister in *Poverty* (2004), while for critical explorations of the idea of social exclusion, Gough et al's *Spaces of social exclusion* (2006), Levitas's *The inclusive society?* (2005) and Byrne's *Social exclusion* (2005) are among the best discussions available. Each seeks to locate poverty in its social and structural contexts. For the relationship between poverty and wealth, see Novak's (1988) *Poverty and the state*, while one of the best all-round accounts, although it is now a little dated, is Scott's *Poverty and wealth* (1994).

For Marxist explanations of equality and inequality, one of the best and most readable accounts is offered by Callinicos in *Equality* (2000). For a Marxist approach to welfare see Ferguson et al's *Rethinking welfare* (2002). Useful general discussions of class are available in Savage's *Class analysis and transformations* (2000) and Sayer's *The moral significance of class* (2005).

References

Alcock, P. (2006) *Understanding poverty* (3rd edn), Basingstoke: Palgrave.

Bendix, R. (1977) *Max Weber: An intellectual portrait*, Berkeley, CA: University of California Press.

Byrne, D. (2005) *Social exclusion* (2nd edn), Maidenhead: Open University Press.

Callinicos, A. (2000) *Equality*, Cambridge: Polity Press.

Cook, D. (2006) *Criminal and social justice*, London: Sage Publications.

Crompton, R. (1998) *Class and stratification* (2nd edn), Cambridge: Polity Press.

Ferguson, I., Lavalette, M. and Mooney, G. (2002) *Rethinking welfare*, London: Sage Publications.

Gough, J., Eisenschitz, A. and McCulloch, A. (2006) *Spaces of social exclusion*, London: Palgrave.

Harvey, D. (2005) *A brief history of neoliberalism*, Oxford: Oxford University Press.

Haylett, C. (2001) 'Illegitimate subjects?: abject whites, neoliberal modernisation, and middle-class multiculturalism', *Society and Space*, vol 19, pp 351-70.

Hughes, J., Sharrock, W. and Martin, P.J. (2003) *Understanding classical sociology: Marx, Weber, Durkheim*, London: Sage Publications.

Jackson, B. and Segal, P. (2004) *Why inequality matters*, London: Catalyst.

Jones, C. and Novak, T. (1999) *Poverty, welfare and the disciplinary state*, London: Routledge.

Lavalette, M. (2006) 'Marxism and welfarism', in M. Lavalette and A. Pratt (eds) *Social policy: Theories, concepts and issues* (3rd edn), London: Sage Publications, pp 46-65.

Lavalette, M. and Mooney, G. (eds) (2000) *Class struggle and social welfare*, London: Routledge.

Levitas, R. (2005) *The inclusive society? Social exclusion and New Labour* (2nd edn), London: Palgrave Macmillan.

Lister, R. (2004) *Poverty*, Cambridge: Polity Press.

Macnicol, J. (1987) 'In pursuit of the underclass', *Journal of Social Policy*, vol 16, no 2, pp 293-318.

Mann, K. (1992) *The making of an English 'underclass'?*, Buckingham: Open University Press.

Marshall, G. (1997) *Repositioning class: Social inequality in industrial societies*, London: Sage Publications.

Mooney, G. (2000) 'Class and social policy', in G. Lewis, S. Gewirtz and J. Clarke (eds) *Rethinking social policy*, London: Sage Publications, pp 156-70.

Morris, L. (1994) *Dangerous classes: The underclass and social citizenship*, London: Routledge.

Novak, T. (1988) *Poverty and the state*, Buckingham: Open University Press.

Novak, T. (1995) 'Rethinking poverty', *Critical Social Policy*, vol 44/45, pp 58-74.

Novak, T. (2001) 'What's in a name? Poverty, the underclass and social exclusion', in M. Lavalette and A. Pratt (eds) *Social policy* (2nd edn), London: Sage Publications.

Orton, M. and Rowlingson, K. (2007) 'A problem of riches: towards a new social policy research agenda on the distribution of economic resources', *Journal of Social Policy*, vol 36, no 1, pp 59-77.

Piven, F.F. and Cloward, R.A. (1977) *Poor people's movements: Why they succeed, how they fail*, New York: Pantheon.

Savage, M. (2000) *Class analysis and transformations*, Buckingham: Open University Press.

Sayer, A. (2005) *The moral significance of class*, Cambridge: Cambridge University Press.

Scott, J. (1994) *Poverty and wealth*, London: Longman.

Sinfield, A. (2004) 'Upstream thinking', *Policy World: Newsletter of the Social Policy Association*, Autumn, no 11 (www.social-policy.com).

Skeggs, B. (2004) *Class, self, culture*, London: Routledge.

Skeggs, B. (2005) 'The making of class and gender though visualising moral subject formation', *Sociology*, vol 39, no 5, pp 965-82.

Tawney, R.H. (1913) 'Poverty as an industrial problem', Inaugural lecture, reproduced in R.H. Tawney, *Memoranda on the problems of poverty*, London: William Morris Press.

UN (United Nations) (2005) *Human development report* (http://hdr.undp.org/).

Walker, A. (1990) 'The strategy of inequality: poverty and income distribution in Britain 1979-89', in I. Taylor (ed) *The social effects of free market policies*, Hemel Hempstead: Harvester Wheatsheaf, pp 29-47.

Walker, A. (1997) 'Introduction: the strategy of inequality', in A. Walker and C. Walker (eds) *Britain divided*, London: CPAG, pp 1-13.

Weber, M. (1978) *Economy and society*, Berkeley, CA: University of California Press.

Welshman, J. (2002) 'The cycle of deprivation and the concept of the underclass', *Benefits*, vol 3, no 1, October, pp 199-205.

Westergaard, J. (1995) *Who get's what?*, Cambridge: Polity Press.

Wilkinson, R.G. (2005) *The impact of inequality*, London: Routledge.

Young, J. (2007) *The exclusive society*, London: Sage Publications.

Part Two

People and place: divisions of poverty and wealth

five

Global inequality, poverty and wealth

Nicola Yeates

Overview

- This chapter reviews the varied meanings of poverty and inequality in a global context.
- It distinguishes between international and global measures of inequality.
- It examines current data on the distribution of income and wealth worldwide.
- It shows that a very large section of the world's wealth is concentrated in the top one tenth of 1% of the population.

Key concepts

global distribution gap; global measures of wealth inequality; global poverty; global social policy; global wealth distribution; global wealth inequality

Introduction

Issues of poverty and inequality have conventionally been approached as ones primarily pertaining to *intranational* distributions of resources and opportunities. Thus, the primary unit of analysis is the individual country and sub-national units thereof (regions, cities and so on). In the UK context, this methodological nationalism pervades poverty research, from the early poverty surveys of Charles Booth and Joseph Rowntree, through to more recent surveys (for example, Hillyard et al, 2002; Pantazis et al, 2006). Alongside this methodologically 'nationalist' tradition sits a methodological transnationalist tradition that relates the structure of poverty and inequality in countries like the UK to its wider global context. This latter tradition maintains that any analysis of the social structure of particular countries is incomplete without reference to their position in the global system of nations, in particular the structures of economic and political power that shape populations' access to and control over resources. This strand of research and analysis can be found in the research and publications of poverty scholar-activists such as Peter Townsend (1993) and Branko Milanovic (2005, 2007).

This globalist strand of poverty and inequality analysis and research forms part of an established field of study known as 'global social policy analysis' (Yeates, 2008). Global social policy concerns the *global* distribution of resources, *global* expressions of social rights and *global* forms of regulation, and the ways in which social policies are co-determined by national and transnational actors and processes. It analyses the world as an integrated world order and focuses on the globally spanning, *transnational* dimensions of social welfare and policy. Thus, the social structures, social relations, social identities and social practices that transcend, or cut across, nation states constitute the primary focus of analysis, together with the ways in which these intersect with and constitute those social processes operating within national borders. Global social policy challenges the prevailing assumption within methodologically nationalist social scientific (including social policy) traditions that the nation state is the only (or best) socio-spatial category for perceiving and understanding social (policy) processes and outcomes – including issues pertaining to the production and reproduction of poverty and other forms of social inequality (Deacon et al, 1997; Deacon, 2007; Yeates, 2007a, 2007b, 2008).

This scholarly tradition finds many sympathies among a variety of civic and social movement activists mobilising around global social justice issues. Like their academic counterparts, for these movements, the production and maintenance of poverty and inequality are best understood in global and transnational terms. Whether the focus of the analysis is the policies and practices of national governments vis-à-vis other countries (as in international development aid, trade and 'security' policies) or those of international organisations such as the World Trade Organization (WTO), World Bank, International Monetary Fund (IMF), United Nations (UN) and European Union (EU) which shape the distribution of resources and wealth worldwide, these movements have successfully raised public awareness in countries like the UK of the need for coherent analyses of the global determinants of poverty and inequality. Through various campaigns such as the 'fair trade' movement, anti-sweatshop and forced labour campaigns, ethical investment schemes and popular musical events such as Live Aid in 1985 and Live 8 in 2005, these activists have been instrumental in raising the profile of and awareness about the social impacts of neoliberal 'globalisation' processes. The creation of World Poverty Day (17 October, annually) and global social fora (World Social Forum and Social Fora in Europe, Africa, Latin America and Asia) are important means through which issues of poverty and inequality are discussed by scholar-activists. While it is difficult to measure with any great certainty the overall impacts of these movements, it cannot be denied that they have been important in forging political climates, political organisations and policy initiatives around poverty.

This chapter discusses issues of poverty, inequality and wealth as a global phenomenon. Its central concern is to explore how 'thinking globally' impacts on the ways in which poverty and wealth are conventionally understood. We explore the shifts in scale and scope involved in adopting a global approach to poverty, inequality and wealth, and the kinds of research and policy issues arising therefrom. The chapter is organised as follows. We first review what this shift to 'the global' means for definitions of 'wealth' and 'poverty' and the ways in which we might go about measuring them on a worldwide basis. We then examine social science evidence about the nature of poverty on a global scale, by reviewing recent research on the global distribution of income and wealth. We conclude by summarising the main themes and issues discussed in the chapter and pose some questions that can be thought about and discussed after reading this chapter.

'Wealth', 'income' and 'poverty' in the world context

As noted in the introduction, questions to do with the distribution of income and wealth are conventionally addressed as a national matter. Recent years have evidenced greater sensitivity to how resources are distributed around the world. This is in turn raising questions about the global dimensions of poverty and inequality, questions such as: is the condition of being rich or poor in a country like the UK equivalent to being rich or poor in countries like Sierra Leone, India, Jamaica or China? How do we measure poverty and inequality on a worldwide basis? And where are the 'global rich' and the 'global poor' most likely to live?

Defining wealth

With regard to how resources such as wealth and income are defined, one of the issues we need to bear in mind is whether the definitions and categories used in countries like the UK are universally applicable. Are different kinds of assets more or less significant when we move outside a country like the UK? In Chapter Two of this volume Karen Rowlingson discussed how assets are commonly divided into three different types: financial ('liquid assets'), housing and pensions. When we look to different countries we can see that the composition of assets can shift significantly even among geographically and economically proximate countries. Thus, in contrast to the UK where the share of financial assets other than liquid assets is high, Japan has a strong and established preference for liquid savings. This preference is borne out of experience, a lack of confidence in property and shares following their poor performance in the 1990s (Babeau and Sbano, 2003, cited in Davies et al, 2006, p 8). In European transition countries (Bulgaria, Czech Republic, Croatia, Romania and Slovakia), liquid assets also constitute a high proportion of total financial assets, but this is due to poorly developed financial markets (Davies et al, 2006, p 8). So the composition of assets can vary quite significantly across countries, with this variation reflecting 'different influences on household behaviour, such as market structure, regulation and cultural preferences' (IMF, 2005, cited in Davies et al, 2006).

These differences in asset composition may be even more pronounced when we move beyond 'developed' countries to 'developing' ones. In developing countries, 'real assets' (housing, land, agricultural and farm assets, consumer durables) are more important while financial assets (savings, income, pensions) are less important. This reflects the greater importance of agriculture to their economies, but also the limited development of financial markets. Thus, in India and Indonesia, which are by global standards low-income 'developing' countries, non-financial wealth assets ('real assets') count for a particularly high share of household assets (Davies et al, 2006, p 3; for a historical comparison between such countries and market economies see also Davies et al, 2006, footnote 12).

So scaling up our analysis from the national (UK) to the global context means we need to be sensitive to a far broader range of assets that are relevant to economic status, resources and well-being: what is important for economic and social well-being in one country context is not necessarily so in another. Variations are related to factors such as whether the agricultural or financial economy is more important, whether private ownership of land is allowed (in parts of China it is not allowed and this is reflected in the composition of household assets), what formal mechanisms exist for retirement income (whether families are expected to look after one another, or whether people are expected to save/invest in pension products etc) and, relatedly, whether these are managed by collective, public schemes or by private companies operating individualised accounts.

Looking at questions of poverty in global context alerts us to the social context of wealth and its ownership. We can expect the non–ownership of land and animal assets in a largely agricultural economy/peasant society to have quite a different – more important – meaning compared to a highly urbanised, service-based economy. This idea that the social context of asset ownership and production is central to any analysis of wealth is poignantly captured by the extract in **Box 5.1**.

Box 5.1: Different societies have different concepts of wealth

In April 1995, some months before the beginning of the UN World Women's Conference in Beijing, Hillary Clinton, the First Lady of the US, visited Bangladesh. She had come to find out for herself what was true of the success stories of the Grameen Bank projects in Bangladeshi villages, of which she had heard so much. The microcredits of the Grameen Bank were said to have remarkably improved the situation of rural women in Bangladesh. Ms Clinton wanted to find out whether the women had really been empowered by these microcredits. For the Grameen Bank and development agencies, 'empowerment for women' means that a woman has an income of her own and that she has some assets.

Hillary Clinton visited the women of Maishahati village and interviewed them about their situation. The women answered: yes, they now had an income of their own. They also had some 'assets': some cows, chickens, ducks. Their children went to school. Ms Clinton was satisfied. The women of Maishahati were obviously empowered. But she was not prepared for the next round of the interview, when the village women turned round and asked her the same questions. Farida Akhter reported the following exchange of questions and answers between the women of Maishahati and Hillary Clinton:

'*Apa* [elder sister], do you have cows?'
'No, I have no cows.'
'*Apa*, do you have your own income?'
'Well, formerly I used to have my own income. But since my husband became president and moved to the White House I have stopped earning my own money.'
'How many children do you have?'
'One daughter.'
'Would you like to have more children?'
'Yes, I would like to have one or two more children, but we are quite happy with our daughter Chelsea.'

> The women from Maishahati looked at each other and murmured. 'Poor Hillary! She has no cow, no income of her own, she has only one daughter.' In the eyes of the Maishahati women Hillary Clinton was not empowered. They felt sorry for her.
>
> *Source:* Bennholdt-Thomsen and Mies (1999, pp 1-2)

An international or global measure of poverty and inequality

If we wish to measure the distribution of resources on a worldwide basis, how should we proceed? What is the appropriate unit of analysis: is it all those who live in the confines of particular nation states, or is it all those inhabiting the earth irrespective of which country they live in? This question, and the kinds of answers it provokes, reflect two quite distinct views of the world system: the internationalist view and the globalist view.

Internationalists hold that the world is a shared place made up of different places (nation states). Thus, although national economies, cultures and polities are ever more interdependent and 'connected', these nations remain essentially distinct places defined by national structures and characteristics and the state has managed to retain overall control of its territorial domain. This internationalist perspective of the world system thus insists that all those living in a particular nation state should be the primary unit of analysis and that the appropriate focus of poverty and inequality analyses is *intranational* distributions and *intercountry* differences.

Globalists see the world as an integrated system, in which the fortunes of peoples and places are intertwined, interdependent and mutually constituted (see Yeates, 2007b, 2008). There are several variants, or kinds, of globalist, each holding different views about the continued importance of maintaining the nation state as a unit of analysis within a global framework. But what they all have in common is the idea that the socioeconomic conditions and opportunities of everyone living on this planet are shaped by their position within global and sub-global hierarchies of wealth and power, as well as the universalist idea that we are all members of a global society of human beings even if we live in different parts of the world politically demarcated into different countries. In this view, the appropriate unit of analysis is the planet.

The implications of these two worldviews for measures of world poverty and inequality are taken up by Milanovic (2005, 2007). He distinguishes between international and global measurements of inequality. *International* measures calculate the inequalities between average resources of different countries, and are typically based on national accounts. In the case of income, gross domestic income or gross domestic income per capita are typically used to calculate this. This way of measuring world inequality is useful for informing intercountry comparisons, but it does not provide a common global measure.

Global measures, on the other hand, take their unit of analysis to be all those currently inhabiting the planet; they approach it as if all those inhabiting it are living in the same nation. This enables them to measure disparities that exist between individuals irrespective of which country they live in. Given that there are no global surveys of inequality, working out a global measure of inequality involves looking in the first instance at national-level household surveys and other sources of data. Unlike the international measures which stop at the nation state, global measures then go on to undertake further statistical work to calculate a global distribution of income (and wealth) between individuals around the world using a common measure of inequality or poverty standard. The World Bank, for example, uses a common, global definition of poverty as all those living on less than a fixed sum per day, typically US$1. From this it then works out how many people living on this amount are living in which countries. More relativist approaches would take account of how much income is needed to maintain them in the context of the particular set of social circumstances pertaining to their place of residence, levels of physical activity, customs and traditions (see Townsend and Gordon, 2002).

Milanovic (2005, 2007) developed this distinction between international and global measures of inequality in the context of income inequality, but these distinctions between international and global measures of inequality are also applicable to our focus on wealth. Thus, international wealth inequality measures calculate the wealth of all those living in a particular nation, while measures of global wealth inequality use a more standardised, global calculation that embraces everyone living in the world.

In the following section, we turn to examine some recent studies of global wealth inequality. Before we do so, it is worth noting that the availability of wealth data around the world has been improving. The largest and most prosperous OECD (Organisation for Economic Co-operation and Development) countries all have relatively extensive wealth data based on household surveys, tax data or national balance sheets. But outside these rich countries, the limitations of wealth data become apparent, particularly among smaller and poorer countries. Studies of wealth are notoriously difficult in capturing the true extent of wealth ownership. These 'sampling errors', as they are known, impact much more on estimates of wealth distribution than they do on income distributions. Wealthy households are much less likely to respond to surveys and they tend to under- or misreport their assets/wealth. These problems make it especially difficult to obtain an accurate picture of the upper end of the distribution scale, especially among the super-rich (Davies et al, 2006). **Box 5.2** below lists some international sources of wealth estimates that can be followed up after reading this chapter.

> **Box 5.2: International sources of wealth estimates**
>
> The World Bank (for example, 2005) compiles national wealth estimates for a large number of countries.
>
> The Luxembourg Wealth Study complements the more established Luxembourg Income Study, and aims to assemble comparable wealth data for OECD countries in cooperation with national statistical agencies and central banks of OECD member states (see www.lisproject.org).
>
> UNU-WIDER commissioned report – Davies et al (2006).
>
> Repeated wealth surveys are available for China and India, and one survey that enquired about wealth is available for Indonesia.
>
> *Forbes* magazine (www.forbes.com\lists) enumerates the world's US$ billionaires and their holdings. Merrill Lynch, an investment bank, also estimates the number and holdings of US$ millionaires around the world in its annual *World wealth report* (www.ml.com/).
>
> *Source:* Davies et al (2006, pp 2-3)

The global distribution gap

Recent debates about global poverty and inequality have mainly focused on the distribution of income. Research shows that the distribution of income worldwide is very unequal and that this inequality has not lessened over recent decades, contrary to what enthusiasts of neoliberal globalisation claim (Townsend, 1993; Wade, 2001; Townsend and Gordon, 2002; Milanovic, 2005, 2007). Milanovic thus reports that:

> the top 5 per cent of highest earners in the world receive one-third of the world income, whereas the bottom 5 per cent receive only 0.2 per cent. Consequently, the ratio of the top 5 per cent to the bottom 5 per cent is 165 to 1. Differently, the top 10 per cent of people in the world get around one-half of world income, leaving

the remaining 90 per cent of the world population the other half
of the global income. (2007, p 40)

These statistics alert us to the yawning global distribution gap – but the
distribution of income only gives us a partial picture of the nature and
distribution of global poverty and inequality. To complete the picture we also
need to look at the distribution of wealth on a global scale. As Pogge (2007)
notes:

> inequalities in wealth are much greater [than inequalities in
> income], because the wealth of affluent people is typically greater
> than their annual income while the wealth of poor people is
> typically smaller than their annual income. In fact, the investment
> income of a few dozen of the world's richest people exceeds the
> total income of the world's poor. (Pogge, 2007, p 132)

We turn now to examine in some detail one recent study commissioned by
the UN (Davies et al, 2006) that measures the world distribution of wealth
using a global measure of inequality.

Davies et al's (2006) study of the world distribution of wealth is the most
advanced attempt so far to study wealth inequality on a global scale. For the
purpose of this study, wealth is defined in the sense of net worth – the value
of physical and financial assets less liabilities. This definition does not include
'social security wealth', that is, the present value of expected net benefits from
public pension plans in household wealth, because estimates are available only
for a few countries. In order to make the study's data as comparable as possible
across as many countries as possible, much of the wealth data Davies et al
used comes from household-level data – notably, Household Balance Sheets
(HBS) – supplemented by other sources such as household wealth survey
data, financial accounts or balance sheets, tax data and other data reported by
financial, government and statistical agencies (for the range of data sources
used, see Davies et al, 2006, appendix II).

The study provides a snapshot of global wealth inequality: it covers a single
year, 2000, since this year provided the best balance of reasonably recent
data and good data availability for the widest range of countries. The study
was concerned with wealth distribution across adults (those over 20 years of
age), on the grounds that those under 20 have little formal and actual wealth
ownership. The countries for which data are available included 56% of the
world's population and more than 80% of its household wealth. In terms of
methodology, the authors analysed the determinants of wealth levels and its
distribution in the countries that have wealth data, and made imputations
for the 'missing countries' to arrive at actual, estimated and imputed wealth

distributions among adults. Through these calculations, they worked out the minimum wealth and wealth share of each percentile in the global distribution of wealth, the number of people that each world region and country supplied to each of the deciles (tenths) and percentile points.

The findings of the study show a wide variation in global wealth and concurred with other research findings that 'globally, wealth is more unequally distributed than income' (Davies et al, 2006, p 11). In the remainder of this section we present some extracts from the report through a series of six tables. *Tables 5.1–5.3* present the global wealth distribution in 2000 using official exchange rates (OER), while *Tables 5.4–5.6* present estimates for global wealth distribution in 2000 using the purchasing power parity (PPP) measure (note that PPPs take account of differences in costs of living in different areas). We set out each of the bases of the estimates and compare the results between these two different bases of measurement. All wealth figures are shown in US dollars.

Table 5.1 summarises global wealth distribution data for 2000, using the official exchange rate basis. While just $2,161 was needed in order to belong to the top half (sixth decile) of the world wealth distribution, to be a member of the top 10% (decile) required at least $61,000; membership of the top 5% required over $150,000 per adult and membership of the top 1% required more than half a million US dollars per adult. The figures for wealth shares show that the top 10% of adults own 85% of global household wealth – so the average member of this group has 8.5 times the global average holding. The corresponding figures for the top 5% and top 1% are 71% (14.2 times the average) and 40% (40 times the average), respectively. This compares with the bottom half of the distribution that collectively owns just 1% of global wealth. The contrast with the bottom decile of wealth holders is even more pronounced: the average member of the top decile owns nearly 3,000 times the mean wealth of the bottom decile, and the average member of the top percentile (1%) is more than 13,000 times richer (Davies et al, 2006, p 26).

Table 5.2 shows how the global wealth distribution breaks down at the level of world regions, showing the number of people each region or country supplies to each of the deciles in the distribution scale, wealth per adult and wealth share by region. Looking first of all at the right-hand side of the table, three regions stand out as having the largest overall share of global wealth – North America (34.3%), Europe (29.5%) and high-income Asian countries (these include Japan, Taiwan, South Korea, Australia, New Zealand and several middle eastern states) (22.9%). These three regions, together with Oceania, also have by far the highest levels of wealth per adult. With the exception of Europe, we can see that the most populous regions have the lowest wealth per adult and lowest share of global wealth, while those with the highest wealth per adult and highest share of global wealth have the lowest population share.

Table 5.1: *Global wealth distribution in 2000 (official exchange rate basis, OER)*

	Decile										Top 5 per cent	Top 1 per cent
	1	2	3	4	5	6	7	8	9	10		
World wealth shares (%)	0.03	0.09	0.2	0.3	0.5	0.8	1.4	2.8	8.8	85.1	70.6	39.9
Minimum wealth (USD)	0.0	192	464	890	1,405	2,161	3,517	6,318	14,169	61,041	150,145	514,512

Source: Adapted from Davies et al (2006, Table 10a)

Table 5.2: *Global wealth distribution in 2000 (official exchange rate basis, USD) – population proportions by region*

	Decile										Top 5 per cent	Top 1 per cent	Population share	Wealth per adult	Wealth share
	1	2	3	4	5	6	7	8	9	10					
North America	0.2	0.5	0.9	1.2	1.8	2.8	4.5	8.0	14.1	27.1	28.6	39.1	6.1	190,653	34.3
Latin America and Caribbean	5.5	6.7	6.9	5.7	6.2	7.9	10.2	13.2	14.7	5.0	3.1	2.1	8.2	18,163	4.4
Europe	8.6	8.3	9.2	7.9	8.8	10.4	12.8	16.8	30.1	36.1	35.7	26.2	14.9	67,232	29.5
Asia: China	6.8	14.6	16.9	36.9	40.8	38.0	35.5	29.1	8.9	0.2	0.0	0.0	22.8	3,885	2.6
Asia: India	27.3	27.5	27.3	19.4	16.5	14.8	11.4	7.4	2.5	0.2	0.0	0.0	15.4	1,989	0.9
Asia: high income	0.0	0.0	0.1	0.2	0.4	0.7	1.6	3.8	12.0	26.3	29.5	31.0	4.5	172,414	22.9
Asia: other	24.1	24.7	24.4	19.3	17.4	17.7	16.6	14.8	12.2	2.5	1.2	0.6	17.4	5,952	3.1
Africa	27.3	17.5	14.1	9.2	7.8	7.4	7.0	6.4	4.4	0.7	0.3	0.2	10.2	3,558	1.1
Oceania	0.2	0.2	0.3	0.3	0.3	0.2	0.4	0.4	1.2	2.0	1.5	0.8	0.6	72,874	1.2
World	100	100	100	100	100	100	100	100	100	100	100	100	100	33,893	100

Source: Davies et al (2006, Table 10a)

Moving towards the left-hand side of the table, the global wealth distribution is broken down by deciles. India, African countries and middle- to low-income Asian countries together contain 43% of the world's population but contain 78.7% of the world's poorest individuals (that is, those having between $0 and $191). On the other hand, North America, Europe and high-income Asian countries, where 25.5% of the world's population lives, contain 92.7% of the world's richest individuals (having $61,041 or more). Nearly four out of ten of the world's top 1% of richest individuals/adults – having $514,512 – live in North America, about one in three live in high-income Asian countries and one in four live in Europe.

The study allows us to ascertain where the UK fits into this global picture. We can already work out from **Table 5.2** that those living in the UK (like the rest of Europe) are among the world's wealthiest people. But **Table 5.2** provides only a regional breakdown, so we need to extract the UK as a country. **Table 5.3** provides some further details on this country, alongside the US and other European countries for the purposes of comparison.

By regional standards, the UK is a wealthy country: it has the highest level of wealth per adult of all the European countries; nearly 6% are members of the top 10% of the world's richest individuals, no one falls into the bottom 20% of the globally poorest groups and just 0.4% of its population are members of the poorest 50% of people in the world. By comparison with Germany and the US, for example, the UK contains a much lower proportion of the global poor – 4.5% of the global poor live in the US and 4.4% live in Germany. But the UK has a greater number of the global poor living there than other European countries – Italy and the Netherlands have none and Spain has 0.2%.

Table 5.3 also allows us to say something about social inequalities within countries. In particular, Germany and the US contain larger proportions of the globally wealthy, but they also have a larger share of the global poor. In Germany's case, this is mainly due to the former East Germany, the population of which was much poorer than that of West Germany. The other European countries presented here have a lower overall wealth per adult but they contain fewer people falling within the globally poor populations. While these figures pertain to global measures of wealth inequality, we can say something about the disparities of wealth within countries, with Germany and the US being particularly unequal (the US especially so), and other European countries (including the UK) having a more equal distribution.

So far we have examined data from the report that relate to the OER measure. There are limitations to this measure, however. As Davies et al (2006) explain:

> For the world's super rich, it is natural to compare the wealth of people in different countries using official exchange rates. In

Table 5.3: Global distribution of wealth 2000 (official exchange rate basis, USD) – UK, US and selected European countries

	Decile										Top 5 per cent	Top 1 per cent	Wealth per adult	Wealth share
	1	2	3	4	5	6	7	8	9	10				
UK	–	–	0.1	0.1	0.2	0.4	0.9	1.7	2.5	5.9	7.8	6.3	169,617	5.9
US	0.2	0.5	0.9	1.2	1.7	2.6	4.2	7.1	11.6	24.9	26.7	37.4	201,319	32.6
Italy	–	–	–	–	–	0.1	0.3	1.1	4.4	6.6	5.0	3.9	122,250	4.5
Netherlands	–	–	–	–	–	0.1	0.1	0.3	1.0	1.7	1.7	1.5	144,406	1.4
France	–	–	0.1	0.1	0.2	0.4	0.8	1.8	4.3	4.2	4.1	5.2	114,650	4.1
Germany	1.4	0.8	0.9	0.4	0.9	0.5	0.4	1.0	3.6	7.6	9.8	3.7	109,735	5.7
Spain	–	–	–	0.1	0.1	0.3	0.5	0.7	3.0	3.9	2.5	1.3	86,958	2.2

Source: Adapted from Davies et al (2006, Table 10b). Blank cells indicate values less than 0.05 per cent.

Table 5.4: Global wealth distribution in 2000 (PPP values, USD)

	Decile										Top 5 per cent	Top 1 per cent
	1	2	3	4	5	6	7	8	9	10		
World wealth shares	0.1	0.3	0.6	1.1	1.6	2.4	3.7	6.2	12.9	71.1	57.0	31.6
Minimum wealth	2	826	1,978	3,693	5,724	8,399	12,749	20,299	35,954	88,035	170,467	523,264

Source: Adapted from Davies et al (2006, Table 11a)

today's world, capital is highly mobile internationally, and rich
people from most countries travel a great deal and may do a
considerable amount of their spending abroad. The wealth of
one millionaire goes just as far as that of another in Monte Carlo
or when shopping in Harrods, irrespective of which country he
[sic] lives in. Lower down the scale, however, the benefits (and
valuations) of asset holdings may depend heavily on local prices
of goods and services. In this case, it may be more appropriate to
evaluate wealth in terms of what it would buy if liquidated and
spent on consumption locally. (Davies et al, 2006, p 28)

To address this point, we now turn to examine a second set of wealth
distribution estimates based on PPP comparisons.

We now set out estimates of global wealth distribution, distinguishing by
decile for the global average (see *Table 5.4*) and by region or country (see *Table
5.5*). Applying the PPP adjustment increases the 'entry price' to each of the
deciles and percentage groups (*Table 5.4*); this reflects an increase in the global
average level of wealth, which rises from $33,893 using OER (*Table 5.2*) to
$43,628 using the PPP basis (*Table 5.5*). The entry price to the top 10% has
now increased from just over $61,000 on the OER basis (*Table 5.1*) to over
$88,000 (*Table 5.4*), while entry to the top 1% increases more modestly from
around $514,000 (*Table 5.1*) to just over $523,000 (*Table 5.4*). We can also
see that the top 10% owns more than two thirds of the world's wealth, while
the top 1% owns nearly one third (*Table 5.4*). The effect of using the PPP
measure can also be observed at the other end of the wealth spectrum: among
the bottom five deciles the entry price into each decile increases significantly,
by about a factor of four, and it owns just 3.7% of world wealth (compared
with 1% using the OER basis, *Table 5.1*). So the effect of the PPP adjustment
is to slightly narrow the disparity between the richest and the poorest deciles
– increasing the world wealth shares of deciles 1 to 9, and reducing them
among the top decile.

We can see from *Table 5.5* that the PPP adjustment factor tends to be greater
for poorer regions and countries in the world and has only small impacts
within the richest ones. Thus, wealth per adult in North America increases
by about $2,500, in Europe it increases by about $14,000 and in Oceania by
almost $27,000. In other parts of the world, wealth per adult increases by a
factor of between two (Latin America and Caribbean) and six (India). Only
in high-income Asian countries, however, does it reduce wealth per adult by
nearly $34,000; most of this effect is due to Japan, whose wealth per adult
declines from $227,600 to $157,146 when measured in PPP terms (Davies
et al, 2006, p 29).

In terms of how global wealth distribution maps across the regions, the wealthiest regions have a reduced ownership of wealth – North America now owns 27% of the world's wealth (compared with 34% using OER, *Table 5.2*), Europe owns 28% (compared with 30% using OER) and high-income Asian countries own 14% (compared with 23% using OER). But all other regions have increased their wealth share, and this is most pronounced in Asia – India has increased its share from less than 1% in OER terms (*Table 5.2*) to just over 4% using PPP, China has increased its share from 2.6% to 8.7%, and other Asian countries have increased their share from 3.1% to 7.3%.

When we compare the proportions of the population by region in each of the deciles, we can see that the wealthiest parts of the world now supply a greater share of the global poor and poorest. So North America, for example, supplies 1.4% of the global poor (compared with 0.2% using OER) and Europe supplies 9.1% (compared with 8.6% using OER); the high-income Asian countries still do not supply anyone in the bottom decile, but start now to supply people in the second decile (0.3% compared with 0% using OER) and supply 3.9% of the global poor (bottom five deciles) compared with 0.7% using OER.

For the purposes of comparison between these estimates of global wealth based on OER and PPP, we also show how the position of the UK and other selected European and North American countries are affected. Again, we can see that the wealth gap has slightly closed, and across the European countries wealth per adult increases while that in the US does not change. But this calculation also produces some surprising results – the wealth per adult is now greater in Spain than in Germany, and Germany is the least wealthy European country shown here. All the countries now supply greater numbers of the global poor but they also supply greater numbers of the global wealthiest people (top 1%). The UK now supplies 2.2% of the global poor (bottom five deciles), although its share of the global wealthiest populations (top 1%) remains at 6.3%.

To summarise, the data presented in the above section show the existence of gross inequality in the global distribution of wealth, in terms of both individuals and regions. Global wealth is concentrated in North America, Europe and high-income Asian countries. The data also show gross inequality in wealth distribution among individuals, with the top 10% of adults owning 85% of global wealth, while 50% of the world's adults own only 1% of global wealth. These data show the existence of what may be termed a 'global distribution gap'.

Table 5.5: Global wealth distribution in 2000 (PPP values, USD) – population proportions by region

	Decile										Top 5 per cent	Top 1 per cent	Population share	Wealth per adult	Wealth share
	1	2	3	4	5	6	7	8	9	10					
North America	1.4	2.6	3.5	3.3	3.5	4.0	5.2	6.2	9.6	21.6	25.7	39.3	6.1	193,147	27.0
Latin America and Caribbean	10.3	9.1	8.1	6.8	6.7	7.5	8.2	9.0	9.3	6.9	6.4	6.1	8.2	34,956	6.6
Europe	9.1	9.2	10.1	9.1	9.3	12.0	14.1	18.1	22.7	35.0	35.8	31.2	14.9	81,890	27.9
Asia: China	6.8	14.3	14.8	33.5	37.5	34.2	32.4	29.4	20.7	4.1	1.4	0.0	22.8	16,749	8.7
Asia: India	21.0	21.9	25.2	18.1	16.3	15.8	14.2	11.6	8.0	2.3	1.2	0.0	15.4	11,655	4.1
Asia: high income	0.0	0.3	0.9	1.2	1.5	2.0	2.4	5.0	12.1	19.6	21.0	17.1	4.5	138,750	14.3
Asia: other	22.2	24.1	23.1	18.7	17.5	17.7	17.2	15.0	11.9	6.4	4.9	3.7	17.4	18,266	7.3
Africa	28.7	17.9	14.0	9.1	7.3	6.6	6.1	5.3	4.6	2.2	1.7	1.2	10.2	11,730	2.7
Oceania	0.4	0.5	0.4	0.2	0.3	0.2	0.2	0.3	1.0	1.9	2.0	1.4	0.6	99,634	1.3
World	100	100	100	100	100	100	100	100	100	100	100	100	100	43,628	100

Source: Adapted from Davies et al (2006, Table 11a)

Table 5.6: Global distribution of wealth 2000 (PPP values) – UK, US and selected European countries

	Decile										Top 5 per cent	Top 1 per cent	Wealth per adult	Wealth share
	1	2	3	4	5	6	7	8	9	10				
UK	0.1	0.3	0.5	0.6	0.7	0.9	0.7	1.2	0.8	5.9	6.0	6.3	172,461	4.7
US	1.4	2.6	3.4	3.1	3.3	3.6	4.6	5.3	8.1	19.6	23.5	36.8	201,319	25.3
Italy	–	–	0.1	0.2	0.3	0.5	0.9	1.7	3.1	5.8	5.5	5.3	148,843	4.3
Netherlands	–	–	0.1	0.1	0.1	0.2	0.2	0.4	0.8	1.4	1.6	1.7	158,484	1.2
France	0.1	0.3	0.5	0.6	0.7	0.9	1.2	1.7	2.6	3.5	3.9	5.6	125,254	3.4
Germany	3.0	1.2	0.8	0.4	0.1	0.7	1.1	1.5	1.9	7.0	8.9	3.9	114,185	4.6
Spain	–	0.1	0.3	0.3	0.4	0.5	0.3	0.7	2.5	3.7	3.2	2.3	116,782	2.3

Source: Adapted from Davies et al (2006) Table 11b; blank cells indicate values less than 0.05 per cent

Conclusion

This chapter has approached the relationship between poverty, inequality and wealth through a focus on the global context of asset ownership. As we have seen, it is problematic to neatly separate questions of inequalities in wealth ownership at national level, in countries like the UK, from questions of where the globally wealthy groups live in the world. The share of global wealth by the population of the UK – and especially the US – is massively disproportionate to its share of population in the world. One of the implications of this is that addressing global inequalities is not only about what other countries 'do', it is also about what happens in our own country and how we relate to different peoples and places around the world, including the ways in which institutional structures, policies and practices maintain unjust distributions of economic resources.

At another level, the chapter has distinguished between different ways of approaching issues of worldwide distributions of wealth (as well as income and other economic resources). We distinguished between internationalist approaches that take as their unit of analysis and measurement the nation state, and globalist approaches that measure differences between all individuals living on the planet, irrespective of which country they live in, and aim to map how current ownership of resources is distributed worldwide. We have argued that the latter approach is the more appropriate to and congruent with globalist politics and policy.

The main body of the chapter was concerned with presenting the main findings of the best available study of the worldwide distribution of wealth. We presented two alternative bases for measuring household wealth globally at global, regional and national levels – the OER and PPP measures. It is important to look closely at how different measures impact on calculations of the extent and nature of, in this case, wealth distribution. This is particularly important as politicians and policy activists make political arguments based on evidence from social sciences research, and may draw selectively to make their arguments for certain policy responses. In terms of the comparisons between the two bases, OER and PPP, we have seen that the use of official exchange rates leads to estimates in which the size and geographical distribution of household wealth is much more concentrated (that is, unequal). As the authors of the UN report put it: 'a somewhat different perspective emerges depending on whether one is interested in the power that wealth conveys in terms of local consumption options or the power to act and have influence on the world financial stage' (Davies et al, 2006, p 29).

Whichever of the two estimates is used, the overall findings of the study are quite staggering in showing the extent to which a very large portion of the world's wealth is concentrated in the top decile of the population (especially the top one tenth of 1%) and the gaping disparities between the richest and the poorest of the world's population. Responding to this appalling situation must be a major research and political priority for national and global social policy activists alike.

Summary

- National analyses of poverty and wealth need to be placed in a global context.
- There are large differences in wealth composition between countries in the developed world, and between countries in the developed and developing world.
- Differing views of the world (held by globalists and internationalists) are reflected in different ways of measuring world poverty and inequality.
- To analyse world poverty we need to examine the global distribution of wealth as well as the global distribution of income.
- Data for 2000 show global wealth to be highly inequitable: the top 10% of adults own 85% of global household wealth, while the top 5% own 71% and the top 1% own 40% of global household wealth.
- Regionally, North America, Europe and high-income Asian countries have the largest share of household wealth, 34.3%, 29.5% and 22.9% respectively. These three regions contain 25.5% of the world's population and 92.7% of the world's richest people.
- Adjusting for PPP reduces the share of global wealth held by these regions – North America has 27%, Europe 28% and high-income Asian countries 14%.
- All measurements show gross inequality in wealth distribution globally (which may be described as a global distribution gap).

Questions for discussion

- Article 11 of the UN Millennium Declaration states 'We will spare no effort to free our fellow men, women and children from the abject and dehumanising conditions of extreme poverty, to which more than a billion of them are currently subjected. We are committed to making the right to development a reality for everyone and to freeing the entire human race from want'. What, in your view, would be the most desirable set of national and global policies to achieve this aim? You may wish to consult the various sources that are listed in the guide to further resources.
- The UK Department for International Development (DfID) has acquired an international reputation as a leading government department in international

poverty reduction and social development. Its current position is set out in *Reducing poverty by tackling social exclusion* (December 2005), available at www.dfid.gov.uk/pubs/files/social-exclusion.pdf. In the light of your answers to the first question, we would like you to think about the following questions:

- Does the policy paper adequately address global inequalities in the distribution of wealth and/or income?
- In your view, is the approach of DfID to tackling poverty and inequality desirable and is it likely to be effective?

Again, you may wish to consult the resources listed below in formulating your ideas and arguments.

Electronic resources

The single most useful web resource for students interested in following up these issues is www.globalpolicy.org. This is the website oif the Global Policy Forum and it contains a useful extensive selection of short and long papers and reports on global income and wealth inequality and poverty issues. The website of the Social Policy Association's International and Comparative Social Policy Group, www.globalwelfare.net, compiles a list of useful websites campaigning around issues of poverty and inequality in a global context.

The journal of *Global Social Policy* (Sage Publications) addresses, as its title suggests, the global dimensions of social policy and welfare. The journal's Digest provides the best available source of up-to-date online information for anyone seeking to keep abreast of contemporary developments in global social policy. Each Digest reviews key policy developments, events and publications during the year, reporting on the publication of important reports such as the one this chapter has drawn on. Each section of the Digest contains hyperlinks to relevant websites and documents. It can be accessed at http://gsp.sagepub.com or via a library, providing it has a subscription to *Global Social Policy*. Alternatively, a pre-publication version of the Digest is available from http://gaspp.org or http://icsw.org.

References

Bennholdt-Thomsen, V. and Mies, M. (1999) *The subsistence perspective: Beyond the globalised economy*, London: Zed.

Davies, J., Sandstrom, S., Shorricks, A. and Wolff, E. (2006) *The world distribution of household wealth*, Helsinki, Finland: UNU-WIDER (www.iariw.org/papers/2006/davies.pdf).

Deacon, B. (2007) *Global social policy and governance*, London: Sage Publications.

Deacon, B. with Hulse, M. and Stubbs, P. (1997) *Global social policy: International organisations and the future of welfare*, London: Sage Publications.

Hillyard, P., Kelly, G., McLaughlin, E., Patios, D. and Tomlinson, M. et al (2002) *Bare necessities – Poverty and social exclusion in Northern Ireland*, Belfast: Democratic Dialogue.

Milanovic, B. (2005) *Worlds apart: Measuring international and global inequality*, Princeton, NJ: Princeton University Press.

Milanovic, B. (2007) 'Globalisation and inequality', in D. Held and A. Kaya (eds) *Global inequality*, Cambridge: Polity Press.

Pantazis, C., Gordon, D. and Levitas, R. (eds) (2006) *Poverty and social exclusion in Britain: The millennium survey*, Bristol: The Policy Press.

Pogge, T. (2007) 'Why inequality matters', in D. Held and A. Kaya (eds) *Global inequality*, Cambridge: Polity Press.

Townsend, P. (1993) *The international analysis of poverty*, Hemel Hempstead: Harvester Wheatsheaf.

Townsend, P. and Gordon, D. (eds) (2002) *World poverty: New policies to defeat an old enemy*, Bristol: The Policy Press.

Wade, R. (2001) 'The rising inequality of world income distribution', *Finance and Development,* vol 38, no 4, pp 37-9.

World Bank (2005) *Where is the wealth of nations? Measuring capital for the XXI century*, Washington, DC: World Bank.

Yeates, N. (2007a) 'The global and supra-national dimensions of the welfare mix', in M. Powell (ed) *Understanding the mixed economy of welfare*, Bristol: The Policy Press, pp 199-219.

Yeates, N. (2007b) 'Globalisation and social policy', in J. Baldock, N. Manning and S. Vickerstaff (eds) *Social policy* (3rd edn), Oxford: Oxford University Press.

Yeates, N. (ed) (2008) *Understanding global social policy*, Bristol: The Policy Press.

six

Spatial divisions of poverty and wealth

Danny Dorling and Dimitris Ballas

Overview

- Poverty/social exclusion cannot be understood out of the context of inequality and hence without an understanding of both the concept and distribution of wealth.
- Both a historical and a geographical perspective are required to appreciate how we got to where we are now – how we achieved the spatial divisions we have – and then to appreciate the current meaning of the extent of inequalities, the depths of poverty and concentrations of wealth among people.
- This chapter concentrates on just one aspect of these requirements: an appreciation of the spatial divisions that are created through inequalities in the geographical distributions of both poverty and wealth.
- Three spatial scales are used to illustrate spatial divisions of poverty and wealth:
    - Firstly, we consider the very local scale, and what divisions are experienced on journeys into and out of a modern-day rich world city, taking the archetypal example of Manchester (England) and showing how a journey into that city has changed since the early 1990s.
    - Secondly, we turn to the nation state and draw extensively on a report recently produced with the help of many colleagues on the changing geographies of poverty and place across all of Britain between 1968 and 2005.

- Thirdly, we end with a consideration of changing world-level inequalities in income and wealth and what they might imply for the future over a longer time period.

Key concepts

social and spatial inequalities; core poor; breadline poor; non-poor, non-wealthy; asset wealthy; exclusively wealthy; poverty/social exclusion

Introduction

In this chapter we describe how both locally and nationally in Britain and worldwide the bulk of the population are destined to live in 'underperforming' regions, more are poor, and the rich are becoming ever more separate from the rest: society is turning 'pear-shaped'. Poverty and wealth are not two sides of the same coin; many people are neither poor nor wealthy. There are thus more sides than two in how we are divided by our access to resources (income) and the uses we put those resources to (expenditure). The very poorest are poor no matter how they are counted, they have low income, low wealth, inadequate possessions and know they are poor and are unambiguously known as poor by others. With colleagues we have termed this group 'core poor' in Britain (see Further reading). In the US the concept of core poor equates best to the eighth of the population living below their miserly poverty line (see *Box 6.1*). Worldwide the concept equates best to the measure of those living on a couple of dollars a day. The core poor in Britain, those beneath the line in the US and those on less than $2 a day in the poor world only just survive. Thus even attempts at absolute measures of poverty have to be relative to be meaningful across the whole world (even at the same point in time – here and now). Quantifying the very richest is more difficult. To a man (it is usually still a man) with access to $1 billion, a man with only $1 million appears a pauper. In between the extremes of core poverty and unimaginable riches runs the gamut of inequity, along which most of us are strung. Being poor or being wealthy are, however, qualitatively different experiences from being a little bit better or worse off along a continuum. Both involve social exclusion from the norms of society. Furthermore, neither could exist without the other, but they are better described as very different-sized facets on a many-sided die rather than opposite side of the coin. We hope to show in this chapter how it is useful to look at the geography of how people find themselves living at, and between, these extremes to get a clearer idea of how we are so divided. We start with a city, then move out to the country and end with the world.

'Manchester: so much to answer for'

We start the analysis at the city level, focusing on Manchester, which is one of the largest and most well-known cities in Northern England. Manchester was the first city in the world to be industrialised. It was the first city in which mass human labour was put to work in a way that so thoroughly dehumanised people. 'Manchester: so much to answer for' were originally the lyrics to a popular song that very few of its younger listeners realise concerned the killers of children known as the 'Moors murderers' ('Suffer little children', The Smiths, 1984, see www.compsoc.man.ac.uk/~moz/lyrics/thesmith/sufferli.htm). But, as the song implies, Manchester, or rather the way of treating human beings first seen in Manchester, has much more to answer for than that.

Box 6.1: The poverty line and the wrong side of the tracks

There is an ongoing debate on where the poverty line should be set (see Rio Expert Group on Poverty Statistics, 2006). Countries such as the US adopt an 'absolute poverty' approach to setting the poverty line, which is much lower than the line set in the European Union (EU), which adopts a 'relative poverty' approach to setting the line (for example, all households below 60% of the national median household income are defined as poor; also see Gordon et al, 2000). This approach is not directly based on the degree to which households are able to satisfy their physiological or other basic needs and recognises that the concept of poverty constantly evolves and that the subsistence approach to the definition of poverty is inadequate. As Gordon and Pantazis (1997) point out:

> The subsistence approach to the definition of poverty is an 'absolute' concept of poverty; it is dominated by the individual's requirements for physiological efficiency. However, this is a very limited conception of human needs, especially when considering the roles men and women play in society. People are not just physical beings, they are social beings. They have obligations as workers, parents, neighbours, friends and citizens that they are expected to meet and which they themselves want to meet. (Gordon and Pantazis, 1997, p 9)

It should be noted that the poverty line also has a spatial dimension, which is best described by the phrase 'wrong side of the tracks'.

Source: www.takeourword.com/TOW134/page2.html

Some speculate that the etymology of this expression dates back to the time when railroads were first built and became a defining characteristic in towns and cities, sometimes dividing them between wealthy and poor areas (Words to the Wise, 2001). According to this theory, the 'wrong side of the tracks' referred to the side of the tracks that due to the wind would receive most of the locomotive's black, sooty smoke. In addition, it has been suggested that at the time when railroad tracks were built and ran through North American towns, soot, smoke and prevailing winds resulted in poor or industrial areas being located on the downwind side of the tracks that may have also given rise to this phrase. Whatever the precise notion behind the 'wrong side of the tracks', it arose in the US, probably in the 19th century, although the *Oxford English Dictionary*'s first record of it is from 1929 (Words to the Wise, 2001). Similar expressions used today include the 'wrong side of town' or the 'wrong side of the street', and they signify the importance of geography: where you live and where you grow up affects your life chances (see also Dorling, 2001). In current terms, people living on the wrong side of the tracks typically receive disproportionately less income and have less wealth and fewer opportunities when compared with those on the right side.

The University of Manchester has the date of its founding now inscribed in the logo of the new unified mega-university: 'Manchester 1824'. This is a date of university founding which is roughly a well-lived lifetime older (75 years) than that of other provincial English cities. It is not by chance that the city boasts of being something special. Take a trip to the Manchester Museum of Science and Industry (www.msim.org.uk/Galleries.asp?menuid=885) and you are walking within a giant warehouse established just a decade after the university. A couple of decades later and Friedrich Engel's *Conditions of the working class* was published (Engels, 1845). Later in the 1850s, the expectation of life's length from birth in Manchester was just 32 years, and fell to 31 years in the 1860s (Szreter and Mooney, 1998, p 88). In Manchester's central district it was as low as 29 by then, exceeded — as worse — only by an all-time life expectancy low of 25 years in those same years in nearby Liverpool (Szreter and Mooney, 1998, p 90). Human life has rarely been valued lower outside of times of war, genocide or in the worst of famines. The urban experience of systemic poverty that can be wrought through capitalism began in Manchester. By the turn of the 20th century standards of living were not much better than during the mid-19th century. In fact, the long hot summer of 1904 saw infants die in Manchester at near to the rates (one in four before their first birthday) at which they now still die in the poorest places on earth a century later (see 'World map of infant mortality', Worldmapper, 2007, map 261, at www.sasi. group.shef.ac.uk/worldmapper/textindex/text_death.html). And it was in Manchester that it was first realised that those deaths were not an act of god, but due to the squalor that accompanies poverty — squalor that was quantified then in the numbers of flies found living around new-born infants:

> By means of a number of beer-traps Dr Niven contrived to count the flies in some dozen houses in Manchester during the summer months of 1904, and from these data he concluded that the advent of the house-fly in numbers precedes by a short time the increase in the number of deaths from diarrhoea. In the fortnight ending August 13th, for instance, the number of flies caught in these traps was 37,521, the maximum in any fortnight, and in the fortnight following the maximum number of deaths from diarrhoea occurred — namely, 192. (Newman, 1906, pp 168-9)

In the century that followed the long hot summer of 1904, life in the city of Manchester changed, for most, almost beyond recognition. However, Manchester the city is still the district of England with the lowest male life expectancy from birth,[1] and this is despite its centre now being one of the most dynamic business districts in the country. The city also now contains some extremely affluent enclaves. In *Box 6.2* a journey you can take through Manchester and out into leafy Macclesfield district is described, and in *Figure 6.1* that same journey is shown on a map in which areas are shaded according to the average incomes of those who live there. How those areas were derived is also detailed in *Box 6.2*. Average incomes in the centre of the city are less than half the average in the rural hinterland of Manchester. Many of those who can do so tend to get out, but still usually drive in for work. These are just the inequalities between averages, not extremes, and between a measure already greatly redistributed before it is counted (it is not earned income that is being shown). Nevertheless, this journey and the accompanying map reveal a great deal when you know more about this city (and most others of its kind).

Box 6.2: A journey you can take through Manchester and out into leafy Macclesfield

Next time you are driving round the north edge of Manchester why not turn in?

Start on the A664 at the M60 Junction 20 (J20), North Manchester. Proceed south through Blackley. Turn left onto the A6010. Turn right onto the A636 into central Manchester. Join the A57 Mancunian Way. Leave on the A5103, pass the universities and Moss Side. Turn left onto the A6010 through Fallowfield. Turn right onto the A34, pass through Didsbury. Join the M60 Westbound for one junction. Leave at J5, turning left onto the A510. Join the M56 at J3, and proceed south west. At J8, leave the M56 and turn left onto the A556, pass through Bucklow Hill. Pass straight over the M6, and turn left onto the A5033 into Knutsford. Leave Knutsford on the A537, and follow all the way to Macclesfield town centre. Leave Macclesfield on the A536 southbound, and proceed to Congleton, where the journey ends.

See *Figure 6.1* for where you have driven and the average income of who you drove past.

To draw *Figure 6.1* it was necessary to divide Manchester and its neighbouring district of Macclesfield up into a series of areas for which averages could be calculated. This was done by first identifying two types of parliamentary constituencies: urban and rural. Urban constituencies have a high proportion of areas defined as urban (above 65%, usually more than 90% of the population), whereas rural constituencies have more rural areas (at least 35% of the population, usually 45%–55%). Where rural constituencies were split by a local authority boundary we treated that boundary as a natural break. The rules we followed for allocating electoral wards to the pair of tracts formed from a constituency differed depending on how we classified the constituency. By far the majority were classified as urban constituencies, so they are described first, by a series of rules. In many constituencies the rules are incompatible, that is, they cannot all be satisfied, but are listed in the order in which we attempted to apply them. For urban constituencies we grouped wards into larger neighbourhoods on the basis of various criteria that included the minimisation of the variance in estimated average income. For rural constituencies we used the population living in urban settlements within those constituencies to define their neighbourhoods. For each of the five years studied, every separate urban area (as defined by the Department of the Environment in 1991) had at least one ward allocated to it (automatically using a GIS [geographic information system] and then edited laboriously by hand). These wards would either be completely or partially located in an urban area. Wards that did not overlap with urban areas were designated as rural. This allowed an approximate calculation of the percentage of people living in rural or urban areas within constituencies. Most of the constituencies classified as rural constituencies contain around 50% of people living in each type of area, which makes them suitable for this method.

More information on the rules that were used to create the 'neighbourhoods' and on the methodology may be found at: www.sasi.group.shef.ac.uk/tracts/ Constructing_tracts.pdf

The difference between incomes are much muted when averaged over many people and when calculated after redistribution in the form of taxes and benefits has occurred (but before housing costs are taken into account). Had we shown instead inequalities in wealth along this journey then the differences would be significantly higher. Had we taken a related measure, but of something very rare – the murder rate – the differences would not be possible to calculate as in places within the city the rate is among the highest in England, whereas it is practically zero in parts of the outskirts. It is not just in the US that such extremes occur. Almost all else in life changes along with the trend in inequalities in incomes as you take this journey through Manchester. First, however, how do we know what the average incomes of people along this route are?

The average incomes shown in *Figure 6.1* are estimates that were produced by the Office for National Statistics (see http://neighbourhood.statistics.gov. uk/HTMLDocs/downloads/Model-Based_Income_Estimates(V2).pdf). They almost certainly underestimate the extent of income inequalities along the route, as they are the products of a statistical model based on relatively limited information. For instance, one of the variables on which these income estimates are based is the proportion of households in each geographical area that are classified as 'professionals and intermediate', masking the considerable income variation within this group.

From the above discussion it becomes obvious that in order to properly analyse socioeconomic inequalities and their spatial manifestations it is necessary to have good quality small area data on income and wealth. Nevertheless, and despite the very strong arguments to measure small area incomes, the UK government decided not to include such a question in the

Figure 6.1: *A journey from less than £200 a week to live on to more than £400 a week*

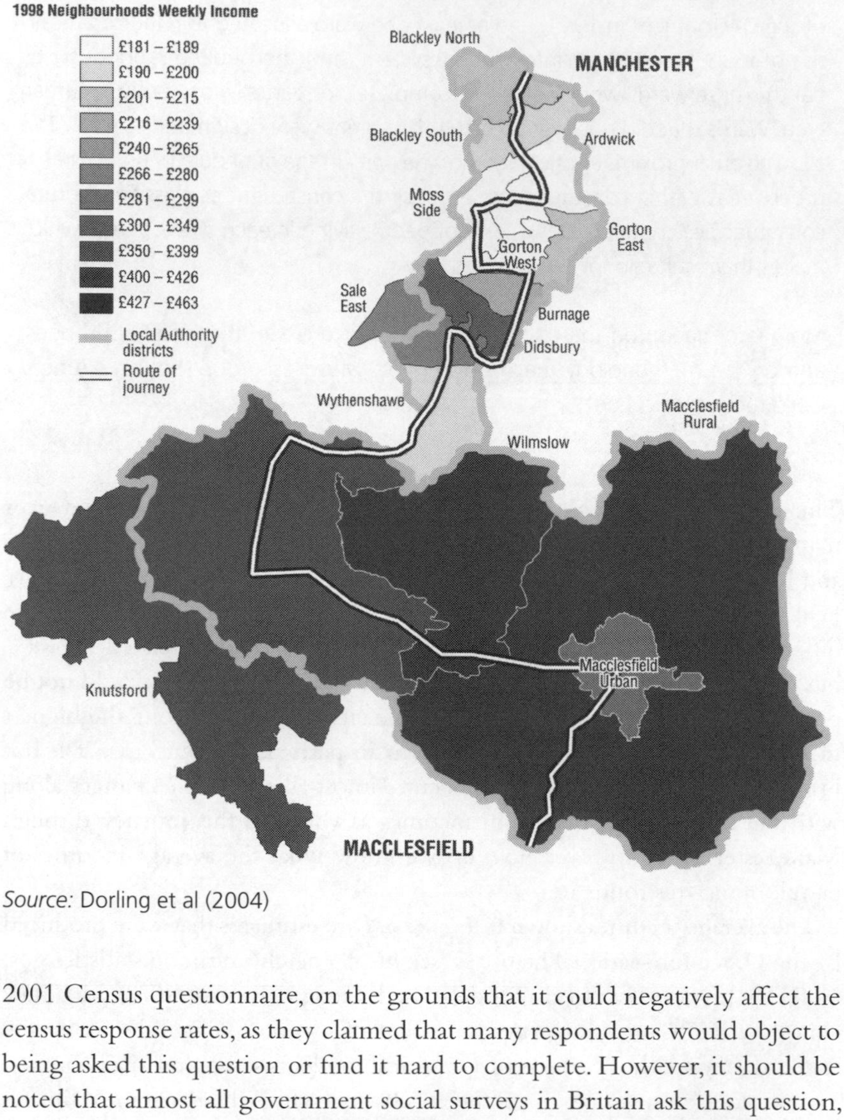

1998 Neighbourhoods Weekly Income

☐	£181 – £189
☐	£190 – £200
☐	£201 – £215
☐	£216 – £239
☐	£240 – £265
☐	£266 – £280
☐	£281 – £299
☐	£300 – £349
☐	£350 – £399
☐	£400 – £426
☐	£427 – £463

Local Authority districts

Route of journey

Blackley North

MANCHESTER

Blackley South

Ardwick

Moss Side

Gorton West

Gorton East

Sale East

Burnage

Didsbury

Wythenshawe

Wilmslow

Macclesfield Rural

Knutsford

Macclesfield Urban

MACCLESFIELD

Source: Dorling et al (2004)

2001 Census questionnaire, on the grounds that it could negatively affect the census response rates, as they claimed that many respondents would object to being asked this question or find it hard to complete. However, it should be noted that almost all government social surveys in Britain ask this question, and it is also successfully asked in other national censuses worldwide. Another argument against the inclusion of an income question in the census is that it would breach confidentiality rules, making it possible to identify individual respondents. Yet it should be noted that individuals' answers to census questions, unlike other government surveys, are confidential and cannot be released from the Office for National Statistics for 100 years under the census legislation (Rees et al, 2002). It can be argued that there are no good statistical or social scientific reasons for not measuring income via the census and that there are possibly other, perhaps political, reasons for keeping people in Britain in the dark over where the rich and poor live. It seems that the government does not want to know too much about the rich – and what an income question tells us most about is the rich – as government ministers seem to be more interested in 'inclusion' rather than 'inequality' (Levitas, 1998). However, if one is interested in how to ameliorate social and spatial inequalities and promote equality it is essential to know about both the richest and the poorest: how many there are and where they live (Marsh, 1993; Rees, 1998; Dorling, 1999). As this book goes to press it now looks almost certain that a question on income will not be asked in the 2011 Census, except perhaps in Scotland. Maybe in 2021?

Given the lack of reliable good-quality geographical income data that would allow a thorough investigation of the spatial distribution of poverty and wealth, there have been considerable efforts within the social sciences to estimate income for geographical areas that are smaller than the levels at which published data exist. In addition, there have been considerable efforts by economists to develop data fusion and related methodologies that aim at combining different sources of data – typically adding 'income' as a variable to data where this information is not present (for instance, see Bramley and Smart, 1996; Noble and Smith, 1996; Davies et al, 1997; Heady et al, 2003; Ballas, 2004; Ballas et al, 2005).

Similar issues arise when analysing social and spatial inequalities in wealth, as this is also something not asked in the census. Social scientists deal with this lack of wealth data by combining information from a wide range of sources including the census of population (number of households and socioeconomic characteristics), building societies and the Land Registry (house price data). A recent study in Britain published for the housing charity Shelter used such methods, revealing the emergence of an unprecedented housing wealth gap (Thomas and Dorling, 2004). In addition, a more recent study (Dorling et al, 2007) extended such methodologies further, and applied them in order to estimate the size and geographical distribution of households that could be considered to be 'asset wealthy' and 'exclusive wealthy' (see the Glossary at the beginning of this book).

Just as it is possible to produce a profile of the changing income distribution along a journey once area data has been estimated, so too can many other aspects of life related to poverty and wealth be measured and depicted. *Figure 6.2(a)–(c)* shows three different transects of our journey from North Manchester through to the rural southern hinterland.

Firstly *Figure 6.2(a)* shows how, despite their rarity in the city centre, detached property is so much higher valued in the suburbs and rural parts of the route. *Figure 6.2(b)* shows that this property increased in estimated value much more in recent years as compared with that in the city centre. *Figure 6.2(c)* shows how the decline in a particular migrant group – those born in Ireland

Figure 6.2(a): *Mean detached house price in £s (2001), Blakely North to Macclesfield Rural*

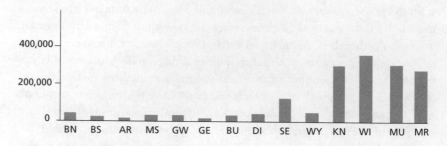

Figure 6.2(b): *Mean detached house price in £s (1995–2003), Blakely North to Macclesfield Rural*

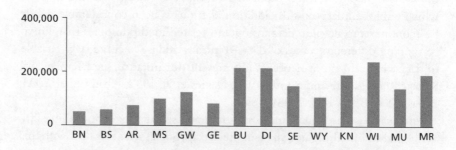

Figure 6.2(c): *Change in the percentage of population born in Republic of Ireland (1991–2001), Blakely North to Macclesfield Rural*

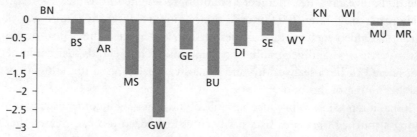

Source: Dorling et al (2004)

– occurs in rough tandem with these trends in income and wealth distribution and redistribution. The centre of Manchester is an area that has been typified by immigration since the first industrial buildings were raised. *Figure 6.2(c)* shows the decline due to death in old age and out-migration of a group who came in large numbers both in the 1840s and 1960s (and often in between), but no longer. New groups from countries further than Ireland now arrive in Manchester in greater numbers, but almost always in greatest proportions where the living is hardest and the incomes and wealth the least.

Manchester was the first model in the world for how income, poverty, wealth and inequality tends to be distributed around a city when much of the market in housing, transportation and wages is left to be free. The present local authority district of the city of Manchester stretches long and thin from north to south, and so it is possible to chart a route – a journey – that covers most of it and does not look too contrived. Journeys have long been a way in which geographical inequalities in Britain have been studied (see *Box 6.3*).

Box 6.3: Travelogues and other spatial journeys

To illustrate social polarisation one typical approach is to take a short journey from affluent suburbs to inner-city estates. It can be argued that these approaches may have been inspired by travelogues such as that of George Orwell, who travelled and spent time living among the poor in mining towns in northern England and wrote an account of his experiences:

> In a Lancashire cotton-town you could probably go for months on end without once hearing an 'educated' accent, whereas there can hardly be a town in the South of England where you could throw a brick without hitting the niece of a bishop. (Orwell, 1937)

A more recent example of this kind of approach is a documentary by Andrew Dilnot in 2001. In it, Dilnot, the (then) director of the UK Institute for Fiscal Studies (www.ifs.org.uk) cycled up and down a hill in Leeds populated by families of varying socioeconomic backgrounds, exploring the geographical and socioeconomic dimensions of income and wealth inequalities. He spoke to four families, starting with a single parent at the bottom of the hill and the income distribution, and ending at the top with a millionaire. In between were a bus driver and his family one third of the way up the income scale, and a council employee and mobile phone company employee two thirds of the way up. Similar approaches to studying socioeconomic polarisation are adopted by lecturers in geography taking fieldtrips of students on coaches from one part of a city to another. Apart from being intrusive, these approaches to studying social polarisation would be very expensive to implement for the whole of a country. So census data and GIS technologies can be used to measure and map local social polarisation nationally to gauge the extent to which it is a long-run phenomenon that social policy makers need to take into account when, for instance, setting targets or designing policy.

Spatial divisions in Britain

The journey into Manchester and out into rural Macclesfield is a journey between extremes, although it is one of many possible such journeys and is certainly not the most extreme that could be taken: *Figures 6.3* and *6.4* show the journey drawn with three small arrows on two maps of the whole of Britain. These are population cartogram maps and each hexagon is a parliamentary constituency. Population cartograms differ from conventional maps of places that show areas as they might appear from space. Looking at a country or a city from space is not the best way to see its economic and social geography. Population cartograms show each area of the country drawn roughly in proportion to the size of its population and it therefore gives the people of the country a 'fairer' representation (for more information on population cartograms, see Dorling, 2005; Thomas and Dorling, 2007). Here we use such cartograms to study the economic geography of Britain. The first of those maps (*Figure 6.3*) shows the proportion of the population that make up the 'core poor' in each small part of the country (see the Glossary at the beginning of this book) and the second map shows how many of those in each place were 'exclusively wealthy' (see the Glossary) by 2000. Without seeing both maps you cannot appreciate that in taking the journey we just have, we have been through some of the areas containing the highest proportions of 'core poor' – and then into places that contain some of the highest proportions of exclusively wealthy households to live in the North of England. Indeed, as *Figure 6.4* shows, the British 'exclusively wealthy' almost exclusively live in a ring of areas to the west of London in the south of England. In this section we discuss how Figures 6.3 and 6.4 were drawn and what their implications are.

Research into the extent and trends in poverty in Britain has generally not produced measures for relatively small areas that can be compared over time. To overcome this problem, with colleagues, we extended the 'Breadline Britain' methodology (Dorling et al, 2007) to produce estimates for small areas across the country around the time of the 1971, 1981, 1991 and 2001 Censuses of population (see *Box 6.4*). Because we mix this data with that from surveys usually taken a few years earlier (1968, 1983, 1990 and 1999), we will use the dates 1970, 1980, 1990 and 2000 from here on. We also used information of housing prices and consumption by affluent individuals to produce estimates for the same areas of the numbers of households that were asset wealthy and exclusively wealthy living in each small area (see the Glossary at the beginning of this book). Our definition of exclusive wealth is the theoretical opposite of what is normally seen as the definition of poverty as relative deprivation. Peter Townsend's standard definition of poverty is that the poor lack the opportunities to enjoy a standard of living commensurate with societal norms,

Figure 6.3: *The geography of where the poorest of the poor lived in Britain in 2000*

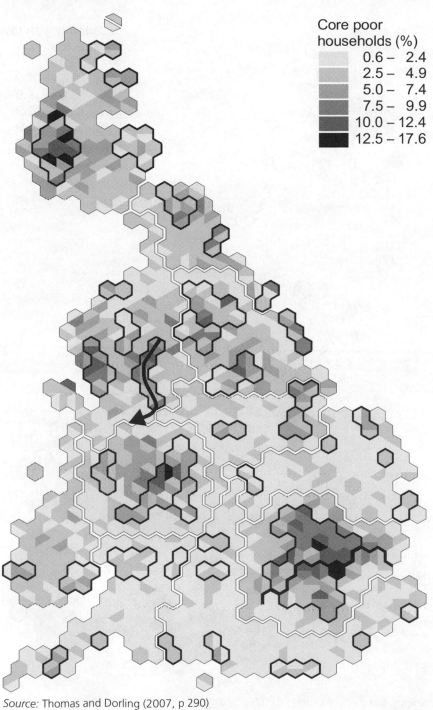

Core poor
households (%)

	0.6 – 2.4
	2.5 – 4.9
	5.0 – 7.4
	7.5 – 9.9
	10.0 – 12.4
	12.5 – 17.6

Source: Thomas and Dorling (2007, p 290)

Figure 6.4: *The geography of where the exclusively wealthy lived most in Britain in 2000*

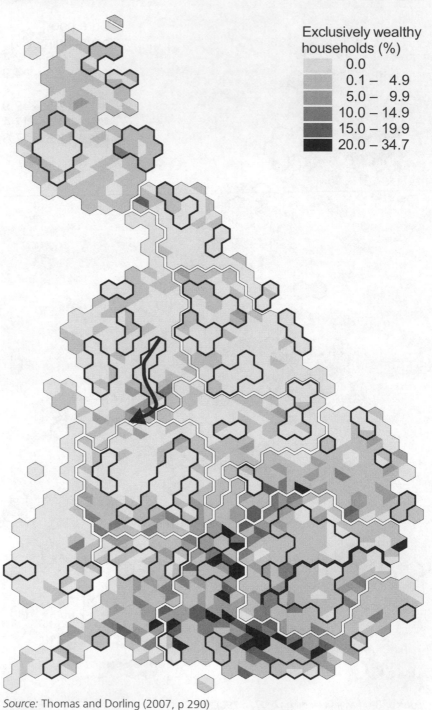

Exclusively wealthy
households (%)

0.0
0.1 –   4.9
5.0 –   9.9
10.0 – 14.9
15.0 – 19.9
20.0 – 34.7

Source: Thomas and Dorling (2007, p 290)

and are thus deprived from participating as full citizens of their society (see Chapter Three, this volume). Exclusive wealth, in contrast, confers privilege through being able to secure benefits by dint of wealth not generally available to the public at large (and certainly not to the poor).

Box 6.4: The 'Breadline Britain' method and units of analysis

The Breadline Britain method (Pantazis et al, 2006) measures relative poverty based on a lack of the perceived necessities of life. This has been widely accepted as a good measure of relative poverty. In Britain, there have been four nationally representative scientific surveys of poverty in the past 50 years, listed below:

- *Poverty in the United Kingdom: A survey of household resources and standards of living*, 1967–9, 2,052 households (Townsend, 1979).
- Living in Britain, 1983, 1,174 households, published as *Poor Britain* (Mack and Lansley, 1985).
- Breadline Britain, 1990, 1,831 households (Gordon and Pantazis, 1997).
- Poverty and Social Exclusion Survey, 1,534 households (Gordon et al, 2000).

These surveys showed that: 'in 1983 14% of households lacked three or more necessities because they could not afford them. That proportion had increased to 21% in 1990 and to over 24% by 1999. (Items defined as necessities are those that more than 50% of the population believes "all adults should be able to afford and which they should not have to do without.")' (Gordon et al, 2000).

Despite the restricted sample sizes, the above surveys reflect a broadly comparable relative approach to the definition and measurement of poverty. By adopting a synthetic modelling approach, it is therefore technically possible to examine the spatial distribution of area poverty over time based on four discrete time slices, using a comparable methodology: 1967–9 (1971 Census); 1983 (1981 Census); 1990 (1991 Census); and 1999 (2001 Census).

When estimating poverty and wealth a critical decision that needs to be made is the unit of analysis – the choice is usually whether to analyse households or individuals. In the examples presented here the unit of analysis is the household and the reason for this is largely pragmatic. In combining the census and the surveys, the most appropriate unit is the household, since that is the sampling unit (for the surveys). It is also the appropriate level for information such as tenure or car ownership. Household size and composition tends to vary with socioeconomic status, but potential bias is controlled in the Breadline Britain method by adjusting household income for these factors. Likewise, given that wealth analysis relies on housing equity, the household is again the most appropriate unit.

It should also be noted that using the household as the unit of analysis is consistent with conventional practices of economists, who assume that the welfare of any one individual in a household will depend not only on their own income, but also on that of other household members. This assumption is, of course, problematic.

The 'exclusively wealthy' can thus be defined as those living above a high wealth line. This has to be a line so high that people are able, living above it, to exclude themselves from participating in the norms of society (if they so wish). To operationalise this definition of a wealth line, data from the Family Expenditure Survey (FES) was used in combination with the households below average income (HBAI) adjustments to the incomes of the very 'rich' (Dorling et al, 2007). The HBAI adjustments are made to account for household size and type when considering household income, and were the same as those used in the Breadline Britain methodology. The adjusted FES data was then used to define the average level of income at which the following exclusive activities tend to occur: children go to independent schools, people use private healthcare, have second homes, have boats, pay private club membership fees, and so on. To estimate the geographical distribution of exclusively wealthy households, housing data were used to estimate the equivalent asset wealth accompanying this exclusive behaviour.

The group that is the mirror image of the exclusively wealthy in theoretical terms are thus living below the relative poverty line: the breadline poor. However, at any one time, just as for every person who is rich there is a subset who are extremely rich; for all who experience poverty, there is a subset who are extremely poor. The group termed the 'core poor' here are those who are suffering from a combination of normative, felt and comparative poverty. That is, respectively, people who are simultaneously income poor (normative), subjectively poor (felt) and necessities/deprivation poor (comparatively poor). This is a subset of those who are comparatively poor but not necessarily felt nor normatively poor: the breadline poor. Finally there are those who are neither poor nor wealthy of any variety. *Table 6.1* shows what proportion of households in Britain we estimate to be in each group at the start of each decade.

Table 6.1 shows that we estimate that currently only half of all households are neither poor nor wealthy (50.4%); however, two thirds are generally included in the norms of society. That two thirds is the non-poor, non-wealthy plus the asset wealthy less the exclusively wealth (50.4 + 22.6 − 5.6 = 67.4%). Note that the middle three columns of *Table 6.1* sum to 100 and that the proportion who are excluded from the norms of society either by dint of their breadline poverty or their exclusive wealth can be calculated by summing the second and fifth column of data in the table. Over 30 years the socially excluded

Table 6.1: *Poverty and wealth measures for Great Britain, 1970 to 2000*

Year	% core poor*	% breadline poor	% non-poor, non-wealthy	% asset wealthy	% exclusively wealthy*
1970	14.4	23.1	n/a**	n/a**	7.4
1980	9.8	17.1	66.1	16.8	6.9
1990	14.3	21.3	55.7	23.0	3.5
2000	11.2	27.0	50.4	22.6	5.6

* Note that 'core poor' and 'exclusively wealthy' are subsets of 'breadline poor' and 'asset wealthy', respectively; see main report for estimates of variability around the exclusive wealth estimates. The middle three columns sum to 100%.

** Housing wealth data were unavailable for 1970; since asset wealth could not be calculated, neither could the proportion of non-poor, non-wealthy at this time.

Source: Dorling et al (2007)

(rich and poor) have grown from 30.5% (23.1% + 7.4%) to 32.6% (27.0% + 5.6%) and were only a quarter of households in 1980 (when the poor were at a minima) and 1990 (when recession in the south hit the wealth of the rich). Note also that we have no estimate of the asset wealthy in 1970 and so can derive no estimate of those households that are non-poor, non-wealthy in that year. Finally it should be noted that there were fewer core poor in 2000 as compared to 1990 – almost certainly due to social innovations such as the introduction of a minimum wage and tax credits for families in lower-paid work. However, it should also be noted that the definition of 'core poor' used here is perhaps a very strict one. For instance, Wolf and de-Shalit (2007) argue that a good definition of who is poor should be based on at least two of the three measures that we used and not necessarily all three of them. A very robust definition of poverty would be that someone is poor if they can tick any two of the following three boxes: (1) they think they are poor; (2) they have a low income; (3) they have low wealth. The low wealth criteria might be that they are breadline poor, or simply that they have almost no savings. The precise definitions of poverty lines become less important when a two-out-of-three criterion is used. Most people understand that someone is poor if they have low income and low wealth – whether they think of themselves as poor or not. Most people are happy that someone with savings who does not think of themselves as poor is not poor, even if they have a low income – and so on. This two-out-of-three criterion was originally proposed by Bradshaw and Finch (2003). We do not use it further here but it is well worth considering for future use, and for measuring much other than poverty. For instance if someone ticks two out of three boxes on thinking they are rich, having a high income and high wealth – might that be a good way to estimate whether they are rich?

Having determined the national proportions of households that can be categorised as asset wealthy, exclusively wealthy, breadline poor and core poor, or none of the above, we next need to estimate how many in each geographical area there are so as to be able to determine the extent of spatial divides in poverty and wealth. *Box 6.5* provides a brief description of the methods used to produce *Figures 6.3* and *6.4* that allow the extent of spatial divides to be estimated.

Box 6.5: The method of estimating 'breadline poor' households by area and the Index of Dissimilarity

In essence, the method uses the information from a detailed poverty survey, carried out on a sample of 1,000 or 2,000 households, to classify each household in the survey as 'poor' or 'not poor'. The survey also includes information comparable to that collected by the census, such as household composition, tenure, car ownership and social class. The survey data can then be analysed to assess the relationship between these census-type variables and the poor/not poor classification of households in the survey. These relationships are applied to census data to estimate the number of poor households in each area for which census data is available. For more details and illustrative examples see Dorling et al (2007).

The Index of Dissimilarity
The Index of Dissimilarity is a summary measure of the relative segregation (or integration) of two population groups across geographical areas. It compares the distribution of the two groups, and calculates what proportion of one group would have to move (geographically) to result in an even distribution of both groups across all areas. While this type of index has frequently been used to study racial/ethnic segregation, it has been used here to compare the distribution of each group of households against all other households (for example asset wealthy households versus all non-asset wealthy households).

The 'symmetrical' version of the index was calculated here, for example comparing the number of breadline poor households to the number of all other households. An index of 30% would indicate that 30% of poor households would need to move to create an even distribution of poor households across all areas. The more segregated and spatially concentrated a group is, the higher the Index of Dissimilarity.

The Index of Dissimilarity defined in *Box 6.5* is simply the minimum proportion of households that would have to move between areas if each area were to have an even proportion of households of a given type. The areas (tracts) that we are interested in households moving between are those defined in *Box 6.2* (above) for all of Britain. *Table 6.2* gives the results and shows that most recently a majority (59.7%) of the exclusively wealthy would have to move out of their neighbourhood to somewhere less exclusive were they to no longer be so extremely clustered (as shown in *Figure 6.4*). That proportion is much as it was in 1990, but much higher than it was in 1980.

Table 6.2: *The Index of Dissimilarity for each of the five measures*

	1970	1980	1990	2000
Core poor	12.3%	15.6%	15.3%	14.1%
Breadline poor	14.7%	16.7%	17.1%	18.3%
Non-poor, non-wealthy	*	15.4%	16.7%	19.8%
Asset wealthy	*	34.9%	34.5%	40.1%
Exclusively wealthy	*	43.6%	60.6%	59.7%

*Small-area estimates of asset wealthy and exclusively wealthy households were not available for 1970, meaning that non-poor, non-wealthy households could also not be estimated at this time.

Of all the five groups shown in *Table 6.2* only the core poor are slightly less spatially concentrated by 2000 as compared to 1990. Those living beneath the breadline have never (at any other time that a breadline measure has been made) been as physically separated from the rest of society by their geography as they are most recently. Similarly those who are 'normal' are less likely by 2000 to be mixing with people who are poor or wealthy, and the asset wealthy are more spatially segregated now in Britain than they were in either 1980 or 1990.

The extents of the spatial divides change slowly. However, those divides are deep and in general they are deepening in cities such as Manchester and across Britain in general. What, then, of the rest of the world?

Spatial divisions worldwide

So far in this chapter we have considered the spatial distribution of poverty and wealth at the local and national scale, showing that there are significant social and spatial inequalities within and between areas at all these levels, or, to use the expression discussed in *Box 6.1*, there are now more and more tracks to live the wrong side of. In countries like Britain, both poor and wealthy households have become more and more geographically segregated from the rest of society over the past three decades. Here we turn our attention to the spatial manifestation of poverty and wealth at the global scale and we critically discuss the ways in which global institutions such as the World Bank, which are meant to deal with global poverty, approach these issues (also see Chapter Five, this volume).

Similar trends of geographical polarisation such as those described at the national and local level above are observed at the global scale, but it is important to remember that when discussing global poverty and wealth we should bear in mind that, as is also discussed in more detail in Chapter Five, different societies have different concepts of wealth. What people want and what people need changes over time and the concept of poverty constantly evolves and therefore (as also discussed in *Box 6.1*) the subsistence approach to the definition of poverty is inadequate:

> By necessities, I understand not only the commodities which are indispensably necessary for the support of life, but whatever the customs of the country render it indecent for creditable people, even of the lower order, to be without. A creditable day labourer would be ashamed to appear in public without a linen shirt. (Smith, 1759, p 383)

As the commodities that the customs of modern countries render indecent for creditable people, wealthy and poor, to be without are constantly changing[2] it can be argued that it is respect that matters the most in people's lives and that we show our respect through the access to resources we allow each other – through income and wealth. Some truths appear harder and take a little longer to grasp than others. In Britain economists have known for over two centuries that a shoe is not merely an aid for walking to work and in social policy for over 100 years that a postage stamp is not just a necessity for paying bills (Smith, 1759; Rowntree, 2000). Adam Smith in the 18th century and Seebohm Rowntree at the end of the 19th explain how a little luxury is also a necessity of life. However, in the pits of the more dismal side of the science of economics this has yet to be grasped (see, for instance, the World Bank myth propogation that nearly everything that matters is improving; as an example, see Kenney, 2005). We end this chapter questioning those myths. By defining 'nearly everything that matters' as what is taken absolutely for granted in the rich world (or 'donor countries' in World Bank speak) Charles Kenney suggests that living standards worldwide are converging (Kenney, 2005) and hence societal inequalities are decreasing. There are many simple mistakes in this work but what matters most is the error in Kenney's (and by implication the Bank's) central tenet that is this: to paraphrase Kenney (2005), if people in the poorest countries of the world begin to receive a little more of what the richest came to expect to receive generations earlier, then the world is becoming fairer. Or, in other words, if more of the world's poor can now afford a cheap pair of shoes (rather than no shoes) and live on nearer $2 a day than $1, then the world has become a fairer place irrespective of the growing incomes of the richest countries or the number and types of shoes worn there, or the fact that people no longer need to walk miles to get water in the rich world.

In his conclusion, Kenney implies that 'donor nations' should not be at all concerned that they may be impoverishing poor nations through debt repayments as the world is set to get fairer anyway. It is possible, of course, that a world that follows his advice would quickly become a very unstable and violent place to live in as, if it became clearer worldwide that this is how people in 'donor nations' think, and if they began to act more like the Bank would like, then the degree of callousness exhibited could well result in violence and a reordering of the world through violence, which almost always harms the poor first and most.

Using the same data as Kenney, *Figure 6.5(a)* shows a somewhat different global trend. It shows how much of the gap between full human development as defined by the United Nations Development Programme (UNDP) is still left to be achieved following progress or lack of progress since 1975. It shows how close to achieving a simple measure of full human development each of 12 regions of the world is as compared to where they were in 1975. At the extremes, in Japan the majority of improvement towards UNDP 'utopia' has been achieved in the past 25 years. Utopia here is defined as living to the age of 85, being educated to tertiary level and having an average income of $40,000. Incidentally, Japan has the most equitable income distribution of the 12 regions. In contrast most of Africa is further from that utopia than it was in 1975. On average central and south-eastern Africa's combined life expectancy, educational enrolment and incomes are worse now in absolute terms than they were in 1975. In between these extremes the remainder of the world forms a diverging continuum. In general those who had most to begin with gained most and those that had least have furthest to go (and further now to go than they had in 1975).

China has achieved a tiny fraction more since 1975 than North America but, other than that, not only has there been overall divergence worldwide (in everything that matters most: health, wealth and learning), there has been uniform divergence everywhere; the richer a set of countries were to begin with, the better they have done. Once countries are grouped as in *Figure 6.5(a)* there are no exceptions. In *Figure 6.5(a)* the 12 regions are comparable. In other words, even if you run things as well as China has done, or as badly as North America has done, you, as a world region, can hardly alter your end position that is determined by where you started in the 'development race'.

The extent of such divergence is also mirrored in the global distribution of income as seen in *Figure 6.5(b)*, which shows the estimated world income by region. *Figure 6.5(b)* is based on income estimates by Angus Maddison (see *Box 6.6*), who developed a time series of historical statistics for the world economy between 1 and 2003 AD (Maddison, 2007).

Box 6.6: Angus Maddison

Angus Maddison (born in 1926, Newcastle upon Tyne, England), a British economist and economic historian, is Emeritus Professor of Economic Sociology at the Faculty of Economics, University of Groningen, the Netherlands. He is a pioneer in the field of the quantification of economic growth in an international comparative and historical perspective.

Maddison has also been a pioneer in the field of the construction of national accounts, where a country's accounts are calculated back in periods of several decades all the way to the year 0. To this end he combined modern research techniques with his own extensive knowledge of economic history and in particular countries' performances in the field of GDP per capita. His work resulted in a deep new understanding of the reasons why some countries have become rich whereas others have remained poor (or have succumbed to poverty). In this vital field, Maddison is regarded as the world's most prominent scholar.

During the past two decades, Maddison has mainly focused on the construction of data and analysis further back in time. He has, for example, published an authoritative study on economic growth in China over the past 20 centuries. This study has strongly boosted the historical debate about the strengths and weaknesses of China and Europe as two of the world's leading economic forces. Furthermore, his estimates regarding the per capita income in the Roman Empire are regarded by many as a breakthrough in economic historiography.

Incidentally, on 27 October 2006 he was awarded the title of Commander in the Order of Orange-Nassau. The ceremony took place during a special symposium held on the occasion of his 80th birthday.

More information and a list of his publications and electronic copies of data and papers may be found at: www.ggdc.net/maddison/

Figure 6.5(a): *Proportion of development gap in 1975 still to achieve by 2002*

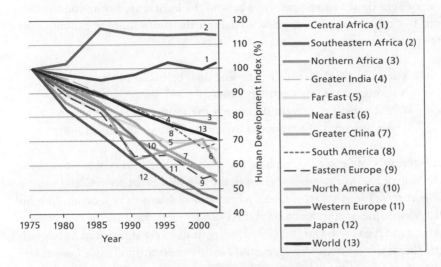

Source: UNDP Human Development Index 2004 (life expectancy, education and income combined)

Figure 6.5(b): *World income estimates (relative to global norm)*

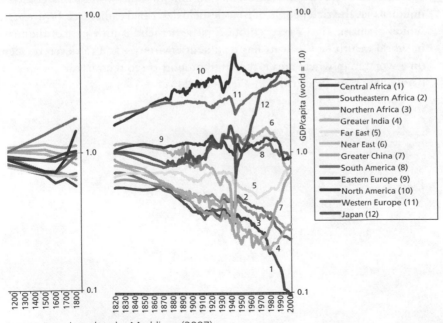

Source: Based on data by Maddison (2007)

It is in the short-term interest of the bankers of the richest people in the richest (donor) nations to present a picture of world living standards converging, of a race where those who began miles behind the leaders are beginning to catch up. A fictional nanny gave good advice on the motivation of banking over four decades ago:

> They must feel the thrill of totting up a balanced book
> A thousand ciphers neatly in a row
> When gazing at a graph that shows the profits up
> Their little cup of joy should overflow! ('Mary Poppins', 1964)

Another way of demonstrating how unequal the world has become is to redraw the map of the world in proportion to the distribution of poverty and wealth. *Figure 6.6(a)* shows a world map where area is drawn in proportion to who has an income of less than $1 a day. As can be seen, the areas of countries in Africa and Asia are by far the largest, whereas it is very difficult to distinguish the shapes of countries in Europe and North America. Similarly, *Figure 6.6(b)* shows a world map where area is drawn in proportion to who has an income of over $200 a day (for more details on how these maps have been drawn, see www.worldmapper.org). In contrast to *Figure 6.6(a)*, European and North American countries dominate this map, whereas the areas of Asian and African countries have shrunk. It is interesting to note that the world has become so unequal that the rich people of Macclesfield described earlier (see *Figure 6.1*), which a century ago was a remote rural settlement, is now part of the map of world wealth – at least its more affluent environs – and can even be seen on a world map where area is drawn in proportion to who has an income of over $200 a day! (See arrow in *Figure 6.6(b)*.)

Figure 6.6(a): *The world drawn in proportion to those living on $1 a day or less*

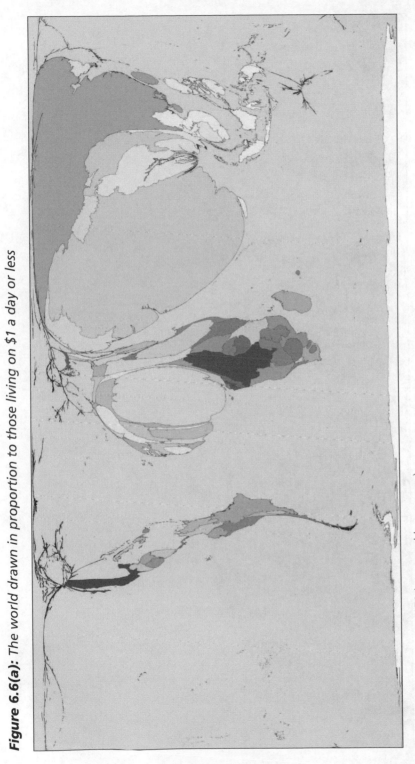

Source: Worldmapper map 179 (www.worldmapper.org)

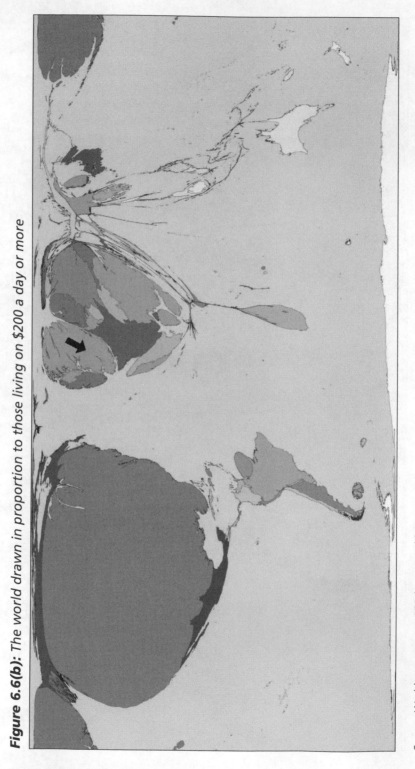

Figure 6.6(b): *The world drawn in proportion to those living on $200 a day or more*

Source: Worldmapper map 158 (www.worldmapper.org)

Conclusion

There are leaps of imagination required to see the true extent of the spatial divisions of poverty and wealth in the world. Here we have tried to show how these can range from taking a journey across the city of Manchester, to looking down on a map of Britain that has been stretched and squeezed so that everyone can be seen equally and both poor and rich are fairly visible, to showing just how distorted a world we live in by distorting it in turn according to average incomes received in each territory. Both locally within Manchester, nationally across Britain and worldwide, the spatial divisions of poverty and wealth are deepening. Locally, this is normally hardest to see and occurs more slowly. At times the trends are reversed. Nationally it is more obvious, especially in countries like those of Britain where a 'pear-shaped' picture of economic development is emerging (Dorling, 2006), where the bulk of the population were destined to live in an underperforming bulge of regions from which the 'productive' winners are moving further and further away. Worldwide the spatial divisions of poverty and wealth have never been as deep, and inequalities across the planet are accelerating.

Acknowledgements
The Manchester research was funded by the Office of the Deputy Prime Minister and conducted by the Social and Spatial Inequalities Group, University of Sheffield (of which we are part) (for the full report see: www.sasi.group. shef.ac.uk/research/pilot_mapping.htm). We are grateful to our colleagues Jan Rigby, Ben Wheeler, Bethan Thomas, Eldin Fahmy, Dave Gordon and Ruth Lupton, who worked on the Joseph Rowntree Foundation report (www. sasi.group.shef.ac.uk/research/transformation.htm). The world inequalities section of this chapter draws on work with colleagues, in the US (Mark Newman) and Anna Barford at the University of Sheffield, as well as some already mentioned (this work can be found at www.worldmapper.org). The authors would also like to thank Graham Allsop and Paul Coles for their help with the illustrations. Danny Dorling and Dimitris Ballas were funded by the British Academy (British Academy Research Leave Fellowship) and the Economic and Social Research Council (research fellowship grant number RES-163-27-1013), respectively, while writing this chapter.

Notes
[1] According to the most recent data available (ONS, 2007), men in Manchester can expect to live to 73 years of age. This is the lowest local authority level male life expectancy in England and it is 10 years less than the respective number for Kensington and Chelsea, which has the highest male life expectancy in Britain. The life expectancy of women in Manchester is 78.6, which is about

nine years less than the age that women born in Kensington and Chelsea can expect to live to. This is the fourth lowest female life expectancy in England, surpassed by Halton, Hartlepool and Liverpool, where a woman can, on average, expect to live to 78.3 years, 10 years less than the female life expectancy of Kensington and Chelsea (ONS, 2007). These gaps are growing.

[2] For instance, Adam Smith's 'linen shirt' would perhaps be, in today's terms (at least for men), a suit of decent style (that is, not the cheapest suit on the shelf). There would also be differences between societies (also see **Box 5.1** in Chapter Five, this volume).

Summary

- The distribution of poverty and wealth has a spatial dimension that can be studied by analysing at different geographical scales and combining information from secondary data sources.
- Geographical methods can be used to map (and analyse geographically) social and economic polarisation and to quantify the degree and the progress of polarisation and segregation.
- Socioeconomic and spatial polarisation has been recently increasing locally, nationally and globally.
- At the local level there is increasing evidence that local socioeconomic polarisation is reaching unprecedented levels. People are becoming socially and spatially graded by large neighbourhoods in many ways more neatly than they were before.
- At the national level already wealthy areas have tended to become disproportionately wealthier, and we are seeing some evidence of increasing polarisation where rich and poor now live further apart. In particular there are now areas in some of our cities where over half of all households are breadline poor.
- Globally, the spatial divisions of poverty and wealth have never been as deep and growth in inequalities across the planet is accelerating.

Questions for discussion

- How would you go about constructing a story that suggests that divisions are narrowing?
- How would you define in today's terms a necessity such as Adam Smith's 'linen shirt'?
- How would your definition differ between places and nations?

- How would you describe and explain geographical patterns of poverty and wealth within: (a) the city or region in which you live; (b) the country in which you live; (c) the world?
- Are inequalities and divisions narrowing in some aspects of life not covered here?

Further reading

Glasmeier, A. (2005) *An atlas of poverty in America: One nation, pulling apart 1960-2003*, London: Routledge.

UN (United Nations) Development Programme (ed) (2006) *Human development report 2006: Power, poverty and the global water crisis*, Basingstoke: Palgrave Macmillan.

Electronic resources

www.msim.org.uk/Galleries.asp?menuid=885 – Warehouse for the world at the Museum of Science and Industry

Inequalities in Britain:
www.sasi.group.shef.ac.uk/ – Social And Spatial Inequalities Group
www.ifs.org.uk/wheredoyoufitin/ – 'Where do you fit in?', Institute for Fiscal Studies

World inequalities:
www.worldmapper.org – Worldmapper
www.ggdc.net/maddison/ – Estimates of world population, GDP and per capita GDP, 1–2003 AD
www.wider.unu.edu/ – World Institute for Development Economics Research
http://hdr.undp.org/UN – Human development reports

References

Ballas, D. (2004) 'Simulating trends in poverty and income inequality on the basis of 1991 and 2001 census data: a tale of two cities', *Area*, vol 36, no 2, pp 146-63.

Ballas, D., Rossiter, D., Thomas, B., Clarke, G.P. and Dorling, D. (2005) *Geography matters: Simulating the local impacts of national social policies*, Joseph Rowntree Foundation Contemporary Research Issues, York: Joseph Rowntree Foundation (free pdf copies available from www.jrf.org.uk/bookshop/details. asp?pubID=659).

Bradshaw, J. and Finch, N. (2003) 'Overlaps in dimensions of poverty', *Journal of Social Policy*, vol 32, no 4, pp 513-25.

Bramley, G. and Smart, G. (1996) 'Modelling local income distributions in Britain', *Regional Studies,* vol 30, no 3, pp 239-55.

Davies, H., Joshi, H. and Clarke, L. (1997) 'Is it cash that the deprived are short of?', *Journal of the Royal Statistical Society A*, vol 160, no 1, pp 107-26.

Dilnot, A. (2001) 'Our unequal society', *The Guardian*, 2 June (http://politics. guardian.co.uk/tax/comment/0,9236,500291,00.html).

Dorling, D. (1999) 'Who's afraid of income inequality?', *Environment and Planning A*, Commentary, vol 31, no 4, pp 571-4.

Dorling, D. (2001) 'How much does place matter? Anecdote is the singular of data', *Environment and Planning A*, vol 33, no 8, pp 1335-40.

Dorling, D. (2005) *A human geography of the UK*, London: Sage Publications.

Dorling, D. (2006) 'Inequalities in Britain 1997-2006: the dream that turned pear-shaped', *Local Economy*, vol 21, no 4, pp 353-61.

Dorling, D., Ballas, D., Thomas, B. and Pritchard, J. (2004) *Pilot mapping of local social polarisation in three areas of England, 1971-2001*, New Horizons Project Report to the Office of the Deputy Prime Minister (www.sasi.group. shef.ac.uk/research/pilot_mapping.htm).

Dorling, D., Rigby, J., Wheeler, B., Ballas, D., Thomas, B., Fahmy, E., Gordon, D. and Lupton, R. (2007) *Poverty, wealth and place in Britain, 1968 to 2005*, Bristol: The Policy Press (free pdf copies available from www.jrf.org. uk/bookshop/eBooks/2019-poverty-wealth-place.pdf).

Engels, F. (1845) *Conditions of the working class in England*, Marx/Engels Internet Archive (www.marxists.org/archive/marx/works/1845/condition-working-class/index.htm).

Gordon, D. and Pantazis, C. (1997) 'Measuring poverty: breadline Britain in the 1990s', in D. Gordon and C. Pantazis (eds) *Breadline Britain in the 1990s*, Aldershot: Ashgate, pp 1-47.

Gordon, D., Pantazis, C. and Townsend, P. (2000) 'Absolute and overall poverty: a European history and proposal for measurement', in D. Gordon and P. Townsend (eds) *Breadline Europe: The measurement of poverty*, Bristol: The Policy Press, pp 79-105.

Heady, P. and Clarke P. et al (2003) *Model-based small area estimation project report*, Office for National Statistics Model-based Small Area Estimation Series No 2, January, London: Office for National Statistics.

Kenney, C. (2005) 'Why are we worried about income? Nearly everything that matters is converging', *World Development*, vol 33, no 1, pp 1-19.

Levitas, R. (1998) *The inclusive society? Social exclusion and New Labour*, London: Macmillan.

Mack, J. and Lansley, S. (1985) *Poor Britain*, London: George Allen and Unwin.

Maddison, A. (2007) *The contours of the world economy 1-2030 AD*, Oxford: Oxford University Press.

Marsh, C. (1993) 'Privacy, confidentiality and anonymity in the 1991 Census', in A. Dale and C. Marsh (eds) *The 1991 Census user's guide*, London: The Stationery Office, pp 111-28.

Newman, G. (1906) *Infant mortality: A social problem*, London: Methuen and Co.

Noble, M. and Smith, G. (1996) 'Two nations? Changing patterns of income and wealth in two contrasting areas', in J. Hills (ed) *New Inequalities: The changing distribution of income and wealth in the United Kingdom*, Cambridge: Cambridge University Press, pp 292-318.

ONS (Office for National Statistics) (2007) 'Inequalities in life expectancy at 65 in UK', News release (www.statistics.gov.uk/pdfdir/expbi1107.pdf, 14/01/08).

Orwell, G. (1937) *The road to Wigan Pier*, London: Victor Gollancz Ltd.

Pantazis, C., Gordon, D. and Levitas, R. (eds) (2006) *Poverty and social exclusion in Britain*, Bristol: The Policy Press.

Rees, P. (1998) 'What do you want from the 2001 Census? Results of an ESRC/JISC survey of user views', *Environment and Planning A*, vol 30, no 10, pp 1775-96.

Rees, P., Martin, D. and Williamson, P. (eds) (2002) *The Census data system*, Chichester: Wiley.

Rio Expert Group on Poverty Statistics (2006) *Compendium of best practices in poverty measurement*, Rio de Janeiro, September (www.ibge.gov.br/poverty/pdf/rio_group_compendium.pdf, 30/11/06).

Rowntree, B.S. (2000) *Poverty: A study of town life* (centenary edn), Bristol: The Policy Press.

Smith, A. (1759) *The theory of the moral sentiments* (reprint 1952), Indianapolis, IN: Liberty Classics.

Szreter, S. and Mooney, G. (1998) 'Urbanization, mortality, and the standard of living debate: new estimates of the expectation of life at birth in nineteenth-century British cities', *Economic History Review*, vol 51, no 1, pp 84-112.

Thomas, B. and Dorling, D. (2004) *Know your place: Housing wealth and inequality in Great Britain 1980-2003 and beyond*, Shelter Policy Library (www.sheffield.ac.uk/sasi/publications/reports/knowyourplace.htm).

Thomas, B. and Dorling, D. (2007) *Identity in Britain: A cradle-to-grave atlas*, Bristol: The Policy Press.

Townsend, P. (1979) *Poverty in the United Kingdom: A survey of household resources and standards of living*, London: Penguin Books and Allen Lane.

Wolff, J. and de-Shalit, A. (2007) *Disadvantage*, Oxford: Oxford University Press.

Words to the Wise (2001) 'The wrong side of the tracts', issue 134, p 2 (www.takeourword.com/TOW134/page2.html, 14/11/06).

seven

Gender, poverty and wealth

Gill Scott

Overview

Gender and poverty have long been the focus of feminist research and policy concern. As a matter of social justice, the concern has been to highlight and provide the tools to address economic and social inequality. The idea that wealth may also be significant in examining gender difference and inequalities has only recently come on to the agenda. The chapter examines the following:

- gendered experiences of wealth and poverty;
- the continuing roles of family, work and state in determining men's and women's access to resources;
- the impact of such inequalities; and
- the role that policy plays or could play in redressing gendered inequalities of wealth and poverty.

Key concepts

poverty; wealth; inequality; intra- and inter-household differences; anti-poverty policy

Introduction

Wealth and poverty represent two dimensions of the problem of economic and social inequality and there can be little doubt that the distribution of income and assets in the UK is marked by patterns of growing inequality. A recent Institute for Public Policy Research (IPPR) report, for example, found that between 1988 and 1999 the top 1% of the population increased their share of personal wealth from 17% to 23% while the number of households without any assets at all doubled from 5% to 10% between 1979 and 1996 (Paxton, 2002). A similar pattern emerges for income inequality. Between 1981 and 1999 disposable income in real terms grew by 38% for those in the top 10% of earners. This was more than five times the rate of growth of 7% for the 10% at the bottom of the earnings league (ONS, 2004). For those interested in social policy, this matters. Increases in income inequality, for example, have been shown to be strongly related to health inequality (Wilkinson et al, 1998; Shaw et al, 2005). Inequalities in health and income exist across all countries in Europe but they do vary between countries, and policy has played a significant role in reducing internal inequalities (see Chapter Eleven, this volume). These broad patterns of inequality impact on men and women differently, primarily because of differences in their life roles and how these are related to the resource systems of family, labour market and welfare systems. This chapter explores the ways in which gender is related to wealth and poverty and considers what that means, particularly for men and women who are 'asset-excluded' and on low incomes, and the role that policy plays and could play.

Gender, poverty and wealth

In 1992, Glendinning and Millar stated that poverty was a consequence of an inability to generate sufficient resources to meet needs and that 'such data as are available suggest that many women are financially dependent on others and are vulnerable to poverty' (1992, p 9). Sixteen years later some would argue that it is time to review the situation. There are, for example, claims that women are accessing wealth in ways previously unimaginable, for example, that changing divorce settlements mean that more women can share pensions and other accumulated wealth even if marriages break down, and that their greater involvement in the labour force throughout their lifetime is leading to much lower gender differentials in earning power (McWilliams, 2005; Rogers, 2007). Such claims are important to explore if they are occurring amidst a cutback in the state's role in responding to those at risk of poverty. The growing expectation too that those previously most vulnerable to poverty in the UK will be able to reduce their risks of poverty once they take up the new childcare and fiscal benefits they are being offered may lead to a paradoxical increase in poverty alongside a potential increase in possibilities to amass lifetime assets. Is it really the case that the link between poverty and gender is fast becoming a thing of the past, and that reductions in poverty are matched by greater access to wealth for women?

Gender and wealth

Measuring and researching wealth is not easy. In comparison with data on income, information on the distribution of wealth is scarce. Defining exactly what is meant by wealth is difficult: the term 'wealth' is used in a variety of ways by different writers and generally combines a notion of a combination of a high income and significant assets. Despite difficulties of measurement, however, there are some well-recognised differences in wealth levels in the UK. For example Banks et al (2002) show, inter alia, through their analysis of British Household Panel Survey (BHPS) data in 2000 that:

- looking at financial wealth (defined as savings plus investments minus debts), half of the population hold £600 or less;
- there is a large variation in the amount of wealth held by the population. One quarter are £200 or more in debt but a further quarter have £9,050 of assets or more. There is more inequality of this magnitude than is found in income distribution.

The Banks et al (2002) study, however, focuses on savings, investments and debts for data. Measuring wealth in detail, as Karen Rowlingson reminds us so clearly in Chapter Two, this volume, can be much more complex. It does, for example, often involve an examination of housing assets and pensions as well as financial savings. Each of these is important when examining gender differences. But why look at gender? A key reason for examining the gender gap in wealth is that, as Warren points out):

> Using wages to indicate gender-based economic advantage and disadvantage is revealing, but it is also somewhat limiting.... Researching wealth enables us to move beyond the snapshot picture of short-term gendered economic inequality that we obtain when we analyse wages and on to exploring the longer term build up of gendered economic inequalities. (2006, p 195)

Researching gender differences, however, poses problems. Income and assets, particularly housing, are likely to be pooled in a household for measurement purposes. This may underestimate marked gender divisions in access to those resources. Indeed Daly and Rake (2003) argue quite forcefully, from their comparative analysis of the gendering of resources, that the average woman in Europe has direct control over less than a third of household income. It is often not clear from available data who built up the assets in a household and who is entitled to keep them should the couple separate. Once we combine age with gender the picture gets even more complex. McWilliams' (2005) study of the very wealthy, for example, highlighted the fact that, in the UK in 2005, among millionaires who were over 65, women outnumbered men by 71,369 to 67,865. This may largely be attributed to women's longer life expectancy and inheritance as widows; they are more likely to inherit from their husbands than vice versa. In fact, in wealthy households, liquid assets may be vested in women's names in order that male partners with high incomes are not liable to higher rate tax on interest/dividends generated.

This does not, however, show by any means that women are more able to save now while working. Warren (2006) has commented that a major reason for researching the gendered distribution of wealth is that it can depict any economic disadvantage women have accumulated over time. If we simply took McWilliams' (2005) study as a key to gender inequalities in wealth, we might assume that women can easily accumulate wealth. In fact, as Warren points out, quite rightly, class remains a major determining factor of wealth accumulation, and most women are simply excluded from it. Furthermore, despite women's increased access to earnings through individual labour market participation and changing government expectations that women will be breadwinners as well as carers (see Lewis, 2002), women are generally still limited in their capacity to accumulate wealth through earnings or assets. The fact that there are more women millionaires over 65 than 10 years ago – many of them are widows or recipients of tax-efficient transfers (Deere and Doss, 2006) – does little to change the wider picture of asset exclusion that the majority of women face and the different patterns of asset holding that exist over a lifetime. It also, largely, fails to fully recognise the way that assets are built up by individuals. Analysis of pensions does this in a more effective way since they are typically one of the few assets held solely by individuals. Such analysis (Ginn, 2003; Warren, 2006; also see Chapter Ten, this volume) shows very clearly that:

- men are more likely to hold pension savings than women;
- women are much less likely than men to have accumulated assets in occupational pensions;
- women's retirement income is boosted significantly by having a partner with a history of well-paid work, but women who have had children and who have separated or divorced face very high risks of pension poverty.

In many ways this last point highlights why gender inequalities in wealth matter but also why it should be tempered with a realisation that wide inequalities exist among women. Changes in patterns of marriage and cohabitation as well as relationship breakdowns and family building patterns, rather than an increase in women's earning and saving capacity, may actually be leading to reduced chances of shared asset building and higher risks of poverty for some women. For lone parents, for example, the situation may be similar to one recently reported in a study of people experiencing poverty in Scotland:

> "After bringing up kids and not working, then going back to work and being too old to take out a pension there's no hope for me. I retire in a year and I've nothing to look forward to, I'm going to be a poor pensioner and that's my future." (Lone parent, quoted in Green, 2007, p 10)

Bellamy and Rake (2005) argue strongly that those women who have moved closest to the male model of employment have been best able to save for retirement as they maintain a closer attachment to the labour market following childbirth. Others with a less tenuous hold in the labour market are not so lucky. Lone parents who have low incomes and tend to spend less time in the labour market are at particular risk, which highlights the tensions between obligations to engage in paid work and obligations to care (see Lewis, 2000; Williams, 2001). Other groups at high risk of poverty in later life include Black and minority ethnic women. They receive less money from their state pension, are less likely to have a private pension, have shorter employment records in the UK and experience the double disadvantage of race and class in the labour market (Ginn, 2000). Savings in this situation are extremely difficult.

Does all this matter? The English Longitudinal Study of Ageing (ELSA) (see Banks et al, 2006), a multidisciplinary study that followed the life experiences of a cohort of people born before 1952 through detailed interviews on many aspects of their life at two-year intervals, shows that it does. In the 2004–05 study, for example, 8,780 people were interviewed on aspects of their life which included: health, work, spending, receipt of healthcare and social participation. Each of these areas was shown to vary according to an individual's level of wealth. Indeed individuals from the poorest fifth of the population were over 10 times more likely to die between the ages of 50 and 59 than their peers from the richest fifth.

Gender and poverty

This last point highlights the positive effect of wealth on a range of social and personal aspects of an individual's life but also reminds us that we know far more about the lives of people experiencing poverty than those of people experiencing wealth. Unlike the study of wealth, the study of poverty has (as

Alcock reminds us in Chapter Three, this volume) been a subject of academic research for some considerable time, and while the concept is much contested, there is certainly more clarity on its gender distribution in comparison to gender and wealth studies. However, there are undoubted difficulties in measuring gender differences in poverty. For example, the most commonly used measure of poverty examines households below 60% of the median national income. But household measurements of poverty assume equal distribution of resources within a household, and this can mask women's poverty. Research shows that women do not necessarily receive their fair share of household income; they are more likely to forgo their own consumption to boost that of their children; and they often have the stressful responsibility for handling tight budgets and debt. So women's poverty is often hidden, both within those households living above the poverty line, and their more dire position within households experiencing poverty (Rake and Jayatilaka, 2002). Nevertheless we know that:

- while 29% of households in the UK are headed by women, 50% of all households at or below the Income Support level are female-headed (Bradshaw et al, 2003);
- 25% of the female population live in households with below 60% of median income, as opposed to 22% of the male population. The odds of a woman being poor are 5% higher than for men (1999/2000 Family Resources Survey);
- women in single-adult households, particularly older women, are at particular risk. Without input from a generally higher male wage or help with caring responsibilities, women are at a higher risk of living in poverty (Bellamy and Rake, 2005);
- women are more likely to suffer recurrent and longer periods of poverty than men (Ruspini, 1998; DWP, 2004);
- lifetime income is lower for women, even without children, but is affected particularly when women become mothers (Bradshaw et al, 2003).

The above figures strongly suggest that gender is a significant factor in the risk of poverty and that the partial economic dependence of most women in households in the UK remains a significant explanatory factor, but we do have to remember that some women are more at risk than others. The risk of poverty for women is not universal. A range of factors can affect the likelihood of poverty, particularly ethnic origin, citizenship status, age and motherhood. Black and minority ethnic women, for example, are more likely to experience poverty than men or White women: 64% of Pakistani and Bangladeshi women live in poverty. Motherhood is another major factor in the dynamics of poverty. Teenage mothers are at very high risk of poverty. Evidence from research by the YWCA suggests that there is a strong link between poverty and early motherhood (Hendessi and Rashid, 2002). Eleven per cent of one-parent families, for example, lived on gross weekly incomes of £100 a week or less in 2005 compared with just 4% of married couples and 5% of cohabiting couples with children (ONS, 2006). This is not to suggest that men do not experience the risk of poverty, but simply that the risks for both men and women are linked to social relations of gender within our society. Higher numbers of women than men live in poverty, women are more likely than men to experience both persistent poverty and hidden poverty and, despite significant changes in employment and welfare policy, motherhood remains a critical event that raises the risk of poverty for a lifetime. On the other hand, men's risk of poverty is mostly connected to their exclusion from the labour market and some groups of men, particularly the long-term unemployed, Black and minority ethnic men and many young men, face problems entering the labour market (Scott, 2005). Similar groups of women face the same issues – lack of qualifications, underdevelopment of skills and geographic location can be significant barriers to employment that could reduce poverty. However, it is clear from existing literature that there are specific gender relations that explain women's higher levels of risk. These include a gender pay gap, the fact that jobs which are predominantly done by women tend to be lower paid, childbirth and caring responsibilities that result in many women, especially those with low education qualifications, having an interrupted profile of labour market activity and much higher rates of part-time work among women than men (Bradshaw et al, 2003).

The importance of poverty

Poverty means diminished life chances. For some it may entail going without essentials such as sufficient food, adequate housing, heating and enough clothing. For many it will also mean having to live without access to the services or social activities that others consider normal, in effect being excluded from taking part in society. Some of the impacts identified by Palmer et al (2004) include fuel poverty, debt and poor health. Drawing on a range of reports their study shows:

- Around three in ten households cannot keep warm at a reasonable cost. Living with fuel poverty has serious consequences for health. It may also mean making cuts in other areas such as food or social activities. Living in poverty means going without necessities; those in poverty spend half the average on food and 75% lack two or more necessary items of clothing.
- Living on a low income also brings with it the threat of falling into unmanageable debt. Low-income households most frequently fall behind

on payments of basic household bills, such as rent and electricity, debts that incur the harshest of sanctions.

• When it comes to health there is abundant evidence that people experiencing poverty suffer poor health as well as low income. The highest mortality rates by a considerable degree are seen among those with persistently low incomes. Looking at the most deprived areas, we find that men die 14 years younger than the national average and women 7 years younger. Both spend the last 13 years of their life in poor health.

Just as important as these quantifiable impacts of poverty on life experiences is the growing evidence from academics, such as McKendrick et al (2004) and Ridge (2002), that poverty is in many ways a socially unacceptable world, heavily imbued with stigma and prejudice. For Wilkinson it is the psychological impact of relative poverty, that is, the differences in resources between those at the bottom and top of the income and resources ladders, that is the most concerning for welfare analysts. Wilkinson (2005) argues that while material living standards do contribute to health inequalities the stresses of low social status and self-esteem attaching to relative poverty are major contributors to poor health. Poverty and inequality are powerful determinants of long-term health and social well-being.

A gendered perspective on the above adds extra understanding to what poverty means. As we saw, the structural causes of women's poverty are to be found in the interaction between dependency, social exclusion and social change within the three resource systems: *family*, *labour market* and *welfare systems*; the structural causes of men's poverty are much more likely to be found in the interaction between just two of these – the labour market and welfare systems. Ruspini comments, for example, that:

> Critical family events – such as lone parenthood, divorce or separation, particularly in the presence of children – will be stronger predictors of poverty transitions for women than for men because of the female economic dependence on a male breadwinner combined with caring responsibilities at home. (Ruspini, 2000, p 300)

But it is not just the risk of poverty that is highly gendered; so too is its impact, and once examined more closely the value of a gendered analysis becomes clearer. Some figures provide a brief idea of how poverty impacts differently on men and women. The impacts for men are often health-related: rates of heart disease, testicular cancer, alcohol abuse, suicide and overall mortality are higher for men experiencing poverty (Ruxton, 2002). Young men living in areas of high unemployment and deprivation are more vulnerable to and more likely to commit violent crime. Women living in poverty are more likely to feel depressed and isolated by their lack of money: 24% compared with 17% of men. Poor women are also more likely than non-poor women to feel unsafe: 49% compared with 40% (Bradshaw et al, 2003). It does seem that women's poverty is a different experience from men's. Women are more likely to be affected by worries about lack of access to money because access to resources in families is not always shared equally and the result is that the responsibility of managing expenditure in low-income households is generally taken by women, and is experienced as a responsibility to manage debt and exclusion, not as consumer choice. In an in-depth study of women in low-income households McKay et al (1999) found that managing a low budget produced sleepless nights, feelings of isolation and stress from managing the competing demands of children and a partner. Managing poverty was time-consuming. Where there were few resources, extra expenditure, even if it was only to cover the extra expenses of children at home during the summer holidays, made it very difficult to maintain, or even establish, an equitable balance in the demands of all family members. Throughout this study the evidence was that, even where husbands were supportive, the activities and stresses of poverty management in a household were largely borne by women. A significant number of women in the study also reflected on how little they spent on themselves as they completed the income/expenditure diaries that were part of the study. Facts about low pay, women's employment, benefits and family distribution of resources paint only a partial picture of the way in which women experience poverty and routes out of poverty. Other studies paint a similar picture: women with young children have to continually juggle spending between household bills and essentials such as food and clothes for the entire family (Kempson,1993); managing household resources and debt can lead to long-term illness (Balmer et al, 2006); balancing children's needs and the transition to training and employment correlates with impaired health for significant numbers of women (Innes and Scott, 2004; Scott and Innes, 2005). As one woman put it in a recent study carried out for the Women's Budget Group:

> "With all the juggling and struggling, I felt demoralised and felt really insecure about whether I could really carry on keeping it all up." (Women's Budget Group, 2005, p 20)

We have to be careful about suggesting that this means that it is only women who suffer the impact of poverty in families. Gender stereotypes may play significant roles in structuring poor people's perceptions of their experiences of poverty. Strier's (2005) analysis of men and women in a poor area of Jerusalem makes a strong case that, regardless of gender, people living in poverty defined it in material, situational and contextual ways. However, gender did contribute to the way these definitions were constructed. For the men in this study, poverty represented not just material deprivation but often involved a painful sense of exclusion from work as a source of independence; women experienced poverty as material deprivation but also as exhaustion and chronic financial management problems involving the household.

Such financial worries become even greater if the relationship between partners is one where financial abuse occurs. Such abuse occurs when one partner (often the male partner) controls and limits the other partner's (usually women's) access to money. This can take the form of being denied access to a bank account, denied enough money to pay the bills or buy food, or women being coerced into servicing a partner's debts (Branigan and Grace, 2005). It may explain why women on benefits who enter new relationships after a relationship breakdown are much more likely than others to retain as much control as they can over money matters (Goode et al, 1998). Financial difficulties often characterise relationship breakdown. Leeming et al's (1994) in-depth qualitative study of 30 lone mothers' patterns of adjustment after a break-up identified the difficulties, financial vulnerabilities and coping strategies that lone parents had to develop when bringing up children on their own.

Many of these are related to housing difficulties, and housing is crucial to an understanding of women's experience of poverty and wealth. Home ownership is an important aspect of housing wealth and although people seldom draw income from their housing wealth, it is a key factor in the quality of life for different income groups. The type of housing to which people have access is a key determinant of their quality of life, both with regard to the adequacy of accommodation in terms of size and condition, and with regard to location, amenity and security. Where people are seeking housing in crisis situations the choices available to them can be very limited, with poor quality housing often being the only type of accommodation available to them. Young mothers trying to set up homes or women leaving after a relationship breakdown or fleeing from a violent partner face particular housing problems, rent and mortgage arrears as well as access to housing. Graham pointed out some time ago that:

> A house provides the physical context in which domestic relationships are built and lived out. It is the place in which women experience what it is like to be a mother and have responsibilities for the health of their children. (1994, p 68)

The connection between poor housing and women's depression and poor health has been well researched in the past (Brown and Harris, 1978; Brown et al, 1994; Wasoff, 1998). Overcrowding, insecurity of tenure, lack of amenities, dampness – each has been shown to be closely related to both poverty and psychological distress among mothers in particular as they struggle to overcome the impact of poor housing on their children as well as themselves. These studies occurred some time ago and there appears to have been little research on the relationships between gender, poverty and housing more recently. Nevertheless, a study in 2001 for the Mayor of London highlighted not only women's disadvantage in terms of access to housing in the city because of their lower earning power and lesser capacity to borrow to finance home ownership but also the particular ways in which aspects of poverty and social exclusion interact with housing (Belcher et al, 2001).

Policy solutions to poverty, wealth and gender inequalities

The significance of the gendered face of poverty and wealth outlined above is a growing concern for many. Women's organisations (for example, Fawcett, Women's Budget Group) have, for example, made numerous representations to policy makers for a more gender-sensitive response over the past decade. In a number of ways, the 10 years between 1997 and 2007 appears to have been a decade when reducing poverty and gender inequalities were central features of policy development. Women had high hopes and expectations of a Labour government in 1997: reflected in equal proportions of men and women voting for Labour for the first time, and resulting in a doubling of women's representation in Parliament, from 60 to 120 Members of Parliament in 1997. The newly elected Labour government proclaimed that it was committed to improving the lives of women and in 2002 it published *Delivering for women*, which set out its main aims and listed 18 initiatives it had undertaken to improve the lives of women. It seemed that tackling obvious and visible forms of injustice against them had been adopted as part of the indispensable task of Labour Party modernisation. At the same time the government made a commitment to reducing child poverty by a half by 2020, and took action to address some of the barriers to women's employment and their potential to increase earned income. This was not just a shift in policy in the UK. Current reform debates in European social policy have increasingly recognised that poverty is gendered and the routes out of poverty need to be made more gender-sensitive (Gillespie, 2003; McKay and Gillespie, 2005). There are, however, a number of questions that need to be asked about the moves that have occurred. We need to ask what form policy has actually taken and to what extent it has been successful in altering gendered patterns of wealth and poverty. In practice the questions we can ask about policy must focus predominantly on the alleviation of poverty rather than the redistribution of wealth as inequalities of wealth have seldom been a major concern of policy makers (see *Box 7.1*).

Box 7.1: Recent key policy changes benefiting women experiencing poverty

Policies addressing women's poverty have been in the areas of childcare, minimum wage legislation, training, employment, social security and taxation. Measures at national level to improve the position of women at greatest risk of poverty include:

- Increased child benefits. As a universal benefit this is of value to all women with children but is likely to have a significant impact on low-income households. Increases in 2007 represented an attempt to redress some of the aspects that have led to a stalling of the child poverty reduction targets.
- The development of a national childcare strategy to increase the supply and affordability of childcare for mothers wishing to enter the labour market. Along with Sure Start this was a way of increasing childcare provision in low-income areas that suited the particular needs of low-income families.
- Enhanced maternity and care leave. This can have a marked impact on labour force participation.
- The introduction of a minimum wage. This was understood to have particular relevance for part-time women workers as part-time work is particularly vulnerable to low pay and women continue to account for the vast majority of part-time workers.
- Expansion of New Deal and European Social Fund-funded training programmes to assist people in entering or returning to the labour market. The Lone Parent New Deal and Employment Zones are programmes that provided benefits, childcare and employment advice as well as financial incentives for some lone parents in their first months of work.
- The introduction of tax credits. These are means-tested benefits for people in low-paid work and include financial support for childcare.
- At devolved, regional and local level there have been further initiatives, often supported by European Commission funds, which have sought to embed strategies on childcare with work–life balance and training initiatives.

Until recently the impact of these policy initiatives could be viewed as positive. The pay gap has narrowed; many more women are working and pensioner poverty (where women predominate) has been falling. There appeared, moreover, to be a recognition in many policies of the impact of costs of caring over a lifetime and the difficulties in returning to the labour market for women with few qualifications and lengthy periods without paid employment. For women with high-paying career jobs the length of time out of the labour market is relatively short; lower-earning women are more likely to have given up work for longer periods (Joshi and Davies, 2000) and support for them has had an impact. There has, for example, been a significant increase in the lone-parent employment rate since 1999 and, because of tax credits, a related reduction in the risk of poverty for lone parents who work but are low paid. Child poverty rates have fallen dramatically at the same time and, given the analysis above, this is of particular significance for mothers managing the family purse.

However, there is still much to be done. One small step would be to improve access to affordable credit through the expansion of credit unions, local financial inclusion partnerships and other locally based, socially just financial inclusion strategies. They could reduce the unmanageable debt that faces many low-income families who are forced to rely on extortionate lending practices of door-to-door money lenders (Rossiter and Cooper, 2005).

Improving earning capacity is another solution but a number of analysts have pointed to the fact that work does not automatically mean a secure route out of poverty for children, men or women. There is evidence that, in the New Deal for Lone Parents, some lone parents were cycling through the programme several times, moving in and out of work (Evans et al, 2003). This implies a lack of sustainable and worthwhile employment/training opportunities. A report by Save the Children (Adelman et al, 2003), moreover, identified that transitions into and out of work are linked to the severest poverty. For the low-qualified female-headed households that make up a large proportion of lone-parent households, work may merely be part of a cycle between low-paid work and welfare. Financial insecurity continues to be a fact of life for such parents when child benefit rates remain low and part-time insecure work offers little in the way of employment promotion, retention and advancement (Manning and Petrolongo, 2005). Flexible, affordable childcare also continues to remain elusive and childcare tax credits have proved to be difficult to administer and slow to increase. The newer forms of childcare provision that have developed also hold an additional risk for women. Childcare work has been an important factor in the government's welfare-to-work strategy but many of the newer childcare jobs are low-paid, insecure and filled by women. Scott et al (2002, p 241) question the sustainability of employment created by childcare and the extent to which it contributes to better employment for the women who fill the posts, particularly when it so often occurs within a volatile and secondary labour market. Low-paid parents remain at risk of poverty (Gregg and Harkness, 2006) but so do low-paid childcare workers. There remains a need to consider and address the 'possibility that childcare and "work–life balance" initiatives may continue to inadvertently fuel class inequalities' (Dean and Shah, 2002, p 77).

It is not just the failure of child poverty strategies and their limited effect on women's and family poverty that concerns us here, however. Gender disparities in the incidence and experience of poverty will continue to be central to the discussion of poverty while a model of women's dependence, albeit a very different one than 40 years ago, remains central to family, work and welfare. There have been significant changes in the patterns of partnering and parenting that have affected the way men and women earn, build up assets or experience the risks of poverty in the UK in the past 40 years. The gendered stereotype of male breadwinner and dependent female carer is no longer appropriate as a description of men and women in the UK. However, there is very little evidence to suggest that the changes have been any more than a modification rather than a transformation (Walby, 1999; Crompton, 2002). Although the situation is changing, the bulk of caring remains a female task and this continues to be the factor that determines the relative lack of power in the labour market for women. The state is increasingly likely to expect women to become workers and consequently to adjust support for women to one more conditional on their participation in work. However, while childcare remains expensive and elusive and employers' and indeed societal attitudes towards work–care balance limits the capacity for women to build up a lifetime's earnings and assets that would fully protect them from poverty, women's risks of poverty remain stronger than men's throughout their lifetime.

Conclusion

It may well be the case that differences between women, particularly those of class and education, are becoming more important determinants of wealth and poverty than simply gender, but the analysis above suggests that the chances of building assets and the risks of poverty remain deeply gendered. Policy solutions to gender inequalities such as equal opportunities legislation, minimum wage legislation, parental leave and increased care provision as well as gender-sensitive training and employment initiatives are just some of the ways the issue of gender equity in welfare can be progressed. Yet the gender dimension in the government's anti-poverty strategy remains largely implicit rather than explicit. The explicit commitments to addressing gender inequality have tended to concentrate on the pay gap rather than the underlying reasons for the continuation of wider and longer-term inequalities, the significance for longer-term asset building and their relationship to deeply gendered social relations. Much of anti-poverty policy has had a positive impact on women but until it explicitly addresses inequalities of opportunity that face men and women and their impact on inequality of outcome, capacity for change will be limited. Why the gender agenda of the early years of New Labour has faltered still needs to be explained, but until the reduction of gendered poverty is integrated with policies to address child poverty the long-term reduction of gender inequality will be difficult to achieve. Without a proper gender analysis gendered wealth inequalities will remain, the lifetime impact of caring will not be addressed and the welfare-to-work agenda will continue to create problems for children, men and women.

Summary

- Wealth and poverty represent two related dimensions of the problem of social and economic inequality.
- Since the 1990s there has been a growing argument that gender differences in wealth and poverty have been changing and that women are accessing wealth in previously unimaginable ways.
- Measuring and researching wealth is not easy. Inherited wealth has led to more women millionaires but analysis of housing and pensions shows a continued pattern of asset exclusion for women.
- Men and women both risk poverty but the causes, experience and impact differ significantly. Men's risks of poverty relate to unemployment, geographic location, ethnicity and lack of qualifications. Women's risks relate more to interrupted employment as they care for children in addition to lack of qualifications, ethnicity and place.
- Poverty means diminished life chances: living without access to services and social activities most people take for granted. Gender differences exist in how this is experienced. Men living in poverty are more likely to express concerns about isolation and exclusion from work, women to express worries about managing family budgets and financial exclusion. For both men and women income and asset inequality are very strongly related to poor health.
- Financial difficulties often affect relationships between men and women and they can have long-term effects on health and housing.
- Policy makers have recognised the existence of gendered poverty to some extent. Key policy changes included increased child benefits, introduction of tax credits and additional support for lone parents in areas of training and employment. Attempts to address women's poverty have generally been framed within the context of child poverty measures and are not always in women's best interests.
- Gender inequalities in pay and employment have been the main focus of policies but, without measures to address financial exclusion and a fuller analysis of gendered wealth inequalities and asset accumulation, wealth inequalities will remain, and the lifetime impact of caring will not be addressed.

Questions for discussion

- What role do the family, the state and the labour market play in gendering access to resources?
- What measures can be taken to reduce the disproportionate effects of poverty on women?
- Would child poverty policies automatically lead to a reduction in women's poverty?
- How should financial institutions be reformed to make it fairer for women?

Further reading

Lister, R. (2004) *Poverty*, London: Polity Press. In this book Lister discusses the meaning and experience of poverty in the contemporary world and makes a case for reframing the politics of poverty as a claim for redistribution and recognition.

In the Women's Budget Group (2005) report, they present a clear analysis of the relationship between women's and children's poverty and a powerful presentation of women's experience of living in poverty.

Bellamy and Rake's (2005) report documents the way in which women continue to be disadvantaged by a gender gap in economic welfare and traces the ways in which women's economic welfare has been affected by a changing policy environment.

Glendinning and Millar (1992) examine whether and, more importantly, why women bear the brunt of increases in poverty.

Warren (2006) provides a thoughtful and very necessary analysis of the relationship between gender and other inequalities in understanding the dynamics of gender, wealth and poverty.

Electronic resources

www.wbg.org.uk/ – The Women's Budget Group is an independent organisation bringing together individuals from academia, non-governmental organisations and trades unions to promote gender equality through appropriate economic policy.

www.equalityhumanrights.com – The **Equality and Human Rights Commission** champions equality and human rights for all in the UK.
www.womenandequalityunit.gov.uk – The Government Equalities Office has responsibility for the government's overall strategy and priorities on equality issues.
www.fawcettsociety.org.uk/ – Fawcett is the UK's campaign for equality between women and men.
www.oxfamgb.org/ukpp/equal/index.htm – Oxfam's UK Poverty Programme focuses on equality between women and men.

References

Adelman, L., Middleton, S. and Ashworth, K. (2003) *Britain's poorest children: Severe and persistent poverty and social exclusion*, London: Save the Children.

Balmer, N., Pleasance, P., Buck, A. and Walker, H.C. et al (2006) 'Worried sick : the experience of debt problems and the relationship with health, illness and disability', *Social Policy and Society*, vol 5, no 1, pp 39-51.

Banks, J., Oldfield, Z. and Wakefield, M. (2002) *The distribution of financial wealth in the UK: Evidence from 2000 BHPS data*, IFS Working Paper WP02/21 (www.ifs.org.uk/publications.php?publication_id=1996).

Banks, J., Breeze, E., Lessof, C. and Nazroo, J. (2006) *Retirement, health and relationships of the older population in England: The 2004 English Longitudinal Study of Ageing (Wave 2)*, London: Institute for Fiscal Studies.

Belcher, Z., Field, S. and Levison, D. (2001) *Homes for London's women*, London: Greater London Authority.

Bellamy, K. and Rake, K. (2005) *Money, money, money: Is it still a rich man's world?*, London: Fawcett Society.

Bradshaw, J., Finch, N., Kemp, P., Mayhew, E. and Williams, J. (2003) *Gender and poverty in Britain*, Working Paper series no 6, Manchester: Equal Opportunities Commission.

Branigan, E. and Grace, M. (2005) 'His money or our money: financial abuse of women in intimate partner relationships', Paper ID31, Australian Social Policy Conference, Sydney.

Brown, G. and Harris, T. (1978) *The social origins of depression*, London: Tavistock.

Brown, A., Breitenbach, E. and Myers, F. (1994) *Equality issues in Scotland: A research review*, Glasgow: Equal Opportunities Commission.

Crompton, R. (2002) 'Employment, flexible working and the family', *British Journal of Sociology*, vol 53, no 4, pp 537-8.

Daly, M. and Rake, K. (2003) *Gender and the welfare state*, Cambridge: Polity Press.

Dean, H. and Shah, A. (2002) 'Insecure families and low paying labour markets: comments on the British experience', *Journal of Social Policy*, vol 31, pp 61-80.

Deere, C.D. and Doss, C.R. (2006) 'The gender asset gap: what do we know and why does it matter?', *Feminist Economics*, vol 12, nos 1-2, pp 1-50.

DWP (Department for Work and Pensions) (2004) *Households below average income 1994/5-2002/03*, London: DWP.

Evans, M., Eyre, J., Millar, J. and Sarre, S. (2003) *New Deal for Lone Parents: Second synthesis report of the national evaluation*, Leeds: Corporate Document Services.

Gillespie, M. (2003) 'Women's social entitlements – Scotland', Paper presented at Network for European Women's Rights, Athens.

Ginn, J. (2000) 'Pension myth-selling gender', *Radical Statistics*, vol 74, pp 26-42.

Ginn, J. (2003) *Gender, pensions and the lifecourse*, Bristol: The Policy Press.

Glendinning, C. and Millar, J. (1992) *Women and poverty in Britain*, Hemel Hempstead: Harvester Wheatsheaf.

Goode, J., Callender, C. and Lister, R. (1998) *Purse or wallet? Gender inequalities within families on benefits*, London: Policy Studies Institute.

Graham, H. (1994) *Hardship and health in women's lives*, Hemel Hempstead: Harvester Wheatsheaf.

Green, M. (2007) *Voices of people experiencing poverty in Scotland*, York: Joseph Rowntree Foundation.

Gregg, P., Harkness, S. and Macmillan, L. (2006) *A review of issues relating to the labour market and economy, particularly in terms of the impact of labour market initiatives on children's income poverty*, York: Joseph Rowntree Foundation.

Hendessi, M. and Rashid, F. (2002) *Poverty: The price of young motherhood in Britain*, London: YWCA.

Innes, S. and Scott, G. (2004) 'After I've done the Mum "things": women, care and transitions', *Sociological Research Online*, vol 8, no 4 (www.socresonline.org.uk/8/4/innes.html).

Joshi, H. and Davies, H. (2000) 'The price of parenthood and the value of children', in N. Fraser and J. Hills (eds) *Public policy for the 21st century: Social and economic essays in memory of Henry Neuberger*, Bristol: The Policy Press.

Kempson, E. (1993) *Housing budgets and housing cost*, London: Policy Studies Institute.

Leeming, A., Unell, J. and Walker, R. (1994) *Lone mothers coping with the consequences of separation*, Department of Social Security Report No 30, London: HMSO.

Lewis, J. (2000) 'Work and care', *Social Policy Review*, vol 12, pp 48-67.

Lewis, J. (2002) 'Gender and welfare state change', *European Societies*, vol 4, no 4, pp 331-57.

McKay, A. and Gillespie, M. (2005) 'Women, inequalities and social policy', in G. Mooney and G. Scott (eds) *Exploring social policy in the 'new' Scotland*, Bristol: The Policy Press.

McKay, A., Scott, G. and Sawers, C. (1999) *What can we afford? A woman's role. Money management in low income households*, Glasgow: Scottish Poverty Information Unit.

McKendrick, J., Cunningham-Burley, S. and Scott, G. (2004) *Families living on a low income*, Edinburgh: Scottish Executive.

McWilliams, D. (2005) *Women and wealth*, London and Liverpool: Centre for Economics and Business Research and Victoria Friendly Society.

Manning, A. and Petrolongo, B. (2005) *The part time penalty*, London: London School of Economics and Political Science and Women and Equality Unit.

ONS (Office for National Statistics) (2004) *General Household Survey 2003* (www. statistics.gov.uk/statbase).

ONS (2006) *General Household Survey 2005* (www.statistics.gov.uk/downloads/ theme_compendia/GHS05/GeneralHouseholdSurvey2005.pdf).

Palmer, G., Carr, J. and Kenway, P. (2004) *Monitoring poverty and social exclusion 2004*, York/London: Joseph Rowntree Foundation/New Policy Institute.

Paxton, W. (2002) *Wealth distribution – The evidence*, London: IPPR.

Rake, K. and Jayatilaka, G. (2002) *Home truths: An analysis of financial decision making within the home*, London: Fawcett Society.

Ridge, T. (2002) *Childhood poverty and social exclusion: From a child's perspective*, Bristol: The Policy Press.

Rogers, L. (2007) 'Divorce – do women win too much?', *New Statesman*, 19 February.

Rossiter, J. and Cooper, N. (2005) *Scaling up for financial inclusion: A national strategy for expanding access to affordable credit and financial services*, Manchester: Debt on our Doorstep.

Ruspini, E. (1998) 'Women and poverty dynamics', *Journal of European Social Policy*, vol 8, no 4, pp 291-316.

Ruspini, E. (2000) 'Engendering poverty research: how to go beyond the feminisation of poverty', *Radical Statistics*, vol 75, pp 25-37.

Ruxton, S. (2002) *Men, masculinities and poverty in the UK*, Oxford: Oxfam.

Scott, G. (2005) *Workstream A: Workless Client Group's final report for employability framework for Scotland*, Edinburgh: Scottish Executive.

Scott, G. and Innes, S. (2005) 'Gender, care, poverty and transitions', in L. McKie and S. Cunningham-Burley (eds) *Families in society: Boundaries and relationships*, Bristol: The Policy Press.

Scott, G., Brown, U. and Campbell, J. (2002) 'Child care, social inclusion and urban regeneration', *Critical Social Policy*, vol 22, no 2, pp 226-46.

Shaw, M., Davey Smith, G. and Dorling, D. (2005) 'Health inequalities and New Labour: how the promises compare with real progress', *BMJ*, vol 330, pp 1016-21.

Strier, R. (2005) 'Gendered realities of poverty: men and women's views of poverty in Jerusalem', *Social Service Review*, vol 79, pp 344-67.

Walby, S. (1999) *New agendas for women*, Basingstoke: Macmillan.

Warren, T. (2006) 'Moving beyond the gender wealth gap: on gender, class, ethnicity and wealth inequalities in the United Kingdom', *Feminist Economics*, vol 12, nos 1-2, pp 195-219.

Wasoff, F. (1998) 'Women and housing', in I. Shaw, S. Lambert and D. Clapham (eds) *Social care and housing*, London: Jessica Kingsley Publishers.

Wilkinson, R.G. (2005) *The impact of inequality: How to make sick societies healthier*, London: Routledge.

Wilkinson, R.G., Kawachi, I. and Kennedy, B. (1998) 'Mortality, the social environment, crime and violence', in M. Bartley, D. Blane and G. Davey Smith (eds) *Sociology of health inequalities*, Oxford: Blackwell.

Williams, F. (2001) 'In and beyond New Labour: towards a new political ethic of care', *Critical Social Policy*, vol 21, no 4, pp 467-93.

Women's Budget Group (2005) *Women's and children's poverty: Making the links*, London: Women's Budget Group.

eight

The intersection of ethnicity, poverty and wealth

Akwugo Emejulu

Overview

- This chapter focuses on the diversity and difference of minority ethnic experiences of poverty and wealth accumulation.
- An understanding of the gender dynamics within different ethnic groups is an important factor for a rigorous analysis of the interaction between ethnicity and economic inequality.
- While some minority ethnic groups have been able to access professional employment and reap the benefits of a high income and high levels of wealth accumulation, the majority of minority ethnic groups are still more likely to be living in poverty with very few assets.
- Current anti-poverty measures are geared towards employment-led solutions to economic inequality and it is not clear that these policies are directly addressing the root causes of minority ethnic poverty and deprivation.

Key concepts

diversity and difference; income and asset-based poverty; labour market discrimination; employment-led solutions to poverty

Introduction

> Ethnicity is not the only – nor necessarily the most important – component of people's identities. Nor is it always the most significant differentiator in terms of disadvantage. (Mason, 2003, p 15)

Focusing on ethnicity when analysing the distribution of wealth and poverty in the UK can be a misleading way to understand inequality. A consensus in the literature on ethnicity and inequality is forming which demonstrates the diversity of experience among minority ethnic groups and the importance of locating ethnicity in the wider socioeconomic context of social class and gender in order to examine the complexity of individual experiences and group outcomes in terms of economic well-being. While it is not new to point out that the UK's minority ethnic population is not a homogeneous group, by isolating ethnicity from wider socioeconomic conditions researchers run the risk of lumping all minority ethnic groups together in a mistaken belief that these groups are all disadvantaged, all suffer discrimination in the same way and that they have not made significant gains since the last wave of migration in the 1960s and 1970s.

Key texts on ethnicity and inequality consistently demonstrate that some groups are prospering (Modood et al, 1997; Berthoud, 1998; Parekh, 2000; Mason, 2003; Pilkington, 2003). Indian and Chinese groups have high levels of employment in stable, professional jobs, good levels of wealth accumulation and high educational achievements. Other groups, however, are not showing such upward mobility. Pakistani and Bangladeshi groups are disproportionately concentrated in low-paid, unstable jobs or excluded from the labour market altogether, and as a result these groups are experiencing endemic, intergenerational poverty and reduced life chances. Black Caribbean, Black African and Other Black background groups, however, are somewhere in between these two extremes with high economic activity rates, average qualifications but poor wealth accumulation (Modood et al, 1997; ONS, 2001; Mason, 2003). Even with these broad characterisations it must be emphasised that there are considerable variations of outcomes within each of the ethnic groups described.

Where possible, this chapter endeavours to present disaggregated data on minority ethnic groups in order to provide a more complex picture of the advantages and continuing discrimination that minority ethnic groups face. It seems less helpful to describe or to analyse using catch-all terms such as 'Asian' or 'Black' because this masks considerable variations of experiences within each of these broad categories. However, due to sample sizes or the lack of disaggregated information in some datasets, some homogenising categories must be used. Attention will be drawn to these data and consideration should be given for future research to refine our categorisation of minority ethnic groups for research purposes.

There is a need, then, to begin telling a different story – to have a more complex and contradictory understanding about the economic well-being of minority ethnic groups. Subverting this narrative about ethnicity with the introduction of gender contextualises, refines and problematises our understanding of ethnicity further. Minority ethnic women's experiences are often lost in the debate about ethnicity even though women's participation in the labour market is a crucial determinant in understanding ethnic differences. Unwittingly it seems that ethnicity is normally analysed from a male perspective while gender is analysed from a White female perspective. Minority ethnic women, as a result, are rendered invisible between these two perspectives and the crucible of gender and ethnicity in determining life chances is not fully appreciated (Mirza, 1997). Several researchers, however, have begun to widen the analysis about gender, ethnicity and economic well-being by demonstrating that gender differences may be more important than ethnicity when determining economic advantage and disadvantage of different minority ethnic groups (Modood et al, 1997; Mason, 2003; Warren and Britton, 2003).

With the complexity of minority ethnic economic situations as the starting point for analysis, this chapter will explore the diversity of experiences among minority ethnic groups in terms of wealth accumulation and levels of poverty. It will begin with a brief demographic overview of minority ethnic groups in the UK, detailing age and geographical distributions and household sizes. The chapter then turns to focus on ethnic differentials in employment and economic activity. There is a focus on employment and unemployment as participation in the labour market is a key variable to understanding differences in outcomes in terms of individual and household income and ability to accumulate assets. The differing levels of labour market participation by women from different ethnic groups will also be highlighted as this is also a key determinant for economic well-being. Income generated from employment is also a key indicator of wealth accumulation, as state pension benefits and the ability to contribute to a private pension are determined by in-work income. The final section considers some of the policy implications of these findings. Consideration by policy makers of the contradictions and diversity of experience of minority ethnic groups, as well as their similarities, makes universal programmes seeking to benefit the most economically marginalised problematic. Targeted, complex policies focusing on the multiple experiences of minority ethnic groups may be the most helpful way forward.

An overview of minority ethnic groups in the UK

The UK population remains overwhelmingly White. According to the 2001 Census, 92% of the total population identified themselves as White, while minority ethnic groups comprised 7.9% of the population (ONS, 2001; General Register Office for Scotland, 2001). Making up almost 23% of the entire minority ethnic population, the Indian group is by far the largest. The Pakistani group and individuals of mixed ethnic backgrounds are the second and third largest groups, comprising 16% and 15% of the minority ethnic population respectively (see *Table 8.1*).

Table 8.1: *Total population by ethnic group*

	Total population (numbers)	Total population (%)	Minority ethnic population (%)
White	54,153,898	92.1	n/a
Mixed	677,117	1.2	14.6
Indian	1,053,411	1.8	22.7
Pakistani	747,285	1.3	16.1
Bangladeshi	283,063	0.5	6.1
Other Asian	247,664	0.4	5.3
All Asian or Asian British	2,331,423	4	50.3
Black Caribbean	565,876	1	12.2
Black African	485,277	0.8	10.5
Black Other	97,585	0.2	2.1
All Black or Black British	1,148,738	2	24.8
Chinese	247,403	0.4	5.3
Other ethnic groups	230,615	0.4	5
All minority ethnic population	4,635,296	7.9	100
All population	58,789,194	100	n/a

Source: Census, April 2001, Office for National Statistics; Census, April 2001, General Register Office for Scotland

It should be noted at this point that because of the proportionately small number of Bangladeshi and Chinese groups, the data samples for these groups might be too small to analyse effectively in other datasets.

The age profile of the minority ethnic population is very different to that of the White population (see *Table 8.2*). A larger proportion of the minority ethnic population is represented in the younger age brackets compared with the White group. Strikingly, 50% of the mixed ethnic group population is under the age of 16 with 38% of the Bangladeshi and Other Black background groups and 35% of the Pakistani group also below the age of 16. Only approximately one fifth of the White group are aged 0–15 (ONS, 2001; General Register Office for Scotland, 2001).

On the other end of the scale, a larger percentage of the White group are aged 65 and over compared with all other minority ethnic groups. This imbalance in terms of the working-age and retirement population will have an impact on different groups' ability to accumulate assets in terms of financial savings,

Table 8.2: *Age distribution by ethnic group*

	Under 16	16–64	65 and over
White	19.19	63.89	16.92
White British	19.52	63.48	17.00
White Irish	5.87	69.31	24.82
Other White	13.81	75.74	10.45
Mixed	49.90	47.13	2.96
Asian or Asian British	28.70	66.05	5.25
Indian	22.89	70.51	6.59
Pakistani	34.90	60.94	4.16
Bangladeshi	38.38	58.39	3.23
Other Asian	23.61	71.22	5.16
All Black or Black British	25.95	67.56	6.48
Black Caribbean	20.35	69.04	10.61
Black African	30.11	67.58	2.32
Other Black	37.83	58.91	3.25
All Chinese or Other	18.95	77.03	4.02
Chinese	18.55	76.35	5.10
Any other ethnic group	19.37	77.75	2.88
All non-White groups	30.11	64.79	5.10
All ethnic groups	20.07	63.96	15.97

Source: Census, April 2001, Office for National Statistics; Census, April 2001, General Register Office for Scotland

mortgages and pensions. The White group is more likely to have accumulated assets because they have had more time in the labour market to earn higher wages and accrue financial savings. (This dimension of wealth inequalities will be discussed later in the chapter.)

The geographical distribution of minority ethnic groups is also noteworthy, as these groups are over-concentrated in urban centres and in London particularly (see *Table 8.3*). A total of 45% of the minority ethnic population resides in London and they make up almost one third of the capital's residents. The next largest concentration is in the West Midlands, at almost 13%, and then the South East followed closely behind by the North West, both at around 8%. Research has found that the concentration of minority ethnic groups in large conurbations is due to migration patterns and the location and availability of employment at the point of migration from the 1950s to the 1970s (Phillips, 1998; Rees and Butt, 2004). Subsequent waves of migration have followed this pattern as groups have become well established. Debate continues within the literature as to whether these urban concentrations constitute ghettos where a large proportion of residents suffer multiple forms of exclusion or whether these neighbourhoods should be viewed in a more positive light, where minority ethnic families make active decisions to live in close proximity to each other because they benefit from shared cultural experiences (Pacione, 1997; Phillips, 1998; Rees and Butt, 2004). While there is not space in this

Table 8.3: *Geographical distribution of minority ethnic groups*

United Kingdom	All non-White groups (%)
North East	1.29
North West	8.07
Yorkshire and the Humber	6.98
East Midlands	5.86
West Midlands	12.79
East	5.68
London	44.63
South East	8.45
South West	2.44
Wales	1.33
Scotland	2.19
Northern Ireland	0.27

Source: Census, April 2001, Office for National Statistics; Census, April 2001, General Register Office for Scotland; Census, April 2001, Northern Ireland Statistics and Research Agency

chapter to explore this debate in more detail, the contested view of minority ethnic geography gives further indication of a need to take a complex analysis of the differences in minority ethnic experience.

Because of the relatively small proportion of minority ethnic groups living in Scotland, research has tended to eliminate them from the point of analysis about ethnicity, poverty and wealth. Scotland collects its own data regarding these issues but the data are not sufficiently disaggregated in order to analyse effectively. More qualitative and quantitative research is required in this area as anecdotal evidence and small-scale research projects seem to point to a very different experience for Scotland's minority ethnic population in comparison with groups in England and Wales (Netto et al, 2001). For instance, the Pakistani group is the largest minority ethnic group in Scotland but it is not clear whether this group experiences the same level of poverty and deprivation as their counterparts in England. Anecdotal evidence suggests that there is a growing Pakistani middle class and this distinct Scottish experience may well yield important lessons for policy makers south of the border. However, not enough hard data exist relating to income levels, assets and poverty of minority ethnic groups in Scotland to be able to come to any firm conclusions about the dynamics of ethnicity, wealth accumulation and poverty north of the border.

The final point to make regarding the demographics of minority ethnic groups is the considerable variation in household sizes and composition (see *Table 8.4*). On average, the Bangladeshi group has 4.5 people living in the same house, the Pakistani group has 4.1 people and the Indian group has 3.3 people. The White and Black Caribbean groups have the smallest household size, with 2.3 people and 2.6 people respectively. The differences in the size of households are due to several factors. Firstly, Asian families – Pakistani and Bangladeshi groups in particular – typically have more children than other ethnic groups. It is worth noting that the relatively large number of children that these groups have is counter to the trend for most other ethnic groups of having fewer children later in life (Modood et al, 1997). Furthermore, the custom of 'dual households' that some Asian groups employ in terms of looking after older relatives and living in extended family structures also impacts on household size. Finally, Asian households are more likely to contain two parents whereas the trend for other ethnic groups is moving towards one-parent families. The size of Asian households does seem to have an impact on the economic well-being for these groups in terms of income levels and financial savings to provide a buffer during economic downturns. However, this will be discussed in more detail later in the chapter.

In contrast to the distinct Pakistani and Bangladeshi situation of larger households and differing compositions, Other Black background, Black Caribbean, Mixed and Black African households differ greatly. They are disproportionately headed by single parents compared with other ethnic groups,

Table 8.4: *Average household size of ethnic groups*

Great Britain	People per household
	Average Household Size
White British	2.31
White Irish	2.15
Other White	2.43
Mixed	2.46
Indian	3.30
Pakistani	4.11
Bangladeshi	4.46
Other Asian	3.19
Black Caribbean	2.26
Black African	2.74
Other Black	2.41
Chinese	2.66
Other ethnic groups	2.79
All households	2.35

Source: Census, April 2001, Office for National Statistics; Census, April 2001, General Register Office for Scotland

ranging from more than one third of Black African families to over 50% of Other Black background families. Indian and Bangladeshi households have the smallest percentage of lone-parent households with dependent children, at 11% and 9% respectively. It is important to note here the unexpected outcomes that gender and ethnicity play in terms of economic well-being and household compositions. Black and Mixed households are more likely to be female-headed lone-parent households subsisting on low incomes (see *Table 8.5*).

Unexpectedly, however, these households tend to have lower poverty rates than Pakistani and Bangladeshi households, which are more likely to have two parents present. As will be shown later, Bangladeshi households are in a very insecure economic situation and are more likely to face long-term deprivation. As the household composition situation demonstrates, the economic well-being of different minority ethnic groups seems to hinge on gender. Bangladeshi couples should be better off than Black single-headed households but because Bangladeshi women typically do not work, and care for more dependent children compared with Black women, this places more financial responsibilities on the single male income (Warren and Britton, 2003). So to understand the economic fortunes of different minority ethnic groups, gender must be in the forefront of our analysis.

Table 8.5: *Lone parent households by ethnic group*

All households with dependent children	
Great Britain	**Percentages**
	Lone parent households
White British	22.12
White Irish	23.13
Other White	17.17
Mixed	38.89
Indian	9.58
Pakistani	12.98
Bangladeshi	11.62
Other Asian	12.21
Black Caribbean	47.81
Black African	36.01
Other Black	52.09
Chinese	15.09
Other ethnic group	18.02
All ethnic groups	22.15

Source: Census, April 2001, Office for National Statistics; Census, April 2001, General Register Office for Scotland

This brief demographic overview demonstrates the incredible diversity among minority ethnic groups and the importance of understanding the substantial differences that exist between ethnic groups in terms of population size, age distribution, geographical location and household size and composition. With the baseline of diversity as the starting point for analysis, we can now turn to examine three key determinants of economic well-being: employment, income level and asset accumulation.

Economic activity, employment and income

Despite continuing discrimination based on gender and ethnicity, minority ethnic groups have made gains in employment over the past 40 years. As will be shown below, it is no longer the case that minority ethnic groups are disproportionately represented in low-skilled, low-paid and low-status work. However, the diversity of experience in the labour market is important to emphasise, with some groups slowly but successfully chipping away at the glass ceiling and gaining access to top managerial positions while other groups continue to be underemployed or excluded from the labour market.

Turning first to economic activity rates, there is wide variation between different ethnic groups. Indian and Black Caribbean men have the highest economic activity rates; they are on a par with White men at 80%. Chinese men have the lowest activity rates at 63%, with several groups of minority ethnic women outperforming Chinese men. Black Caribbean women have the highest rate of economic activity among minority ethnic women, almost on a par with White women at 74%, while Bangladeshi and Pakistani women are noteworthy for their very low activity rates, at 25% and 31% respectively (see *Table 8.6*).

There are several potential explanations for the differing rates of economic activity between minority ethnic groups. With a longer history of settlement in the UK, Indian and Black Caribbean groups are more established and have longer employment and educational experiences than more recent migrants such as the Chinese groups (Modood et al, 1997; Platt, 2005). As was noted earlier, Pakistani and Bangladeshi households are bucking the trend of having fewer children later in life. Since most Pakistani and Bangladeshi women have more children in their early to mid-20s and then also step off the career ladder to be full-time carers, their economic activity rates tend to be much lower compared to other groups. As will be shown later in this section, the intersection of gender discrimination in the workplace combined with the differing cultural expectations about women and employment also plays a key role in explaining ethnic differences.

Table 8.6: *Economic activity rates by ethnic group and gender*

Great Britain	Males (%)	Females (%)
White British	84.2	74.8
White Irish	82.5	74.9
Other White	83.2	70.9
Mixed	77.9	65.6
Indian	81.1	66.1
Pakistani	71.7	30.8
Bangladeshi	70.5	25.3
Other Asian	77.3	59.9
Black Caribbean	80.3	73.8
Black African	72.0	56.8
Other Black	72.6	71.4
Chinese	62.7	55.8
Any other ethnic group	71.9	53.6
All ethnic groups	83.3	72.8

Note: Black shaded figures indicate the estimates are unreliable and any analysis using these figures may be invalid. Any use of these shaded figures must be accompanied by this disclaimer.

Source: Annual Population Survey, January–December 2004, Office for National Statistics

Analysing employment and occupational patterns[1] between minority ethnic groups is striking (see *Table 8.7*). The polarisation of experience is what is surprising about employment and unemployment, with more variation within the minority ethnic population than between the White and minority ethnic groups. It is here that we see the way gender and ethnicity interact and produce different outcomes for different parts of the minority ethnic population. Again it is Indian and Chinese men who fare the best in the labour market, with relatively low unemployment rates and an even distribution throughout different occupations.[2] Even though Indian and Chinese men have higher unemployment rates compared with the White group, they are well represented in professional occupations. One fifth of Chinese and Indian men are in senior management positions in the labour market and they slightly outperform White men in this regard. Interestingly, Indian and Chinese men are less likely to be represented in low-skilled and low-paid occupations and this is a very different experience compared with other minority ethnic groups.

It is still unclear why Indian and Chinese men perform relatively well in the labour market compared with other groups, but one explanation is that Indian and Chinese men tend to have higher qualifications and these educational achievements may give them an extra advantage when competing in the labour market (Connor et al, 2004). What remains unclear, however, is why other groups with good qualifications, namely African men, still fare so poorly in the job market.

Even with good progress in the labour market over the past 40 years it is the experience of Pakistani, Bangladeshi, Black Caribbean and Black African men that should be scrutinised. These groups have unemployment rates that are three times higher than the White group, and they are more heavily concentrated in lower-paid, lower-status occupations. Whether these minority ethnic men leave school with no qualifications or whether they are highly qualified workers, they are more likely to be employed in lower-skilled jobs or to be excluded from the labour market completely. The explanation for this so-called 'ethnic penalty' is straightforward: ongoing discrimination. There can be no escaping the fact that endemic racism is the cause of the systemic disadvantage of these groups of men in the labour market. The persistence of both direct discrimination, in terms of the recruitment and selection of job candidates, and indirect discrimination, in terms of stereotypical judgements about a candidate's ability to fit into the work environment, results in these unequal outcomes in the workforce (Modood et al, 1997; Mason, 2003).

Turning to women's experiences, gender and ethnicity interact differently (see *Table 8.8*). Some minority ethnic women have lower rates of unemployment compared with their male counterparts, so it seems that some women may be better able to negotiate the ethnic penalty when competing for jobs. As was noted earlier, the cause of high unemployment among Pakistani and

Table 8.7: *Unemployment rates by ethnic group and gender*

Great Britain	Male (%)	Female (%)	All (%)
White British	4.5	3.7	4.2
White Irish	4.9	3.5	4.2
Other White	6.1	6.1	6.1
Mixed	12.6	11.6	12.1
Indian	6.5	7.7	7.0
Pakistani	11.0	19.7	13.6
Bangladeshi	12.9	12.6	12.9
Other Asian	11.3	7.0	9.4
Black Caribbean	14.5	9.1	11.7
Black African	13.1	12.3	12.8
Other Black	19.0	18.1	18.6
Chinese	9.7	7.1	8.5
Other ethnic groups	10.4	11.5	10.9
All ethnic groups	5.1	4.3	4.7

Note: Black shaded figures indicate the estimates are unreliable and any analysis using these figures may be invalid. Any use of these shaded figures must be accompanied by this disclaimer.

Source: Annual Population Survey, January–December 2004, Office for National Statistics

Bangladeshi women appears to be the result of these groups leaving the labour market to become the primary carer at home. Many Pakistani and Bangladeshi women do not seem to return to the labour market after the birth of their children and this probably keeps these women's unemployment figures artificially high (Mason, 2003; Warren and Britton, 2003).

Despite the differing traditions about the role of work in women's lives and the interaction between work and motherhood that affects women's participation in the labour market, what these minority ethnic women have in common is the 'glass ceiling' – systematic labour market segregation and discrimination – which prevents them from accessing higher-paid and higher-status occupations. All women, regardless of ethnic background, are still unevenly distributed throughout occupations and they still seem to be in a pink-collar ghetto, concentrated in semi-professional roles and under-represented in senior management positions (see Chapter Seven, this volume).

Almost one fifth of minority ethnic women work in some kind of administrative or secretarial role in the workplace, and their participation drops significantly when moving up the occupational scale or examining 'non-traditional' roles for women as in the manufacturing sector. Similar to their male counterparts, only Chinese and Indian women are on a par with

Table 8.8: *Occupation by ethnic group and gender*

Great Britain	Managers and senior officials	Professional occupations	Administrative and secretarial	Process, plant and machine operatives	Elementary occupations
Males					
White British	18.6	13.0	4.8	12.3	11.6
White Irish	22.6	16.4	4.0	10.3	9.6
Other White	19.2	16.8	4.2	9.5	12.4
Mixed	13.8	10.9	4.3	9.3	15.2
Indian	20.5	20.6	7.6	10.6	10.1
Pakistani	14.1	11.7	6.7	27.1	13.3
Bangladeshi	17.1	7.1	4.0	9.7	21.9
Other Asian	20.3	15.6	5.4	8.8	15.1
Black Caribbean	11.9	8.7	4.5	11.7	15.8
Black African	7.5	18.8	7.1	10.2	26.0
Other Black	16.0	14.9	0.6	9.9	30.2
Chinese	20.9	24.8	5.1	5.3	12.1
Any other ethnic group	17.4	17.9	3.3	8.1	17.2
All ethnic groups	18.5	13.4	4.9	12.1	11.9

continued

167

Table 8.8: (continued)

Great Britain	Managers and senior officials	Professional occupations	Administrative and secretarial	Process, plant and machine operatives	Elementary occupations
Females					
White British	10.8	10.7	22.4	2.3	11.3
White Irish	13.6	15.5	14.0	2.3	11.0
Other White	11.2	16.8	18.1	1.6	12.1
Mixed	8.0	12.6	19.6	1.2	8.6
Indian	10.1	14.3	21.6	4.9	10.9
Pakistani	6.4	14.9	15.0	4.1	9.4
Bangladeshi	6.6	9.2	18.6	2.1	8.1
Other Asian	7.4	10.2	17.6	2.2	14.1
Black Caribbean	8.4	10.2	22.3	2.0	10.4
Black African	6.5	8.5	15.5	2.4	15.0
Other Black	5.1	6.1	26.6	6.0	8.2
Chinese	12.5	16.7	14.6	1.3	16.1
Any other ethnic group	8.8	16.5	16.1	2.5	10.7
All ethnic groups	10.7	11.2	21.9	2.3	11.4

Note: Black shaded figures indicate the estimates are unreliable and any analysis using these figures may be invalid. Any use of these shaded figures must be accompanied by this disclaimer.

Source: Annual Population Survey, January–December 2004, Office for National Statistics

White women in accessing senior positions. It is also worth noting that only African men fare equally as poorly as the rest of minority ethnic women in being disproportionately concentrated in low-paid low-status work.

Looking at economic inequality from the point of employment is telling. Different minority ethnic groups experience both successes and failures in trying to enter the labour market or making progress up the career ladder. It is no longer useful to discuss minority ethnic groups in terms of wholesale disadvantage in comparison with the White group. While all groups still have higher unemployment rates than the White group, Indian and Chinese men and women have been able to make substantial gains within the labour market and their achievements should be better acknowledged and understood. Other groups, however, are not faring so well and the ongoing discrimination faced by men from African, Caribbean, Pakistani and Bangladeshi backgrounds is a cause for considerable concern. The experience of minority ethnic men, however, is only one half of the story. Minority ethnic women have a different experience. Traditional gender roles still seem to play a significant role in determining the participation of women in the labour force. For those working women, their labour market participation is typically clustered in semi-professional administration roles and they are noticeably missing from senior management positions. Only Indian and Chinese women have been able to make some significant gains into the higher echelons of the workforce.

Understanding the interaction between gender and ethnicity helps bring a more complete and complex picture to the experiences of minority ethnic groups in the UK. By exploring how ethnicity and gender affect different groups in different ways we can begin to have a better analysis about inequality and how it manifests itself in terms of the unequal distributions of poverty and wealth. By combining data on minority ethnic households and the differing outcomes for minority ethnic groups in the labour market, we can begin to construct a complex picture about the economic well-being of Britain's minority ethnic communities.

Income, wealth and poverty

Although employment is a key indicator of economic well-being it is important that this analysis takes into account the income generated both from employment and state benefits and also the ability of different groups to make long-term use of income and other resources through the accumulation of wealth and assets. Income is an important starting point for assessing the economic situation for a particular minority ethnic group. Analysing income gives us an immediate indication of how well a particular group is faring. Income, however, as a measure of economic well-being, should be used cautiously because it only provides a snapshot in time for groups as it is highly unstable and fluctuates over time because of individuals moving into and out of the labour market. This discussion of income will be supplemented with an analysis of wealth accumulation that provides a long-term economic view of a group's ability to build assets and savings over time.

The discussion on the relationship between ethnicity and income is complex because of the diversity of experience among minority ethnic groups. The economic situation for pensioners versus recent migrants versus young people just entering the labour market is very different. Unfortunately there is not the space in this chapter nor the disaggregated data available to discuss the discreet experiences of specific groups within the minority ethnic population. Instead, this section focuses on the experience of working-age adults, the largest section of the minority ethnic population. Specific notable experiences based on gender, age and other factors will be highlighted for further consideration.

Despite high levels of economic activity for minority ethnic groups and Indian and Chinese men's entry into higher occupational positions, minority ethnic groups are still more likely than the White group to be living on low incomes (Berthoud, 1998; DWP, 2006a). Using the after housing costs (AHC) data from the Households below average income (HBAI) 2004/05 survey (DWP, 2006a) the experience of working-age minority ethnic groups cautions against hasty conclusions about the improvements in the economic well-being of minority ethnic groups (see *Table 8.9*).[3]

Using the White group as a baseline for comparison, they are the most evenly distributed group throughout the income scale, ranging from 17% of households in the bottom quintile to 26% in the top quintile. Minority ethnic households, however, are disproportionately concentrated in the two lowest income brackets and, in some cases, twice as many minority ethnic households are located in the bottom quintile compared with the White group. But, keeping in line with the diversity of experience, some ethnic groups appear to be doing better than others.

Consistent with their improving performance in the labour market, the Indian group is the most evenly distributed minority ethnic group, with representation in the top quintile almost in step with their White counterparts at 22%. This group's fairly even distribution on the income scale is noteworthy as it seems to demonstrate the culmination of several socioeconomic factors. With relatively few lone-parent households, a greater likelihood of having a qualification and greater access to higher-earning jobs for both men and women, the income distribution of the Indian group seems to show a variety of experience that appears to question the traditional idea of wholesale minority ethnic disadvantage. Certainly, with 43% of working-age Indian households living on the lowest incomes, some Indian groups are experiencing poverty and an insecure economic position. However, with 40% of Indian households located in the top two income quintiles this makes

Table 8.9: *Quintile distribution of AHC income for working-age adults*

Ethnic group	Net equivalised disposable household income					All working-age adults (millions)
	Bottom quintile	Second Quintile	Middle quintile	Fourth quintile	Top quintile	
White	17	15	20	23	26	30.8
Mixed	30	17	24	12	18	0.3
Asian or Asian British	35	22	14	13	16	1.7
of which						
Indian	28	15	17	18	22	0.8
Pakistani/Bangladeshi	49	28	12	6	5	0.6
Black or Black British	32	18	18	17	15	0.8
of which						
Black Caribbean	24	15	24	19	18	0.4
Black Non-Caribbean	40	20	12	15	12	0.4
Chinese or Other Ethnic Group	33	17	20	14	16	0.6

Source: DWP (2006a)

working-age Indian households unique among minority ethnic groups for not being disproportionately concentrated in the lowest income brackets.

Analysis of the 'Chinese or other ethnic group' category should be treated with caution since several different groups have been combined to form this artificial grouping. The income of Chinese or other ethnic group households is intriguing because the income distribution does not seem to match with employment figures. With unemployment rates twice as high as for the White group it is perhaps not surprising that 50% of this group are concentrated in the bottom two income brackets. However, there does seem to be a disconnection between the occupational position of this group and their available income AHC. For instance, nearly 45% of Chinese men are in professional or senior management positions but only one third of the working-age population have incomes that place them in the top two income quintiles. While there is not a simple link between occupational position and household income, there seems to be a discrepancy between the labour market experiences of this group and the income available to the household.

The groups that are in the most vulnerable position based on household income, however, are the Pakistani and Bangladeshi groups. Forty-nine per cent of these groups are concentrated in the bottom quintile of income, and 77% of all Pakistani/Bangladeshi groups are living on the lowest incomes. Pakistani/Bangladeshi groups are virtually shut out of the higher-income brackets given their over-concentration in the lowest occupational sectors and high levels of unemployment, which are almost three times higher than for the White group. Furthermore, as discussed earlier, because Pakistani and Bangladeshi women are more likely to be full-time carers for their children, this means that these households are over-reliant on an unstable combination of low-income male earnings and state benefits. These socioeconomic factors add up to entrenched poverty among Pakistani and Bangladeshi groups that places them in a precarious economic situation and makes these two groups extremely vulnerable to downturns in the economy and reforms to the state benefit system.

It is crucial to now turn to analyse the differentials in wealth accumulation of ethnic groups because understanding wealth is the key to understanding the long-term impact of economic inequality. The ability to accumulate wealth is a key variable that determines economic stability and social mobility for households. However, before interrogating the data on wealth it is important to bear in mind that the traditional idea of wealth – household savings, investments and pensions – is as a socially constructed good. Minority ethnic groups interpret 'wealth' in ways that can differ from the dominant understanding of wealth accumulation. For instance, for many Muslim households in the UK the accumulation of interest is prohibited, and as a result financial savings are channelled into assets such as land and property rather than in traditional interest-bearing investments. Also, a higher proportion of minority ethnic wealth is transferred overseas through remittance and investments in foreign land and property, and this can skew the data when comparing White and minority ethnic wealth accumulation. However, despite these culturally defined understandings of wealth, significant asset-based inequalities exist between different ethnic groups and socioeconomic factors such as school qualifications, high-earning employment and household size seem to be key determinants in understanding why these inequalities exist and persist (Warren and Britton, 2003; Warren, 2006).

Using Warren and Britton's (2003) valuable analysis of data from the Family Resources Survey and focusing on working-age adults, we find that the White, Indian and Chinese groups have the highest levels of assets in terms of pensions, savings and mortgages. Their average level of assets is £37,000. This is in contrast with Bangladeshi and Black African groups, whose average level of assets is only £5,000. The Other Black background group is in the most precarious economic position, with an average asset portfolio of only £2,500 (Warren and Britton, 2003, p 112). The variations of wealth between the different minority ethnic groups is not surprising given the earlier analysis about the diversity of experience in terms of labour market discrimination, household income levels, qualification levels and occupational positions of different groups.

Taking a closer look at the favourable economic position of the White, Chinese and Indian groups suggests that women's relative success in the labour market is a key determinant to effectively contributing to wealth accumulation in the household. The 'formula' for successful wealth accumulation seems to be two-parent households, a small number of dependent children to support and both adults working in fairly high-earning jobs. With the lowest female unemployment rates, a higher number of women in professional and senior management occupations and smaller household sizes it seems White, Indian and Chinese groups are more likely to have enough AHC disposable income to build up wealth.

In contrast, Bangladeshi, Pakistani, Black African, Black Caribbean and Other Black background households do not conform to this wealth-generating 'formula' and as a result find themselves in an unequal position in their ability to effectively accumulate wealth. The situation of Bangladeshi and Pakistani groups in terms of wealth accumulation is particularly problematic because these households overwhelmingly consist of two parents. While two-parent households are often seen as an important determinant of individual household economic stability in terms of dual-earning couples, with differing cultural norms about women's participation in the labour market, many Bangladeshi and Pakistani households are actually in a disadvantaged position in their ability to generate income and, as a result, their ability to accumulate wealth (Ginn and Arber, 2001; Warren and Britton, 2003; Warren, 2006). Without the female income, many Bangladeshi and Pakistani groups are over-reliant on either state benefits or a low-waged male income because of high unemployment rates and high levels of occupational segregation that prevent Bangladeshi and Pakistani men from entering the labour market or from moving off the lowest rungs of the labour market ladder. As a result, there is very little money left to effectively accrue assets AHC.

For Black African, Black Caribbean and Other Black background groups, wealth accumulation is made difficult because of the over-representation of female lone-parent households. Black female lone-parent households are similar to the Bangladeshi and Pakistani households in the sense that these households are dependent on a single unstable income composed of state benefits and low-waged work, and as a result there is very little AHC disposable income left to contribute to building up an effective wealth portfolio. Although Black women have higher employment and economic activity rates than their Pakistani and Bangladeshi counterparts, they are disproportionately concentrated in unstable, part-time and low-paid work which depresses their earning and savings potential.

The unequal distribution of wealth among minority ethnic groups is not surprising given the structural inequalities that exist within the labour market, which prevent different minority ethnic groups from securing well-paying jobs that bring real economic benefits in terms of higher incomes, the ability to build up savings and private pensions contributions. The impact of these wealth inequalities is intergenerational and reinforces existing inequalities. The immediate effect of being asset-poor is that Bangladeshi, Pakistani, Black African, Black Caribbean and Other Black background groups are more likely to live in poverty. However, the long-term effect of being asset-poor is that for those groups living in poverty this inequality will stretch into old age and will be passed on to their children. Without the protection of a private pension or higher National Insurance contributions for a reasonable state pension, those groups living in poverty until old age will be over-reliant on other poor relatives to care for them. Thus the intergenerational ramifications of being asset-poor continue. Being asset-poor also means that wealth is not inherited and as a result children of asset-poor adults are disadvantaged in terms of lacking the economic security of assets to finance education, purchase a home, start a business or better withstand downturns in the economy or unemployment due to a long-term illness.

Analysing the income and assets of different minority ethnic groups is problematic because the experiences of these groups are so varied. Focusing on working-age adults, the causes of wealth inequalities are complicated and diverse and an appreciation of the varied causes of this inequality may be the key to forming effective policy solutions to tackle these problems.

Social policy conundrums

Tackling unequal distribution in wealth among different ethnic groups is a complicated process for those concerned with social policy. Finding policy solutions to these deep-seated problems is further problematised by the current policy trend of employment-led routes out of poverty, as seen in the proposed changes to the benefits system and the national action plan for social inclusion (DWP, 2006b, 2006c). However, measures that might have the most impact on supporting wealth creation and tackling labour market discrimination are neither straightforward nor popular in current thinking on anti-poverty policies.

Ongoing gender and racial discrimination in the recruitment and retention of women and minority ethnic workers is a direct barrier preventing wealth accumulation for these groups. However, with over 25 years of research findings and reports discussing the persistence of labour market discrimination and occupational segregation, and despite equal opportunity and positive action measures, it remains to be seen how this embedded inequality will be systematically addressed (Modood et al, 1997; Parekh, 2000; Cabinet Office Strategy Unit, 2003; Pilkington, 2003). Due to lack of action to root out racism and sexism in the labour market, women and Black and minority ethnic groups are left in a precarious and dubious position of negotiating institutionalised discrimination on an individual basis.

The failure of government intervention to tackle racist and sexist attitudes in the workplace is made worse by other factors that seem to determine the ability of households to accumulate wealth. Returning to the idea that there is a 'formula' that can help to predict asset-rich households is another major barrier that policy makers face when attempting to reduce wealth inequalities. Since it appears that a dual-earning professional couple with a small number of children is the norm for asset-rich households, the policy question is whether this is a legitimate set of standards to which asset-poor minority ethnic groups should conform in order to increase the likelihood of effective wealth accumulation. A policy dilemma seems to exist about the recognition of 'difference' in the choices that minority ethnic groups make in their family life and how this difference interacts with dominant anti-poverty and wealth accumulation strategies.

As long as the discourse on routes out of income and asset poverty are centred on getting individuals back into work, then the issues to do with accepting, recognising and supporting difference in household compositions will remain unaddressed.

Certainly a key area for investigation is about creating space and support for different types of family formations and supporting those choices that different ethnic groups make regarding their household compositions. By not understanding and recognising difference, structural inequalities are reinforced. For instance, in addition to negotiating the ethnic penalty in the labour market, minority ethnic groups are further penalised in their private lives for the different decisions they make. The active choice of some minority ethnic women to stay at home and look after children or elderly relatives should not reduce their chances for economic stability, but the evidence suggests that this is exactly what is happening. Being a single parent with dependent children should not prevent women from climbing the employment ladder and accumulating wealth but the likelihood is that these types of households will disproportionately be living in poverty (see Chapter Seven, this volume).

Policy solutions to date have emphasised conformity to a work-based model as an effective route out of poverty. Perhaps it is time to reconsider this approach and instead explore ways in which support can be given to households as they actually exist, rather than how policy makers would wish them to be, in order to effectively support measures of employment, adequate incomes and wealth accumulation by minority ethnic groups.

Conclusion

This chapter has attempted to outline the complex way in which ethnicity impacts on wealth accumulation in the UK. Since the 1970s, some minority ethnic groups, such as Indian and Chinese groups, have experienced an increase in social mobility through higher education qualifications and entry into professional and senior management employment. These two groups are enjoying the economic benefits of this improved labour market experience via an increase in wealth accumulation. Bangladeshi, Pakistani, Black African, Black Caribbean and Other Black background groups, however, have not made such impressive economic improvements and are more likely to be shut out of higher-paying employment and be living in poverty with very few assets.

An important aspect to understanding the way in which ethnicity and wealth interact, however, appears to be gender. The ability of women to work and to combine a relatively high income with the male wage seems to mark out the difference between households being asset-rich or asset-poor. The problem with addressing wealth inequalities, however, is that the UK's anti-poverty strategies are based on a policy failure in terms of tackling embedded racist and sexist attitudes in the labour market that lock several minority ethnic groups into unstable and low-paying work but also the favouring of one type of family structure over another. The movement away from addressing structural inequalities in the labour market to focusing on up-skilling individual minority ethnic workers in a sense only reinforces the hostility to difference and pressure on minority ethnic households to conform to a dominant idea of household composition in order to increase assets.

Wealth inequalities and the wider problem of labour market discrimination which causes asset poverty will continue to persist unless policy makers begin to expand their remit from 'getting people back into work' to increasing state benefits for those who cannot work because of a disability or caring responsibilities, adequate incomes for those in insecure or part-time employment and also supporting the choices of minority ethnic households, and women in particular, who decide to make different choices in the structure of their family life.

Notes

[1] This chapter is using unemployment statistics from the ONS Annual Population Survey because the traditional source of these statistics, National Statistics' First Report Labour Market Survey, does not disaggregate the data to be able to analyse for ethnic differences.

[2] While it is not entirely clear why Chinese men have low economic activity rates, one reason may be migration patterns for this group. Perhaps economic activity rates are artificially low because these groups are still establishing themselves in the labour market. What counts, however, is that once Chinese men are established in the labour market, they tend to outperform other minority ethnic groups.

[3] Due to small sample sizes Pakistani and Bangladeshi groups have been combined in this dataset. The data on Mixed and Black or Black British may be unreliable because of a small sample size and as a result Mixed, and Black or Black British groups will not be analysed in this particular section of the chapter.

Summary

- Diversity and difference are important concepts to be embedded in analysis about the experiences of minority ethnic groups in the UK.
- Gender is an important indicator for helping to determine the economic position of ethnic groups.
- Indian and Chinese groups are slowly prospering with high educational attainment rates, access to higher-paid and higher-status employment and wealth accumulation in line with White groups.
- However, Bangladeshi, Pakistani, Black African, Black Caribbean and Other Black background groups are experiencing endemic labour market discrimination which disproportionately concentrates them in low-skilled, low-waged work and this has a direct impact on their ability to accumulate wealth.
- Current anti-poverty strategies are focused on employment-led solutions to economic inequality and these policies do not adequately address labour market discrimination or the differing household compositions of minority ethnic groups.

Questions for discussion

- Labour market discrimination is an ongoing problem that disproportionately concentrates minority ethnic groups in low-paying and low-skilled work. What are some practical measures that can be put in place to overcome this form of discrimination?
- Is it appropriate for policy makers to make space for different choices that minority ethnic groups make in terms of household composition and women's participation in the labour market? How might 'difference' be recognised in social policy?
- Do you think employment-led routes out of poverty are the most effective way to tackle economic inequality? What are the alternatives to this approach?

Further reading

Conley, D. (1999) *Being black, living in the red: Race, wealth, and social policy in America*, Berkeley, CA: University of California Press. Despite the closing gap in incomes between Whites and African-Americans, economic inequalities are widening in North America. This award-winning study explores how ongoing racial inequality in North America is better understood through the analysis of class differences and differences in wealth accumulation rather than through employment and income comparisons between different ethnic groups.

Young, I.M. (1990) *Justice and politics of difference*, Princeton, NJ: Princeton University Press. Young's reinterpretation of social justice represents a landmark in 'race', class and gender studies. By shifting the focus of social justice from redistribution to the recognition of cultural differences, Young persuasively argues that a transformation of society's norms and values combined with the redistribution of wealth is the only way to achieve real justice.

Electronic resources

www.equalities.gov.uk – Government Equalities Unit

www.dwp.gov.uk/asd/hbai.asp – Department for Work and Pensions, Households Below Average Income

www.equalityhumanrights.com/en/Pages/default.aspx – Equality and Human Rights Commission

www.fawcettsociety.org.uk – The Fawcett Society

www.jrf.org.uk/default.asp – Joseph Rowntree Foundation

References

Berthoud, R. (1998) *The incomes of ethnic minorities*, ISER Report 98-1, Colchester: Institute for Social and Economic Research, University of Essex.

Cabinet Office Strategy Unit (2003) *Ethnic minorities and the labour market*, London: The Stationery Office.

Connor, H., Tyers, C., Modood, T. and Hillage, J. (2004) *Why the difference? A closer look at higher education minority ethnic students and graduates*, DfES Research Report RR552, Nottingham: DfES.

DWP (Department for Work and Pensions) (2006a) *Households below average income 2004/05*, London: The Stationery Office (www.dwp.gov.uk/asd/hbai/hbai2005/pdf_files/chapters/chapter_5_hbai06.pdf, accessed 15/7/06).

DWP (2006b) *A new deal for welfare: Empowering people to work*, Consultation Report, London: The Stationery Office (www.dwp.gov.uk/welfarereform/docs/welfare_reform_response.pdf, accessed 15/7/06).

DWP (2006c) *Working together: UK national action plan on social inclusion 2006-08*, London: The Stationery Office (www.dwp.gov.uk/publications/dwp/2006/nap/WorkingTogether.pdf, accessed 13/10/06).

General Register Office for Scotland (2001) *Census*, April (www.scrol.gov.uk/scrol/common/home.jsp).

Ginn, J. and Arber, S.L. (2001) 'Pension prospects of minority ethnic groups: inequalities by gender and ethnicity', *British Journal of Sociology*, vol 52, no 3, pp 519-39.

Mason, D. (2003) *Explaining ethnic differences: Changing patterns of disadvantage in Britain*, Bristol: The Policy Press.

Mirza, H.S. (1997) 'Gender, ethnicity and difference', in T. Modood, R. Berthoud, J. Lakey, J. Nazroo, P. Smith, S. Virdee and S. Beishon, *Ethnic minorities in Britain: Diversity and disadvantage*, London: Policy Studies Institute.

Modood, T., Berthoud, R., Lakey, J., Nazroo, J., Smith, P., Virdee, S. and Beishon, S. (1997) *Ethnic minorities in Britain: Diversity and disadvantage*, London: Policy Studies Institute.

Netto, G. et al (2001) *Audit of research on minority ethnic issues in Scotland from a 'race' perspective*, Edinburgh: Central Research Unit, Scottish Executive (www.scotland.gov.uk/Resource/Doc/156758/0042145.pdf, accessed 15/7/06).

Northern Ireland Statistics and Research Agency (2001) *Census*, April (www.nisra.gov.uk).

ONS (Office for National Statistics) (2001) *Census 2001: Focus on ethnicity and identity*, April (www.statistics.gov.uk/focuson/ethnicity/, accessed 15/7/06).

ONS (2004) *Annual population survey January 2004–December 2004* (www.statistics.gov.uk/statbase/ssdataset.asp?vlnk=6588&More=Y, accessed 15/7/06).

Pacione, M. (1997) *Britain's cities: Geographies of division in urban Britain*, London: Routledge.

Parekh, B. (2000) *Rethinking multiculturalism: Cultural diversity and political theory*, Basingstoke: Macmillan.

Phillips, D. (1998) 'Black minority ethnic concentration, segregation and dispersal in Britain', *Urban Studies*, vol 35, no 10, pp 1681-702.

Pilkington, A. (2003) *Racial disadvantage and ethnic diversity in Britain*, Basingstoke: Palgrave Macmillan.

Platt, L. (2005) *Migration and social mobility: The life chances of Britain's minority ethnic communities*, Bristol: The Policy Press.

Rees, P. and Butt, F. (2004) 'Ethnic change and diversity in England, 1981–2001', *Area*, vol 36, no 2, pp 174-86.

Warren, T. (2006) 'Moving beyond the gender wealth gap: on gender, class, ethnicity, and wealth inequalities in the United Kingdom', *Feminist Economics*, vol 12, nos 1-2, pp 195-219.

Warren, T. and Britton, N.J. (2003) 'Ethnic diversity in economic well-being: the added significance of wealth and asset levels', *Journal of Ethnic and Migration Studies*, vol 29, no 1, pp 103-19.

nine

Children's and young people's experiences of poverty and social exclusion

Petra Hölscher[1]

Overview

- This chapter provides an overview of poverty and social exclusion among children and young people.
- It analyses recent trends in child poverty rates and identifies which groups of children have not benefited from recent declines in child poverty.
- There is a focus on children's and young people's experiences of poverty and the pathways through which poverty affects their well-being and future life chances.
- Policies are assessed to tackle the poverty of children and young people.

Key concepts

child poverty; social exclusion; child well-being; UN Convention on the Rights of the Child

Introduction

Child poverty is high on the political agenda. Almost 10 years after the UK government's ambitious pledge to end child poverty by 2020 and the implementation of a range of new measures, child poverty rates have decreased considerably. By 2005, 700,000 children had been lifted out of poverty. Although this reduction in the number of children experiencing poverty was a dramatic achievement, it fell short of the stated target to reduce child poverty by 25% by 2005. Poverty is still a reality for between 2.8 and 3.8 million children (depending on whether or not the costs for housing are taken into account) below the age of 16 (DWP, 2007). A further 1.4 million young people aged 16–24 also still experience poverty in the UK (European Commission, 2006). Moreover, the worst-off children have not benefited from the reduction in poverty – severe poverty among children remained largely unchanged between 1999 and 2005 (Magadi and Middleton, 2005).

A family's economic situation has a strong impact on a child's well-being. It determines children's housing conditions and the neighbourhood that they grow up in, their nutrition, clothing and other resources, their participation in activities of their peer group as well as their access to healthcare, childcare, social services and high-quality education. But growing up in poverty can also mean coping with difficult family situations, such as experiencing parents' divorce, unemployment or having parents with mental health problems. Thus it is not surprising that child poverty is linked to poor health and education outcomes as well as children's psychosocial problems (Duncan and Brooks-Gunn, 2000; Beresford et al, 2005; NICHD, 2005). Some children may experience additional structural disadvantages and discrimination because they belong to a minority ethnic group, have a disability, are refugees or live in temporary housing. Children's experiences of poverty therefore have to be understood not only in terms of their personal development, but also in the context of their relationships with family and peers and their experiences of public services. Against this background, this chapter analyses children's and young people's experiences of poverty in relation to three conceptual frameworks:

- the United Nations Convention on the Rights of the Child (UNCRC)
- social exclusion
- child well-being.

The UN Convention on the Rights of the Child

The political discourse on child poverty is often focused on the child as the adult of the future, particularly in relation to their education and future employability. The UNCRC, which has been almost universally adopted, brings in a different perspective. Children are not only dependent on their families but at the same time independent citizens and bearers of rights and entitlements. They have the right to be heard on issues that concern them and to have their views taken into account (Article 12). Thus child poverty has to be understood both in terms of children's current well-being and its impact on children's future life chances. The UNCRC recognises the complexity of children's lives by promoting a holistic view of the child, in which children's civic, political, social, economic and cultural rights are given equal weight. It highlights that these rights are interrelated, universal and indivisible. From this perspective, child poverty and social exclusion point to violations of children's rights, for example the right to non-discrimination (Article 2) and an adequate standard of living (Article 27). The fight against poverty is therefore not least a response of governments to children's legitimate claims on society (Sabatini and Alexander, 2004).

Social exclusion

Poverty and social exclusion (see Chapter Three, this volume) are complementary and interacting concepts that depict, in spite of overlaps, different aspects of children's life situations. Concepts of poverty help to understand the material situation of families who have inadequate resources to cover basic essentials that are considered to be a normal part of everyday life and to monitor the dynamics of poverty such as changes in the number of children and young people in poverty or the duration and depth of poverty spells. The concept of social exclusion, on the other hand, shifts the focus from a relatively static understanding of children's living conditions to the underlying social processes that either create or limit children's and young people's opportunities for participation, for example in community activities, sports or education. This view of the concept highlights the agents that lead to social exclusion: discriminatory practices and institutional barriers that prevent access to public services and political participation (Lister, 2004). At the same time the concept of social exclusion helps to better understand how children and their families interact with their immediate environment as well as wider society and resulting processes of social exclusion and inclusion. It is important to recognise that people's lives are multidimensional and that social exclusion and inclusion can be experienced simultaneously. People may be socially included within their local community and live in close-knit social networks but may be excluded from participation in the wider society, so that they, for instance, may work in the shadow economy but are unable to find regular employment. Another example could be a child belonging to a minority ethnic group who may experience close family ties but at the same time exclusion from her peer group at school or live in a deprived community with a lack of sporting or leisure activities. Against this background it is not easy to identify specific individuals as entirely 'included' or 'excluded', for example children who are excluded from adequate incomes because their parents are in low-paid work might be included in an after-school football club. It is as possible to be poor but socially included as it is to be excluded without being poor. Understanding children's and young people's experiences of social exclusion and inclusion can help to appreciate what it means to live in disadvantaged circumstances and to investigate how complex social processes operate to the advantage of some children and young people, while excluding others.

Child well-being

There is no simple definition as to what child well-being is. From a child rights perspective child well-being can be understood as the realisation of children's rights and the fulfilment of the opportunity for every child to be all he or she can be. But even if families and society put all conditions in place, children still play an active role in creating their own well-being. Child well-being is not static. It is the result of the interplay between resources and risk factors concerning the personal situation of the child, his or her family, friends and neighbourhood, school and the wider society. These factors are constantly changing and children – with their evolving capacities – create their well-being actively by mediating these different factors. Child well-being therefore has to be understood as inherently multidimensional, focusing on how children themselves feel about their world. Attempts to understand child well-being in practice, therefore, have to take into account not only children's living conditions, health and education but also their relationships and emotional well-being. Child poverty in terms of children's material well-being is only one, albeit important, dimension of child well-being, although deprivations in other dimensions may be linked to poverty (Bradshaw et al, 2007a, 2007b).

The big picture

Child poverty has emerged as one of the priority issues in the European Union (EU) social inclusion process. In 2004, 15 million children in the EU – one in five – were living in poverty. In the majority of rich countries, child poverty rates have been rising over the past decade so that it is not surprising that in most EU member states children have a higher poverty risk than the general population (Förster and d'Ercole, 2005; UNICEF, 2005).

Within the EU, this has led to a growing recognition of the inadequate living conditions of many children. One of the milestones in this process was the independent report by Atkinson et al (2005) for the Luxembourg EU presidency that called for the mainstreaming of children in the EU social inclusion process and for the development of better indicators to monitor the well-being of children in Europe. By 2006, child poverty had become a priority for the EU with the EU Council of Ministers calling on member states 'to take the necessary measures to rapidly and significantly reduce child poverty, giving equal opportunities to all children regardless of their social background' (EU, 2006, p 24).

Figure 9.1 shows that child poverty rates vary widely across the EU from less than 10% in Denmark and Slovenia to 30% in the Slovak Republic. While the UK was one of the first countries to address child poverty it is – five years after its commitment to end child poverty – still one of the EU countries with the highest child poverty rates, well above the EU average of 20%.

Figure 9.1: *Children (0–15 years) in EU households with net income below 60% of the national equivalised median income*

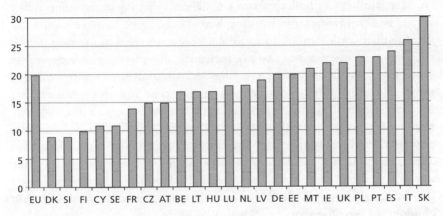

Source: European Commission (2006, data: 2004)

Risk of experiencing poverty in childhood

Children have the lowest risk of experiencing poverty if they live with two parents who are both working. The risk of experiencing poverty rises if parents' access to the labour market is limited or if income is not sufficient to provide for the family, for example because of insecure or low-waged employment. As in other EU countries, children in the UK are more likely to be poor if they:

• live in lone-parent families
• have two or more siblings
• have very young parents
• are immigrants (especially from non-EU countries) or belong to a minority ethnic group

- live in workless families, or
- are in families with a disabled or chronically sick household member (Hölscher, 2004).

Based on income after housing costs (AHC) in 2005/06, 23% of children in two-parent families but 50% of children in lone-parent families lived in poverty (measured as income below the 60% median income line; DWP, 2007). However, looking at lone parents' employment status, only 14% of children whose single mother or father was in full-time work experienced poverty, but this increased to 75% for those whose parent was out of employment. Similar rates can be found for children growing up with two parents who are both out of work (DWP, 2007). Parents' employment status thus seems to be the strongest predictor for child income poverty. Nevertheless, there are more poor children living in families in which at least one parent is working than in workless families (2.1 million versus 1.6 million), pointing to the vulnerability of children in low-income working households. Large families need more income than small families to make ends meet, so work alone may not be sufficient to provide for the family, increasing the poverty risk substantially – one in three children with two siblings and half of all children with three or more siblings are poor. In similar ways families' time and expenses for caring for a chronically ill family member or a family member with a disability may not be adequately compensated by social benefits, again increasing children's poverty risk. More children from minority ethnic groups live in poverty than White children. But the situation is different for different minorities. Nine out of 10 children of Pakistani/Bangladeshi background belong to the lowest two income quintiles, with 66% in poverty, while the poverty risk of Indian children, on the other hand, is 27% (DWP, 2007).

Some groups of children are very vulnerable to poverty and social exclusion but their situation is not captured in household surveys. They may slip through the social net and live in very severe conditions. This includes homeless children, refugees, Roma and traveller children as well as victims of child trafficking.

What has changed since 1999?

To back up the commitment to end child poverty by 2020 the UK government set two intermediate targets: the reduction of the number of children in poverty by 25% by 2005 and by half by 2010. A range of new policy measures was put into place: child benefits and cash transfers to families with children were raised, support to bring parents into work became more personalised and flexible, and access to childcare and social services for poor families improved (Hölscher, 2004). By 2004/05 the number of children in poverty was reduced by 700,000, missing the target of a 25% reduction by 100,000 (income before housing costs, or BHC) and 400,000 (income AHC) respectively. Nevertheless, the decline in child poverty is substantial.

The Institute for Fiscal Studies (Brewer et al, 2006) looked into how child poverty rates changed for different groups of children (see *Table 9.1*). This detailed analysis of changes in child poverty rates between 1998/99 and 2004/05 showed that, on the one hand, fewer children live in workless families and, on the other, that children in lone-parent families and children who have no parent working full time have benefited most from poverty reduction, although they remain the groups most vulnerable to poverty.

If a large part of the reduction in child poverty was achieved by bringing parents into work, it is likely that poverty reduction strategies mainly reached those families close to the poverty line who had the capability to find employment. For those families unable to escape poverty through employment, more generous social security benefits may be the only way to tackle poverty. Flexible and user-friendly cash transfer systems and adequate benefit levels are crucial to reach children in severe and persistent poverty. In fact there has been little progress in reducing severe and persistent poverty. Magadi and Middleton (2005) analysed data from the British Household Panel Survey (BHPS) 1994–2002, comparing it with their previous analysis for 1991–99

Table 9.1: *Details of changes in relative child poverty after housing costs, 1998/99–2004/05*

	Percentage of child population		Poverty rate (%)	
	1998/99	2004/05	1998/09	2004/05
Children in lone-parent families				
Full time	4.0	4.7	16.9	13.0
Part time	5.0	7.0	44.8	27.4
Workless	13.8	12.8	78.7	72.3
Children in couple families				
Self-employed	11.5	11.8	30.5	28.6
Two full-time earners	11.2	11.6	1.1	2.1
One full time, one part time	25.0	23.8	6.7	6.5
One full time, one not working	18.0	17.7	27.8	21.0
One or two part time	4.3	4.5	57.42	48.6
Workless	7.2	6.1	82.2	71.7
All children	100.0	100.0	32.5	27.2

Note: Rows and columns may not sum exactly to totals due to rounding.

Source: Brewer et al (2006, p 46)

(Adelman et al, 2003).They define children (0–18) as living in severe poverty if they live in households with incomes less than 27% of the median. Children are regarded as living in persistent poverty if they experienced poverty in at least three out of five years. *Table 9.2* shows the changes in persistent and severe child poverty between the two periods.

Table 9.2: *Severe and persistent child poverty in the UK*

Poverty group	Per cent of children	
	1994–2002	**1991–1999**
No poverty	53	50
Short-term poverty only	18	18
Short-term and severe poverty	4	4
Persistent poverty only	18	20
Persistent and severe poverty	7	9
Unweighted numbers	2,113	2,103

Source: Magadi and Middleton (2005, p 14)

Persistent poverty particularly affects younger children, while young people (aged 15-19) more often experience short-term severe poverty.The findings show that periods in which parents move into and out of work make families particularly vulnerable to severe poverty, suggesting that benefits and social services are not flexible enough to smooth over transition periods (Magadi and Middleton, 2005).

   In summary, while child poverty rates have come down in recent years, they still remain high in comparison with other EU countries.A large part of the decline seems to have been achieved by increases in cash transfers and by bringing more parents, particularly single parents, into work.These policies, however, have not yet reached those children and families in the most difficult situations.

It's not all about money

Data on income poverty alone are not enough to understand the life situations of children and young people and what is needed to ensure their well-being and well-becoming. It is crucial to consult children and young people themselves and to listen to their experiences of poverty and social exclusion. Children have a right to be heard in all matters that affect them (Article 12 of the UNCRC). Children in poverty and their families are experts about their own situation and know best what needs to change in their communities, in school, social security benefits and social services. Policy development that takes into account the experiences of children and involves them in the process of policy and service development will lead to solutions that are closer to the reality of children and families and more likely to meet their needs (Bennett and Roberts, 2004; Hölscher and Sabatini, 2006). This next section focuses on children's experiences of poverty and processes of social exclusion.

'I just want to fit in ...'

How children experience material deprivation and related stressful conditions depends on the severity, timing and duration of poverty. The impact of poverty on children's health, cognitive and social development becomes more severe with the persistence and severity of poverty (NICHD, 2005; Magadi and Middleton, 2006). Young children's experiences of poverty are mainly mediated through their family situation and immediate environment, while older children and young people have to deal directly with the experience of having less money than others. For them, poverty manifests in many daily situations: in not being able to wear the 'right' clothes, in not having the money to participate in school trips, in being singled out for free school meals, in not being able to go to a friend's birthday party or to celebrate their own. Poverty excludes children from the activities of their peer group:

> 'I just want to fit in the group, 'cos it's like I get ..., people take the mick out of me because I can't afford things. Like my trainers are messy and they don't suit me and I need new trainers and new clothes ... I can't get decent clothes like everyone else does.' (Bella, 12 years, quoted in Ridge, 2002, p 69)

Whether or not clothing becomes a yardstick for belonging to a peer group depends partly on children's and young people's self-confidence, but also on the rules and policies that schools have in place. In schools in which bullying is not tolerated brand name articles seem to lose importance (ATD Fourth World, 2000; Hölscher, 2003). The World Health Organization (WHO) Health Behaviour in School-aged Children (HBSC) Study shows that bullying and fighting is a widespread problem in the UK. A total of 35.8% of 11-, 13- and 15-year-old students report experiences of bullying in the previous two months (Currie et al, 2004). Experiences of peer violence are linked to a range of negative outcomes. Immediate impacts include higher levels of social anxiety and depressive symptoms, feelings of loneliness and lower self-esteem. These symptoms can again increase children's vulnerability and reinforce the bullies' behaviour so that children may get caught up in a cycle of victimisation (Craig, 1998).

High levels of bullying in the UK go along with a low level of social cohesion in the peer group. According to the HBSC Study only 43.3% of children see their peers as kind and helpful, placing the UK at the bottom of the league of OECD (Organisation for Economic Co-operation and Development) countries (Currie et al, 2004; Bradshaw et al, 2007b). Nevertheless, friendship belongs to the strongest protective factors in the lives of poor children. Research on young people's experiences of poverty in Germany shows that for both girls and boys a best friend is often the only person with whom they talk about poverty, parents' unemployment and family problems (Ridge, 2002; Hölscher, 2003):

> 'If my parents now are quarrelling so much that my father says, I'm leaving you, then I always think no, that can't be happening after all these years.... My friend has had exactly the same problems as me and that has brought us together more. And then I thought that doesn't really help us if we know each other's problems but can't do anything about it. It would be better to talk to adults who know more about adults' problems.' (girl, 14 years, quoted in Hölscher, 2003, pp 183-4; translated by the author)

'I would rather go without'

Children are very aware of their parents' struggle to make ends meet and show a high level of understanding for their family situation. A 14-year-old girl in Germany explains the changes in her life after her parents' divorce:

> 'Well, the things that one liked to do, cinema or swimming or that, you couldn't do that any more, maybe because there was no money for it. Or not buying clothes so often any more. I didn't run around like the last tramp but to say, let's go into town to buy something, that wasn't possible. Actually that was a hard time, but I'm not somebody who says, oh, I have to go swimming. I've understood my mother. She just had no money and so I didn't have to do these things.' (quoted in Hölscher, 2003; translated by the author)

Children learn early to accept that their parents cannot give them what they want. Seventeen-year-old Nell remembers "I would ask my parents to buy me things and then I realised that my parents couldn't afford things. 'Cos I'd sit down and listen to their conversation and then I stopped asking for things and saved up for them. And that's been ever ... since I was about eight, because I was a quick learner" (quoted in Ridge, 2002, p 69).

Box 9.1: Experiencing child poverty: Nadja's story

Poverty and social exclusion have many faces. Fifteen-year-old Nadja is a Russian immigrant who came to Germany two years before I talked to her. Rather than getting a German language course she was enrolled in a grade two years below her age, making it very difficult for her to become integrated in her new environment. For a long time she felt excluded until she finally confronted her peers. "I need my classmates, I still have to stay in this school for a long time. I just asked them what they've got against me. Then they said, because you are so arrogant, though they didn't even talk to me before. And then they said we didn't know that you are so ok. And now, when they do this with others, I tell them, well, go to them and talk." Her parents are unemployed and in training, since their qualifications have not been recognised in Germany. She explains that her friends know about her parents' unemployment and that it was okay because as they were trying to find work she did not feel ashamed about the situation. At 15 years old Nadja has already become financially almost independent, working in a department store after school. "Well, actually I needed more money sometimes, because I always needed something. I couldn't get so much from my parents. I always had to ask my parents and I needed a bit more, you know." Nadja has a very proactive way of coping with her life situation. Close, supportive relationships with her parents, a good understanding of her family's situation and her job appear to be the factors that are most helpful in dealing with the challenges in her life.

Source: Adapted from Hölscher (2003, chapter 11)

While younger children seem to resign themselves to accepting their families' tight financial situation, older children start taking responsibility for their own needs. Poor children are less likely to get pocket money than their better-off peers and the amount of money they get is often not reliable and comes from different sources, with not only parents but also grandparents or older siblings contributing. Many young people also start working very early and start paying for their own clothes or school materials, often relieving the family budget substantially. While young people enjoy the experience and gain self-confidence and peer acceptance, interviews also show their vulnerability to exploitation and the difficulties of combining schoolwork with employment (Ridge, 2002; Hölscher, 2003).

'That's because of all the stress'

The quality of family relations is the most important factor for the well-being of children. Children and young people who report a trusting relationship with at least one parent seem to be able to cope with poverty and other difficulties. A 15-year-old boy in Germany put it this way: "My mother always finds a solution. That's what mothers are there for" (Hölscher, 2003, p 183; translated by the author). Research on resilience of low-income families confirms the importance of family cohesion and a sense of togetherness. Children whose parents maintained warm and nurturing relationships while being clear on rules and consequences did well in their transition to adolescence and young adulthood (Conger and Conger, 2002; Orthner et al, 2004).

However, poverty and social exclusion are by definition linked to an increased exposure to stressful conditions and events: economic loss or chronic economic stress (for example, difficulties in making ends meet) and a growing constriction of choices and participation in all areas of life (for example, choice of neighbourhood, school and education, recreation, healthcare and transport). As a consequence feelings of depression and anger may become more frequent and lead to an increased risk of mental health problems. This in turn may lead to more conflictual and strained interaction between parents, making it more difficult to maintain warm, supportive and consistent child-rearing practices (Conger et al, 1997; Duncan and Brooks-Gunn, 2000).

While some studies show that child poverty is associated with low levels of subjective well-being, the evidence is inconclusive (Hölscher, 2004; Magadi and Middleton, 2005; Quilgars et al, 2005). Living in complex disadvantaged life situations seems to have a stronger impact than low income by itself. Qualitative research in Germany shows that poor children from difficult family situations report low levels of subjective well-being and tend to face more problems at school and in their peer group (Hölscher, 2003). An analysis of the Health Survey for England found three family risk factors for children's emotional and behavioural problems: living in a lone-parent family with low socioeconomic status, changes in family structure (for example, living with a step-parent) and parents' psychological problems (McMunn et al, 2001).

Box 9.2: Family and poverty: Sara's Story

A good relationship with at least one parent is one of the most important factors for children's well-being. Poverty and social exclusion can, however, impact on the quality of family relations or exacerbate already difficult family situations. Thirteen-year-old Sara comes from a very difficult family background. Her father is unemployed and doing odd jobs but the money is not enough to make ends meet. Sara does not get any regular pocket money. "Of course I would like to have pocket money and also money for clothes. But if you don't have it, then you have to buy either cheap stuff or save somehow." She likes going to school because it is the only way she can escape her family and meet friends, even though she is struggling and often has trouble with her teachers. One reason for this is that her living conditions make it very difficult for her to do homework. The family – her parents, herself and her little sister as well as an aunt – live in a small flat. Sara shares her bed with her aunt. There is no space for her to do her homework. "I do it in the living room and when it gets too loud I can't do it. I want to, but where? And then I don't do it and I get into this cycle again, the teachers ask, why don't you have your homework and I want to improve at school and then it's not possible. And I have no chance to explain to my parents, they would just hit me again." Sara rarely has a chance to escape the conflicts and violence at home. She explains that she has nobody to talk to about her problems. She has started to smoke and to self-harm because she feels that gives her some relief. Children who are overburdened can easily find themselves in a downward spiral of poverty, family problems and problems at school, making it very difficult for them to find a way out – unless teachers or social workers recognise their vulnerability and give support.

Source: Adapted from Hölscher (2003, chapter 11)

Parents' chronic illness, disability, mental health problems or substance abuse increase families' poverty risk. For example, only 24% of people with long-term mental health problems in England and Wales are in employment. A conservative estimate puts the number of children experiencing poverty in these families at 368,000 (Gould, 2006). A substantial number of these children care for their parents. The 2001 Census found that among all children aged 5–15 in the UK 114,000 provided informal care at home. Studies with young carers show that they live in more deprived circumstances than their peers and that many are forced into taking on caring responsibilities due to lack of money for alternative support. Often children and their parents also avoid asking for additional support out of a fear that their children may be placed into care. Many young carers are overburdened with their situation, which is reflected in worries about their parents, but also self-harm and thoughts of suicide, and they face a higher risk of child abuse and neglect. At the same time children display high levels of loyalty to their parents and would resist separation from their parents by almost any means (Mayhew et al, 2005).

Education: opportunities lost

The relationship between social background and children's educational attainment has been shown in many studies. While income is directly associated with children's cognitive development, mothers' educational status, parents' interest in children's educational achievements, their aspirations for their children and access to educational resources are likewise important (Peters and Mullis, 1997; Baumert and Schümer, 2001; for an overview see Hölscher, 2004). Finally, children in deprived neighbourhoods or in rural areas may have less access to good schools, depriving them of a chance of high-quality education.

Educational disparities in the UK are substantial – in 1998/99 children with parents in professional work were more than five times more likely to be in higher education than children whose parents were in unskilled labour (Glennerster, 2001). However, the same study also found that the gap is narrowing. Data on children's educational attainment in England and Wales show that, in 2002, 77% of young people with parents classified as 'higher professional' achieved at least five or more GCSEs, compared with only 32% of children in both the 'routine' and 'other' group. Compared with 2000 there have been improvements across all groups, with the two lowest groups catching up most. However, disparities persist for children from some minority ethnic groups. African-Caribbean, Pakistani and Bangladeshi students have benefited the least from rising levels of attainment (Coles and Richardson, 2005; see also Chapter Eight, this volume).

Many children and young people in poverty have ambivalent feelings about school. Many like going to school. Those with a very difficult family background may enjoy school as a place where they do not have to deal with family problems. School is also a place to meet friends, especially when poverty and/or their family situation make it difficult to spend time with friends outside of school. But many adolescents also perceive school as a chance to escape from poverty and to work hard. At the same time school life seems to be more difficult for poor children and adolescents than for their better-off peers. Their achievements are lower, and they are also less self-confident about their capabilities. They report more conflicts with teachers and show more behavioural problems. Young people experiencing poverty, especially boys, are more likely to be truant or be expelled from school. Truancy again is linked to experiences of bullying and exclusion (Ridge, 2002; Hölscher, 2003; Coles and Richardson, 2005).

Parents living in poverty highlight barriers in the education system, which make it difficult for them to play an active role as partners in their children's education. In particular, parents with children in secondary school and those whose children had problems at school did not always feel sufficiently informed and taken seriously as partners in their children's education. For some this has led to a detachment from their children's school. "I think what puts parents off is when the teachers are very negative about the kids … it's heartbreaking actually when you go up and they just hurl all this negativity at you before you even got to know them" (quoted in ATD Fourth World, 2000, p 14). In similar ways parents' poverty and low level of education can become a barrier to their participation in parents' evenings and parent–teacher associations. One parent noted, "If they could have understood that just because I wasn't a professional person … if they had accepted that I had something to offer other than signing a cheque or donating stuff, if somebody had made me feel more welcome, it would have made a big difference" (quoted in ATD Fourth World, 2000, p 16). Finally, expenses for children's education, including school uniforms, trainers, books and stationery, school trips and expected contributions to fundraising events, pose substantial difficulties to parents. Even where schools have arrangements to support low-income families, these are either difficult to access or insufficient in coverage:

> 'I'm going to find it really, really hard the last three years to keep her at school, but I'll do it, if I have to work 24 hours a day. I would never discourage her from continuing her education because of lack of money. But that's why a lot of kids leave school because there's no help for them. They're screaming that they want kids to get qualifications but they're not giving us the help and support to get the qualifications.' (Quoted in ATD Fourth World, 2000, p 39)

Children's experiences of poverty and disadvantaged life situations are complex. Not all children growing up in poverty have poor outcomes. Children's family relations and their inclusion in their peer group are protective factors that mediate their experiences of poverty. Persistent poverty, the experience of multiple deprivations and social exclusion can, however, have long-term consequences that impact on children's well-becoming. The following section looks into young people's transitions into adulthood.

Transition into adulthood

Experiences of poverty and social exclusion in childhood increase the risk for experiencing poverty and social exclusion in adulthood. According to data from the European Commission (2006), 18% of 16- to 24-year-old young people in the UK live in households with less than 60% median income (BHC). Unlike the child poverty rate, this is below the EU average of 21%. On other indicators, however, the UK compares less favourably with other EU countries. Only 75.9% of young people aged 15–19 are in education, while 9.4% are not in education, employment or training (OECD, 2005a). Moreover, more than a third of 15-year-olds aspire to low-skilled work. Compared with other EU countries, only France has lower levels of young people's labour market outcomes (Bradshaw et al, 2007a).

Walther and Pohl (2005) point out that young people's demotivation starts at school. In particular students in lower secondary education perceive what they are taught as having little relevance for their lives. They miss individual recognition and personalised relationships with teachers. This continues into career guidance: many young people feel that they are forced into a certain direction rather than getting support in finding out what they want.

Low educational achievement and qualifications are the main factors for young people not being in employment, education or training. There are gender differences: while living in the inner city is a risk factor for boys, for girls the interest parents have in their education is an important factor for continuing education and training. Among the girls in the study, many were teenage mothers, with immediate implications for their educational and vocational careers (Bynner and Parsons, 2002). The OECD (2005b) has analysed the transition of young adults (aged 20–24) with low educational achievements from education into work. They identified low parental education as a key factor for the low educational achievement of young people. Foreign-born young adults were particularly disadvantaged, both in regard to educational qualifications and labour market participation. This study also identified gender differences. Young men were more likely to have a low level of education and not to be in education than young women. However, within this group young men with low levels of education were more likely to be working than young women. One reason for this can be seen in early family formation and childbearing.

With 28 live births per 1,000 teenage girls, the UK has one of the highest rates of teenage fertility in the OECD (Bradshaw et al, 2007b). Teenage pregnancies in today's societies are seen as a major policy concern, as they are linked to a range of disadvantages, including school drop-out and lack of educational qualifications, poverty and unemployment. The reasons based on which teenagers become pregnant and decide to have their child are complex, depending much on the girl's social background, sex education at school, the availability of contraception and the availability of social services and benefits (UNICEF, 2005; Cater and Coleman, 2006). Interviews with teenage mothers in England showed that many girls had low expectations and a weak attachment to education before becoming pregnant. In fact, new educational opportunities, combined with the reality of motherhood, created opportunities for young women to re-engage with their education (Hosie, 2007). Pregnancies were unplanned and many girls were actually using contraception, but it either failed or was not used correctly. Many girls had a strong orientation towards motherhood and did not perceive having a child as a major obstacle in their lives (Arai, 2003). In discussions with young people about their views of teenage pregnancies, they showed that well-off students were more likely than their disadvantaged peers to consider abortion, as they perceived pregnancy as a major obstacle for their education and future life chances and did not expect to be supported by their family, friends and school. While disadvantaged students shared a negative view on teenage pregnancies they were more likely to consider having the child and to believe that they would receive support from their families, partner and friends (Turner, 2004).

What does it take to end child poverty?

Following the historic pledge to end child poverty by 2020 the UK government has introduced a range of measures. Work is seen as a main route out of poverty, and more personalised and targeted employment services along with a new system of tax credits were introduced to bring more people into work, to make work pay and provide higher incomes for parents. This was combined with targeted social services for children and young people and increased cash transfers to families. By 2004/05 this brought 700,000 children out of poverty, although missing the target of a 25% reduction. The families that benefited most were those close to the poverty line or with the capabilities to take up employment. For the poorest groups of children, those in severe or persistent poverty, however, little has changed. This suggests that further substantive reduction of child poverty has to reach out to those families that live in the most deprived circumstances.

For achieving the next target of halving child poverty rates by 2010, welfare-to-work policies are likely to have only limited impact on child poverty rates. Piachaud and Sutherland (2000) examined the potential impact of UK policies to reduce child poverty. They came to the conclusion that as many as 51% of poor children lived in households that could not reasonably be expected to take up employment of more than 16 hours per week. These children had parents who were looking after at least one child under five, were chronically sick or had a disability, were on maternity leave, were full-time students or were working for very low wages. Thus half of poor children live in families that are unable to get out of poverty through employment. Similarly Esping-Andersen (2002) estimated (based on European Community Household Panel [ECHP] data) that only about 40% of workless households – many of them with children – were likely to be integrated into the labour market. Among those who were likely to be permanently excluded were a large group of mainly women who never had any real labour market attachment, sick and disabled people and those long-term unemployed and low-skilled workers who had not worked for the past five years. This points to the need for flexible, accessible and user-friendly systems of benefits and tax credits that ensure families' adequate living standard. Parents themselves highlight the importance of having the choice between working and caring for children and of better opportunities to reconcile work and family life. Parent-friendly employment policies need to recognise that parents who decide not to work in order to care for their children still make a valuable contribution to society (Hirsch, 2006).

The Joseph Rowntree Foundation analysed, partly with microsimulation, what was needed to end child poverty. They conclude that to meet the 2010 target of halving child poverty, a substantial increase in benefits and tax credits worth 0.3% of GDP (gross domestic product) would be necessary. They recognise, however, that lifting the second half of children out of poverty is much more difficult and would require, on the one hand, raising the relative value of the income of non-working families above the poverty line and, on the other hand, improving the incomes from earning for the lowest-income working families. This would have to go together with more investments in the education of disadvantaged children to equip them with the skills and qualifications needed to earn a decent living when entering work (Hirsch, 2006).

Conclusion

Children are the population group with the highest risk of living in poverty, with long-term consequences for their present well-being and future life chances. But not all children have negative outcomes. Some manage to cope with adverse living conditions and develop the resources they need for an independent and successful adult life. The most important protective factors for children's well-being are good parent–child relationships and children's social inclusion in school and their peer group. Other children, however, face high risks of remaining in disadvantaged situations later in life.

Experiences in the EU confirm that the reduction of child poverty can only be achieved with a multidimensional, integrated strategy of child and family-friendly policies that prioritise the realisation of children's rights and the eradication of child poverty, secure and increase the financial resources of families, enhance child development and well-being and include the most vulnerable.

Note

[1] The views expressed in this chapter are those of the author and do not necessarily reflect the policy or views of UNICEF.

Summary

- Fifteen million children, one in five, in the EU lived in poverty in 2007 (measured as families with income less than 60% of the national median BHC).
- In the UK the respective child poverty rate is 23%, while 18% of young people aged 16–24 are poor.
- Following the UK government's 1999 pledge to end child poverty within a generation, child poverty rates were reduced from 32.5% in 1998/99 to 27.2% in 2004/05 AHC. While the decline is considerable, the target to reduce child poverty rates by 25% in 2004/05 was missed.
- A substantial part of the reduction in child poverty has been achieved by increasing the employment level of parents, in particular single mothers, through the introduction of new services for children and young people and by increasing cash transfers. A further decline in child poverty requires more investments in benefits and tax credits as well as in education. Strategies to reduce poverty have to go together with efforts to prevent poverty and social exclusion.
- The impacts of poverty on the well-being and well-becoming of children are complex. Poverty affects children's health, cognitive and social development, psychosocial well-being and educational outcomes.
- Not all children who experience poverty have negative outcomes. Among the mediating factors are the quality of family relations, parents' education and interest in children's education, children's inclusion in their peer group and the quality of schools and neighbourhoods.
- Poverty and social exclusion as well as low educational achievements disadvantage young people and are the main factor for young people not managing a successful transition into the labour market.

Questions for discussion

- Why is the eradication of child poverty important for the social and economic development of a country? What are the costs of not ending child poverty?
- Identify steps towards the prevention of poverty and social exclusion among children.
- How can children, young people and their families participate in decisions about how policies are designed and implemented? What difference would

it make to include the experiences of people experiencing poverty when designing policies?

Further reading

In the run-up to the first assessment of whether the UK government reached its target of reducing child poverty by 25%, the Joseph Rowntree Foundation published a series of papers to discuss progress made and persisting challenges, including Hirsch (2006).

The UNICEF Innocenti Report Card series periodically analyses the life situations of children across OECD countries. The two latest reports focused on child income poverty and, in a broader perspective, the well-being of children in different dimensions, including data on children's relationships and subjective well-being. See UNICEF (2007) *Child poverty in perspective. An overview of child well-being in rich countries*, Innocenti Report Card No 7, Florence: UNICEF Innocenti Research Centre and UNICEF.

Electronic resources

www.cpag.org.uk – Child Poverty Action Group
www.unicef.org/crc – UN Convention on the Rights of the Child
www.jrf.org.uk – Joseph Rowntree Foundation
http://ec.europa.eu/employment_social/social_inclusion/index_en.htm
– European Commission: The Social Protection and Social Inclusion Process

References

Adelman, L., Middleton, S. and Ashworth, K. (2003) *Britain's poorest children: Severe and persistent poverty and social exclusion*, London: Save the Children.

Arai, L. (2003) 'Low expectations, sexual attitudes and knowledge: explaining teenage pregnancy and fertility in English communities. Insights from qualitative research', *The Sociological Review*, vol 51, no 2, pp 199-217.

ATD Fourth World (2000) *Education: Opportunities lost. The education system as experienced by families living in poverty*, London: ATD Fourth World.

Atkinson, A.B., Cantillon, B., Marlier, E. and Nolan, B. (2005) *Taking forward the EU social inclusion process*, Final Report, Luxembourg: Government of Luxembourg.

Baumert, J. and Schümer, G. (2001) 'Familiäre Lebensverhältnisse, Bildungsbeteiligung und Kompetenzerwerb', in Deutsches PISA-Konsortium (ed) *PISA 2000. Basiskompetenzen von Schülerinnen und Schülern im internationalen Vergleich*, Opladen: Leske und Budrich, pp 323-407.

Bennett, F. and Roberts, M. (2004) *From input to influence. Participatory approaches to research and inquiry into poverty*, York: Joseph Rowntree Foundation.

Beresford, B., Sloper, T. and Bradshaw, J. (2005) 'Physical health', in J. Bradshaw and E. Mayhew (eds) *The well-being of children in the UK* (2nd edn), London: Save the Children, pp 65-107.

Bradshaw, J., Hoelscher, P. and Richardson, D. (2007a) 'An index of child well-being in the European Union', *Journal of Social Indicators Research*, January, vol 80, no 1, pp 133-77.

Bradshaw, J., Hoelscher, P. and Richardson, D. (2007b) *Comparing child well-being in OECD countries: Concepts and methods*, Innocenti Working Paper, Florence: UNICEF.

Brewer, M., Goodman, A., Shaw, J. and Sibieta, L. (2006) *Poverty and inequality in Britain: 2006*, London: Institute for Fiscal Studies.

Bynner, J. and Parsons, S. (2002) 'Social exclusion and the transition from school to work. The case of young people not in education, employment or training (NEET)', *Journal of Vocational Behaviour*, vol 60, pp 289-309.

Cater, S. and Coleman, L. (2006) *'Planned' teenage pregnancy. Perspectives of young parents from disadvantaged backgrounds*, York: Joseph Rowntree Foundation.

Coles, B. and Richardson, D. (2005) 'Education', in J. Bradshaw and E. Mayhew (eds) *The well-being of children in the UK* (2nd edn), London: Save the Children, pp 262-88.

Conger, R.D. and Conger, K.J. (2002) 'Resilience in midwestern families: selected findings from the first decade of a prospective, longitudinal study', *Journal of Marriage and Family*, vol 64, pp 361-73.

Conger, R.D., Conger, K.J. and Elder Jr, G.H. (1997) 'Family economic hardship and adolescent adjustment: mediating and moderating processes', in G. Duncan and J. Brooks-Gunn (eds) *Consequences of growing up poor*, New York: Russell Sage Foundation, pp 288-310.

Craig, W.M. (1998) 'The relationship among bullying, victimisation, depression, anxiety, and aggression in elementary school children', *Personality and Individual Differences*, vol 24, pp 123-30.

Currie, C., Roberts, C., Morgan, A., Smith, R., Settertobulte, W., Samdal, O. and Barnekow Rasmussen, V. (eds) (2004) *Young people's health in context. Health Behaviour in School-aged Children Study (HBSC)*, International report from the 2001/02 study, WHO Regional Office for Europe.

Duncan, G. and Brooks-Gunn, J. (2000) 'Family poverty, welfare reform, and child development', *Child Development*, vol 71, no 1, pp 188-96.

DWP (Department for Work and Pensions) (2007) *Households below average income (HBAI) 1994/95-2005/06* (www.dwp.gov.uk/asd/hbai/hbai2006/contents.asp).

Esping-Andersen, G. (2002) 'A child-centred social investment strategy', in G. Esping-Andersen, D. Gallie, A. Hemerijck and J. Myles, *Why we need a new welfare state*, Oxford and New York: Oxford University Press, pp 26-67.

European Commission (2006) *Joint report on social protection and social inclusion*, Brussels: European Commission.

European Union, Council of (2006) *Brussels European Council, 23/24 March 2006, Presidency Conclusions*, 7775/1/06 REVI, Brussels: European Union.

Förster, M. and d'Ercole, M. (2005) *Income distribution and poverty in OECD countries in the second half of the 1990s*, OECD Social, Employment and Migration Working Papers, Paris: OECD.

Glennerster, H. (2001) *United Kingdom education 1997–2001*, CASEPaper 50, London: Centre for Analysis of Social Exclusion, London School of Economics and Political Science.

Gould, N. (2006) *Mental health and child poverty*, York: Joseph Rowntree Foundation.

Hirsch, D. (2006) *What will it take to end child poverty? Firing on all cylinders*, York: Joseph Rowntree Foundation.

Hölscher, P. (2003) *Immer mußt du hingehen und praktisch betteln. Wie Jugendliche Armut erleben*, Frankfurt/Main and New York: Campus Verlag.

Hölscher, P. (2004) *A thematic study using transnational comparisons to analyse and identify what combinations of policy responses are most successful in preventing and reducing high levels of child poverty*, Brussels: European Commission.

Hölscher, P. and Sabatini, F. (2006) 'Beyond statistics – participatory approaches to researching poverty and social exclusion among children in the CEE/CIS', in A. Minujin, E. Delamonica and M. Komarecki (eds) *Poverty and children: Policies to break the vicious cycle*, New York: The New School and UNICEF, pp 133-56.

Hosie, A. (2007) '"I hated everything about school": an examination of the relationship between dislike of school, teenage pregnancy and educational disengagement', *Social Policy and Society*, vol 6, no 4, pp 333-47.

Lister, R. (2004) *Poverty*, Cambridge: Polity Press.

McMunn, A.M., Nazroo, J.Y., Marmot, M.G., Breham, R. and Goodman, R. (2001) 'Children's emotional and behavioural well-being and the family environment: findings from the Health Survey for England', *Social Sciences and Medicine*, vol 53, pp 423-40.

Magadi, M. and Middleton, S. (2005) *Britain's poorest children revisited: Evidence from the BHPS (1994–2002)*, CRSP Research Report 3, Loughborough: Centre for Research in Social Policy.

Mayhew, E., Finch, N., Beresford, B. and Keung, A. (2005) 'Children's time and space', in J. Bradshaw and E. Mayhew (eds) *The well-being of children in the UK* (2nd edn), London: Save the Children, pp 161-81.

NICHD (Early Child Care Research Network) (2005) 'Duration and developmental timing of poverty and children's cognitive and social development from birth through to third grade', *Child Development*, vol 76, no 4, pp 795-810.

OECD (Organisation for Economic Co-operation and Development) (2005a) *Education at a glance 2005*, Paris: OECD.

OECD (2005b) *From education to work. A difficult transition for young adults with low levels of education*, Paris: OECD.

Orthner, D.K., Jones-Saupei, H. and Williamson, S. (2004) 'The resilience and strengths of low-income families', *Family Relations*, vol 53, pp 159-67.

Peters, H.E. and Mullis, N.C. (1997) 'The role of family income and sources of income on adolescent achievement', in G. Duncan and J. Brooks-Gunn (eds) *Consequences of growing up poor*, New York: Russell Sage Foundation, pp 340-81.

Piachaud, D. and Sutherland, H. (2000) *How effective is the British government's attempt to reduce child poverty?*, CASEPaper 38, London: Centre for Analysis of Social Exclusion, London School of Economics and Political Science.

Quilgars, D., Searle, B. and Keung, A. (2005) 'Mental health and well-being', in J. Bradshaw and E. Mayhew (eds) *The well-being of children in the UK* (2nd edn), London: Save the Children, pp 134-60.

Ridge, T. (2002) *Childhood poverty and social exclusion: From a child's perspective*, Bristol: The Policy Press.

Sabatini, F. and Alexander, G. (2004) 'Investing in children: an obligation to build a just society', Background paper for the Second Intergovernmental Conference 'Making Europe and Central Asia Fit For Children', 13-15 May, Sarajevo.

Turner, K.M. (2004) 'Young women's views on teenage motherhood: a possible explanation for the relationship between socio-economic background and teenage pregnancy outcome?', *Journal of Youth Studies*, vol 7, no 2, pp 221-38.

UNICEF (2005) *Child poverty in rich countries, 2005*, Innocenti Report Card No 6, Florence: UNICEF Innocenti Research Centre.

Walther, A. and Pohl, A. (2005) *Thematic study on policy measures concerning disadvantaged youth*, Brussels: European Commission.

Poverty and financial inequality in later life

Jay Ginn

Overview

- This chapter examines the prevalence of poverty among older people and the measures used.
- It looks at inequality in income and material assets in later life.
- It shows how private pensions reinforce structured inequalities arising in the working life.
- The experience of poverty and inequality among older people, and the effects on social inclusion, health and well-being are explored.
- Pension policy is examined in the context of an ageing society and alternative options.

Key concepts

relative poverty; deprivation; income inequality; means testing; pension privatisation; neoliberal ideology

Introduction

The UK is ageing, like most developed countries, due to rising longevity and falling fertility. Rising life expectancy is an achievement that benefits societies: older people's long and diverse experiences are a valuable asset in any paid work, in their care for grandchildren and other relatives and in voluntary work in the community. But ageing societies also face challenges: ensuring that there are suitable jobs for those who want to continue in paid work and that older people can be socially included and maintain a good quality of life. A crucial element in this is freedom from the hardship, anxiety and indignity of poverty.

Ways of meeting these challenges are controversial, but, through all the debate about pension policy (in think-tanks and the media), older people's voices through their own organisations are rarely heard. In Britain older people seem to be politically invisible, despite being a growing group numerically.

In this chapter I examine the financial circumstances of older people, including how and why income and material assets vary among population groups. I then consider how poverty is experienced among older people. Finally, I discuss pension policy options in the context of an ageing society.

Poverty and inequality

Low income

There were 10 million people in the UK aged over 65 in 2005, comprising 4.3 million men and 5.7 million women in a population of just over 60 million (ONS, 2007). Among older people, about 2.2 million are estimated to live in poverty, according to the official indicator of relative poverty, used also by the European Union (EU), which is having an income less than 60% of national median income, adjusted for household size. This indicator of poverty has the disadvantage that it gives no idea of the depth of poverty, nor of the proportion who are near-poor, with incomes slightly above 60% of median national income. It also ignores other dimensions of poverty than low income.

Another measure of pensioner poverty is the proportion receiving means-tested Income Support (now known as Guarantee Credit) that tops up income to a certain level (£114 per week in 2006 for a single pensioner). A total of 2.12 million pensioners received Guarantee Credit in 2005, the majority of them single (that is, not married) women. This measure has several drawbacks. The proportion receiving Income Support underestimates the extent of poverty because it misses those pensioners – estimated as up to 40% of all those eligible – who fail to claim the benefit (DWP, 2006). Like the official poverty measure described above, the means test assumes equal sharing between couples, making partnered women's low income invisible. And, like the official poverty measure, the threshold for Income Support has no scientific basis in terms of the minimum income required to meet the physical or social needs of older people.

A different approach is to define poverty as deprivation, measured as lack of a range of goods, services or activities deemed by the public to be essential in their society. A related approach to pensioner poverty – the Budget Standards method – estimates the minimum income necessary for an acceptable standard of living as perceived by the general public (see Chapter Three, this volume). The Family Budget Unit estimated a 'low cost but acceptable' income for a lone pensioner aged 65–74 in 1999 as about £20 per week higher than the means-tested minimum (Parker, 2000). A 'modest but adequate' income was estimated as £159 per week for a lone pensioner woman homeowner in 2002; about half of pensioner households had less than this amount (Parker, 2002). Similarly, a team of experts calculated older people's 'Minimum Income for Healthy Living' in 2005 – including a good diet, sufficient physical activity, adequate housing, social participation, hygiene, mobility and clothing – as £122 per week for a lone pensioner and £192 for a couple (Morris et al, 2006). This study excluded the cost of rent, mortgage, Council Tax and any extra costs of disability. It is clear, however, that the Guarantee Credit (£109 per week in 2005) is insufficient to allow a lone pensioner to maintain a healthy life, even if no Council Tax, rent or mortgage were payable.

The official poverty rate among pensioners was 19% in 1981, following the previous Labour government's legislation indexing the basic pension to national average earnings. During the subsequent Conservative administration, indexing to earnings was replaced by indexing to prices (the Retail Price Index, or RPI). For this and other reasons, the pensioner poverty rate rose substantially by 1991 to 31%. According to calculations by the Institute for Fiscal Studies, the pensioner poverty rate was 22% in 1996, declining slightly to 21% by 2003; thus there was no significant fall in this measure of poverty during seven years of the Labour administration (Brewer et al, 2005). For the population as a whole, the government figure for poverty was 17% in 2003 (ONS, 2006a, Table 5.19).

Persistent poverty (lasting for at least three out of four years measured) affected 90% of pensioners whose income was below the official poverty line. Nearly a fifth of older people experienced persistent poverty: 17% of pensioners living in a couple and 21% of lone pensioners. For the population as a whole, persistent poverty affected only 11% of individuals, although among lone parents 23% were persistently poor (ONS, 2006a, Table 5.20). For low-income pensioners, unlike most working-age adults, there is usually no way, short of a win on the lottery, to escape poverty: it is a lifelong sentence. I examine next how income sources and amounts vary among pensioners.

Income inequality

The income distribution among pensioners – as for the whole population – is skewed, with the majority bunched towards the lower end of the income scale. The distribution of pensioner household incomes is shown in *Figure 10.1*. The modal value (or peak frequency) in 2004 was £200 per week, slightly higher than the official threshold for poverty at £180 per week (Goodman, 2007). Thus, a large proportion of pensioners had incomes close to the poverty level.

Figure 10.1: *Frequencies, pensioner incomes (2004/05)*

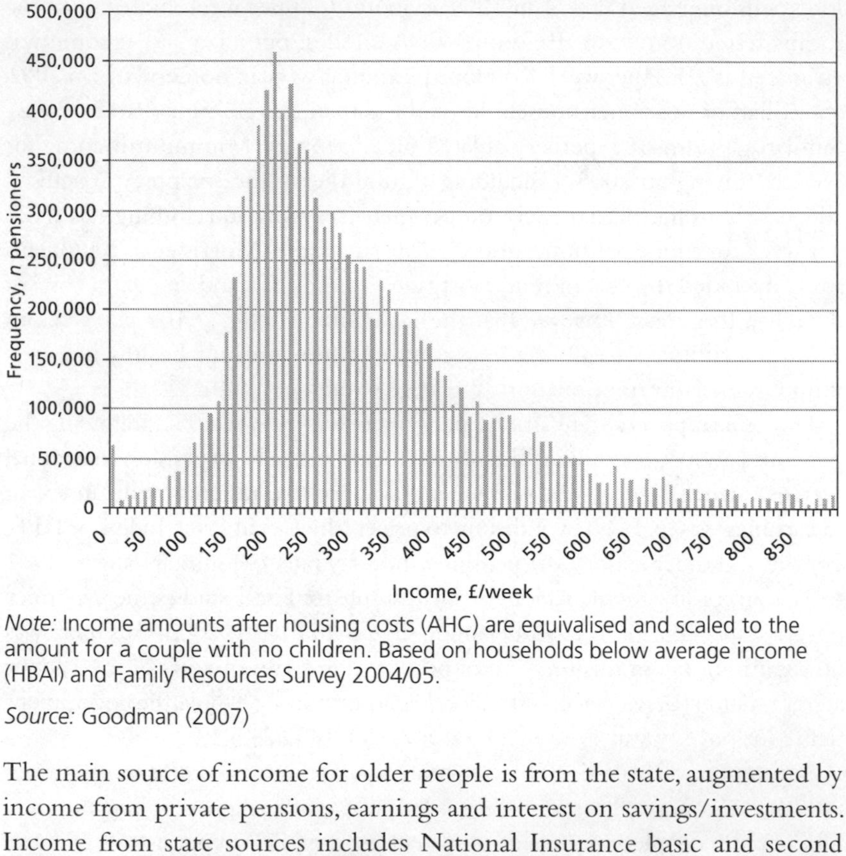

Note: Income amounts after housing costs (AHC) are equivalised and scaled to the amount for a couple with no children. Based on households below average income (HBAI) and Family Resources Survey 2004/05.

Source: Goodman (2007)

The main source of income for older people is from the state, augmented by income from private pensions, earnings and interest on savings/investments. Income from state sources includes National Insurance basic and second pensions, disability benefits and, for the poorer half of pensioners, means-tested Pension Credit (Guarantee Credit plus any Savings Credit). The mean total individual income from state and private sources is shown in *Figure 10.2* for men and women and by age group. State pensions and benefits have a fairly even distribution between men and women and across age groups. In contrast, private income differentiates strongly by gender and age group. *Box 10.1* shows the main types of pension schemes in 2007.

Box 10.1: Outline structure of British pension system in 2007

THIRD TIER — Additional voluntary contributions (AVCs), Freestanding AVCs, or personal pensions, all defined contribution (DC)

SECOND TIER — Mandatory State Second Pension (replacing SERPS from 2002) or final salary occupational pension (defined benefit, DB) or money purchase occupational pension (DC) or personal pension (DC)

FIRST TIER — Basic state pension, flat rate, mandatory

Notes

1. State pensions are based on Pay-As-You-Go, like other National Insurance benefits. The pensions allow credits for periods spent caring for children or others. (a) *Basic pension:* flat rate, £87/week in 2007 for single pensioner with a full National Insurance record. (b) *State Second Pension:* earnings-related but boosted for the low paid. State pensions are indexed to prices (RPI) in payment.

2. Private (occupational or personal) pensions are a funded alternative to the State Second Pension. Employees may opt out of the state scheme, with National Insurance rebates paid into the private scheme and tax relief allowed on contributions. (a) *Final salary occupational pensions* are DB; the pension is based on years in membership and salary in the last few years. Employers tend to contribute more than the minimum required to replace the State Second Pension but rules and practice vary among schemes. Schemes based on the employee's average earnings during membership of the scheme are becoming more common and many schemes are closing to new members. (b) *Money purchase occupational pensions* are defined contribution (DC); contributions are paid into a fund, invested in equities and bonds, then annuitised (converted to a pension) after retirement. The pension depends on investment performance and annuity rates. (c) *Personal pensions* (including stakeholder). These are money purchase schemes operated by insurance companies. They are independent of the employer, therefore portable across jobs. Charges levied as a percentage of the fund significantly reduce the pension received.

3. Details of spousal and survivor pensions are provided in Ginn (2003).

4. The pension system will change as a result of the 2007 and 2008 Pensions Acts. For details and analysis see Pensions Policy Institute website (www.pensionspolicyinstitute.org.uk/).

Figure 10.2: *Individual income[a] of pensioners from state and private sources*

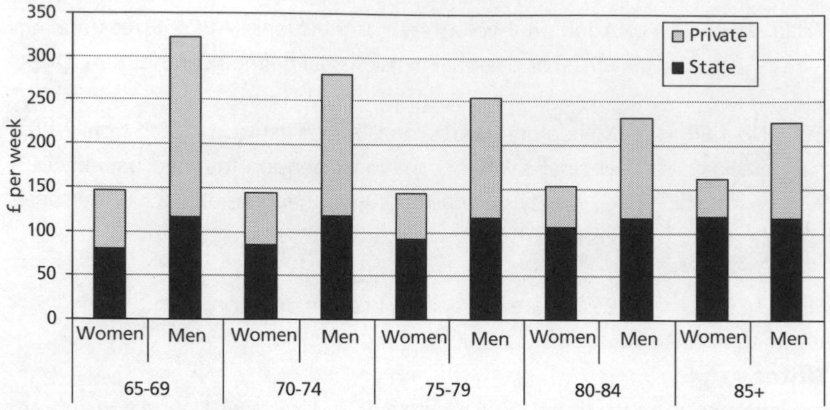

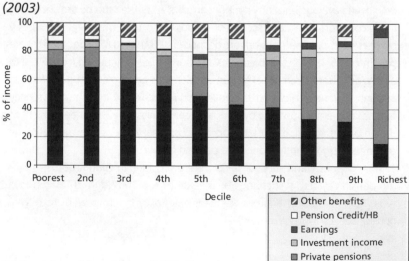

Note: [a] Mean total income, at 2004 prices, based on three years of Family Resources Survey data combined. Pension Credit for a couple is recorded as the income of the individual who claims. Other household-level state benefits are excluded, mainly Council Tax Benefit and Housing Benefit.
Source: DWP (2006, Figure 2.i)

Figure 10.3 shows sources of pensioner income in each decile of the income distribution, confirming the major role played by private pensions. In the poorest decile of pensioners, 70% of their income is from the state and only 11% from private pensions. In contrast, those in the richest decile receive 16% of their income from the state and 55% from private pensions.

Figure 10.3: *Income sources of pensioner households, by decile (2003)*

Source: Adapted from Dornan (2003, Figure 5.3)

There is a gulf between the modest amounts of private pension that ordinary households receive after a working life of employment and family caring and the large amounts received by a powerful minority. For example, £760 per week private pension is payable to Members of Parliament after only 20 years in their job. If Gordon Brown and Tony Blair had retired in 2006, they would have received a weekly private pension of £1,777 and £3,123 respectively. Even these inflated pensions are exceeded by those of company directors, 112 of whom expect a private pension of over £4,000 per week, retiring at the age of 60. The richest 27 of these will have a pension of over £9,600 per week (LRD, 2006). According to the Trades Union Congress, a typical FTSE 100 company director received an occupational pension of £3,230 per week, nearly 24 times greater than the average for their staff, at £137 per week.

Earnings from employment make a much smaller contribution to income inequality among pensioner households than private pensions (see *Figure 10.3*). Among men aged over 65, 10% were employed and among women over 60, 12% (DWP, 2007). Despite a widespread expectation that age discrimination in employment and training would be banished following the EU Employment Directive in 2000, the Employment Equality (Age) Regulations of 2006 still permit employers to implement a normal retirement age of 65. Besides employers' unwillingness to retain employees over the age of 65, other barriers to supplementing pensions with earnings include lack of training to update skills, poor health and family care commitments. For the poorest pensioners, those receiving means-tested benefits, only £5 per week of earnings is disregarded, any greater amount being withdrawn from benefits. Despite the willingness and ability of many pensioners to continue working, government employment policies are targeted at those below state pension age.

Inequalities in pensioner income are structured by gender, previous occupational class and current marital status (Arber and Ginn, 1991; Ginn and Arber, 1991). Research using data from the General Household Survey illustrates these inequalities (Arber and Ginn, 2004). *Figure 10.4* shows the median weekly individual income of men and women aged over 65 by age group, class and marital status.

The effect of previous occupation on income in later life is striking. Men who had been employed as professionals or managers had the highest gross weekly income, with a median amount over twice as high as that of male routine and manual workers. The advantage conferred by previous high occupational status was less marked among women. Those in the highest occupational group had a median income only half that of similar men, whereas in the two lower occupational groups women's median income was over two thirds of men's.

Married men had the highest income but among women it was single (never-married) and widowed women who had most. The ratio of women's

Figure 10.4: *Individual income[a] of men and women aged 65+, by age group, occupational class[b] and marital status*

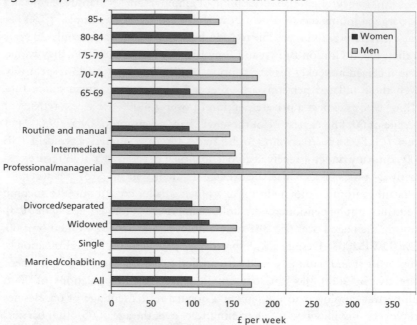

Note: [a] Median income. [b] Based on own occupation and classified according to the National Statistics Socioeconomic Classification (NS-SEC).

Source: Arber and Ginn (2004, Table A.10, using General Household Survey 2001/02)

median income to men's, within each marital status, was highest for single women at 85% and lowest for married at only 33%. The precarious financial position of older divorced women, who have usually interrupted their paid employment to raise children, is evident. Although their income was higher than that of married women, they had no prospect of inheriting a widow's pension. Overall, women's median individual income was 57% of men's (Arber and Ginn, 2004).

Accumulating a good private pension depends on above-average lifetime earnings and long membership of a generous occupational pension scheme. In both of these, women and manual workers are disadvantaged. **Table 10.1** shows the proportions of men and women aged over 65 receiving private pensions and the median amounts for those with such pensions in 2001. The class differential is clear, especially for men. In the highest occupational group – professional and managerial – 90% of men had a private pension, with a median amount from this pension of £172 per week, compared with only £50 per week for the 62% of men previously in a routine or manual job. Only two fifths of older women had any private pension income, including widows' pensions based on their deceased husbands' private pensions, compared with over 70% of men. Among those with a private pension, women's median amount was just over half of men's (*Table 10.1*, last column). Men's receipt and amount of private pensions were higher than women's within each occupational class group. A relatively high proportion, 61%, of single (never-married) women had some private pension income and their median amount was higher at £70 per week than that of ever-married women and single men. Among divorced women, only a third had any private pension income.

Thus in terms of individual income, marriage is linked with advantage for older men but disadvantage for older women. This reflects the domestic division of labour, in which mothers who care for their children and other family members forfeit some years of employment, career advancement, earnings and private pension contributions (Ginn and Arber, 1991; Ginn, 2003). The hourly gender gap in pay before women have a child is 9% but rises to 33% for mothers compared with fathers, reducing mothers' ability to

Table 10.1: *Private* pensions of men and women aged 65+ by (a) marital status and (b) occupational class^*

	a) % receiving private pension		b) Median amount for those with private pension		
	Men (%)	Women (%)	Men (£/wk)	Women (£/wk)	Women's/ men's (%)
(a) Marital status:					
Married/cohabiting	74	28	92	34	37
Single	52	61	65	70	108
Widowed	70	56	62	46	75
Divorced/separated	57	36	78	48	62
(b) Occupational class:					
Professional/ managerial	90	64	172	95	55
Intermediate	60	51	84	43	51
Routine and manual	62	34	50	28	56
All	71	43	83	44	53
n	1,474	1,882	891	694	

Notes: *Occupational or personal pension, including survivor pensions

^ Based on own occupation and classified according to the National Statistics Socioeconomic Classification (NS-SEC)

Source: Arber and Ginn (2004, Table A.11, using General Household Survey 2001/02)

contribute to private pensions (Giles and Taylor, 2006). Motherhood restricts employment, hours of work, earnings and pension contributions at all levels of education and the reduction is greatest for lone mothers (Ginn and Arber, 2002). Divorced mothers have very limited scope for building private pensions (Ginn and Price, 2002). However, gender roles have much less effect on state pension income (see *Figure 10.2*). This is due to redistributive features in the basic pension such as the flat rate structure, widows' benefits at 100% of the husband's entitlement, and the right of divorcees to use their ex-husband's National Insurance record during the period of the marriage to improve their entitlement.

The interaction between gender and marital status in influencing risk of low income is highlighted by Arber's (2004) research, in which the odds of low income are compared with those for married men, defined as 1.00 (see *Figure 10.5*). *Figure 10.5(a)* shows the odds of living in a household whose income was in the bottom quintile (the lowest 20% of the income distribution) while *Figure 10.5(b)* shows the odds of having personal income under £100 per week. These two measures reflect a similar likelihood of low income, but the first measure assumes equal sharing between married couples.

In terms of household income, older married men and women have equally small odds of a low income, due to the assumption of equal sharing (see *Figure 10.5[a]*). Divorced women and widows had odds of low income five times and three times as high as married men, respectively, while never-married women had an odds ratio of two. In terms of personal income, however, married women were the most disadvantaged group, with odds of low income 15 times as high as for married men (*Figure 10.5[b]*). Thus a household-based measure hides women's low income during marriage. It re-emerges after breakdown of the marriage through widowhood or divorce.

Comparing ethnic groups, in the mid-1990s the median income of individuals aged over 60 was higher for the White group than for minority ethnic groups. The gender difference in income was substantial in all ethnic groups except for Black people (see *Figure 10.6*). The risk of personal poverty was highest for women in the Pakistani/Bangladeshi group (Ginn and Arber, 2000). These income inequalities are mainly due to differences in private pension income. White men had a substantial advantage in private pension income over all other ethnic-gender groups. Pakistani and Bangladeshi men and women, and Indian women, were particularly disadvantaged. Gender and ethnicity interact in their effects, so that gender inequality in private pension income was least among Black people. This reflects both the disadvantaged position of Black men in the labour market relative to White men and the greater propensity of Black women, relative to women in all other ethnic groups, to maintain full-time employment (Ginn and Arber, 2000).

Figure 10.5: *Odds of low income by marital status, age 65+*

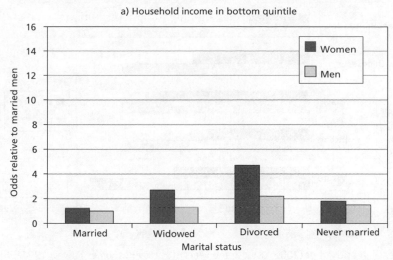

a) Household income in bottom quintile

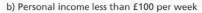

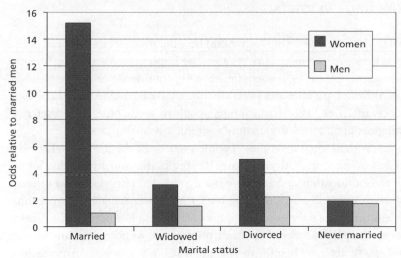

b) Personal income less than £100 per week

Source: Arber (2004, Table 5.2)

Research on income is more plentiful than that on wealth, at all ages. However, several measures of wealth among older people are available: housing tenure, access to a car in the household and amount of savings. These three are considered next.

Figure 10.6: *Mean individual income, by ethnic group*

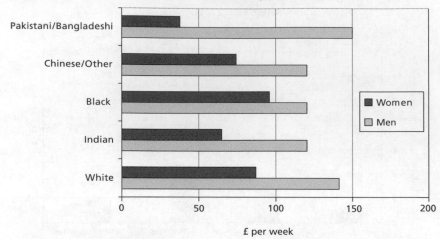

£ per week

Source: Ginn and Arber (2000, using three years of Family Resources Survey, 1994–96)

Disadvantage in assets

Inequalities in asset ownership (or wealth) have been subject to less social policy attention than income inequality.Yet assets are important in providing security, in enabling people to plan their future with confidence and in expanding choices.Although income and assets are strongly correlated (Arber et al, 2003), pensioners are more likely than younger people to be 'income-poor, asset-rich' (Rowlingson et al, 1999) due mainly to home ownership.

A home is the largest asset most people own, once the mortgage has been repaid, and ownership is advantageous. Rented homes usually provide lower-quality accommodation, and are more often located in poorer neighbourhoods where crime and pollution tend to be higher. Moreover, tenants must continue to pay rent, unless they are poor enough to qualify for Housing Benefit.Among pensioner couple households, a high proportion, 81%, were homeowners in 2001, compared with 69% in the population as a whole. Among lone pensioners, who are more likely to be women and older, the proportion was only 58% (ONS, 2004).There are differences among ethnic groups in rates of home ownership. In the population aged over 60, home ownership was 76% among the White group, 83% among the Indian and Chinese groups and 71% among the Black, Pakistani and Bangladeshi groups (Ginn and Arber, 2000). Despite providing independence, home ownership is not an unambiguous benefit to older people. The average net housing expenditure of older home owners was £30 per week, compared with £27 per week for tenants, because only the latter can receive Housing Benefit (Hancock et al, 2007).The expense of professional maintenance and repair can be unaffordable on a low income, while 'do-it-yourself' solutions become more onerous with advancing age, especially for widows who may have relied on a husband's practical experience in the past. Thus renting may be a less costly option for older people.

Homeowners with a low income theoretically have the option of releasing capital by downsizing if their home is large. However, this could mean leaving a home full of family memories, and moving away from a valued social network. Another option is equity release but both main types of scheme have drawbacks. The owner may raise a loan (mortgage) against the value of the house, but interest on the loan depletes the value in the property year by year, potentially to zero. Or the owner may agree to sell a percentage of the property in return for a lump sum or monthly income, but this may restrict their ability to sell up and move at a time of illness or bereavement. Thus home ownership is not necessarily a substitute for having an adequate income.

Having a car in the household is important in maintaining older people's independence and enabling visits to friends and relatives. With advancing age, walking, cycling and use of public transport can become limited by chronic illness or disability. In addition, older people are more likely than younger people to fear for their safety after dark, if walking alone. Lack of a car for shopping and hospital visits is particularly restrictive in rural areas where public transport is scarce, while closure of local post offices exacerbates difficulties in obtaining cash. Not surprisingly, since access to a car in the household depends on having sufficient income to afford fuel and maintenance, lack of a car is linked to low income (Arber et al, 2003). Among pensioner households, 79% of couples had a car but only 31% of lone pensioners. This compares with 80% of households of all ages that had at least one car (ONS, 2006a). In later life, having a car in the household becomes less common with advancing age and is less likely for women than men in each age group. Among those aged over 65, married women are almost as likely as married men to have access to a car, but non-married women are disadvantaged. Compared with married men, the odds of never-married women having no car were over five times as high, while those of widows and divorced women were over seven times as high (Arber, 2004). Thus the adverse effects of loss of a partner are often compounded for older women by a new restriction on their mobility. Ethnic groups differ in rates of car ownership, with Black people and Pakistani/Bangladeshi older people less likely than White, Indian and Chinese/Other groups to live in a household with a car. Over half of older Black people and Pakistani/Bangladeshi men lacked a car compared with only 31% of White men. The gender gap in access to a car in later life was widest among White people but Black women were the group least likely to have access to a car (Ginn and Arber, 2000).

Household savings for older people provide a measure of security, given that they can no longer rely on wage increases to pay for steeply rising utility bills or new costs connected with illness, disability or bereavement. Among pensioner couples, 54% had under £10,000 in savings in 2001, but among lone pensioners three quarters had less than this amount, the same as the proportion in the whole population of households (ONS, 2004, Table 5.27). Like income, financial assets are related to gender and marital roles in earlier life. About three quarters of pensioners have some savings, and about 6% have stock market investments. Among men aged over 60 with a savings account, the median amount was £7,000, while among women it was £6,000 in their 60s and £3,500 if they were over 70 (Fawcett Society, 2007). The distribution of wealth is considered more fully in Chapter Two, this volume.

To summarise this section, the main driver of income inequality in retirement is private (occupational and personal) pension incomes. Because of the low level of state pensions, the presence or absence of substantial private pensions plays a pivotal role in determining pensioners' position in the income distribution and whether they have an adequate retirement income. Ability to build private pension entitlements depends on level of earnings, occupation, access to a good occupational pension scheme and maintaining continuous full-time employment. These factors place White middle-class men at an advantage, relative to women (particularly mothers and carers) and to working-class men, with Asian women experiencing the most severe disadvantage. As individuals, older women receive a little over half of older men's income. Possession of a car, home and substantial savings are less common among lower-income pensioners, mainly the non-married.

Statistics on income and assets cannot convey how the experience of poverty impacts on the quality of older people's lives, to which I turn next.

Older people's experiences of poverty and inequality

Material deprivation

A third of pensioners could not afford to have a day out with friends, go for a meal, spend an evening at a pub, entertain at home or pursue a hobby, while two fifths could not afford a holiday, according to an ICM poll (Churchill, 2006). Among the most disadvantaged pensioners, food, heating and clothing were prioritised, while inviting friends for a meal, visiting friends and family, carpets and home contents insurance were not always regarded as essential. Ways of coping included buying food past its sell-by date and stretching food to make it last (Scharf et al, 2006). These investigations show how low incomes limit older people's ability to participate fully in society, compelling them to focus on basic survival.

One of the reasons for such deprivation is the relatively large proportion of pensioners' income absorbed by unavoidable costs. For example, Council Tax takes no account of income so that 'a recurring issue is the fairness of council tax … on older people, especially in the light of increases … above the rate of inflation' (Orton, 2006, p 2). For a D band property, Council Tax rose by 123% between 1993 and 2006 (www.isitfair.co.uk). Fuel is another cost that is difficult to avoid, except by putting health at risk. About 2.5 million households in England (all ages) are projected to be in fuel poverty in 2007 – that is, spending over 10% of their income on gas and electricity (Hancock et al, 2007). Fuel costs rose over the decade from 1997 to 2007 by 20% above inflation. The rise was dramatic from the beginning of 2004 to the end of 2006, by 67% for gas and 41% for electricity in real terms (FPAG, 2007). Private tenants and low-income homeowners tend to live in less energy-efficient housing (Palmer et al, 2006, p 90), so face particularly steep rises in fuel costs. The Winter Fuel Payment has been frozen at £200 per week for pensioner households since 2000 (£300 for the over-80s). As a result of escalation of Council Tax and utility bills, it has been estimated that pensioners' cost of living for the year up to September 2006 rose by 8.9% (Bootle and Loynes, 2006), while the basic pension was uprated by only the RPI increase of 3.6%. These reports imply that rapidly rising unavoidable costs are eroding pensioners' standard of living year by year, a trend not captured by measured changes in the pensioner poverty rate.

Research on deprivation typically identifies the goods and services deemed necessary by the majority of the public, then asks the subjects of the research how many of these they lack, to construct deprivation scores (see also Chapter Three, this volume). Respondents may also be asked if they cannot afford the items. Despite relatively high deprivation scores, older people do not report the expected degree of hardship (Berthoud et al, 2006). Similarly, qualitative research on vulnerable groups of pensioners shows that they do not recognise the extent of their material disadvantage (Scharf et al, 2006). Several interpretations have been suggested for the mismatch between objective and perceived disadvantage: that low expectations result from having internalised the experience of poverty, for example during wartime scarcity; that pride makes pensioners reluctant to admit they cannot afford items, so they say they do not want them; or that practical and social support from family and neighbours enable an older person to maintain a sense of independence despite difficult circumstances and material deprivation.

Nevertheless, pensioners do express a sense of injustice about the inadequacy of the basic pension, high levels of Council Tax relative to their income, loss of local post offices, banks and transport, and the unfair and intrusive nature of means testing (Scharf et al, 2006). Older people are sensitive to social exclusion, or "social and economic apartheid", as one older woman attending a conference put it. She and her neighbours felt physically and spiritually shut off from the mainstream of city life, with its new jobs, designer shopping, festivals and cafe culture (Young, 2007). The importance of income for the health and well-being of older people is considered next.

Health

Older people have identified health and independence as priorities for giving their life quality, with financial resources seen as necessary to maintain these (Bowling et al, 2001). Socioeconomic disadvantage is associated with poorer health, including depression and decline in cognitive ability (SHARE, 2005). Self-assessed health and mobility were better for older men and women who had a high income, owned their home and had access to a car, after controlling for age group and previous occupational class (Arber and Ginn, 1991, 1993). Health was also better among those who saw their local area positively, in terms of being safe and clean, without problems of drug and alcohol abuse (Ginn and Arber, 2004).

There are two main ways in which low income may threaten health: directly, through an inability to afford a nutritious diet, adequate physical activity and a warm comfortable home, and indirectly, through stress and stress-related behaviours. A good diet and recommended levels of physical activity are both more common among older people living in advantaged economic circumstances (Cooper et al, 1999). A healthy diet for a pensioner has been calculated, in the Minimum Income for Healthy Living study, to cost at least £32 per week, but those in the bottom 40% of the pensioner income distribution spent only £23 per week on average, 30% less than required for a healthy diet, thus risking their health (Morris et al, 2006). Malnutrition, due partly to poverty, affects over 10% of people aged over 65, but is often overlooked (The European Nutrition for Health Alliance, 2006). Exercise can improve strength, flexibility and balance, reducing the risk of falls, while a safe warm home is essential to physical health. Yet these incur costs that may put them out of reach of those in poverty. In qualitative research with older people, a pensioner summed up the role of an adequate income:

> "With income you can do all them things, without it you can do none of them. I mean, somebody mentioned good health and … leisure centres. But to get to a leisure centre you need money. You're in a catch-22 because you need the money to go to the leisure centre to keep fit…." (quoted in Smith, 2001, p 3)

Older people are often reluctant to risk the large fuel bills they fear will result from heating their home adequately (see above). Among those aged over 75, there were an estimated 20,200 excess deaths in England and Wales during the winter of 2005 (December to March), compared with deaths in the same period during non-winter months (ONS, 2006b). The inference that an inadequately heated home was responsible for these deaths seems inescapable.

The indirect effect of poverty and inequality on health is less obvious, yet research has established a link and indicated the mechanisms. Longitudinal research on male civil servants has shown a relationship between ill-health and status anxiety among those low in the occupational pecking order (Marmot and Wilkinson, 1999). These authors argue that low self-esteem and inability to control one's circumstances can generate chronic stress. This has physiological effects harmful to the circulatory system and the immune system. Moreover, inability to afford the standard of living of the rest of society can be damaging to a sense of personal worth, leading to depression and neglect of health. This may explain the link between relative poverty and smoking found by Marsh and McKay (1994) as well as other risky health behaviours such as excessive drinking and over-consumption of junk food. Given the low social visibility of older people and the prevalence of age discrimination, low income can only reinforce an already negative self-image (see also Chapter Eleven, this volume).

A related idea linking income inequality and poor health is that of social capital, a concept which embraces social cohesion, trust, civic engagement and supportive networks in the community. In areas where income is relatively equal, mortality rates are also lower than average (Wilkinson, 1996; Kawachi et al, 1997). Inequality, it is argued, reduces the social capital that individuals need to thrive, increasing chronic stress levels. Better self-assessed health is associated not only with favourable economic circumstances, but also with greater social capital at the individual level (Ginn and Arber, 2004). It may be that material disadvantage has adverse effects on both social capital and health, as argued by Gillies et al (1996). Poverty often prevents older people from leading full and active lives, leading to isolation, depression, illness and dependency (House of Lords, 2005). Thus low income can harm older people's health in several ways. In addition, the source of income and the manner of obtaining it – whether as a pension or through claiming means-tested benefits – are relevant to older people's well-being and sense of dignity.

Means testing: damaging to dignity

Since 2003, means-tested Income Support for pensioners has been named Pension Credit. It consists of Guarantee Credit to top up a lone pensioner's income to £114 per week in 2006 (£174 for a couple) and Savings Credit, a tapered 'reward' for additional income above the basic pension. Pension

Credit has stabilised the pensioner poverty rate, but has brought nearly half of pensioners into means testing, an unprecedented expansion.

This policy, and associated language from politicians and the media, divides the pensioner population into two groups with different implied moral status – those who have been 'responsible' by making sufficient pension provision for themselves, and those who become 'a burden on the state' because they are poor and have to claim Pension Credit. What effect does this moral dichotomy, and the language of 'burden' have on older people's self-image? Whereas pensioners see National Insurance pensions as an entitlement they have earned and can accept with dignity, claiming means-tested benefits is seen as signifying shameful dependency; Pension Credit seems merely the latest version of the Poor Laws of past centuries, in which applying for relief was the ultimate social disgrace. Claiming means-tested benefits is experienced as confusing, intrusive and demeaning – hence the persistent problem of low take-up. A large sum, variously estimated as between £2.5 billion and £4 billion, of means-tested benefits goes unclaimed by pensioners each year. The perception of stigma persists despite the fact that means-tested supplements are only required because British state pensions are 'among the least generous in the developed world' (Pensions Commission, 2004, p 10). It is mainly long-term sick/disabled people and women who need to claim Pension Credit. Their poverty is due to a pension system designed for full-time continuous employment, rather than to any lack of personal responsibility. Indeed, it is women's commitment to their family's needs that has limited their pension building (Ginn, 2003). To the injury of hardship is added the insult, as pensioners see it, of having to parade their poverty to obtain a little extra income. A further drawback of the means test for married and cohabiting older women is joint assessment, so that a partner's income or savings may disqualify the couple from benefits, leaving the woman with little or no income of her own and thereby reinforcing female dependency in marriage (see also Chapter Seven, this volume).

In sum, older people's experience of low income and lack of wealth incurs psychological and health costs as well as limiting participation in society. Means testing, intended to target income at the poorest pensioners, comes at the price of excluding over a third of these because they do not claim, while robbing many of those who do claim of their dignity. Council Tax and utility bills for pensioners are rising faster than their RPI-linked income, reducing their standard of living and entrenching social exclusion.

In the next section, I turn to policy alternatives, questioning whether the current preference for shifting towards a more privatised pension system is necessary or desirable.

A policy challenge

Population ageing is occurring throughout the developed world, an achievement due to public health improvements, family planning and medical advances. In Britain around 1980, men's life expectancy at age 65 was 14 years but by 2000 it was 19 years and is expected to be over 21 years by 2020. Women's life expectancy is about 3.5 years longer than men's and has seen similar increases. Since 1950, the average time in retirement has increased from 18% to 31% of adult life (Pension Commission, 2004). Meanwhile, fertility is below replacement level. A quarter of British women born in 1972 are predicted to be still childless by age 45, compared with 11% of women born in 1943 (FPSC, 2000). The average number of children fell from 2.5 for women born in 1934 to 1.75 for women born in 1990 (projected) (ONS, 2006a). As a result of these changes, the proportion of adults over state pension age is predicted to rise from 27% in 2006 to 48% in 2050. These developments present a challenge for the pension systems of developed societies, but the magnitude of the problem depends on employment rates and productivity as well as age structure. There are alternative policy options, and how societies can best respond is controversial.

Pension policy trend

Since the 1980s a neoliberal ideology has dominated policy in western countries, promoting welfare retrenchment and privatisation of public assets and services. Across the Organisation for Economic Co-operation and Development (OECD), policy makers aim to reduce state Pay-As-You-Go (PAYG) pensions and promote private-funded pensions (mainly personal pensions) to replace them wholly or in part. Chile's pension privatisation of 1981 (now facing serious problems) was held up as a role model for Latin America, while the World Bank's (1994) report advocating similar reforms has been influential. For some central and eastern European countries, pension privatisation after 1989 has been radical (Mueller, 2006) following conditions set by US-dominated international loan agencies. However, in most EU member states reforms to PAYG social insurance schemes have been more gradual, due to resistance from organised labour and pensioners. Reforms have consisted mainly of tightening the requirements for a maximum state pension, reducing the benefit formula and increasing the contribution rate (Queisser, 2006), and have started from a more generous base than in Britain. In the US, Bush's aim to privatise social security has met strong opposition from workers and pensioners.

Britain's pension system was already heavily privatised by 1997, with about 40% of all pension income provided by the private sector. Conservative administrations had reduced state pensions since 1979, using National Insurance funds to pay generous incentives to those leaving the State Second Pension or an occupational pension in favour of a personal pension plan – the notorious mis-selling scandal. This 'funding obsession' (Hill, 2007, p 135) continued under New Labour, who very quickly announced their aim to increase private pension provision from 40% to 60% of the total (DSS, 1998). They claimed state pensions were unsustainable due to population ageing; that reducing their value and expanding private provision would solve this problem; that private pensions would increase national savings and hence economic growth; and that private saving encourages self-reliance and responsibility. All these claims have been challenged by academic analysts, think-tanks, charities, trade unionists and pensioners.

Are British state pensions unsustainable?

Policy measures can improve sustainability of pension schemes. The relevant ratio in assessing scheme viability is the number of pensioners to the number employed. It is estimated that this ratio would be the same in 2030 as in 1999 if 2 million more of the 9 million non-employed working-age individuals were able to find jobs (Catalyst, 2002). Many men and women effectively retire before state pension age (65 for men and 60 for women). Thus at age 62 only half of men are employed and at age 59 only half of women. Reasons for early exit include the decline of heavy industry (especially in the North East), ageism, ill-health, disability and family caring commitments. However, labour market policies introduced since 1997 to increase employment among the over-50s (Taylor, 2002) are proving moderately successful. Among those aged between 50 and state pension age, 73% of men and 68% of women are employed, the highest rates in the EU. At the same time, younger women's employment rate is also rising, helped by better policies on maternity and childcare.

Mullan (2000) points out that the increase in pensioners between 2030 and 2040 will be temporary. Moreover, productivity growth of only 1.75% a year (less than has been the norm) will mean that the average worker produces twice as many goods and services in 2045 as in 2005. Recently, a business-led group has also challenged the doom-laden pension orthodoxy among policy makers, concurring with Mullan that rising productivity will dwarf any effect of an ageing population (Sadler, 2005). Fertility rates are also responsive to social policy (Esping-Andersen, 1999). Cross-national comparison shows fertility is higher in states where: 'the caring activities are better shared between men and women, public caring infrastructure is more developed, part-time jobs are more available and legislation is more family-friendly' (Eurostat, 2001, p 28).

Does shifting to private pensions help?

Most economists agree that any type of pension is ultimately paid from the productive capacity of the working population. As one put it, 'funded and unfunded pensions alike have to be provided out of ... contemporary real resources which pension funding cannot alter' (Crawford, 1997, p 39). If population ageing presents difficulties for state PAYG pensions, there are equivalent problems for private-funded pensions, whether occupational or personal schemes (Toporowski, 2000; Minns, 2001). The truth of this has become increasingly evident, as personal pensions deliver lower annuities than contributors were led to expect for a given fund, while many occupational final salary schemes are in deficit and employers are retreating from this provision. It is only in the public sector that such schemes remain relatively unscathed (for civil servants and NHS staff, for example) but these schemes are not pre-funded. Even before the present crisis in private pensions, their image of reliability was tarnished due to fraud (Maxwell in the 1990s), incompetent management of funds (Equitable Life), mis-sold personal pensions from 1988 to 1993, Enron's collapse in the US, and the risk exemplified by a sinking world stock market from 2000 to 2004. In Latin America, the US-prescribed private pension experiment has failed to live up to claims made by its advocates (Mesa-Lago, 2006). Continuing turbulence in stock markets due to the 2006–08 credit squeeze in banking suggests that uncertainty is here to stay.

To summarise, fears of a 'demographic time bomb' threatening state but not private pensions are misplaced, at least in Britain. Even the government belatedly recognised (in 2002) that private pension saving was not filling the gap created by declining state pensions. Indeed the prospect of means testing affecting 80% of pensioners by 2050 was a disincentive to saving and many private pensions are in financial difficulty. Ministers also acknowledged that the pension system had not worked fairly for women. The Pensions Commission was set up to explore solutions to these problems.

Alternative policies: investing in private pensions or in better state pensions?

The Pensions Commission provided a comprehensive analysis of British pensions, including acknowledging women's long-standing pension disadvantage (Pensions Commission, 2004). It proposed a new scheme of auto-enrolled personal accounts with low charges. Employers would be compelled to contribute 3% of wages for employees opting to stay in the scheme. The basic state pension would be re-linked to average earnings from 2010 and the state pension age gradually raised above 65. For working-age women, state pensions would be more inclusive of carers and the state second pension would shift rapidly to a flat rate structure (Pensions Commission, 2005).

The 2007 Pensions Act broadly accepted the recommendations but delayed earnings-linking the basic pension until 2012 or even 2015. The measures to ensure better inclusion of carers in state pensions in future have been widely welcomed and the idea of personal accounts accepted. However, there is still concern at the extent of pensioner means testing from 2030, with a range of one third to two thirds of pensioners being eligible, as estimated by the independent Pensions Policy Institute (2007). The prospect of means testing on this scale could discourage saving and undermine the success of personal accounts. A major omission from the Act is any improvement for current pensioners. Even if the basic pension is linked to earnings in 2012, the gain will be only £1.40 per week in that year and the value of the pension will have declined to about 14% of average earnings. An estimated 3 million pensioners will have died between 2007 and 2012 without seeing any increase in their basic pension above inflation. Clearly the Act does not aim to reduce poverty, inequality and means testing among current pensioners. While a target has been set to reduce child poverty by half from 1998 to 2010, there is no corresponding target for pensioners.

A wide range of organisations, including some in the private pensions industry who fear that a high level of means testing threatens the viability of personal accounts, have urged the government to raise the basic pension to the level of the Guarantee Credit (about 22% of average wages), to make it more inclusive and to index it to average earnings well before 2012. Some have argued for a citizen's pension at Guarantee Credit level. The Treasury claims none of these proposals is affordable.

Affordability

In 2005, it was estimated that paying a universal pension at the threshold for means testing (£105 per week at the time) would cost £7.3 billion extra in the first year (Churchill and Mitchell, 2005). There is reason to believe such a reform is affordable. First, the increased cost is only a third of the amount spent annually to incentivise saving through private pensions. In 2005 the net cost of tax relief on private pension contributions was £21 billion or 1.8% of GDP (PPI, 2005). Tax relief is highly regressive, with half the benefit received by the top 10% of taxpayers and a quarter by the top 2.5% (Agulnik and Legrand, 1998), mainly men. Second, National Insurance receipts could be increased substantially by abolishing the upper earnings limit on contributions. Third, Government Actuary figures show the National Insurance Fund had a surplus of £38.5 billion in 2007, forecast to rise to £74 billion by 2012, a growing surplus as long as contributions are earnings-related while benefits are only price-indexed. The surplus is used to buy government bonds, providing the Treasury with a cheap source of extra money for general spending. Pensioners argue that the surplus should be used to help pay improved state pensions and other National Insurance benefits. Britain's state pension spending, at about 5% of GDP, is only half the EU average, leaving ample room to spend more without affecting international competitiveness.

Conclusion

Despite a high poverty rate among older people and the evident failures of private pensions – fraud, mismanagement, mis-selling, investment risk and insolvency – the Blair government and the Conservatives (hardly an opposition party) have rejected a substantial improvement in the generosity of state pensions. Instead, yet another new type of personal pension is to be promoted for working-age employees, with the usual tax incentives that disproportionately reward high earners. State pensions will become more inclusive of women in the future but the amounts may be insufficient to prevent poverty without additional private pensions. Since private pensions make no allowance for periods of unpaid caring work, women will continue to be pension-poor, perpetuating their predominance among those who need to claim means-tested benefits in later life. The alternative of a universal basic state pension above poverty level and indexed to national earnings would not only end poverty among older people and free them from the indignity of the means test; it would also ensure that any extra saving during the working life was not rendered futile by means testing.

The weakness of the case for pension privatisation has led some analysts to conclude that a state pension crisis has been socially constructed in order to present a political choice as an economic imperative (Walker, 1990; Vincent, 1999). According to these writers, ideological opposition to public welfare, rather than economic reasons, has motivated welfare retrenchment. 'Arguments for privatisation ... are political arguments for changing the distribution of costs and benefits' (Willmore, 1998, p 2). The choice for policy makers is a political one: whether to promote the transmission of labour market inequalities into retirement, or to embrace redistributive pension policies that ensure a fairer deal in later life for the low paid and for the millions of unpaid family carers on whom our society depends.

Acknowledgements
I am grateful to the Department of Sociology at the University of Surrey for the use of facilities and computer support while writing this chapter.

Summary

- Poverty affects at least one fifth of older people.
- Low income impacts on older people's health, independence and well-being, excluding them from the mainstream of society.
- Lack of financial and material resources reflect gender, class and ethnic inequalities during the working life.
- Older women have a higher risk of poverty than men in later life, due to lower pay and the caring roles that restricted their ability to build good pensions.
- Private pensions are the chief means of transmitting these inequalities into later life.
- New Labour, like the Conservatives, favours the promotion of private pensions while limiting the role of state pensions.
- Means testing will remain widespread in the future.
- The alternative of improving state pensions is both popular and viable.

Questions for discussion

- What are the advantages and disadvantages of relying on means testing to compensate for inadequate state pensions?
- Why do some governments prefer private(-funded) pensions to state (Pay-As-You-Go) pensions?
- Why do many EU states have lower poverty rates for older people than the UK and less gender inequality?

Further reading

Ginn (2003) examines how shifting gender relations interact with evolving pension policy, creating new patterns of poverty and income inequality in later life. The effect of pension privatisation and alternative policies are discussed, with EU comparisons.

Davies, B. et al (2003) *Better pensions: The state's responsibility*, London: Catalyst. This booklet provides a critical analysis of pension policy over the past three decades, making the case for restoring the centrality of state pensions.

Pensions Commission (2004, 2005) analyse trends and challenges for the British pension system, consider alternative reforms and provide policy recommendations.

Electronic resources

Government statistics relevant to pensioners can be found at:

www.statistics.gov.uk
www.dwp.gov.uk/asd/pensioners_income.asp

Independent analysis of alternative pension reforms and accessible information on the changing British pension system can be found in reports and briefings at **www.pensionspolicyinstitute.org.uk**

A wide range of independent information on older people's circumstances is provided by Age Concern (**www.ageconcern.org.uk**) and Help the Aged (**www.helptheaged.org.uk**).

References

Agulnik, P. and Le Grand, J. (1998) 'Tax relief and partnership pensions', *Fiscal Studies*, vol 19, no 4, pp 403-28.

Arber, S. (2004) 'Gender trajectories: how age and marital status influence patterns of gender inequality in later life', in S. Daatland and S. Biggs (eds) *Ageing and diversity: Multiple pathways and cultural migrations*, Bristol: The Policy Press, chapter 5.

Arber, S. and Ginn, J. (1991) *Gender and later life: A sociological analysis of resources and constraints*, London: Sage Publications.

Arber, S. and Ginn, J. (1993) 'Gender and inequalities in health in later life', in M. Stacey and V. Olensen (eds) *Social Science and Medicine*, special issue on 'Women, men and health', vol 36, no 1, pp 33-46.

Arber, S. and Ginn, J. (2004) 'Ageing and gender. Diversity and change', *Social Trends No 34*, London: Office for National Statistics, pp 1-14.

Arber, S., Price, D., Davidson, K. and Perren, K. (2003) 'Re-examining gender and marital status: material wellbeing and social involvement', in S. Arber, K. Davidson and J. Ginn (eds) *Gender and ageing*, Maidenhead: Open University Press, chapter 10.

Berthoud, R., Blekesaune, M. and Hancock, R. (2006) *Are poor pensioners deprived?*, DWP Research Report No 364, London: Corporate Document Services.

Bootle, R. and Loynes, J. (2006) 'What's *your* inflation rate?', *UK Economics Focus*, 30 November, London: Capital Economics.

Bowling, A., Gabriel, Z., Banister, D. and Sutton, S. (2001) 'Older people's views on quality of life', *Growing Older Newsletter*, vol 2, p 2.

Brewer, M., Goodman, A., Shaw, J. and Shephard, A. (2005) *Poverty and inequality in Britain: 2005*, London: Institute for Fiscal Studies.

Catalyst (2002) *The challenge of longer life. Economic burden or social opportunity?*, London: Catalyst.

Churchill, N. (2006) 'Second class citizens in a first-world country?', *Reportage*, April, p 5.

Churchill, N. and Mitchell, M. (2005) *Labour's pension challenge: Building a progressive settlement*, London: Age Concern England.

Cooper, H., Ginn, J. and Arber, S. (1999) *Health-related behaviour and attitudes of older people: Secondary analysis of national datasets*, London: Health Education Authority.

Crawford, M. (1997) 'The big pensions lie', *New Economy*, vol 4, issue 1, Spring.

Dornan, P. (2003) 'Social security policies in 2005', in L. Bauld, K. Clarke and T. Maltby (eds) *Social Policy Review 18: Analysis and debate in social policy 2006*, Bristol: The Policy Press for the Social Policy Association, chapter 5.

DSS (Department of Social Security) (1998) *A new contract for welfare: Partnership in pensions*, Cm 4179, London: The Stationery Office.

DWP (Department for Work and Pensions) (2006) *Pension credit estimates of take-up in 2004/2005*, London: DWP.

DWP (2007) *Economic and Labour Market Review*, vol 1, no 3, March (www. statistics.gov.uk/elmr/).

Esping-Andersen, G. (1999) 'The household economy', in G. Esping-Andersen, *Social foundations of post-industrial economies*, Oxford: Oxford University Press, chapter 4.

European Nutrition for Health Alliance, The (2006) *Malnutrition among older people in the community*, London: ENHA/ILC (www.european-nutrition. org).

Eurostat (2001) *The social situation in the European Union 2001*, Luxembourg: Office for the Official Publication of the European Communities.

Fawcett Society (2007) Personal communication based on analysis of BHPS 2000.

FPAG (Fuel Poverty Advisory Group) (2007) *Fifth annual report 2006*, London: FPAG.

FPSC (Family Policy Studies Centre) (1998) *Families and childcare*, Family Briefing Paper 6, London: FPSC.

Giles, C. and Taylor, A. (2006) 'Gender pay gap vanishes among young', *Financial Times*, 27 October.

Gillies, P., Tolley, K. and Wolstonholme, J. (1996) 'Is AIDS a disease of poverty?', *Aids Care*, vol 8, no 3, pp 351-63.

Ginn, J. (2003) *Gender, pensions and the lifecourse*, Bristol: The Policy Press.

Ginn, J. and Arber, S. (1991) 'Gender, class and income inequalities in later life', *British Journal of Sociology*, vol 42, no 3, pp 369-96.

Ginn, J. and Arber, S. (2000) 'Ethnic inequality in later life: variation in financial circumstances by gender and ethnic group', *Education and Ageing*, vol 15, no 1, pp 65-83.

Ginn, J. and Arber, S. (2002) 'Degrees of freedom: can graduate women avoid the motherhood gap in pensions?', *Sociological Research Online* (www. socresonline.org.uk/7/2/).

Ginn, J. and Arber, S. (2004) 'Gender and the relationship between social capital and health', in A. Morgan and C. Swann (eds) *Social capital for health. Issues of definition, measurement and links to health*, London: Health Development Agency, chapter 8, pp 134-56.

Ginn, J. and Price, D. (2002) 'Do divorced women catch up in pension building?', *Child and Family Law Quarterly*, vol 14, no 2, pp 157-73.

Goodman, A. (2007) 'The progress so far in reducing pensioner poverty', Presentation to Help the Aged conference, September.

Hancock, R., Askham, J., Nelson, H. and Tinker, A. (2007) *Home ownership in later life*, York: Joseph Rowntree Foundation/YPS.

Hill, M. (2007) *Pensions*, Bristol: The Policy Press.

House of Lords (2005) *Ageing: Scientific aspects*, Report of Science and Technology Committee, London: The Stationery Office.

Kawachi, I., Kennedy, B.P., Lochner, K. and Prothrow-Smith, D. (1997) 'Social capital, income inequality and mortality', *American Journal of Public Health*, vol 87, no 9, pp 1491-8.

LRD (Labour Research Department) (2006) 'Why some piggy banks overflow', *Labour Research*, September, pp 19-21.

Marmot, M. and Wilkinson, R. (eds) (1999) *Social determinants of health*, Oxford: Oxford University Press.

Marsh, A. and McKay, S. (1994) *Poor smokers*, London: Policy Studies Institute.

Mesa-Lago, C. (2006) 'Structural reform of social security pensions in Latin America', *International Social Security Review*, vol 54, no 4, pp 67-92.

Minns, R. (2001) *The cold war in welfare: Stock markets versus pensions*, London: Verso.

Morris, J., Dangour, A., Deeming, C., Fletcher, A. and Wilkinson, P. (2006) *Minimum income for healthy living: Older people*, London: Age Concern.

Mueller, K. (2006) 'Perspectives on pensions in Eastern Europe', in H. Pemberton, P. Thane and N. Whiteside (eds) *Britain's pension crisis. History and policy*, Oxford: Oxford University Press/British Academy, chapter 15.

Mullan, P. (2000) *The imaginary time bomb. Why an ageing population is not a social problem*, London: IB Taurus.

ONS (Office for National Statistics) (2004) *Social trends 2003*, London: The Stationery Office.

ONS (2005) *The pensioners' income series 2003/4*, London: The Stationery Office.

ONS (2006a) *Social trends no 36*, London: The Stationery Office.

ONS (2006b) 'Winter mortality' (www.statistics.gov.uk/cci/nugget. asp?id=574).

ONS (2007) 'Population estimates' (www.statistics.gov.uk/cci/nugget.asp?id=6).

Orton, M. (2006) *Struggling to pay council tax. A new perspective on the debate about local taxation*, York: Joseph Rowntree Foundation.

Palmer, G., MacInnes, T. and Kenway, P. (2006) *Monitoring poverty and social exclusion*, York: Joseph Rowntree Foundation.

Parker, H. (ed) (2000) *Low cost but acceptable incomes for older people. A minimum income standard for households aged 65–74 years in the UK*, Bristol: The Policy Press.

Parker, H. (ed) (2002) *Modest but adequate: A reasonable standard of living for people aged 65–74 years*, London: Age Concern England.

Pensions Commission (2004) *Pensions: Challenges and choices*, London: The Stationery Office.

Pensions Commission (2005) *A new pension settlement for the twenty-first century*, London: The Stationery Office.

PPI (Pensions Policy Institute) (2005) *Facts on pensions*, London: PPI.

PPI (2007) *Incentives to save and means-tested benefits*, London: PPI.

Queisser, M. (2006) 'Pension reforms: towards a new system of retirement?', Paper presented at the 'Situation of Ageing Persons' Conference, Social, Health and Family Affairs Committee of the Parliamentary Assembly of the Council of Europe, Paris, 13 September.

Rowlingson, K., Whyley, C. and Warren, T. (1999) *Wealth in Britain: A lifecycle perspective*, London: Policy Studies Institute.

Sadler, P. (2005) *The ageing population, pensions and wealth creation*, London: Tomorrow's Company.

Scharf, T., Bartlam, B., Hislop, J., Bernard, M., Dunning, A. and Sim, J. (2006) *Necessities of life. Older people's experiences of poverty*, London: Keele University Centre for Social Gerontology/Help the Aged.

SHARE (Survey of Health, Ageing and Retirement in Europe) (2005) www. share-project.org

Smith, A. (2001) 'Defining quality of life', *Growing Older Newsletter*, vol 2, p 3.

Taylor, P. (2002) *New policies for older workers*, Bristol: The Policy Press.

Toporowski, J. (2000) *The end of finance*, London: Routledge.

Vincent, J. (1999) *Politics, power and old age*, Buckingham: Open University Press.

Walker, A. (1990) 'The economic "burden" of ageing and the prospect of intergenerational conflict', *Ageing and Society*, vol 10, pp 377-96.

Wilkinson, R. (1996) *Unhealthy societies: The afflictions of inequality*, London: Routledge.

Willmore, L. (1998) *Social security and the provision of retirement income*, Pensions Institute Discussion Paper No PI-9805, London: Pensions Institute (http://papers.ssrn.com/sol3/papers.cfm?abstract_id=93824).

World Bank (1994) *Averting the old age crisis*, New York: Oxford University Press.

Young, A. (2007) 'A paucity of ideas for how to tackle poverty', *The Herald*, Glasgow, Features, 23 February.

eleven

Health and disability

Mary Shaw, Ben Wheeler, Richard Mitchell and Danny Dorling

Overview

- Poverty, inequality and poor health have a long and closely entwined relationship in British history.
- Despite marked and continued overall improvements in life expectancy we can still observe health inequalities such that income and wealth have a marked influence on life and death.
- A range of data sources show evidence of social and geographical inequalities in Britain in terms of mortality, morbidity and disability.
- Health inequalities can be explained by a combination of materialist, lifestyle and psychosocial factors operating over the lifecourse. The relative importance of these factors is disputed.
- Inequalities in health are further entrenched when there are inequities in the provision of healthcare.
- Policies that reduce poverty and inequality are key to tackling health inequalities. Social security policies have a vital role to play in ensuring adequate income levels.

Key concepts

inequality; inequity; lifecourse; morbidity; disability; health

Introduction

The intimate and inextricable connection between poverty, inequality, wealth and health – that people experiencing poverty are more likely to suffer sickness and to die young, whereas the wealthy are more likely to enjoy good health and longevity – is a theme that can be traced throughout British history. Across the 19th and 20th centuries, despite the economic, political and technological transformation of society, authors documented evidence of this relationship between poverty and ill-health with notable consistency (see Davey Smith et al, 2001). Again and again the difficult living conditions of people in poverty were described and the impact on their health observed; the better life chances of the rich on the other hand were duly noted but rarely scrutinised.

In 1833 the Factory Inquiry Commission Report presented information on the working conditions of children in factories (see ***Box 11.1***). Legislation in that year prohibited the employment in mills of children under the age of nine; those under 18 could not work more than 12 hours a day. In 1845 Engels published *The condition of the working class in England*, in which he documented and discussed the health consequences of capitalist industrialisation and urbanisation. In all areas of life the working class systematically faced the most treacherous conditions, or in Engels' words 'The workers get what is too bad for the property owning class' (cited in Davey Smith et al, 2001, p 61) – living in dank overcrowded cellars, wearing worn-out clothes of the poorest quality, only able to buy the rancid and half-decayed food left over at market. For Engels this amounted to 'social murder' – 'when society places hundreds of proletarians in such a position that they inevitably meet a too early and an unnatural death' (cited in Davey Smith et al, 2001, p 67).

> ## Box 11.1: An extract from the Factory Inquiry Commission Report
>
> That this excessive fatigue, privation of sleep, pain in various parts of the body, and swelling of the feet experienced by the young workers, coupled with the constant standing, the peculiar attitudes of the body, and the peculiar motions of the limbs required in the labour of the factory, together with the elevated temperature, and the impure atmosphere in which that labour is often carried on, do sometimes ultimately terminate in the production of serious, permanent, and incurable disease, appears to us to be established. From cases detailed in the evidence, and the accuracy of which has been strictly investigated, we do not conceive it to be possible to arrive at any other conclusion. The evidence, especially from Dundee and Glasgow, from Leicester, Nottingham, Leeds, and Bradford, from Manchester and Stockport, in a word, from all the great manufacturing

towns, with the exception, perhaps, of those in the western district, in which there is little indication of disease produced by early and excessive labour, shows that grievous and incurable maladies do result in young persons from labour commenced in the factory at the age at which it is at present not uncommon to begin it, and continued for the number of hours during which it is not unusual to protract it.

Source: Davey Smith et al (2001, p 28)

In the 20th century, while absolute living standards had generally improved, scholars, reformers and campaigners continued to present the realities of living in conditions of dire poverty to the public. In 1913 Maud Pember Reeves published *Round about a pound a week*, which described how working-class women cooked, washed, cleaned and scrimped to feed a family and how they coped with cold, damp, vermin and sickness (see Davey Smith et al, 2001). After the First World War and on the eve of another, in 1939 Margery Spring Rice also documented the lives of *Working class wives*, revealing a picture in which 'monotony, loneliness, discouragement and sordid hard work are the main features' (Davey Smith et al, 2001, p 216) and 'Happiness, like health, can suffer an almost unperceived lowering of standard, which results in a pathetic gratitude for what might be called negative mercies, the respite for an hour a day, for instance, from the labouriousness of the other eleven, twelve or thirteen' (Davey Smith et al, 2001, pp 216-17).

Undoubtedly, living conditions have improved substantially over the past two centuries (see Chapters Two and Six, this volume) and death rates have declined accordingly. *Figure 11.1* shows life expectancy in the UK for males and females across the 20th century, increasing some 30 years over this period and with improvements continuing to the present time.

Continued inequalities

Despite overall improvements in life expectancy we can still observe health inequalities such that income and wealth have a marked influence on life and death. (For the definitions of 'inequality' and 'inequity' see *Box 11.2*.)

Figure 11.1: *Improved life expectancy over the 20th century, males and females, UK*

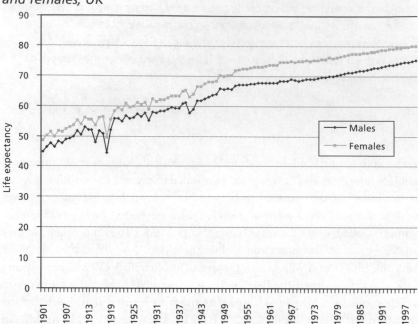

Source: Government Actuaries Department (drawn by the authors)

Box 11.2: Defining inequality and inequity

Inequality is said to exist when there is a difference in the distribution of a resource (such as income) or outcome (such as mortality or educational achievement) across groups of people or places (for example, by socioeconomic group, by gender or by age group) (Shaw et al, 2007).

Inequity and **equity** refer to how *fairly* services, opportunities and access are distributed across groups of people or places, according to the need of those groups. Inequities are said to occur when services do not reflect health needs (Shaw et al, 2007).

One traditional method of looking at the 'health' of a population and to analyse inequalities is to look at mortality. Recent figures on UK life expectancy show that inequalities in mortality persist and even continue to widen. Figures for local authorities for 2003–05 showed the highest life expectancy to be 82.2 years for men and 86.2 for women, in Kensington and Chelsea, one of the wealthiest parts of the country. The lowest figures were found in Glasgow, at 69.9 years for men (12.3 years lower than the highest figures) and 76.7 for women (a difference of 9.5 years) (National Statistics, 2006). These figures demonstrate the very substantial differences in death rates across different parts of the UK. Referring to figures for previous years tends also to show the gap to be widening; life expectancy increases everywhere, but it increases most in those areas where it is already highest (Dorling et al, 2005).

Looking instead at morbidity – illness – ***Figure 11.2*** shows some results from the Whitehall II Study, a longitudinal survey of white-collar civil servants in London. This demonstrates a strong trend of decreasing prevalence of self-reported poor health with increasing household income, for both men and women. It is interesting to note here that there is no obvious attenuation of the trend in the very high-income groups. Even the group with an average household income of £80,000 tend to fare worse than those in the highest income bracket. At the other end of the income scale there has been research into the minimum income required to keep a person in good health (see ***Box 11.3***.)

Figure 11.2: *Age-adjusted prevalence (%) of poor self-rated health in the Whitehall II Study by household income band (1997–99)*

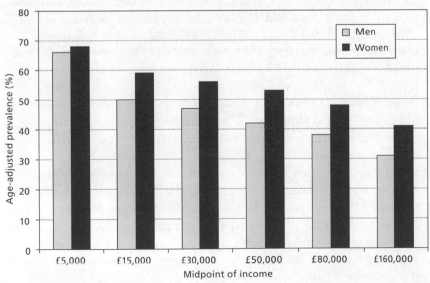

Source: Adapted from Martikainen et al (2003)

Box 11.3: A minimum income for healthy living?

In the early 1930s, the British Medical Association (BMA) appointed a committee:

> To determine the minimum weekly expenditure on foodstuffs which must be incurred by families of varying size, if health and working capacity are to be maintained, and to construct specimen diets. (Hannington, 1937, p 198)

The report from the BMA committee found that the majority of unemployed people, and a reasonable proportion of the employed population, earned an income below this minimum expenditure. This was reflected in John Boyd Orr's studies around the same time, which concluded that a healthy diet could only be achieved with an income level above that of half of the population (Boyd Orr, 1936).

A more recent study, inspired by the introduction of a national minimum wage (and the lack of any health input in setting its level), attempted a more comprehensive assessment of the minimum income required for healthy life in the UK (Morris et al, 2000). This assessment considered not only the costs of material sustenance such as nutrition and housing, but also the expense of 'psychosocial' goods necessary for health and well-being, such as participation in social networks beyond the immediate family and telephone bills. In 1999 prices, the estimated minimum income (defined for a single young man) was £132 per week. This was compared to the wage that would be earned for a 38-hour working week at the minimum wage of £105 to £121 per week, or basic level social security payments of between £40 and £51 per week. Sixty or seventy years on, the findings were not so different to those of Boyd Orr and the BMA committee.

Morris et al's figures have been updated with some allowances for inefficiencies, and were found to indicate that a single healthy man working a standard full-time week (37.5 hours) would, if aged 18–21, still have an income approximately £20 per week less than the minimum required for healthy living. A man aged 22–24 would fare somewhat better, with weekly income around the minimum, while a man aged 25–30 and qualifying for working tax credits would exceed the minimum by £11 per week (Deeming, 2005).

The census provides a useful source of information on the nature and extent of inequalities in morbidity in the UK, especially given that it covers the vast majority of the population. In 2001, two questions were asked of each person about their health. The first asked the person to rate their general health over the previous 12 months as 'good', 'fairly good' or 'not good'. The second asked whether the person had a long-term illness, health problem or disability that limits daily activities or work (a 'limiting long-term illness', or LLTI). ***Table 11.1*** shows the prevalence of LLTI for all people aged 16–74 by their National Statistics Socioeconomic Classification (NS–SEC, the occupational measure of socioeconomic classification that has replaced the Registrar General's Social Class). The table clearly shows increasing prevalence of long-term illness with decreasing socioeconomic position as measured by NS–SEC (these are crude rates; age-standardisation makes very little difference to the pattern; see National Statistics, 2006). The prevalence of LLTI among people in higher managerial and professional occupations is around 6%; among those in routine occupations it is around 15%. The prevalence rates among those who have never worked and long-term unemployed people are even higher (although this is somewhat circular given that some people will have never worked or stopped working because of LLTIs).

Table 11.1: *Limiting long-term illness prevalence (%) by National Statistics Socioeconomic Classification (NS-SEC), Census 2001, England and Wales, all people aged 16–74.*

NS-SEC group	% with LLTI
Higher managerial and professional occupations: large employers and higher managerial occupations	6.3
Higher managerial and professional occupations: higher professional occupations	6.3
Lower managerial and professional occupations	8.3
Intermediate occupations	8.8
Small employers and own account workers	12.5
Lower supervisory and technical occupations	11.5
Semi-routine occupations	12.3
Routine occupations	14.6
Never worked	39.9
Long-term unemployed	21.3
Full-time students	5.5
Not classifiable for other reasons	47.0
ALL	17.5

Source: 2001 Census, commissioned table M194.

Measuring morbidity

There are many ways of measuring morbidity in a population. This can include looking at the prevalence rates of individual conditions that have been clinically diagnosed, such as diabetes. For some diseases, such as cancer, there are disease registers (see *Box 11.4*) that are useful tools for monitoring disease trends and analysing patterns or morbidity. The advantage of using data based on clinical diagnosis in this way is that it brings a high level of validity; 'doctor diagnosis' is considered to be the 'gold standard' of health status measurement.

Box 11.4: Four characteristics of disease registers

1. Registers are based on people not events.
2. People registered have a feature in common.
3. Information held about these people is updated in a defined and systematic manner.
4. The register is based on a geographically defined population.

Source: Donaldson (1992), cited in Newton and Garner (2002)

Indirect measures of health status, such as number of consultations with a general practitioner (GP) or use of hospital services, can also be used to analyse patterns of morbidity, although in these cases it is often the case that ecological rather than individual-level analyses have to be performed. For instance the relationship with area-level deprivation is often the focus of research as data on individual socioeconomic circumstances is often either of poor quality or absent from health services data.

The data presented above in *Figure 11.2* from the Whitehall II Study (a longitudinal survey) and in *Table 11.1* from the 2001 Census (a survey of the whole population) are both based on self-rated measures of health whereby respondents are asked to give an overall assessment of their health in a single item. Versions of this have been used in surveys worldwide (Bowling, 2005). Although a single, and simple, question, with generally three or four response categories, this has been shown to be significantly and independently associated with specific health problems and the use of health services (Bowling, 2005). Self-rated health has also been shown to be closely associated with mortality.

Figure 11.3 illustrates the potentially high value and validity of morbidity measures, since they can be very strongly related to objective measures of poor health, in this case death rates (expressed as life expectancy at birth). Local authorities with high LLTI prevalence tend to have lower life expectancy rates, and the association between the two is strong and linear. The LLTI

Figure 11.3: *The association between the prevalence of LLTI in 2001 and life expectancy at birth 1999–2001 across Britain's 406 local authorities*

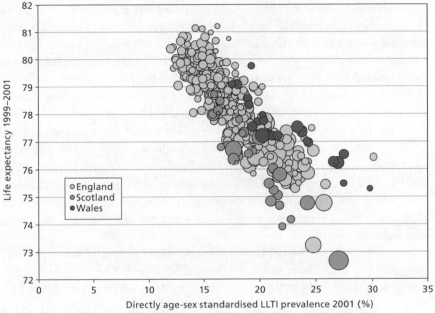

Note: Each local authority is represented by a circle with area proportional to population (the largest circles are the local authorities with the largest populations).

Sources: 2001 Census (LLTI, Standard Tables 16 and 65); National Statistics (2004)

prevalence measure was calculated from data output from the 2001 Census, and is standardised to account for varying age/sex population mix across different local authority areas. Life expectancy figures are calculated by National Statistics based on mortality data from death certificates. Both measures are therefore derived from almost 100% count data (as opposed to survey samples), and are extremely reliable indicators. The close match between the two (correlation coefficient $-0.83, p < 0.001$) also supports the validity of self-reported morbidity measures, since census data are derived from self-completed questionnaires.

Self-rated health measures such as these may not be clinically validated (although many who rate their health as poor will have formal diagnoses; similarly many people with a GP's diagnosis may not consider their health to be poor) but instead it is arguably a better reflection of people's own subjective assessment of their health status. 'Health', as Blaxter (2004) has so eloquently discussed, is a slippery and complicated concept with multiple meanings.

Disability and poverty

Another approach to considering the distribution of health within a population is to look at disability, and its consequences, more specifically. As with morbidity, many different measures have been used, and there is a certain amount of overlap with chronic illness. The Health Survey for England is one source of data on the prevalence of disability. Its questions cover limitations in functional activities (seeing, hearing, communication, walking and using stairs) and in activities of daily living: getting in and out of bed or a chair, dressing, washing, eating and going to the toilet. The prevalence of disability from this survey, by age group, is shown in *Table 11.2*. From this we can see that the prevalence of disability increases with age, with almost a quarter of the population experiencing moderate or severe disability by the age of 55–64, and a third of men and 42% of women aged 85 and over experiencing severe disability. Disability is not the preserve of the old, however, nor is it an inevitable consequence of ageing – over a quarter of those aged 85 report no disability.

Disabled people are more likely than non-disabled people to live in poverty; disability can be a cause and consequence of poverty. The poverty rate for adults with disabilities is 30%, twice that for adults without a disability. The main reason for this is worklessness (Palmer et al, 2006), although it is the level at which social security benefits are set that determines whether worklessness results in poverty. Not only are the incomes of people with disabilities lower, but their living costs are higher, further compounding their difficulties. Recent

Table 11.2: *Prevalence of disability (%) in the Health Survey for England, 2001*

AGE	16–24	25–34	35–44	45–54	55–64	65–74	75–84	85+	TOTAL
Men									
No disability	96	95	92	86	75	66	57	28	83
Moderate disability	3	4	6	11	18	25	39	39	13
Serious disability	1	1	2	3	7	9	14	33	5
Women									
No disability	95	94	91	86	77	68	49	27	82
Moderate disability	4	5	7	11	17	23	32	32	13
Serious disability	1	1	2	3	6	9	19	42	5

Source: Health Survey for England, 2001

research conducted for the Joseph Rowntree Foundation has highlighted the additional costs of living that people with disabilities face in order to meet their needs (Smith et al, 2004). This research looked at what people with disabilities need in order to achieve a 'level playing field' with people without disabilities and constructed the disabled person's budget standard totals. This included major expenditure on equipment essential for independence as well as ongoing higher expenses for items such as food, clothing, utilities and recreation. The disabled person's budget standard totals were compared to maximum benefit levels and it was found that even if receiving these maximum benefit levels people with disabilities still face a substantial shortfall in income – approximately £200 a week less than the weekly amount required for them to ensure a minimum standard of living. Policies that define the levels of benefits are again highlighted as being crucial in determining whether people with disabilities live in poverty.

Disability, and the poverty that is often associated with it, also has an impact on children. *Table 11.3* shows child poverty rates for different forms of household composition. These figures show that a family that contains a child or adult with a disability has a higher chance of being in poverty, and if there is both a child *and* an adult with a disability, then poverty is even more likely. However, these figures have been coming into line with the rate for all children in recent years – although this is still markedly high at over

Table 11.3: *Trends in child poverty rates, by household composition*

	Children in households					
	All children	No disabled adult	One or more disabled adults	No disabled child	One or more disabled children	Disabled adult and disabled child
1999/00*	32	29	45	31	40	50
2000/01	30	28	43	30	36	39$
2001/02	30	27	43	29	35	46
2002/03	28	26	39	28	31	40
2003/04	28	26	38	27	31	36
Composition of child population	100	83	17	90	10	4

Notes: * Figures exclude the self-employed.

$ This figure is out of line with the trend and may reflect sampling or clerical error in the series.

Source: CPAG Poverty magazine, Issue 123

a quarter (28%). For the most recent period for which data are currently available (2004/05) the percentage of all children living in poverty was 27% (Palmer et al, 2006).

As with mortality, geographical inequalities in the distribution of disability can be observed across the country. The map in ***Figure 11.4*** shows the substantial geographical variations in the proportion of the working-age population claiming Incapacity Benefit. It highlights that while much of southern England has social security claimant rates below 5%, these rates increase to the north and west of Britain. The highest rates are found in the

Figure 11.4: *Proportion of the working-age population claiming Incapacity Benefit, Britain (August 2005)*

% working age population claiming IB
- <5.0
- 5.1 - 7.5
- 7.6 - 10.0
- 10.1 - 15.0
- 15.1 - 33.7

Note: The areas mapped here are tracts, each of which is approximately half a parliamentary constituency; the tracts therefore have very similar populations. The map on the right shows the same information as that on the left, but is a cartogram – it affords each tract the same area on the map, and is a fairer representation of the data.

Source: Department for Work and Pensions Longitudinal Study

deindustrialised cities of the north and Midlands, the valleys of south Wales, and in and around Glasgow.

Recent government policy, as outlined in the welfare reform Green Paper (DWP, 2006), aims to actively encourage and support people with disabilities to find work, reflecting the fact that many people with disabilities are keen to work. However, the proposals have been criticised for the reduction in the value of benefits that will be incurred if people do not engage in work-related activities. Furthermore, work is not necessarily a route out of poverty. The research conducted by Smith and colleagues (2004) described above found that people with low to medium-level needs would need to receive the national average wage before their costs would be covered (and this is without taking into account any costs for personal assistance).

Health and wealth

Health inequalities have usually been studied with people experiencing poverty and deprivation as the groups of interest. In order to truly understand these inequalities, it is perhaps important to also understand the life circumstances and health experiences of those at the wealthy end of the socioeconomic spectrum. Deprivation indices and measures of poverty, such as the Townsend and Breadline Britain indices (see Shaw et al, 2007), have frequently been used to help us understand the nature of health inequalities. However, they are explicitly indices of poverty or deprivation, and those areas or populations at the 'least deprived' ends of the scales are just that; they cannot necessarily be said to be affluent or wealthy. The dearth of studies of wealth and health has been highlighted only recently, along with the recognition that good-quality wealth data is not easily available (Baum, 2005). This lack of wealth data should begin to be rectified with the advent of the National Statistics Wealth and Assets Survey, which began in mid-2006, which should give some insight into the details of wealth held in the UK and could prove useful in investigating associations between wealth and health. Work has also been carried out to calculate small-area wealth estimates, using a methodology and theoretical basis similar to the Breadline Britain poverty indices (Dorling et al, 2007).

The health circumstances of the affluent have rarely been commented on, other than to describe their advantage. In one discussion of a report on variation in cancer survival rates across the UK, one of the authors commented that:

> Your chances depend on the area in which you live, and if the survival rates of all patients were as good as those achieved in affluent areas we would avoid many deaths. (Michael Coleman, quoted in Anderson, 1999, p 1163)

There is little or no research that has specifically set out to investigate the mechanisms for better health among the wealthy. However, it is apparent in conceiving wealth as the opposite of poverty that similar mechanisms are likely to be involved. Where poverty implies a lack of resources to participate in material and social norms, wealth implies sufficient resources to exceed those norms. Affluence is likely to bring secure access to material necessities – healthy food, high-quality housing, a relatively clean and spacious environment in which to live – and luxuries. It can also mean that the time and money required to participate in social networks and cultural experiences are not barriers. With wealth can also come the option to actually exclude oneself from societal norms, such as waiting on a list for health services. These clear advantages that are likely to accompany wealth are all potentially associated with improved health and well-being.

What explains inequalities in health?

In advanced industrialised societies such as the UK – where poverty is a relative rather than an absolute condition and the National Health Service (NHS) provides healthcare free at the point of access – we might reasonably ask the question: why, and how, does poverty still lead to poor health? Indeed, why is it that even at the high end of the income scale we see an association such that higher income is related to better health (see *Figure 11.2* above)? It is not just that poverty is related to the worst outcomes, but that inequalities in health can be observed across the entire social spectrum. Various explanations have been put forward and their relative importance is actively debated (for a full discussion, see Bartley, 2004).

One of the explanatory factors is the **materialist** position, where it is argued that it is the material circumstances of living and working conditions that are vital in determining health outcomes. This includes factors such as the quality of housing and the safety of working conditions. Looking at the specific conditions and causes of death that can be attributed to the material environment, these have been estimated to account for about a quarter of all deaths (Bartley, 2004).

An alternative position is that it is not material conditions that lead directly to health inequalities but the different **lifestyle** choices made by people that are the key determining factor. The social class gradient in smoking is often cited as support for this position, as well as participation in leisure-time exercise and diets high in salt, fat and sugar. While this explanation is often seen as blaming the individual, an alternative stance emphasises the constrained choices that face many people living in difficult circumstances and the cultural identities associated with various patterns of consumption.

A more recent strand of explanation relates to **psychosocial** factors that lie at the interface of the social and the psychological, such as control at work, autonomy, social support, depression and social capital (Shaw et al, 2007). Here the focus is on 'how feelings that arise because of inequality, domination or subordination may directly affect biological processes' (Bartley, 2004, p 80). Control over work, effort–reward imbalance, social support, position in the status hierarchy and 'stress' more generally are all areas which are receiving attention as possible explanations for health inequalities.

Epidemiological studies often focus on one set of explanatory factors and use statistical techniques to 'control' for a range of other confounding factors, using the logic of 'all other things being equal', for example, looking at the relationship between income and mortality controlling for smoking behaviour as if it did not vary by income. While necessary in an analytical sense, this approach encourages a particularist and inaccurate way of thinking about the social world. In reality, of course, these three explanatory factors outlined above, which are so often seen as competing against one another, are clustered together, such that, for example, people with low incomes tend to work in more dangerous jobs, are more likely to smoke and have lower levels of control over their work. These factors compound each other and accumulate over time. The **lifecourse** perspective focuses on this issue of the accumulation of disadvantage through life, rather than taking a cross-sectional, snapshot view at one point in time, and provides a way of bringing a range of explanatory factors together conceptually (see *Figure 11.5*). Far less attention has been paid to the accumulation of *advantage*, however.

Figure 11.5: *Various indicators of socioeconomic position (SEP) combined in a lifecourse framework*

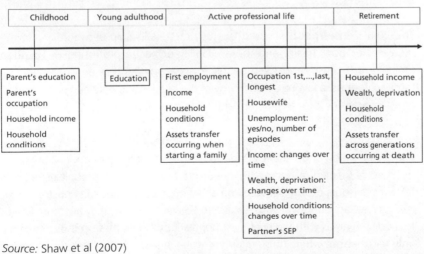

Source: Shaw et al (2007)

What of **healthcare**? The provision of healthcare for all that is free at the point of use through the NHS has done nothing to reduce health inequality, contrary to initial expectations at the time of the inception of the NHS (Bartley, 2004). It has been suggested that health inequalities have persisted because by the time people come to use health services their disease is already established and the effects of living conditions and lifestyle have taken their toll. This is not to say that healthcare is ineffective, rather that it is not able to redress the socioeconomic distribution of poor health. Moreover, there is evidence that although everyone in the population has access to healthcare in theory, in practice there are issues of equity in achieving that access, which may in fact further compound existing inequalities.

Inequalities in health and the NHS

Julian Tudor Hart proposed the inverse care law in 1971. The law states that those most in need of healthcare are least likely to receive it; that those with the best health status tend to receive the highest quality healthcare; and that the law is most evident where healthcare provision is subject to the greatest market forces (Tudor Hart, 1971). The inequities in the provision of health services have been incompatible with the central tenets of the UK NHS since its inception in 1948, but continue to the present day (see **Box 11.5**; Shaw and Dorling, 2004; Guthrie et al, 2006).

If provision of adequate and appropriate healthcare is one mechanism by which inequalities in health may be explained and addressed, then the inequities described by the inverse care law would need to be reversed.

> **Box 11.5:** Using the 2001 Census to investigate healthcare supply and demand
>
> The 2001 Census has been used to study the relationship between area-level measures of poor health and the availability of health professionals. For the first time, this census also asked people to state whether they provided care for family or friends, allowing similar study of the relationship between poor health and the provision of informal, unpaid care (Shaw and Dorling, 2004; Wheeler et al, 2005).
>
> The graphs below show the relationship between a measure of poor health and measures of (a) medical doctors; (b) dental practitioners; and (c) people providing 50 or more hours of care per week on an informal basis. These demonstrate the inverse care law operating with respect to GPs and dentists; they are more likely to live in the areas with the healthiest populations. While these census data not only tell us about where these health practitioners live, rather than where they

practise, the geographical patterns are nationwide rather than local (that is, they cannot be simply explained by health professionals commuting from 'healthy' to 'unhealthy' areas to work).

The relationship between three measures of healthcare provision (GPs, dentists and informal/unpaid care) and the proportion of the population with both LLTI and poor health in the previous 12 months

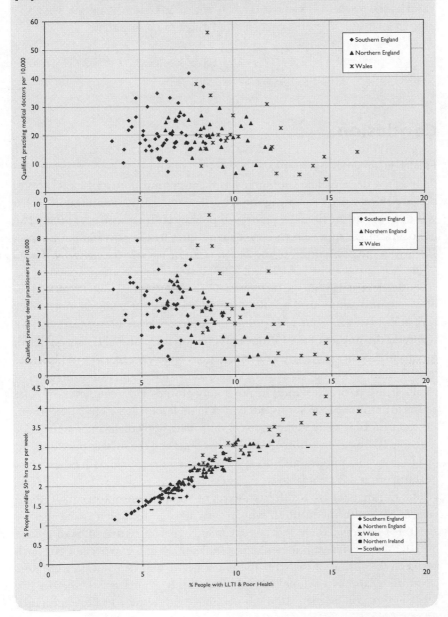

Conversely, the relationship between poor health and the provision of informal care demonstrates an extremely strong positive relationship; care is provided in almost direct proportion to need (making the reasonable assumption that the poor health measure is a good proxy of need).

Notes: Data are from the 2001 Census, and are for counties, unitary authorities and former metropolitan authorities of England and Wales, Scottish council areas and Northern Ireland as a whole. Data on medical professionals are only available for England and Wales, hence the limited extent of those graphs.

Source: Adapted from Wheeler et al (2005)

Conclusion

Health inequalities have received a varying amount of policy attention over the past few decades. The Labour government-commissioned Black Report of the late 1970s was effectively ignored by the Conservative administration that was in power by the time the report was published (Townsend et al, 1988). The next substantive approach to health inequalities by the government came in 1998 with the publication of the *Independent Inquiry into Inequalities in Health* ('The Acheson Report') (Acheson, 1998) that had been commissioned by the recently elected Labour government. This comprised an extensive analysis of health inequalities in the UK, along with a series of wide-ranging policy recommendations, from advocating the promotion of breast feeding to a review of the impact of the European Common Agricultural Policy on health inequalities. Some of these recommendations were very specific and have fed directly into public health activities, such as the requirement for directors of public health to produce local health equity profiles and to undertake regular audits to monitor progress towards equity in their local areas. However, others, although laudable, were vague and very difficult to implement and monitor (for example, Recommendation 14 was 'We recommend the further development of a high-quality public transport system which is integrated with other forms of transport and is affordable to the user').

The Department of Health has a series of Public Service Agreement (PSA) targets on health inequalities, which currently are supposed to be met by 2010. For example, there is a target for life expectancy that aims to reduce by 10% 'the relative gap (ie percentage difference) in life expectancy at birth between the fifth of areas with the worst health and deprivation indicators ... and England as a whole' (DH, 2006, p 3). It is unclear whether or not these targets will be met, although certainly with respect to life expectancy this seems unlikely (see our previous discussion of life expectancy figures). Moreover, as an *inequality* target, this does not really pass muster, as it does not relate to the entire social spectrum.

Aside from these specific health inequalities policies, more general poverty and related social policies could have a substantial impact on public health and inequality. The evidence presented here connecting poverty and poor health outcomes shows the fundamental and urgent need for policies that tackle poverty and low income. For example, the government's target of eliminating child poverty by 2020, if achieved, would potentially impact on the entire lifecourse of health risks and outcomes for children. Current policy, however, focuses on improving low incomes almost entirely through paid work, an approach that does nothing to improve the incomes of those who cannot work, such as some people with disabilities. Moreover, the level at which benefits are set may not be adequate to maintain healthy living (as outlined in ***Box 11.3***). It may not be as fashionable (or as cheap) as focusing on building social capital or sending in teams of health trainers to a few selected deprived areas, but social security policy has a vital role to play in tackling poverty and low incomes and thereby addressing inequalities in health.

Summary

- Poverty, inequality and poor health have a long and closely entwined relationship in British history.
- Despite marked and continued overall improvements in life expectancy we can still observe health inequalities such that income and wealth have a marked influence on life and death.
- A range of data sources show evidence of social and geographical inequalities in Britain in terms of mortality, morbidity and disability.
- Health inequalities can be explained by a combination of materialist, lifestyle and psychosocial factors operating over the lifecourse. The relative importance of these factors is disputed.
- Inequalities in health are further entrenched when there are inequities in the provision of healthcare.
- Policies that reduce poverty and inequality are key to tackling health inequalities. Social security policies have a vital role to play in ensuring adequate income levels.

Questions for discussion

- What is the relationship between poverty, wealth and health outcomes?
- Will the government reach its goal of eradicating child poverty by 2020?
- What policies could be instigated to attempt to reverse the inverse care law?

Further reading

See Bartley (2004) for a broad introduction to the theories, concepts and methods involved in researching health inequality.

Davey Smith et al (2001) is a historical overview of original sources on poverty, inequality and health in Britain.

Shaw, M., Davey Smith, G. and Dorling, D. (2005) 'Health inequalities and New Labour: how the promises compare with real progress', *BMJ*, vol 330, pp 1016-21 is a more recent exploration of the Labour government's progress to date in tackling health inequalities.

Tudor Hart, J. (2006) *The political economy of health care: A clinical perspective*, Bristol: The Policy Press. This is a passionate analysis of the historical development, current state and potential future shape of the National Health Service.

Electronic resources

Community health profiles: **www.communityhealthprofiles.info/**

2006 government report on tackling health inequalities: *Health challenge England – next steps for choosing health:* **www.dh.gov.uk/en/Publicationsandstatistics/ Publications/PublicationsPolicyAndGuidance/DH_4139514**

Health Poverty Index Visualisation Tool: **www.hpi.org.uk/**

References

Acheson, D. (1998) *Independent inquiry into inequalities in health*, London: The Stationery Office.

Anderson, P. (1999) 'Study demonstrates link between cancer survival and wealth', *BMJ*, vol 318, p 1163.

Bartley, M. (2004) *Health inequality: An introduction to theories, concepts and methods*, Cambridge: Polity Press.

Baum, F. (2005) 'Wealth and health: the need for more strategic public health research', *Journal of Epidemiology and Public Health*, vol 59, pp 542-5.

Blaxter, M. (2004) *Health*, Cambridge: Polity Press.

Bowling, A. (2005) 'Techniques of questionnaire design', in A. Bowling and S. Ebrahim (eds) *Handbook of health research methods: Investigation, measurement and analysis*, Maidenhead: Open University Press.

Boyd Orr, J. (1936) *Food, health and income*, Extract reprinted in Davey Smith et al (2001).

Davey Smith, G., Dorling, D. and Shaw, M. (2001) *Poverty, inequality and health in Britain: 1800–2000: A reader*, Bristol: The Policy Press.

Deeming, C. (2005) 'Keeping healthy on a minimum wage: Is not easy in the United Kingdom', *BMJ*, vol 331, pp 857.

DH (Department of Health) (2006) *Health inequalities* (www.dh.gov.uk/healthinequalities, accessed 11/12/06).

Donaldson, L. (1992) 'Registering a need', *BMJ*, vol 305, pp 587-8.

Dorling, D., Mitchell, R., Orford, S., Shaw, M. and Davey Smith, G. (2005) 'Inequalities and Christmas yet to come', *BMJ*, vol 331, p 1409.

Dorling, D., Rigby, J., Wheeler, B., Ballas, D., Thomas, B., Fahmy, E., Gordon, D. and Lupton, R. (2007) *Poverty, wealth and place in Britain 1968 to 2005: Understanding the transformation of the prospects of places*, York: Joseph Rowntree Foundation.

DWP (Department for Work and Pensions) (2006) *A new deal for welfare: Empowering people to work*, June, Cm 6730, London: DWP.

Guthrie, B., McLean, G. and Sutton, M. (2006) 'Workload and reward in the Quality and Outcomes Framework of the 2004 general practice contract', *British Journal of General Practice*, vol 56, no 532, pp 836-41.

Hannington, W. (1937) *The problem of distressed areas*, Extract reprinted in Davey Smith et al (2001).

Martikainen, P., Adda, J., Ferrie, J.E., Davey Smith, G. and Marmot, M. (2003) 'Effects of income and wealth on GHQ depression and poor self rated health in white collar women and men in the Whitehall II study', *Journal of Epidemiology & Community Health*, vol 57, pp 718-23.

Morris, J.N., Donkin, A.J.M., Wonderling, D., Wilkinson, P. and Dowler, E. (2000) 'A minimum income for healthy living', *Journal of Epidemiology & Community Health*, vol 54, pp 885-9.

National Statistics (2006) 'Life expectancy at age 65 continues to rise', News release 21/11/2006 (www.statistics.gov.uk/pdfdir/liex1106.pdf).

Newton, J. and Garner, S. (2002) *Disease registers in England: A report commissioned by the Department of Health Policy Research Programme in support of the White Paper entitled Saving lives: Our healthier nation*, Oxford: Institute of Health Sciences.

Palmer, G., MacInnes, T. and Kenway, P. (2006) *Findings: Monitoring poverty and social exclusion in the UK 2006*, York: Joseph Rowntree Foundation.

Shaw, M. and Dorling, D. (2004) 'Who cares in England & Wales? The positive care law: a cross-sectional study', *British Journal of General Practice*, vol 54, pp 899-903.

Shaw, M., Galobardes, B., Lawlor, D.A., Lynch, J., Wheeler, B. and Davey Smith, G. (2007) *The handbook of inequality and socioeconomic position*, Bristol: The Policy Press.

Smith, N., Middleton, S., Ashton-Brooks, K., Cox, L. and Dobson, B. (2004) *Findings: Disabled people's living costs*, York: Joseph Rowntree Foundation.

Townsend, P., Davidson, N. and Whitehead, M. (1988) *Inequalities in health: The Black report and the health divide*, Harmondsworth: Penguin.

Tudor Hart, J. (1971) 'The inverse care law', *Lancet*, vol 1, pp 405-12.

Wheeler, B., Shaw, M., Mitchell, R. and Dorling, D. (2005) *Life in Britain: Using millennial Census data to understand poverty, inequality and place*, Bristol: The Policy Press.

Part Three

The role of the state

twelve

State approaches to wealth

Michael Orton

Overview

- This chapter discusses ways that better-off citizens are able to accumulate wealth and sustain their privileged position.
- It explores how systems of taxation affect inequality and wealth, and how better-off citizens can gain from fiscal welfare (or 'tax breaks').
- It examines how better-off citizens can benefit from publicly funded services such as the National Health Service (NHS), which aim to be available on an equal basis.
- It looks at how citizenship rights and responsibilities are applied differently to the poor and rich, and can advantage the better-off.
- It considers the voluntary social exclusion of the wealthy.
- It challenges the commonly held assumption that the better-off pay taxes and the poor receive the benefits.

Key concepts

wealth; fiscal welfare/tax breaks; progressive and regressive taxes; direct and indirect taxes; the inverse care law; advantage; privileged access to resources

Introduction

This chapter looks at the ways in which government policies can affect wealth and, what might appear surprising, how this can benefit the better-off over poorer people. In the UK, the government's approach to wealth contrasts with its approach to poverty (see Chapter Thirteen, this volume). While poverty is seen as a problem, the generation of personal wealth is generally viewed more positively by the state and no explicit policies on wealth exist. As we saw in Chapter Two (this volume), some extremely wealthy people live in the UK, such as Lakshmi Mittal, who reportedly spent £30 million on his daughter's wedding, and the Duke of Westminster, who owns vast estates as well as property portfolios in central London. There are a wide range of factors and powerful processes that enable better-off citizens to accumulate wealth and sustain their privileged position. For example, the Duke of Westminster inherited most of his wealth. The reasons why wealth inequality has increased since the mid-1990s include the stock market boom in the late 1990s and rising house prices (Hills, 2004). There is an increasing link between educational qualifications and earnings, and rising incomes (for some people) mean there is an opportunity to accumulate savings and other assets. Huge bonuses, for example to financiers in the City of London, are another source of wealth accumulation (according to the *Sunday Telegraph*, 18 February 2007, a 'record 4,200 City workers will this year rake in bonuses of more than £1 million each, on top of their six-figure annual salaries').

From policy on housing to education there is, then, potential for government to affect wealth and inequality; but there are two particularly important policy areas: taxation, and the provision of welfare benefits and public services. The amount of tax that people pay, and how this changes over time, is due to decisions made by the government and impacts directly on levels of inequality and wealth. But the way that systems of taxation operate, and how they impact on different groups of people, is rarely considered. Inequality and wealth are also directly affected by the state's provision of cash benefits (for example, Income Support and Child Benefit) and the provision of universal public services (meaning services available to all citizens on an equal basis, for example, the NHS – public services are sometimes referred to as 'benefits in kind'). Figures from the Office for National Statistics (Jones, 2007) show that, before taxes and benefits (cash and in kind) are taken account of, the richest 20% of households have an average income 16 times higher than the poorest 20% of households. After taxes and benefits are taken account of, however, the average income is four times higher. Taxes and benefits therefore reduce inequality. This can, however, lead to the commonly held assumption that the rich pay taxes and the poor get the benefits (Sinfield, 2003). But this is not necessarily the case, as shall be seen in this chapter.

This chapter is in two parts. The first examines wealth and taxation. It considers how different taxes, and forms of taxation, impact differently on rich and poor households, and how fiscal welfare (or 'tax breaks') can benefit the better-off. The second part considers who benefits most from universal services, including discussion of the specific examples of health and education, citizenship rights and responsibilities, and the voluntary social exclusion of the wealthy. We begin with wealth and taxation.

Wealth and taxation

Table 12.1 shows the amount of tax paid by different income groups. The population is divided into fifths, or quintiles, based on income. The bottom quintile is made up of the 20% of households that have the lowest incomes. The second bottom quintile is the next 20% of households, through to the top quintile that is the 20% of households with the highest incomes. The table shows that households in the bottom quintile (those households with the lowest incomes) paid, on average, £3,910 in taxes in 2005/06, whereas the top quintile (those households with the highest incomes) paid £25,000 on average. In cash terms, higher-income households paid more in taxes than low-income households.

Table 12.1: *Amount paid in taxes by households in each income quintile, 2005/06*

	Bottom quintile	2nd	3rd	4th	Top quintile	All households
Amount paid in taxes	£3,910	£5,660	£9,150	£13,800	£25,000	£11,500

Source: Compiled from Jones (2007, p 9, Table 4)

However, if we look instead at the proportion of household income that is spent on paying taxes, the position is very different (see *Table 12.2*). *Table 12.2* shows that taxes account for 36.4% of income for households in the bottom quintile (those with the lowest incomes), but account for only 35.5% of income for households in the top quintile (those with the highest incomes). Looked at in this way, the poorest households pay proportionately more tax than people with the highest incomes. See *Box 12.1* for a discussion of paying tax.

Table 12.2: *Tax as a percentage of gross household income, 2005/06*

	Bottom quintile	2nd	3rd	4th	Top quintile	All households
Tax as a % of gross household income	36.4%	32.1%	34.6%	35.7%	35.5%	35.1%

Source: Jones (2007, p 7, Table 3)

> **Box 12.1:** Paying tax: cash amounts versus tax as a proportion of income
>
> To use a simplified example, imagine if you had a job and earned £100 per week, while your friend earned £180 per week. If you had to pay £50 a week in tax, and your friend paid £60 in tax, in cash terms your friend would be paying more tax than you. But as a proportion of income, tax would be half (50%) of your income, but only a third (33%) of your friend's income. You would be paying proportionately more tax than your friend.
>
> Do you think the fairness of taxes should be considered in relation to who pays most in cash terms, or as a proportion of income?

Progressive and regressive taxes

Table 12.3 provides more detail about different taxes, and what proportion of household income they account for, for households in each of the quintiles. An important distinction between taxes, and how they impact on different households, is whether they are **progressive** or **regressive**. A progressive tax takes a greater proportion of income from people with higher incomes, and proportionately less from people with lower incomes. A regressive tax does the opposite, that is, it takes a greater proportion of income from people with lower incomes, and proportionately less from people with higher incomes. In *Table 12.4*, income tax is an example of a progressive tax, and value added tax (VAT) is an example of a regressive tax. Whether governments choose to raise money through progressive or regressive taxes impacts directly on inequality and wealth.

Direct and indirect taxes

The taxes in *Table 12.3* are divided into 'direct taxes' and 'indirect taxes', and this is another important distinction in understanding how different taxes impact on poor and rich households. Direct taxes are those paid directly to the government (for example, income tax). Indirect taxes are collected by an intermediary and then passed to the government (for example, if you buy a pint of beer in a pub the price you pay includes alcohol duty, which is then passed to the government). What is important in understanding how taxes affect different households is that as a general rule (and there are exceptions such as the current system of local tax, which will be discussed later) **direct taxes** are **progressive** but **indirect taxes** are **regressive**. This means that the balance between direct and indirect taxes will have different impacts. In the 1980s Conservative governments reduced levels of direct taxation and increased indirect taxes. This shift from direct to indirect taxes reduced the amount of tax paid by the better-off, and increased the amount of tax paid by poorer people.

Table 12.3: *Taxes as a percentage of household income, 2005/06*

% of gross household income	Bottom quintile	2nd	3rd	4th	5th	All households
Direct taxes						
Income tax	2.8	6.3	10.2	13.2	18.3	13.5
Employees' NI contributions	1.5	2.9	4.6	5.4	4.7	4.4
Local tax	5.2	3.9	3.2	2.7	1.7	2.7
All direct taxes	9.5	13.1	18.0	21.2	24.7	20.6
Indirect taxes						
VAT	10.5	7.8	6.9	6.3	5.0	6.3
Duty on alcohol	1.4	1.1	1.1	0.9	0.6	0.9
Duty on tobacco	2.9	1.8	1.3	0.8	0.3	0.9
Vehicle related duties	2.9	2.1	2.1	2.0	1.3	1.8
Other indirect taxes	9.2	6.3	5.2	4.5	3.5	4.7
All indirect taxes	26.9	19.1	16.6	14.4	10.8	14.5
All taxes	36.4	32.1	34.6	35.7	35.5	35.1

Source: Jones (2007, p 7, Table 3)

Examples of individual taxes, and how they impact on different households, will now be discussed in more detail.

Income tax

Income tax is a tax on income, which includes earnings from employment or self-employment, interest on most savings and income from shares (called dividends). *Table 12.4* shows the different rates of income tax for 2007/08. Looking at earned income, 10% (or 10p in every £1) is paid in income tax on earnings from £1 to £2,230. For earned income of £2,231–£34,600, 22% (or 22p in every £1) is paid in tax. The highest rate is 40% for earned income over £34,600. *Table 12.4* also shows that different tax rates apply to earned income, savings and dividends from shares.

It is up to the government to decide the different rates of income tax, and changing income tax rates has a major impact on inequality and wealth. In 1979 the top rate of income tax on earned income was 83%. By 1988 it had been cut to 40%, and has not changed since. Cutting the top rate from 83% to 40% left people on high incomes with much more money.

The different rates of income tax for different kinds of income can also be looked at critically. For example, why should income from dividends on shares be taxed at a lower rate than earned income? If shares are more likely to be owned by better-off citizens, does this mean the income tax system is favouring the better-off?

The income tax system is much more complicated than this summary suggests. There is a whole set of rules about exempted income, allowances and reliefs, some of which will be discussed later. But the key point at this stage is that tax rates are the result of political decisions, and they greatly affect levels of inequality and wealth.

Table 12.4: *Income tax rates, 2007/08*

Income tax band	Income tax on earned income	Income tax on savings	Income tax on dividends
Starting rate: £1–£2,230	10%	10%	10%
Basic rate: £2,231–£34,600	22%	20%	10%
Higher rate: £34,601 and above	40%	40%	32.5%

Source: DirectGov (2007)

Value added tax

Value added tax (VAT) is a tax that you pay when you buy goods and services. It is normally included in the price of the goods or service when you buy them (for example, if you look at the receipt for a meal in a restaurant, the amount of VAT will be shown as a separate item). But VAT is not payable on all goods. For example, VAT is not payable on food, books or children's clothes. Also, there are two separate rates of VAT. The standard rate is 17.5% (for example, if you buy a coat that costs £100, the total price will be £117.50 because VAT of 17.5% is added). But there is also a reduced rate of 5% for some things, such as gas and electricity, and children's car seats.

As can be seen from *Table 12.3*, VAT is a very regressive tax. But its impact depends on government choices as to what items should be included/excluded, and at what rate the tax should be levied. For example, 'luxury' goods likely to be purchased by the better-off could be taxed at a higher rate than 17.5%. The imposition of VAT on fuel bills was very controversial because it affects all households, including the very poorest. If fuel, or other basic items were exempted from VAT, its impact could be very different.

Taxing inheritance, and other assets

As mentioned earlier, inheritance is one of the key ways that wealth can be accumulated and passed on within families to maintain a privileged position. When you die, your financial assets form what is called your 'estate'. For 2007/08, if your estate is valued at under £300,000 no inheritance tax is payable. Anything over £300,000 is taxed at 40%. Self-evidently, the rate at which inheritance tax is levied impacts directly on the amount of money that wealthy people can pass on, or receive, through inheritances. One of the changes to taxation that took place in the 1980s was having much lower rates of tax on large inheritances than in the preceding four decades (Hills, 2004). Given such a change, it is not surprising that wealth inequality should increase (just as, conversely, increasing death duties led to a fall in wealth inequality in the 1920s; Scott, 1994).

With assets more generally, governments also have to decide on relevant tax rates. In the 1970s, income on some forms of assets attracted a tax rate of 98% (this was a period when the Chancellor of the Exchequer in the Labour government said he would tax the rich 'until the pips squeaked'). But in the 1980s, Conservative governments sharply cut levels of tax on assets (Hills, 2004). Indeed, in the 1970s rates of tax on investment income were higher than rates of tax on earnings (from employment). But by the 1990s the reverse was the case, again creating the conditions for greater asset accumulation and increasing wealth inequality.

Box 12.2 provides an example of how another type of tax, Council Tax, impacts differently on households that have different levels of wealth.

Box 12.2: Council Tax: 'protecting' the rich?

Council Tax is the current system of local taxation in Britain. It involves properties being valued and then placed in one of eight bands, A–H, dependent on the value of the individual property. A different amount of tax is payable for each band with the liability for a band H property being three times that for a band A property. *Table 12.3* shows that Council Tax is very regressive. It accounts for 5.2% of income for households in the bottom quintile, but only 1.7% for households in the top quintile. Because properties are placed in valuation bands, there is a strict ceiling put on the amount of Council Tax that has to be paid irrespective of how high an income a person has or the extent of their wealth. Consistent with changes in income tax and National Insurance rules that took place in the 1980s, the assets of the rich are 'protected' by Council Tax being limited, and those on lower incomes have to pay proportionately more of the tax.

Source: Orton (2002)

The above examples have shown how different types of taxes affect different income groups, and contribute to inequality and wealth. Another way tax affects wealth is through what is called 'fiscal welfare' (more commonly known as 'tax breaks') which work specifically to the advantage of better-off citizens. Fiscal welfare is a very neglected field of social policy analysis, but will be discussed next.

Fiscal welfare: 'tax breaks' and the hidden welfare state

Contemporary debates about welfare have become very narrowly focused on social welfare, for example, welfare benefits provided by the state (Dwyer, 2000), but there are in fact three different types of welfare (Titmuss, 1958). In addition to social welfare, the other two types of welfare provision are: occupational welfare (provided by employers – also known as the 'fringe benefits' of a job) – and fiscal welfare (more popularly known as tax loopholes or tax breaks). While social welfare involves giving cash payments to people, fiscal welfare is about enabling people to minimise the amount of tax they have to pay through loopholes or tax breaks, more properly called 'allowances' or 'reliefs'. The cost of providing cash benefits (social welfare) is easy to calculate. Fiscal welfare 'costs' the government money in that including allowances and reliefs in tax systems means the government forgoes income, in the form of tax revenue, that would otherwise be collected (for a helpful introduction to fiscal welfare, see Sinfield, 2007).

The importance of fiscal welfare is that it is a hidden issue, and one that potentially benefits better-off citizens over poor citizens. For example, Hacker (2002, p xii) argues that fiscal welfare remains 'beneath the surface of popular consciousness and political debate', with academic studies focusing overwhelmingly on public social programmes, while Howard (1997, pp 3-5) describes fiscal welfare as being largely absent in the study of social policy, forming a 'hidden welfare state' and a 'blind spot in the academic literature'. Hacker (2002, p xiii) argues directly that this form of welfare is 'far more favorable to the privileged'. But the idea that better-off citizens may benefit from welfare systems, when defined broadly rather than simply as social welfare, remains 'subterranean' and 'hidden'. This also contrasts sharply with the very great policy and media interest given to benefit 'scroungers' and 'cheats' (that is, people who may be fraudulently claiming social welfare benefits).

One of the reasons why fiscal welfare is a hidden issue is simply because it is so complicated. Indeed, one of the ways the better-off are able to preserve their wealth is by having access to the (very expensive) accountants and financial experts whose detailed knowledge of tax systems enables those with very high levels of assets to protect those assets through minimising the amount of tax they have to pay (Scott, 1994). As Mann (2001) puts it, without an extensive knowledge of accountancy it is difficult to disentangle the complex systems of tax allowances, rebates and exemptions woven into the UK system. While tax evasion (the non-payment of taxes for which one is liable) is illegal, tax avoidance (the use of tax regulations to minimise the amount of tax one has to pay) is entirely legal. To illustrate this point, we consider two examples.

Fiscal welfare benefiting the better-off: tax avoidance, the legal way

All citizens are subject to the same laws relating to tax, but in practice there is great scope for those with high levels of assets to avoid or minimise the taxes they pay. Lansley (2006, p 181) illustrates this through the example of 'non-domiciliary status'. Under this rule, residents in Britain who were born abroad can register as 'non-domiciles' (this is simply a categorisation for tax purposes and has no other standing). They then only pay tax on that part of their income that is sent back to Britain or is derived in the UK. An estimated 60,000 rich British residents benefit from this arrangement. One person who gained from this is Mohamed al-Fayed, the multi-millionaire owner of Harrods, the Paris Ritz and Fulham football club. The 2007 *Sunday Times* Rich List estimated al-Fayed's wealth as £507 million. In 1985 al-Fayed reached an agreement with the Inland Revenue that he would pay a fixed annual level of tax of £240,000. This only came to light through a high-profile libel case in 1999, during which it emerged that while al-Fayed drew no salary from Harrods, tens of millions of pounds in dividends were paid to an offshore trust in Bermuda some of which was seeping back into Britain untaxed. For most people £240,000 a year is in cash terms a very large amount of tax – but for a multi-millionaire like al-Fayed it represents a tiny fraction of their wealth. In plain terms, 'non-domiciliary status' allows the rich to avoid paying taxes that would contribute to the provision of public services, and instead maintain their wealth and privilege.

Fiscal welfare favouring the better-off: pensions

Tax reliefs on pensions provide an example of how an apparently universal system in fact favours the better-off in accumulating assets (in the form of pension provision). For each pound you contribute to a pension scheme, the pension provider (company) claims tax back from the government at the basic rate of 22%. In practice, this means that for every £78 you pay into your pension, you end up with £100 in your pension fund. People who pay the higher income tax rate of 40% are further advantaged because they receive a relief of 40%, that is, higher rate taxpayers only have to pay £60 into their pension scheme to end up with £100 actually going into their pension. So the more tax a person is liable to pay the greater the tax subsidy they get from paying into a pension. The better-off get a disproportionately generous subsidy.

The cost of providing these tax reliefs, in terms of the amount of tax that would otherwise be collected, is very high. Throughout the 1990s tax reliefs on pensions was between £7.3 and £9.9 billion, but this could be an underestimate by as much as £2 billion (Mann, 2001). More recently, it has been estimated that the net cost of tax relief on non-state pensions in 2005/06 was £13.7 billion, a sum greater than all means-tested assistance to the poorest older people, prior to the introduction of the Pension Credit (Sinfield, 2007). The injustice of the UK system is compounded by the fact that employee contributions into the state's National Insurance scheme (used primarily by those on lower incomes) do not get tax relief. This means the poorest pay tax on their pension contributions and receive the lowest pensions; thus, 'Despite the existence of a supposedly "universal" system of public pensions, the pattern in the UK is ... clearly unfair' (Mann, 2001, p 44).

Box 12.3 provides another example of how fiscal welfare arrangements can favour wealthy citizens.

Box 12.3: Fiscal welfare: the rich and famous

According to Lansley (2006, p 183):

> Entrepreneurs, businessmen, City dealers, footballers, pop stars and
> television presenters are known to use a variety of schemes dreamt up by
> highly paid accountants to minimise their tax bills. When Bianca Jagger
> divorced Mick Jagger, she revealed how the wealthy pop star was obsessed
> with avoiding paying taxes not just in Britain but in any country he feared
> might seek to claim them. "Throughout our married life, he and I literally
> lived out of a suitcase in a nomadic journey from one place to another
> in his quest to avoid income taxes." Some top British footballers use a
> perfectly legal offshore scheme devised by accountants Deloitte & Touche
> that funnels performance-related bonuses into special accounts to minimise
> their tax bills.

This section has been about how tax affects inequality and wealth. Money
collected in taxes is used to fund public services like health and education.
It is often assumed that poorer people benefit more from the provision of
these universal services, that is, services that should be available to everyone
on an equal basis. But is this really the case? This issue is considered in the
next section.

Who benefits most from public services?

Who benefits most from public services is a controversial issue. For example,
Le Grand (1982) characterised the 1970s' UK welfare state as pro middle class.
Townsend's (1979, p 222) study of poverty found that, 'contrary to common
belief, fewer individuals in households with low rather than high incomes
received social services in kind of substantial value'. However, Glennerster
(2003) argues that the poorest fifth of households now benefit twice as much
as the richest fifth from public spending. Of course, wealthy citizens can
opt out of public services and purchase their own, private, provision of (say)
healthcare and education. This can mean avoiding waiting times for operations,
or purchasing expert specialist health advice which may be difficult to access
through the NHS. Private schools spend more per pupil than state schools,
providing smaller class sizes, better sports facilities and so on. However, private
provision is very limited. For example, only 10.8% of adults have their own
private medical insurance (Wallis, 2004). So the provision of public services
is important for the vast majority of people.

To try to make sense of who benefits most from public services, the next section focuses on the example of healthcare. Healthcare is of central importance to our lives: enjoying good health is critical to a person's quality of life; good health leads to longer life expectancy (quite literally the number of years our life will last); poor health can lead to poverty and vice versa (see Chapter Eleven, this volume). The NHS aims to provide equal access to healthcare; health services and treatments available to individuals should depend only on their need for treatment, and not on factors that are irrelevant to that need (Dixon et al, 2003). In particular, access to the service should be independent of individuals' socioeconomic status, except in so far as this affects need. But in direct contradiction to this, and the assumption that people experiencing poverty benefit most from public services, it has been argued that areas which are poorer and therefore have greater health needs are less well served by the health service than wealthier (and healthier) areas – this is known as 'the inverse care law' (Tudor Hart, 1971; also see Chapter Eleven, this volume).

How the better-off can gain more from health services: 'the inverse care law'

Dixon et al (2003) undertook a review of available research evidence to examine whether the NHS is equitable. The key findings (Dixon et al, 2003, pp 31-2) were:

- the position is not clear-cut, but there continues to be evidence that people with low incomes and low educational qualifications use health services less, relative to their needs, than people who are more affluent and better educated;
- there is strong evidence that lower socioeconomic groups use services less in relation to need than higher socioeconomic groups for specific NHS services including: cardiac, diagnostic and surgical care; elective procedures for hernia, gallstones, tonsillitis, and grommets; inpatient oral surgery; immunisation for diphtheria, pertussis, measles, mumps and rubella; and diabetes clinics and diabetes reviews; and
- lower socioeconomic groups may also receive less time per GP consultation.

The reasons for this inequality include: lack of suitable transport; restrictions on available time limiting access to services; and differences in beliefs about severity of illness and the need to seek medical attention.

However, a very important factor is the superior 'voice', connections and communications by middle-class patients influencing treatment once the service is accessed. Dixon et al (2003, p 25) discuss this in the following terms:

The view that the middle classes get more out of the health service because they are better at expressing their need and working the system is well known ... they are more adept at using their 'voice' to demand better and more extensive services. They are more articulate, more confident, and more persistent. Moreover, the medical practitioners who are taking the relevant treatment decisions are themselves from the middle class and hence are more likely to empathise with middle class patients. Hence the latter are well placed to ensure they get as much treatment as they want – which may or may not be as much as they need ... higher socio-economic groups are more likely to have family or friends who work in the health services. Even if these contacts are not directly used to gain access to services they act as an important source of advice on how to work the system.

For example, a qualitative study of patients who experienced chest pain found that 10 out of 30 affluent patients were personally connected with the medical profession, compared with none of the patients from a deprived area.

The ability of better-off citizens to 'play the system' so as to gain from universal services is sometimes referred to as 'the sharp elbows of the middle class' (see **Box 12.4** for some examples of how this operates in relation to health) and can also be seen in a second example – education.

Box 12.4: Some examples of the inverse care law at work

Studies of healthcare have found that:

- people in the bottom two social classes had 10% fewer health preventive consultations than people in the top two social classes, after standardising for other determinants;
- hip replacements were 20% lower among lower socioeconomic groups, despite people in lower socioeconomic groups having a roughly 30% higher need than people in higher socioeconomic groups;
- if people are ranked on a seven-point deprivation scale, the amount of time a GP spent with a patient fell by 3.4% for each point on the scale, that is, the better-off the person, the more time the GP spent with them;
- socioeconomic inequalities in both outcomes and use of antenatal care are well recognised, and women from the most disadvantaged groups are up to 20 times more likely to die in childbirth than women in the two highest social classes.

Source: Dixon et al (2003)

Education: the sharp elbows of the middle class

Education is also critical to life chances with strong links between qualifications and earnings (see, for example, Hills, 2004); it is also another example of how the better-off can gain advantages from a universal system that aims to apply equally to all citizens. For example, people with higher incomes are able to buy homes in the catchment area of popular schools (for example, schools with good academic records), leaving poorer people to send their children to less popular schools. Better-off people can afford to employ private tutors to coach their children in preparation for examinations, and pay for extra-curricular activities such as music and sport.

In 2007, in an attempt to overcome some of these issues, Brighton Council announced that places at oversubscribed schools would be decided by a lottery. In theory this means poorer children now have as much chance of gaining a place at popular schools in Brighton as those whose parents are able to buy homes in the catchment areas of those schools. However, Frank Field, Labour Member of Parliament and former Minister of Welfare Reform (1997–98), argued that:

> if the lottery idea catches on, can anyone sensibly think that the elbow-wielding middle classes will passively accept their forced movement down the queue when their whole aim in life is about getting to and staying out in front? We have already seen some parents moving closer to the school of their choice even though they are currently in the catchment area for fear that, as the school becomes even more popular, the geographical catchment areas for eligibility will be reduced. No one should be surprised at such actions. Since the 1960s middle-class parents have been able to work the rules of the schools system to the advantage of their offspring. (www.frankfield.com/type2show.asp?ref=422&ID=21, 19/06/07)

Advantage in school education also provides a greater chance of going into higher education (which again enhances the likelihood of higher earnings and consequent advantage). But participation in higher education is very unequal. There are broad and deep divisions in the chances of going into higher education, according to where you live. People living in the most advantaged 20% of areas are five to six times more likely to enter higher education than those living in the least advantaged 20% of areas (HEFCE, 2005). Many cities and towns are educationally divided, containing both neighbourhoods where almost no one goes to university and neighbourhoods where two out of three (or more) young people will enter higher education.

The purpose here is to illuminate how the assumption that the rich pay taxes while people experiencing poverty receive the benefits is not necessarily correct. Poor citizens do need welfare benefits to avoid absolute destitution, and much attention is devoted to social welfare and issues such as 'welfare dependency'. But if we begin to look more critically, we can begin to see that who benefits from state spending is far more complex. However, there is to a large extent a lack of information and research to draw on and, as with fiscal welfare, the issue of who benefits from public spending is one that is often hidden.

This section has looked at how publicly funded services can work to the advantage of better-off citizens. *Box 12.5* provides an additional example of how richer citizens can benefit from public spending – this time in relation to transport. The next section takes a slightly different approach, and examines whether the more fundamental (universal) status of citizenship applies equally to poor and rich people.

Box 12.5: Who benefits most from public spending?

The example of transport

Table 12.5 shows which households benefit most from government subsidies for different types of transport. The poorest households (in the bottom quintile) gain most from the bus subsidy, but least from the rail subsidy. Households in the top quintile gain most from the rail subsidy, and least from the bus subsidy. A decision as to whether to give a greater subsidy to bus or rail transport may appear to have nothing to do with inequality and wealth but in fact it impacts directly on the financial position of rich and poor households – and can favour the better-off over poorer households.

Table 12.5: *Benefits of travel subsidies for non-retired households 2005/06*

	Bottom quintile	2nd	3rd	4th	Top quintile	All non-retired households
Rail subsidy	£20	£24	£29	£48	£95	£43
Bus subsidy	£62	£52	£48	£48	£52	£52

Source: Adapted from Jones (2007, p 25, Table 16A)

State approaches to the rich and poor: citizenship rights and responsibilities

For the purposes of this chapter 'citizenship' is used to mean a universal status, which provides rights and responsibilities that apply equally to all members of society (Dwyer, 2004, provides a very helpful introduction to more complex and contested views of citizenship). The question to consider is whether rights and responsibilities do apply equally to all citizens, or whether there are differences in how they relate to poor and rich citizens? Responsibility is discussed first.

Citizenship responsibilities: asking less of the rich and more of the poor?

Tony Blair's first speech as Prime Minister included a section on citizenship and responsibility. He stressed the importance of responsibility, and argued that what he called 'The ethic of responsibility' applied 'as much at the top of society as at the bottom' (Blair, 1997, p 8). However, in terms of policy development it is more difficult to see evidence of responsibility having been applied equally to all citizens. For example, as Wilson (1994) argues, there is a particular belief that a welfare ethos exists which encourages the poor to avoid their obligations as citizens to work, to support their families and to obey the law. Considerable policy attention has been given to the responsibilities of poor people, with increased job search obligations placed on benefit claimants a highly visible example. Poor citizens therefore face increasing responsibilities.

Better-off citizens, however, appear to be facing less responsibilities. This is tied to changes in taxation mentioned earlier. Lister (1998, p 317) argues that Conservative governments (1979–97) placed less emphasis on the payment of tax as a citizenship obligation and instead contended that for 'better-off citizens ... citizenship responsibility was about time and commitment and not just paying taxes'. Paying tax did remain a citizenship obligation, but what was asked of wealthy citizens was reduced dramatically with (as noted earlier) the top rate of income tax being cut from 83% in 1979 to 40% by 1988. Instead, the wealthy were exhorted to express their citizenship responsibility in different ways. In practical terms the tangible obligation of wealthy citizens to pay tax has reduced and is replaced by rather vague, and unenforced, calls to give 'time and commitment'. As Dwyer (2000) notes, obligation has certainly been applied in relation to those seeking to claim welfare benefits but not to the fiscal and occupational benefits of the middle class. There appears to be an imbalance between the citizenship responsibilities of poor and rich citizens, with it being possible to argue that the privileged face less responsibilities than do those in poverty (for a fuller discussion, see Orton, 2006). We now consider citizenship rights.

Citizenship rights

There are three categories of citizenship rights (Marshall, 1963) and they should apply equally to all citizens. The three categories are: civil rights (for example, the right to own property); political rights (for example, the right to vote); and social rights (for example, the right to claim welfare benefits). Historically, there are clear examples of rights being available only to wealthy citizens. For example, in the 19th century the political right to vote was restricted at least in part on the basis of wealth. In addition, receipt of public assistance could mean the loss of political and/or civil rights (Lister, 2004).

In the 21st century, citizenship rights might not be restricted on such an explicit basis but there certainly remains a question as to whether rights do apply equally to rich and poor citizens. For example, receipt of welfare benefits no longer means a loss of civil or political rights but, as Lister (2004, p 164) argues, 'poverty and welfare receipt can still mean that these rights are compromised in practice'. A specific example of this is that homeless people without a fixed address are unable to vote. To focus on social rights, it can be argued that through mechanisms such as means tests, receipt of welfare benefits can carry a strong sense of stigma. While (say) the right to vote indicates inclusion as a citizen, claiming welfare benefits can be seen in the opposite terms, that is, attached to it is a sense of exclusion. This contrasts with better-off people claiming the kinds of tax relief discussed in the section on fiscal welfare, with which there is no sense of stigma or problem of take-up (see, for example, Sinfield, 2007). The application of rights is therefore different for rich and poor citizens. As Deacon and Bradshaw (1983) argue, some rights are, in a negative rather than positive sense, 'reserved for the poor'.

A key point to emphasise here is the difference between **formal** citizenship rights (based on the formal equality of citizenship; see Dean, 2002) and how rights work in practice. For example, Dean with Melrose (1999, p 90) argue that in reality social rights are subordinate to civil and political rights: '[w]hile civil rights are enforceable through the courts and political rights through the electoral system, social rights are altogether more vulnerable, having no distinctive forum for their expression or realisation'. The distinction between formal equality under the law and social reality is illustrated by Hall and Held's (1989) example that there may be no laws preventing someone from entering the Ritz but whether they have the means to do so is a different matter. Social rights do not provide the resources and conditions that would allow all citizens to exercise their formal rights equally.

What is also important is an understanding of the differential impact of rights. For example, ownership of land and property is critical to the accumulation of large levels of wealth by the very richest people. The civil right to own property is therefore very important to wealth accumulation. That right applies equally to all citizens (in a formal sense) but, as has already been seen, whether one has the resources with which to buy property is a different matter. Social rights mean that the poorest citizens can claim welfare benefits (without which people would be destitute and potentially face starvation). But, as Taylor (1996, p 164) argues, '[r]ights can only be meaningful if they raise the possibility of access to and control over the resources necessary to realise the human need for self-development'. Social rights might mean poor citizens avoid starvation, but they still leave people living in poverty and do not provide the basis for self-development. Civil rights, however, do provide the basis for the better-off to develop their wealth accumulation and asset holding. If we look critically, therefore, it can be seen that the (social) rights of citizenship do not enable poor citizens to escape poverty, but the (civil) rights of citizenship do enable the rich to protect and enhance their wealth. With the creation of the welfare state it was argued that social rights would alleviate poverty and promote greater equality (Dean, 2002), but as seen throughout this book (see in particular Chapters One, Three and Thirteen) this has self-evidently not been the case. While there may be a formal equality of citizenship under the law, in practice there is a differential application and impact of citizenship rights in relation to poor and rich citizens. *Box 12.6* considers citizenship rights and responsibilities for wealthy people.

Box 12.6: Citizenship and wealth

New Labour figure Peter Mandelson (2002) has argued that there needs to be 'an honest debate about the position of Britain's new super-wealthy.... The right for those on high incomes to make good ... has to be balanced with the obligation of stewardship and responsibility to wider society'.

What do you think should be the balance between rights and responsibilities for wealthy citizens? What responsibilities do you think wealthy citizens should have?

One of the things that underpins the issue of wealth as considered in this chapter is that wealth is seen as being entirely positive, and wealth accumulation should be encouraged, for example, 'Our economic policies [are] ... supporting enterprise and wealth creation' and the 'Government ... must support the wealth creators' (Labour Party, 2005, pp 14, 18). But wealth also creates privilege, which is the opposite social condition to poverty (Scott, 1994). Poverty is very much a focus of policy concern (see Chapter Thirteen, this volume). The final section of this chapter considers whether privilege should also be the focus of social policy attention.

Should privilege be the focus of policy attention?

There are a number of reasons why an interest in privilege is relevant (also see Orton and Rowlingson, 2007). As mentioned earlier, the dominant view of wealth is as being positive, and that wealth creators should be supported. An alternative argument is that privilege should be a cause for concern if it threatens social cohesion. This is sometimes referred to as the voluntary social exclusion of the wealthy (in contrast to the involuntary social exclusion of poor people).

Voluntary social exclusion of the wealthy

Scott (1994) argues that there has been decreasing participation in the public sphere by wealthy citizens who are able to withdraw into an insulated and exclusive 'world'. Gated communities (private housing developments, quite literally, with a gated entrance to prevent entry to others) occupied by middle-class people can be seen as separating their occupants from contact with different social groups, creating 'havens of social withdrawal' and contributing to the creation of 'time–space trajectories of segregation' (Atkinson and Flint, 2004, p 875). There is also evidence that better-off citizens in gated communities may seek to withdraw from systems of local services and local taxation (Blandy et al, 2003).

So while poor citizens may face enforced social exclusion, there may be voluntary social exclusion of the better-off (Le Grand, 2003). Barry (2002) argues that the voluntary exclusion of the wealthy through use of private education and health, and withdrawal from regular social interaction into gated communities or exclusive rural retreats, does have broader consequences for social relations and social solidarity. Barry argues that social exclusion should be seen alongside social differentiation and social polarisation. The isolation of rich citizens in private schools and hospitals means they can buy advantage denied to others and their support (financial and political) for broader public services is likely to reduce. But while poorer people are compelled to pursue social inclusion through paid work, the exclusionary practices of the privileged go unchallenged by the state. Giddens (2004) argues that the earnings of the rich should be a policy concern if high levels of income set the wealthy apart from the rest of society, but this has not to date been reflected in government policy.

Conclusion

This chapter has examined ways in which the state affects inequality and wealth, particularly through taxation and the provision of benefits and public services. Government decisions about rates of taxation, in particular changes that took place in the 1980s, have encouraged the accumulation of wealth by better-off citizens, and enabled the wealthy to sustain a privileged position through higher incomes and ownership of assets. This privileged position allows the wealthy greater opportunities and well-being, for example in relation to increased life expectancy, that is, the rich literally live longer than poor people (see Chapter Eleven). Not only can the wealthy benefit from being able to afford the private provision of services such as health and education, they can also gain disproportionately from the provision of universal public services. It can also be argued that the privileged face less citizenship responsibilities than do those in poverty.

It has also been seen, however, that the ways the rich benefit from tax systems and public services are hidden. Indeed, the entire system of fiscal welfare that can benefit the wealthy can be described as a 'hidden welfare state'. But it is only through exploring some of these issues, and looking critically at the assumption that the rich pay taxes and the poor receive the benefits, that we can begin to understand how governments affect wealth and inequality, and better-off citizens are able to accumulate assets and preserve a position of privilege.

Summary

- This chapter has shown that there is considerable scope across a range of policy areas for the government to influence wealth accumulation and inequality, particularly in relation to taxation and the provision of public services.
- Different taxes, and forms of taxation, impact differently on affluent and low-income households. In particular, 'tax breaks' and 'legal' tax avoidance act to preserve wealth and protect assets. These fiscal advantages are only part of the 'hidden welfare state' that disproportionately favours the wealthy.
- The assumption that 'the rich pay taxes and the poor receive the benefits' has been examined critically and wealthy people have been shown to receive considerable fiscal advantages through 'tax loopholes' and 'allowances'.
- There is also evidence that better-off citizens can gain disproportionately from universal public-funded services like health and education.

- The voluntary self-exclusion of the richest, serviced by private education and healthcare and living in gated communities, is also a significant concern. This voluntary exclusion of the wealthy contrasts with the enforced social exclusion of those in need and can have repercussions on social cohesion.

Questions for discussion

- What would a fair system of taxation look like? Should taxes be progressive or regressive?
- How could you find out who gains the most from universal public services?
- Should the voluntary social exclusion of the wealthy be a policy concern? What could be done about it?

Further reading

Compared with all the empirical reports and textbooks written on poverty there is very little on wealth. Scott's (1994) account of poverty, wealth and citizenship is a key starting point, along with Dean and Melrose's (1999) book that covers the same themes but draws on a qualitative research study including interviews with wealthy citizens. Lansley (2006) examines the super-wealthy, and issues of taxation. Orton (2006) presents findings from research into better-off citizens' views of citizenship.

Beyond academic work, newspapers such as *The Sunday Times* and *Sunday Telegraph* regularly have features on wealth. The satirical magazine *Private Eye* (whose editor, Ian Hislop, is one of the team captains on the BBC TV programme 'Have I Got News For You') also contains (critical) stories of wealth and the wealthy.

Electronic resources

www.direct.gov.uk/en/MoneyTaxAndBenefits/Taxes/ BeginnersGuideToTax/index.htm – The Directgov website guide to money, tax and benefits: 'The beginner's guide to tax'
www.statistics.gov.uk/StatBase/Product.asp?vlnk=10336 – 'The effects of taxes and benefits on household income' is published each year by the Office for National Statistics, usually in May.

www.cipa-apex.org/toomuch/tmweekly.html – *Too Much* is a US-based website which describes itself as 'An online weekly on excess and inequality' and provides topical stories and statistics on wealth

www.ifs.org.uk/ – The Institute for Fiscal Studies website has useful reports and data relating to inequality and wealth

References

Atkinson, R. and Flint, J. (2004) 'Fortress UK? Gated communities, the spatial revolt of the elites and time-space trajectories of segregation', *Housing Studies*, vol 19, no 6, pp 875-92.

Barry, B. (2002) 'Social exclusion, social isolation and the distribution of income', in J. Hills, J. Le Grand and D. Piachaud (eds) *Understanding social exclusion*, Oxford: Oxford University Press, pp 13-29.

Blair, T. (1997) Speech at the Aylesbury Estate, Southwark, 2 June, London: Social Exclusion Unit.

Blandy, S., Lister, D., Atkinson, R. and Flint, J. (2003) *Gated communities: A systematic review of the research evidence*, CNR Article 12, Bristol: ESRC Centre for Neighbourhood Research.

Deacon, A. and Bradshaw, J. (1983) *Reserved for the poor: The means test in British social policy*, Oxford: Blackwell.

Dean, H. (2002) *Welfare rights and social policy*, Harlow: Pearson Education Limited.

Dean, H. with Melrose, M. (1999) *Poverty, riches and social citizenship*, Basingstoke: Macmillan.

Directgov (2007) 'The beginner's guide to tax' (www.direct.gov.uk/en/ MoneyTaxAndBenefits/Taxes/BeginnersGuideToTax/index.htm).

Dixon, A., Le Grand, J., Henderson, J., Murray, R. and Poteliakhoff, E. (2003) *Is the NHS equitable? A review of the evidence*, LSE Health and Social Care Discussion Paper 11, London: London School of Economics and Political Science.

Dwyer, P. (2000) *Welfare rights and responsibilities*, Bristol: The Policy Press.

Dwyer, P. (2004) *Understanding social citizenship: Themes and perspectives for Social Policy*, Bristol: The Policy Press.

Giddens, A. (2004) 'We can and should take action if the earnings of the rich set them apart from society', *New Statesman and Society*, 27 September, pp 50-1.

Glennerster, H. (2003) *Understanding the finance of welfare: What welfare costs and how to pay for it*, Bristol: The Policy Press.

Hacker, J. (2002) *The divided welfare state*, Cambridge: Cambridge University Press.

Hall, S. and Held, D. (1989) 'Citizens and citizenship', in S. Hall and M. Jacques (eds) *New times*, London: Lawrence and Wishart, pp 173-88.

HEFCE (Higher Education Funding Council for England) (2005) *Young participation in higher education*, Bristol: HEFCE.

Hills, J. (2004) *Inequality and the state*, Oxford: Oxford University Press.

Howard, C. (1997) *The hidden welfare state*, Princeton, NJ: Princeton University Press.

Jones, F. (2007) *The effects of taxes and benefits on household income, 2005/06*, London: Office for National Statistics.

Labour Party (2005) *Manifesto*, London: The Labour Party.

Lansley, S. (2006) *Rich Britain*, London: Politico's.

Le Grand, J. (1982) *The strategy of equality*, London: Allen & Unwin.

Le Grand, J. (2003) *Individual choice and social exclusion*, CASEPaper 75, London: London School of Economics and Political Science.

Lister, R. (1998) 'Vocabularies of citizenship and gender: the UK', *Critical Social Policy*, vol 18, no 3, pp 309-31.

Lister, R. (2004) *Poverty*, Cambridge: Polity Press.

Mandelson, P. (2002) 'Third way is the only way', *The Guardian*, 10 January.

Mann, K. (2001) *Approaching retirement*, Bristol: The Policy Press.

Marshall, T.H. (1963) 'Citizenship and social class', in T.H. Marshall, *Sociology at the crossroads and other essays*, London: Heinemann, pp 67-127.

Orton, M. (2002) 'Council Tax: who benefits?', *Benefits*, vol 10, no 2, pp 110-15.

Orton, M. (2006) 'Wealth, citizenship and responsibility: the views of better-off citizens in the UK', *Citizenship Studies*, vol 10, no 2, pp 251-65.

Orton, M. and Rowlingson, K. (2007) 'A problem of riches: towards a new social policy research agenda on the distribution of economic resources', *Journal of Social Policy*, vol 36, no 1, pp 59-78.

Scott, J. (1994) *Poverty and wealth: Citizenship, deprivation and privilege*, London: Longmans.

Sinfield, A. (2003) 'Changing tax welfare', Paper presented at the ESPANET conference 'Changing European Societies – The Role For Social Policy', Copenhagen, 13-15 November.

Sinfield, A. (2007) 'Tax welfare', in M. Powell (ed) *Understanding the mixed economy of welfare*, Bristol: The Policy Press, pp 129-48.

Taylor, D. (1996) 'Citizenship and social power', in D. Taylor (ed) *Critical social policy: A reader*, London: Sage Publications, pp 156-67.

Titmuss, R.M. (1958) *Essays on the welfare state*, London: Allen & Unwin.

Townsend, P. (1979) *Poverty in the United Kingdom*, Harmondsworth: Penguin.

Tudor Hart, J. (1971) 'The inverse care law', *Lancet*, pp 405-12.

Wallis, G. (2004) 'The demand for private medical insurance', *Social Trends*, no 606, pp 46-56.

Wilson, W.J. (1994) 'Citizenship and the inner-city ghetto poor', in B. van Steenbergen (ed) *The condition of citizenship*, London: Sage Publications, pp 49-65.

thirteen

State approaches to poverty and social exclusion

Tess Ridge and Sharon Wright

Overview

- This chapter outlines the principles underlying the history and development of state approaches to dealing with poverty and social exclusion.
- It outlines key areas of policies to address poverty and social exclusion at the UK and devolved levels.
- It investigates the possible efficacy of paid employment as a solution to poverty, in the light of welfare-to-work policies.
- It considers the role and adequacy of social security benefits and tax credits in addressing poverty and social exclusion.

Key concepts

poverty; social exclusion; anti-poverty policy; social security; tax credits; welfare-to-work

Introduction

In stark contrast to the generation of wealth and amassment of assets (see Chapter Twelve, this volume), the experience of poverty is recognised as a social problem in the UK. Poverty, and more recently social exclusion, have been distinct fields of policy intervention for several decades. In fact, there has been a proliferation of policies at supranational (especially European Union, or EU), national and devolved administration (in Scotland, Wales and Northern Ireland) levels. However, despite more than 60 years of a welfare state that was designed to eradicate 'want', and a decade of the commitment to eradicate child poverty within a generation, the UK still has one of the worst records of poverty of all rich nations (see UNICEF, 2007). It is clear that there is no lack of policy activity in this sphere. Therefore, the main question that this chapter seeks to answer is: why have the anti-poverty policies operating within the UK proved so far to be so ineffectual?

In answering this question, we must first of all recognise that poverty is a controversial and highly politicised issue. Throughout the course of the past two centuries, politicians and policy makers have diagnosed the 'problem' of poverty in different ways. Unsurprisingly, this has led to different prescriptions of the solution. Social and political constructions of poverty and their underpinning ideologically influenced assumptions play a fundamental role in determining whether or not there is the political commitment to respond to poverty and, crucially, what policies are seen as necessary and how they are implemented. As Gerry Mooney argued (in Chapter Four, this volume), we can broadly distinguish between explanations of poverty that blame individuals and those that recognise structural causes for the existence of poverty. In the first section of this chapter we examine the principles on which policies have been based: whether or not policy makers have recognised poverty, how they have defined and conceptualised the issues and how these assumptions have influenced their policy design.

Of course, there are many ways in which the state can and does respond to poverty with policies generated across a wide range of areas including health, education, housing and neighbourhoods. However, for the purposes of this chapter we will focus on two key policy areas: employment policy and income maintenance (through social security and tax credits). In the next section we examine the role of key strategies, namely paid employment and social security, in tackling poverty and social exclusion. We consider the role and adequacy of social security benefits and tax credits in addressing poverty and social exclusion and identify key debates in the provision of financial support for people experiencing poverty. In conclusion, we draw together the previous sections to emphasise both continuity and change in the approaches of policy makers to the problems of enduring levels of poverty and social exclusion in the UK at the beginning of the 21st century.

History and development of anti-poverty policies in the UK

In this section we overview the main principles underlying key phases in the historical development of state approaches to poverty in the UK. In each period, it is evident that the government of the time took a distinctive approach to diagnosing the problem of poverty and designed policies to prescribe a solution. Interpreting the dominant ways in which social problems were understood during particular time periods and how these understandings fed into the policy-making process is a complex and imperfect exercise. What we present below is inevitably a simplification, but we highlight the assumptions behind the actual policies that are judged to have the greatest impact on people experiencing poverty.

Nineteenth-century Poor Laws: state intervention to deter pauperism

When we consider the origins of anti-poverty policies in the UK, it is important to recognise the significance of the Victorian Poor Laws as a definitive early stage of state intervention. The Poor Laws[1] established an enduring British perspective on the experience of poverty by firmly distinguishing between the 'deserving' and 'undeserving poor' (Fraser, 2003). This moralistic diagnosis saw 'the problem' as being caused by the individual behaviour of unmotivated working-age men who were thought to be able, but unwilling, to work (Thane, 1996). Based on this false assumption, the harsh workhouse system was 'not intended to reduce poverty but to deter pauperism' (Fraser, 2003, p 50) so that publicly funded support would only be offered as a last resort for those who were completely destitute.

The implementation of the system was met with concerted opposition, particularly in the north of England, where wages were paid at such a low level that it was often not possible to make living conditions less comfortable within the workhouses than it was for 'deserving' working-class people in employment. Even in the early years of the system, it became apparent that those at greatest risk of poverty and destitution were not, as predicted, fit working-age men, but, more often than not, women, people who were ill or had a disability, older people and children. The policy was based on a misdiagnosis of the problem and the punitive system that had been designed for one target group was, in practice, applied to a broad group of people with very different personal characteristics and needs, resulting in a large-scale incarceration of people experiencing poverty. The harsh conditions (envisaged as a deterrent and a punishment for people who were too lazy to work) were applied to people with complex needs, for whom no other formal services existed. Thus, the Poor Laws did not alleviate poverty, because they were never designed to.

Early 20th-century intervention: setting up areas of state responsibility for meeting needs

In the early 20th century, state approaches to understanding the issue of poverty began to change dramatically. New social investigators like Rowntree (2000, originally 1901) and Booth (1903) had drawn public and political attention to the nature and extent of poverty in York and London. The experience of the failing Poor Laws had highlighted areas of unmet needs among certain social groups, particularly in relation to older age, ill-health and unemployment. Understandings of poverty were moving away from moralism, towards more collectivist concerns for national efficiency (including the need for a fit and healthy fighting force). Push-and-pull factors created conditions that made it acceptable for the first time for the British government to take responsibility for making arrangements for these 'deserving' groups (Thane, 1996).

The Liberal government of the time opted for a mixed approach in welfare provision through direct services and social insurance. The first old age pensions were introduced in 1908. Significantly, these were funded through taxation and did not require employees to make contributions towards the scheme. In 1911, the UK's first government-led insurance-based schemes were introduced for unemployment and health. These were only available to particular groups of workers and mainly benefited male workers, rather than women, but nevertheless, this development marked a step-change in the state's understanding of poverty and anti-poverty action. For the first time the Westminster government recognised that it was responsible for assisting citizens to meet needs by providing them with money when they could not earn it themselves.

Establishment of the postwar welfare state: comprehensive action intended to prevent and alleviate poverty

The postwar welfare state was fundamentally intended, both explicitly and implicitly, to tackle poverty. The main assumptions of arrangements were that men would provide for their families through paid work, when they would contribute to insurance-based benefits. Women's contribution to the postwar reconstruction project was primarily intended to be in bearing and rearing children (Williams, 1989; Lewis, 1992). The problem was seen to be interruptions in earnings and the solution was a comprehensive system of social security benefits, which were to be paid at times when people were not able to provide for themselves, for example, if they were unemployed, pregnant, ill or disabled. An important principle of the system was that it was respectable and reciprocal – workers paid National Insurance contributions when in work, in order to earn their entitlement to benefits in times of need. The system was intended to be holistic – to provide for people 'from the cradle to the grave'. Social security benefits were intended to ensure people had income to prevent them experiencing poverty. It is difficult to understate the significance of these reforms, which gave ordinary people (and women in particular) access to services and cash benefits that had not previously been imagined. The principles and the policies of the postwar welfare state were solidly based on the prevention (through full employment, good health and adequate housing) and alleviation (via social security benefits) of poverty.

This was a crucial juncture for policy design, which offered a golden opportunity for eradicating poverty. However, the greatest flaw in the postwar strategy for tackling poverty was that steps were not taken to ensure that people would actually have enough income to afford basic necessities – either through paid work (because Beveridge's (1942 and 1944) proposals for a relatively generous minimum wage were ignored) or through adequate social security benefits for times when people were unable to work (see Timmins, 2001). The value of payments was never linked to calculations of the minimum costs of living (Brown, 1990; Atkinson, 1995). Social security benefits have therefore never provided even for the most basic level of subsistence and have been judged as one of the most austere of the postwar reforms (Tomlinson, 1998, p 74).

The implications of this approach had become apparent by the 1960s. Significant holes could be seen in the safety net that the postwar welfare state was intended to create (Lowe, 2004). Academics, principally Abel Smith and Townsend (1965), 'rediscovered' poverty (of course, for those experiencing poverty the deficiencies of policies were already quite apparent). It became clear that the welfare state was not living up to expectations – not only did poverty exist, but the problem was getting worse, rather than better. This recognition of poverty led to high-profile anti-poverty campaigns from organisations like the newly established Child Poverty Action Group (CPAG), which lobbied for changes to social security benefits.

Rolling back the state: Thatcherism and the denial of poverty

In 1979, Margaret Thatcher came to power with an ideologically driven commitment to 'roll back the frontiers of the welfare state'. In the 1980s, mass unemployment (see Whiteside, 1991) was met with what some have termed a 'dismantling' (Pierson, 1994) of the welfare state, involving reducing spending, withdrawing from state finance and direct provision of services and creating an individualisation of the social rights that had been collectivised three decades earlier.

Under the Conservative governments (1979–97), individual responsibility became the order of the day and even the word 'poverty' disappeared from official documents and policy discourse. The political environment changed very radically towards neoliberal understandings of social problems, with a return to Victorian moralism and a reinterpretation of social divisions that reduced the problem of poverty merely to the experience of social inequality – which was seen as necessary for creating competition in the free market. For 18 years, the UK government denied the existence of poverty and designed policies that primarily benefited wealthier citizens – reducing higher rates of income tax and creating tax breaks, while simultaneously reducing the real value of social security benefits (with annual uprating of benefits being changed in line with prices, rather than wages) and tightening the criteria for entitlement. This policy approach resulted in rises in income inequality, as well as increased poverty. By deliberately ignoring and misinterpreting the problem of poverty, the Conservative governments set in place priorities (that is, cost-cutting and the economic priority of controlling inflation), policies (especially in tax and social security) and delivery arrangements (for example, the marketisation of welfare services) that have left a lasting legacy which has proven hard to shift. The results of this approach towards poverty and wealth were seen in increased poverty rates and increased income inequality (see Chapter One, this volume).

Throughout the past two centuries, different governments have understood the problem of poverty in different ways. Broadly speaking, for two thirds of the 20th century, understandings of poverty developed incrementally and benefited from insights from social research. State interventions largely seemed set on a trajectory towards increasing intervention to tackle poverty that peaked with the collectivist postwar reforms, which had the potential to eradicate poverty (although this was never fully realised). During 1979–97, however, there was a major break in this trajectory when the Conservative governments came full circle in understanding poverty in the moralistic terms of the Victorians. In the late 20th century, this led to an enduring state-endorsed public stigmatisation of people experiencing poverty. The following section outlines the deep-seated tensions in Labour's new approaches to poverty (from 1997 onwards), which combine the ground-breaking commitment to eradicate child poverty with a continued adherence to moralistic views of adults who experience poverty.

Into the 21st century: New Labour and 'work for those who can'

Following the rapid increase in relative poverty levels under the Thatcher and Major administrations, the 1997 Labour government inherited some of the worst levels of poverty among rich countries, combined with public attitudes that had been hardened towards the experience of poverty. Although Labour initially stuck to the tight fiscal plans of the outgoing Conservative government (including the abolition of One Parent Benefit and the Lone Parent Premium of Income Support – a deeply unpopular move with anti-poverty groups), their recognition of poverty was radically different from that of their predecessors. However, considerable tensions persist in the current Labour government's diagnosis of the problem of poverty. On the one hand, their adoption of a relative definition of poverty demonstrates an accurate understanding of what poverty is and how it affects people. On the other hand, the Labour governments since 1997 have sought to redefine citizenship rights and responsibilities (through policy design and the discourse that surrounds it) in a way that stigmatises involuntary experiences (such as unemployment), personal circumstances (illness and disability) and activities (caring work, either for children or for ill or disabled adults, including older people) that were previously recognised as legitimate causes for absence from the labour market. Examples of Labour's adoption of aspects of individual behavioural explanations of poverty are clear in documents that aim to move adults 'off benefits and into work', where the 'problem' is at least partly presented as 'dependency' (see, for example, DWP, 2006, 2007b). Citizens are primarily expected to contribute to wider society through their engagement in paid work and this is presented as the door to 'independence'. There are several key dimensions to Labour's approach to poverty and social exclusion and these are outlined below.

Ending child poverty?

In 1999, Tony Blair promised to 'end child poverty forever' (Blair, 1999). Following this pledge, progress milestones were established to reduce child poverty by a quarter by 2004/05 and halve it by 2010/11 on the route to eradicating child poverty by 2020. The Labour government consulted widely on how to define and measure poverty and this led to a well-informed understanding of the problem that they had committed to tackling. A very detailed set of targets and indicators were set out in the *Opportunity for All* (1999) report (see **Box 13.1**), which have subsequently been monitored annually in order to measure progress towards the goals. The combination of an ambitious target tied into a specific timescale with a transparent and unequivocal system for measuring progress makes this the most robust strategy for eradicating child poverty that the UK has ever seen. Should the government fail to meet their targets, change their commitment or alter the emphasis of their goals, this will be immediately apparent to independent observers.

> **Box 13.1: *Opportunity for All***
>
> Since 1999, the UK government has produced annual reports in the *Opportunity for All* series (see www.dwp.gov.uk/ofa/). These reports detail progress towards meeting a series of specific goals in tackling poverty and social exclusion; in some cases targets relate to Britain, although many are only for England because responsibility for policies in fields such as education lies with devolved governments in other parts of the UK. There are 41 indicators in total, relating to the following groups:
>
> - children and young people, for example, proportion of children and young people in relative poverty or in inadequate housing, teenage pregnancies, smoking;
> - people of working age, for example, proportion of people: in employment, rough sleeping;
> - people in later life, for example, proportion of older people being helped to live independently;
> - communities, for example, life expectancy, fear of crime, road accidents in deprived areas, fuel poverty.
>
> Each report monitors progress in terms of change since 1999 and the direction of recent change (that is, trend moving in the right or wrong direction or broadly staying the same). This series of reports is a demonstration of the UK government's commitment to tackling poverty and social exclusion.

So, how have they done so far? According to the main headline figure (the number of households with incomes below 60% of the median), child poverty fell sharply for the six years following the pledge (Hirsch, 2006). Such rapid progress is unprecedented and shows that the policy approach was initially effective. This progress has been achieved primarily by a Work First approach (Finn, 2003), underpinned by a fundamental reform of the tax and social security systems (Millar, 2003), which has depended on moving large numbers of parents into work. The lowest earnings have been protected for the first time by the introduction of the National Minimum Wage in 1999 and low wages have been topped up using the Working Tax Credit (which replaced the Working Families' Tax Credit and Disabled Person's Tax Credit in 2003[2]). This strategy of 'making work pay' has also been paralleled with a set of policies to 'make work possible' (Millar, 2002), which has included the National Childcare Strategy (which has had some success in increasing the availability of high-quality affordable childcare) and employment information and advice provided by personal advisers to a range of benefit recipients through New Deal programmes and work-focused interviews. In addition to this, some increased financial support has also been directed to low-income families through the Child Tax Credit (CTC, introduced in 2003), which provides extra money for households with children and can partly be used to contribute to the costs of childcare for working parents. The CTC is quite a different sort of intervention because it does not contain a work incentive and its coverage is close to universal; therefore it is much more concerned with longer-term social investment in children (see Ridge, 2003; Lister, 2004).

By 2005, 700,000 fewer children were living in poverty than in 1999. This was a major achievement, with a rate lower than at any time in the previous 15 years and meaning that the UK no longer had the highest child poverty rate in the EU (Harker, 2006). Unfortunately, this equated to a 17% reduction in child poverty by the date of the first milestone and fell short of the 25% that was aimed for. As Hirsch argues, although this 'record is impressive relative to the past, it risks looking wholly inadequate relative to the stated ambitions for the future' (2007, p 2). Furthermore, in 2007, reductions in child poverty rates flattened off for the first time since the pledge and showed that progress was losing momentum (Hirsch, 2007). Analysts have argued that 'if no further action is taken on policy, the child poverty rate is unlikely to fall significantly' (Harker, 2006, p 11). The Work First strategy is stalling and a step-change in policy is required, along with substantial new resources, in order for child poverty to be reduced by half by 2010 and eradicated by 2020.

Older people

Alongside the stated commitments over reducing child poverty, Labour at the same time illustrated its concerns over pensioner poverty, with relatively substantial increases to Income Support for pensioners channelled through the Minimum Income Guarantee and now Pension Credit (both means-tested benefits). Additional small financial increases have been given through winter fuel payments.

Work for those of working age: constructing discourses of desert

It is noteworthy that Labour's most high-profile anti-poverty interventions have been directly aimed primarily at those who can be readily characterised as 'deserving'. Certainly, there is a dispassionate justification for tackling child poverty as a priority since, in 1997, poverty rates were higher for children than for people of working age or those over the age of 65. However, since child poverty was only a few percentage points higher (Hirsch, 2006), it is conceivable that children were chosen as the primary target group because of their 'deserving' status. Policy developments that have been designed for adults of working age have been presented in a much less sympathetic light. A series of welfare reforms have reinforced the distinction between people currently in work, who are presented as independent and 'deserving', and people who are currently out of work, who are presented in a derogatory way as 'dependent' with a strong implication that they are undeserving of financial support from the state. This division is confused by giving the false impression that having a job necessarily alleviates poverty (see, for example, DWP, 2007b). This view means that:

> dependence on state benefits is now believed by New Labour as well as Conservatives to sap character and to result in undesirable, passive behaviour … welfare is held to destroy incentives to work and the capacity for living an independent existence. (Lewis, 1998, p 4)

Labour's policy has been to increase the proportion of the population in work and enhance their support through more generous tax credits. Although the government has significantly increased payments for children through the new CTC, these increases have to some extent been diluted by the lack of increased support for non-working parents. There has been no increase in adult payments of Income Support or Jobseeker's Allowance and these means-tested assistance benefits have continued to reduce in relation to average earnings.

Area-based anti-poverty initiatives

Historically, the UK government has placed a large degree of emphasis on a categorical approach to anti-poverty interventions, mainly through transferring cash according to types of circumstances, for example, for unemployed people, people who are sick or disabled, or lone parents. However, particularly since the 1960s (see Berthoud et al, 1981), another important approach has been to identify specific geographical locations where disadvantages are concentrated and to fund local projects for limited time periods to tackle specific aspects of poverty in these places. Such area-based anti-poverty initiatives have been an important part of the way that central government has organised anti-poverty intervention and have been significantly revived by the Labour government since 1997 (Alcock, 2006). Focusing on particular localities can have advantages in understanding specific situated experiences since the spatial distribution of poverty and wealth is unequal (see Chapter Six, this volume). However, this approach is problematic because any given place is likely to contain greater numbers of people who do not experience poverty than those who do; conversely more people who experience poverty will live outside of the area than in it (Townsend, 1979). This means that some people who do not need extra support will be eligible for it, whereas, perhaps more importantly, other people who need support will not qualify for it. Placing neighbourhoods at the centre of attention can also be related to the assumption that poverty is mainly caused by individual (mis)behaviour, thereby diminishing the importance of wider inequalities, economic events, labour market changes and social relations in explaining poverty and neglecting the importance of more wide-ranging policy solutions, such as ensuring the adequacy of wages and social security benefits (Alcock, 2006).

Locality-based projects have tended to be short-term and target-driven. They are coordinated and funded by central government (or devolved administrations) through competitive tender processes. A range of organisations, including the voluntary sector and private companies, deliver services that are mainly intended for people in very specific locations. In England, the Social Exclusion Unit played an important cross-departmental role in coordinating these activities. Its role changed in 2002, when it was moved to the Office of the Deputy Prime Minister, from where it now works with other parts of government, such as the Neighbourhood Renewal Unit and the Homeless and Housing Support Directorate to tackle social exclusion in England. The Social Exclusion Task Force continued to head a cross-departmental approach to tackling social exclusion. Recent area-based initiatives, such as the New Deal for Communities, Action Zones for Employment, Health or Education, and Sure Start, have emphasised partnership working, the involvement of local communities and evidence-based service development (for further details, see Alcock, 2006). Although these initiatives are intended to be more long-term than preceding area-based initiatives, they are still time-limited and another criticism of this type of approach is that effective services can be curtailed because of a lack of funding, rather than a lack of need.

Changing state: devolution and the potential for diverse approaches to anti-poverty policy within the UK

The Labour government instigated another very important shift in state approaches to tackling poverty when they held referenda on devolution in Scotland and Wales. Since 1999, the central UK 'state', in the form of the Westminster government apparatus, has relinquished control over key areas of social policy to the Scottish Parliament and the Welsh Assembly, including health, education, transport and social justice. The process of devolution has been much more complex and disjointed in Northern Ireland, but it should be noted that distinct arrangements already existed pre-1997 and since then have been developed partially under the auspices of the Northern Ireland Executive and Assembly. Overall, the implications of this decentralisation of power for the development of anti-poverty policy are mixed. Firstly, the ruling parties in Scotland, Wales and Northern Ireland have matched the UK government's goal of eradicating child poverty by 2020. This is highly significant because it reflects a broad cross-party recognition of both the existence of poverty and the need to take active steps to reverse the pattern of increasing poverty that was set in place by the Conservative governments (1979–97). Furthermore, this convergence around the commitment on child poverty firmly reinforces the high priority of anti-poverty policies – in contrast to the preceding policy-making era, when such an agreement would have been unimaginable.

However, the devolved administrations are limited in their capacity to fundamentally challenge poverty because Westminster retains reserved powers over the three crucial policy areas that influence people's incomes: social security,[3] taxation[4] (including tax credits) and employment (including Minimum Wage legislation). This means that although there is scope for some divergence in the strategies pursued by different administrations within the UK, it is the Westminster government that has the greatest role in setting and adjusting the policy instruments that have the capacity to directly and immediately reduce (or, alternatively, perpetuate) poverty. Nevertheless, in Scotland, Wales and Northern Ireland a number of separate policies and initiatives have been funded to prevent and alleviate different aspects of poverty and disadvantage. In Scotland, for instance, there has been a development of universal in-kind policies: for example, free eye tests for all, students in higher education do not directly pay tuition fees, long-term care for older people is free and all primary school pupils in Years 1-3 receive their school meals free (in five pilot areas). In a similar vein, the Welsh Assembly introduced free prescriptions. The devolved administrations each conduct research on poverty and have developed a series of policy documents for tackling child poverty, which continue to exert pressure on Westminster to increase the incomes of people experiencing poverty, regardless of employment status. Devolution also allows for a more localised understanding of the patterns and causes of poverty, which may lead to diverse policy solutions (see Kenway et al, 2006; Kenway and Palmer, 2007; McKendrick et al, 2007). Overall, the new strategies pursued in Scotland, Wales and Northern Ireland have tended to be less conditional on participation in paid employment and less punitive. While this is undoubtedly a reflection of their spheres of policy influence, it may also signify essential differences in the principles of policy making – with some signs of favouring universalism over selectivity.

Asset-based welfare[5]

In the early years of the New Labour administration, asset-based welfare was popular in political and academic debate as a significant new principle for provision (particularly in relation to citizenship rights and responsibilities). Asset-based welfare policies move beyond the traditional territory of state anti-poverty action, by providing and promoting asset holding, especially for those experiencing poverty (see Collard and McKay, 2006; Gregory and Drakeford, 2006; Paxton and White, 2006; Sodha and Lister, 2006). In principle, this approach has the capacity to address some of the fundamental inequalities in wealth that exist in the UK (see Chapter Two, this volume), since it acknowledges that the accumulation of assets, as well as income and living conditions (for example, housing or health services), plays and important role in preventing poverty.

Although there have been signs that asset-based welfare policies would develop (HM Treasury, 2000; DTI, 2005), particularly in order to promote personal savings for financial independence and to avoid over-indebtedness, actual policy developments have been limited. Of particular interest are the Child Trust Fund and the Saving Gateway. The Child Trust Fund was introduced in 2005 and gives every newborn child (since 1 September 2002) £250 as a lump-sum endowment, which they can access when they turn 18. Children in the poorest 40% of families receive an additional £250. A further government endowment is planned for children aged seven (again with a higher payment for those with the lowest incomes). This fits with a social investment model of welfare provision (Ridge, 2003; Lister, 2004). Similarly, the Saving Gateway scheme, which offers a matched savings account for low-income families, has been piloted twice in specific areas of England. At this stage it is not certain whether or not the Saving Gateway will be developed nationally. Evaluations of the pilots have shown positive signs that it can help promote saving, although it continues to be very difficult for people experiencing poverty to save money since their incomes are inadequate to meet basic needs (Collard and McKay, 2006). While these developments are significant in principle, the potential of new asset-based approaches to welfare provision remain largely unrealised.

In historical context, New Labour have been pioneers in committing to eradicate child poverty and have established a watershed in both the recognition of poverty (now acknowledged by all major political parties) and the necessity for action to tackle it. However, in practice there are strong tensions in Labour's discourse and policy design for different groups. On the one hand, a social investment approach has informed the development of socially just approaches to measuring child poverty and monitoring progress towards eradicating it. However, on the other hand, Labour have failed to rid themselves of the Victorian moralism that the preceding Conservative governments returned to. This tension has, as yet, prevented the radical policy changes (such as increasing benefit levels to ensure that they allow people to afford basic necessities and increasing minimum wages to a level that ensures working families can escape poverty) that are required to change the UK's position in international poverty leagues. The next section of this chapter examines in greater depth the efficacy of key strategies for tackling income poverty: employment and social security.

Evaluating the efficacy of key strategies in tackling poverty

For almost a century, UK governments, like the administrations of other rich nations, have depended very heavily on paid employment and social security as the primary means of ensuring that citizens are able to provide for their basic needs and thereby prevent or alleviate poverty. However, unlike the majority of European countries, poverty levels in the UK have remained persistently high into the 21st century. So what has the UK done differently? In this section, we examine the reasons why the anti-poverty potential of employment and social security have not yet been realised in the UK.

Paid employment

State interventions to prevent or alleviate poverty have always afforded a central role for paid employment. However, the potential for paid work to provide adequate resources to protect against poverty is not as straightforward as it might at first seem. The capacity for earnings to meet basic needs depends on their value in relation to: the cost of essentials (like housing, energy bills, clothing, food, travel and social activities); tax payments (for example, Council Tax, income tax, Value Added Tax); debt repayments (for instance to the Social Fund or for student loans); and child maintenance payments. Household income is also affected by income other than earnings (for example, child maintenance, which is critical for lone parents on low incomes, or interest on investments), and the regularity and reliability of other sources of income is a crucial consideration for people managing on a low income. In fact, despite the government conviction that 'work is the best route out of poverty' (DWP, 2007a), half of all children experiencing poverty live with a working parent (Hirsch, 2007). Added to this is the UK's overall high employment rates and long working hours.

Like many other countries, the UK has developed welfare-to-work policies since the late 1990s that individualise the responsibility for self-provision through paid employment (see Lødemel and Trickey, 2000; Peck, 2001; Clasen, 2002; Bryson, 2003b; Handler, 2003). This has served to emphasise the strategy of paid employment as the main route out of poverty and to delegitimise absence from the labour market. As pointed out earlier in this chapter, work is seen as the main route to 'independence'. However, there are two major problems with this approach to tackling poverty. Firstly, wages may be insufficient to prevent poverty and, secondly, not all citizens are able to work. The two main reasons for not being economically active are substantial caring responsibilities (either for children or sick/disabled adults) or being ill or disabled. Thus an inbuilt flaw of a Work First strategy to tackling poverty is that it:

> does not address the need that all societies have for unpaid work in the form of caring for the young and the old; work that is performed mostly by women, lone mothers included. Indeed, it effectively devalues this form of work. (Lewis, 1998, p 4)

Although policy has sought to address the standard of living for children and for pensioners, the focus on adults of working age has been preoccupied with facilitating employment. There have been considerable efforts to encourage and enable adults to take up paid work, both by tackling unemployment and by increasing the number of adults looking for work, including by the New Deal programmes, tax credits and efforts to increase childcare availability (see HM Treasury, 2004). The current aspiration is to raise the employment rate to 80%, well above the UK current rate (already high in international terms). Within this umbrella aspiration there are specific targets to increase the employment rates of: lone parents (a 70% employment rate target by 2010); disabled adults (an intention to reform Incapacity Benefit and to reduce the numbers on it by one million over 10 years); and older workers (see DWP, 2006).

Social security: state-provided income maintenance

The social security system is one of the most important means by which the state can ensure a measure of economic security through the redistribution of income. This redistribution can happen in several ways, through vertical redistribution (from richer to poorer), or through horizontal redistribution (between people whose circumstances differ, for example from those without children to those with children). Social security can also ensure that people have an income through their lifecourse, paying into the system (through National

Insurance contributions) when they are earning and drawing out (according to their payment records) in times of need like retirement or unemployment.

In addition to social security benefits, tax credits – wage top-up payments and payments for children delivered through the tax system – have come to play an increasingly significant role in the lives of low-income families. Tax credits, like social security benefits, are means tested and also have qualifying criteria such as age, family status and hours worked, although they tend to be considerably more generous than social security benefits.

Persistent tensions in welfare provision

As we have seen, social security has developed and changed over time. The term 'social security' and the ideals that underpin it are important, as Millar (2003) explains, 'the word "social" indicates that this is a shared system, we are all part of it – as contributors, as recipients, as tax payers, as citizens – and social security provisions involve various forms of redistribution that are an expression of our values as a society and our commitment to social and economic justice' (2003, p 7). Social security policy can have several different goals, it can be used to support people at times of need, but it can also play a significant role in reducing poverty and promoting social justice. However, as Millar also points out:

> views about goals and specifically the normative question of what
> policy goals should be, rest in turn upon different ideologies of
> welfare, upon different views about state and citizenship, and upon
> different views about human nature and motivation. (2003, p 2)

These different approaches and understandings of social security policy result in persistent tensions in the social security system about the role of social security, entitlement, generosity of payments and delivery mechanisms. *Box 13.2* sets out some of these long-standing debates.

Box 13.2: Ongoing debates in social security

Contributory benefits versus means testing
Should entitlement to benefits be earned or paid according to needs? **Contributory benefits** are strongly linked to rights. You pay money into a scheme through National Insurance contributions and you receive a benefit as of right in times of need, such as contribution-based Jobseeker's Allowance or a state pension. This stems back to the postwar Beveridge rights-based model of welfare. **Means-tested benefits** are different. To receive them your income

---

and assets are taken in to account. If you have more than the state allows then you are not entitled to the benefit or you receive a reduced amount. Means-tested benefits tend to be rule bound, restricted and often stigmatised, and this affects their take-up.

Universal versus targeted benefits, and the new 'progressive universalism'

Should benefits be paid to everyone or only those most in need? Universal benefits are non-contributory and non-means-tested, for example Child Benefit is paid to all families with children, and, because there is no stigma attached to the benefit and delivery is straightforward, the take-up rates are consistently high. Targeted benefits are directed at very low-income households and tend to be means tested and more stigmatised. 'Progressive universalism' is a new alternative that creates a compromise between the traditional debate of universalism and targeting. The best example of this is Child Tax Credit, which almost everyone with the main caring responsibility for dependent children is eligible for (hence something close to universalism is achieved) and payments are graduated according to income, with the highest payments going to people on lowest incomes.

Cash versus in-kind support

Should financial assistance be offered in cash or indirectly, for example, by voucher or free access to services? Most social security benefits are delivered in the form of **cash** for people to spend as they see fit. **In-kind** services are provided free or through vouchers. In some cases, eligibility to certain benefits operates like a 'passport' to entitlement for free goods or services, like free school meals for school children in England. This raises the issue of whether people should be entitled to spend their money in whatever way they wish, or whether the state should intervene in a more paternalistic way by providing more 'in-kind' support, for example to ensure the welfare of children through free school meal provision.

Benefits as a respectable right versus benefits as stigmatising

Should benefits be paid as a respectable right or as a stigmatising last resort? Notions of poverty that draw on stereotypes of the 'deserving' and 'undeserving poor' have a long history and are still prevalent in society today (see above). This can have a profound impact on how people are treated by the welfare state, especially through the social security system, where discourses of 'welfare dependency' pathologise people who need to rely on social security benefits to survive. Furthermore, as Lister argues (2004, p 111), 'in the UK a recurrent discourse of "fraud and abuse" continues to de-legitimize social security recipients'.

Social security and the relief of poverty

While social security is intended to provide support and security for those who cannot support themselves, the generosity of that support and its adequacy for people's needs is of central importance. Payments are concerned not only with support but also with incentives, and the social security system is often used as leverage to reward and/or penalise certain behaviour. Therefore, the system is about support but with control in mind.

Adequacy

A key issue in evaluating the capacity for social security benefits to prevent and alleviate poverty is the adequacy of the level at which they are paid. Quite simply, do benefits give people enough money to afford basic necessities? As Alcock argues 'social security may not have removed poverty; but it has certainly reduced its extent and depth' (1999, p 215). While benefits in the UK play an important role in protecting people from becoming destitute, they have never been paid at an adequate level to allow people to afford all of the basic necessities. This is one of the main reasons why poverty levels remain persistently high in the UK. Sainsbury and Morissens' (2002) comparison of 13 European countries examined the effectiveness of social security benefits in alleviating poverty. The study found that social security benefits in the UK were less effective in alleviating poverty than almost all of the other countries in the study. During the period of the study (the 1990s), in the UK, only four out of every 10 people were lifted out of poverty by social security. UK benefits are paid at a flat rate, which is set at a low, residual level and, unlike many other European countries, payments are not connected either to an individual's actual previous earnings or to average earnings of the whole population.

For people who have to rely on social security benefits for long periods of time – for example, lone parents and their children, pensioners and the long-term sick and disabled – the adequacy of social security benefit payments is critical to their well-being. Research evidence shows that long-term reliance on means-tested benefits has severe consequences, with many people experiencing considerable hardship, including ill-health, debt, poor housing and nutrition and a lack of the basic necessities that more affluent people take for granted in their daily lives (Howard et al, 2001; Hirsch, 2006). Kempson et al's (1994) meta-study of life on a low income showed that it was almost impossible to manage on a day-to-day basis while receiving means-tested benefits for any length of time, no matter how hard people tried to budget. The work of the Family Budget Unit at the University of York, which produces detailed baskets of goods and services to estimate the costs of a modest but adequate or low-cost but acceptable budget standard, have consistently highlighted the disparities between social security benefit payments and what is required for families to manage their needs and living costs (see Electronic resources below).

The adequacy of basic levels of benefit payments are further undermined by deductions in weekly benefit allowances of payments made for loan repayments and utility services, and in many cases people experience multiple deductions. This means that many families are trying to manage on weekly incomes that are well below the poverty line. Chief among these deductions are repayments for Social Fund loans that accounted for over 50% of deductions being made in 2005 (DWP, 2007a).

Delivery

How social security is administered and delivered is also a key issue. It is possible for the state to provide assistance that is supportive, facilitative, liberating, sustaining and protecting. However, policies can also be experienced as demeaning, controlling, humiliating and stigmatising. Both policy design and implementation can affect people's lives in very significant ways. *Box 13.3* provides one example of the importance of getting delivery right – free school meals for the children of benefit recipients in England and Wales.

Box 13.3: Being on the receiving end: free school meals for benefit recipients in England and Wales

In England and Wales, free school meals are usually only available to children whose parents receive means-tested social security benefits. This is a targeted approach for those with very low incomes. Research shows how the method of delivering selective free school meals in schools can be a critical factor in determining whether children and their families feel comfortable taking up their entitlement (Ridge, 2003; Tanner et al, 2003).

The method of delivery varies considerably between schools but in general it has been characterised by highly stigmatised rules. Different discriminatory practices include: lining up separately, having a paper/metal token, eating at a separate time and having your name called or kept on a list at the cash register. Understandably many children find the process of claiming their free meals to be too stigmatising and either opt out of provision or suffer considerable anxiety about the process. Here is Lisa talking about how difficult she found the process in her school:

'We used to have a paper token, which is little bits of paper and I'd go to the office and as soon as they'd give it to me I grab it in my hand and screw it in my pocket. I do this every day.... I just think the word benefits

---

sounds so harsh and like puts you really down so.' (Lisa, quoted in Ridge, 2005, pp 82-3)

The case of free school meals highlights how an important initiative – the provision of adequate nutrition to children who need it – can be undermined by insensitive delivery. Better systems are possible and there is now a growing trend towards the use of swipe cards for all children to pay for school meals. This system is proving very popular with children who are entitled due to their parents' receipt of benefits, since they can have their entitlement programmed into the card.

Buck and Smith (2003) argue that the operation and delivery of specially targeted schemes – like the Social Fund designed to support people in extreme financial hardship and crisis – gives us fundamental insights into how 'society' believes people who are living in poverty should be treated. 'Recurrent questions about the extent to which certain categories of people in poverty are to be deemed "deserving" or "undeserving" are effectively decided by the manner and extent to which their needs are met when they turn to the state for help in a crisis' (Buck and Smith, 2003, p xiii). *Box 13.4* sets out some of the problems associated with the Social Fund.

Box 13.4: The Social Fund

The Social Fund is a system of discretionary, cash-limited, lump sum loans and payments. Intended to provide support for social security claimants in exceptional hardship, it has been a cause of considerable controversy not least because of its single failure to meet people's needs.

The Social Fund is a discretionary system – decisions are made according to officials' discretion rather than hard and fast rules. Discretion in administration can be problematic for benefit recipients, as while some decisions respond appropriately to individual circumstances, many others appear inconsistent and irrational; discretion can also lead to discrimination against certain groups, including for people in minority groups (Platt, 2003; Rowe, 2003; Wright, 2003).

Below is the oral evidence from a Social Fund applicant Liz Forest given to the House of Commons Social Security Select Committee in 2001, which gives some idea of the challenges that asking for a Social Fund loan can present for people who are in extreme circumstances:

'You feel you are always in the wrong. You are very intimidated. They [agency staff] do not come across as real people. They do not accept that

your situation is probably the most distressing thing in your whole life....
They are very hard-hearted.' (quoted in Buck and Smith, 2003, p 94)

The Social Fund has been characterised by inadequate provision, inappropriately high repayment rates and the refusal of support to some of the most disadvantaged people on the grounds that they would be unable to repay the loan. There is substantial evidence that the Social Fund 'contributes to poverty and hardship for many people on low-incomes rather than alleviating it' (Becker, 2003, p 112).

Tax credits

Tax credits such as the Working Tax Credit are a key element of the government's welfare-to-work policies. They act as in-work wage supplements to support low-income families whose wage is inadequate. The policy intention is to encourage workless people into employment, even poorly remunerated employment, by rewarding work over welfare. Tax credits are considerably more generous than out-of-work support in the form of Income Support or Jobseeker's Allowance, continuing the principle of 'less eligibility' that was established by the Victorians. Tax credits linked to employment are believed to be more socially acceptable to claimants than highly stigmatised social security benefits (Millar, 2003).

Child support has also been used by the Labour government to provide incentives for lone mothers to seek low-paid employment. Unlike mothers receiving Income Support, lone mothers who move into employment receive all child support payments without deductions or means testing. This has contributed to the creation of a further hierarchy between working and non-working lone-mother families. With employed lone mothers receiving the more generous tax credits and full child support (if available), and workless lone mothers receiving more stigmatised, less generous Income Support with little or none of their child support (if available).

The social security and tax credit system has experienced considerable upheaval and change as a result of Labour's policy drive to end child poverty. By investing so heavily in 'making work pay' and welfare-to-work measures, tax credits have played a central role as incentives to employment. Furthermore, many people receiving tax credits are working at the most unstable end of the labour market, cycling between in-work tax credits and out-of-work Income Support, and research shows that some of the severest child poverty can be found in families that move between work and the benefits system (Harker, 2006).

Conclusion

This chapter has charted the development of state responses to poverty in the UK from the Poor Laws onwards. This illustrates different diagnoses of the 'problem' of poverty, particularly relating to dominant understandings of what poverty is and what it is caused by – broadly distinguishing between the individualistic models of human behaviour and responsibility and structural explanations that take a broader view of the context of social relations. Our account of the history and development of state responses to poverty also demonstrated the traditions and legacies of policy making, for instance in relation to the low levels of benefit payments in the UK. Another recurrent issue is the connection between judgements about human behaviour and provision of financial and in-kind support according to whether people are viewed as deserving of assistance or not.

In the early 21st century, reducing child poverty has proved very difficult and calls have been made for the Labour government to commit substantial resources to providing adequate support for families both inside and outside of the labour market. This raises challenges for the Work First approach that fundamental reform of the tax and benefit system has been based on. Furthermore, the consistency between the assumptions of governments led by opposing political parties means that there is now a consensus on previously contentious issues (Tonge, 1999; Bryson, 2003a) of conditionality and compulsion for benefit recipients. In this way, the Labour governments since 1997 have adopted significant aspects of individual behavioural explanations of poverty that have now come to be seen as almost indisputable. The tensions created by this ambivalence about the causes of poverty can be seen in the government's policy choices concerning different target groups. Paradoxically, while the Labour government of the early 21st century has adopted the most advanced understandings of poverty and social exclusion of any UK government and has made the historical commitment to eradicate child poverty, they have returned to the values of Victorian moralism to guide a substantial proportion of policy reforms.

Notes

[1] The main piece of legislation was the 1834 New Poor Law in England, although there were separate, parallel, systems operating in other parts of Britain. The 1834 Poor Law was not the first (the 1601 Poor Law was long established by this time), but the 1834 Act was significant for its radical centralisation and attempted comprehensiveness of approach.

[2] These were introduced in 1999 by the incoming New Labour government, but actually replaced previous in-work benefits that served the same function of topping up low wages (Family Credit was the direct predecessor). In fact it

was the Conservatives who first introduced this type of benefit in the 1970s (Family Income Supplement).

[3] Northern Ireland has historically had greater power than Scotland or Wales in determining social security policy, but since Westminster holds the purse strings, policies have rarely diverged significantly.

[4] The Scottish Parliament holds tax-varying powers but these have not yet been invoked.

[5] Many thanks to Michael Orton for the policy details and references provided in this section.

Summary

- This chapter has identified inadequate benefit rates and wage levels as important reasons for disproportionately high poverty levels in the UK.
- The history and development of state approaches to intervening in the field of poverty in key time periods have been outlined, highlighting: the ideologically driven diagnosis of the problem, the policy prescribed as the solution and the relationship between this and levels of poverty.
- The main aspects of current anti-poverty policies in the UK have been outlined.
- The efficacy of two key anti-poverty mechanisms, paid employment and social security, have been investigated.

Questions for discussion

- What relationships can we draw between a government's values and a government's commitment to tackle poverty?
- Why have high employment levels in the UK failed to eradicate poverty?
- Should social security benefits be paid at a level that ensures people are lifted out of poverty?
- How could caring responsibilities and activities be better valued in the UK?
- What policies would need to be implemented for poverty to be eradicated in the UK?

Further reading

For detailed accounts of the establishment of state intervention in anti-poverty policy see Fraser (2003) for the 19th and early 20th centuries; and Lowe (2004) and Timmins (2001) for insight into the postwar welfare state. Glennerster, H. (2006) *British social policy 1945 to the present* (Oxford: Blackwell) supplements these sources for the postwar period and provides further information for the 1970s, 1980s and 1990s. Use Alcock (2006), Millar (2003) and Pantazis, C. and Gordon, D. (eds) (2000) *Tackling inequalities: Where are we now and what can be done?* (Bristol: The Policy Press) for greater detail on the more recent policy situation.

Electronic resources

Policies continually change, so in order to keep up with developments, we recommend looking at the following websites.

UK
www.dwp.gov.uk – Department for Work and Pensions
www.cpag.org.uk – Child Poverty Action Group
www.unicef.org – UNICEF
www.oxfam.org.uk – Oxfam
www.poverty.org.uk – The Poverty Site
www.cabinetoffice.gov.uk/social_exclusion_task_force.aspx – Cabinet Office Social Exclusion Task Force
www.neighbourhood.gov.uk – Department for Communities and Local Government
www.york.ac.uk/res/fbu/ – The Family Budget Unit

Scotland
www.povertyalliance.org – The Poverty Alliance
www.cpag.org.uk/scotland – Child Poverty Action Group Scotland
www.povertyinformation.org – Scottish Poverty Information Unit
www.scottish.parliament.uk – The Scottish Parliament
www.scotland.gov.uk – The Scottish Government

Wales
www.childreninwales.org.uk/1725.html – Children in Wales
www.funkydragon.org.uk/en/fe/page.asp?n1=2 – Funky Dragon
www.makepovertyhistorywales.org.uk – Make Poverty History
new.wales.gov.uk

Northern Ireland
www.northernireland.gov.uk/ – Northern Ireland Executive
www.niapn.org – Northern Ireland Anti-poverty Network

References

Abel-Smith, B. and Townsend, P. (1965) *The poor and the poorest*, London: Bell.

Alcock, P. (1999) 'Poverty and social security', in R.M. Page and R. Silburn (eds) *British social welfare in the twentieth century*, Basingstoke: Macmillan.

Alcock, P. (2006) *Understanding poverty* (3rd edn), Basingstoke: Palgrave.

Atkinson, A.B. (1995) *Incomes and the welfare state: Essays on Britain and Europe*, Cambridge: Cambridge University Press.

Becker, S. (2003) '"Security for those who cannot": Labour's neglected welfare principle', in J Millar (ed) *Understanding social security: Issues for policy and practice*, Bristol: The Policy Press, pp 103-22.

Berthoud, R. and Brown, J. with Cooper, S. (1981) *Poverty and the development of anti-poverty policy in the UK*, London: Heinemann.

Beveridge, W. (1942) *Social insurance and allied services*, Cmd 6404, London: HMSO.

Beveridge, W. (1944) *Full employment in a free society*, London: Allen and Unwin.

Blair, T. (1999) 'Beveridge lecture', Toynbee Hall, 18 March (www.bris.ac.uk/poverty/Publication_files/Tony%20Blair%20Child%20Poverty%20Speech.doc, accessed 2/11/07).

Booth, C. (1903) *Life and the labour of the people in London*, London: Macmillan (original volume on East London published 1889).

Brown, J.C. (1990) *Victims or villains – Social security benefits in unemployment*, York: Joseph Rowntree Memorial Trust

Bryson, A. (2003a) 'Permanent revolution: the case of Britain's welfare-to-work regime', *Benefits*, vol 11, no 1, pp 11-17.

Bryson, A. (2003b) 'From welfare to workfare', in J. Millar (ed) *Understanding social security: Issues for policy and practice*, Bristol: The Policy Press, pp 77-101.

Buck, T. and Smith, R. (eds) (2003) 'Introduction'. in T. Buck and R. Smith (eds) *Poor relief or poor deal?: The Social Fund, safety nets and social security*, Aldershot: Ashgate, pp xiii-xviii.

Clasen, J. (2002) 'Unemployment and unemployment policy in the UK: increasing employability and redefining citizenship', in J. Goul Andersen, J. Clasen, W. van Oorschot and J. Halvorsen (eds) *Europe's new state of welfare: Unemployment, employment policies and citizenship*, Bristol: The Policy Press, pp 59-73.

Collard, S. and McKay, S. (2006) 'Closing the savings gap? The role of the Saving Gateway', *Local Economy*, vol 21, no 1, pp 25-35.

DTI (Department of Trade and Industry) (2005) *Tackling over-indebtedness: Annual report 2005*, London: DTI.

DWP (Department for Work and Pensions) (1999) *Opportunity for all: Tackling poverty and social exclusion*, First Annual Report, London: The Stationery Office.

DWP (2006) *A new deal for welfare: Empowering people to work*, London: The Stationery Office.

DWP (2007a) *Working for children*, London: The Stationery Office.

DWP (2007b) *In work, better off: Next steps to full employment*, London: The Stationery Office.

Finn, D. (2003) 'The "employment first" welfare state: lessons from the New Deal for Young People', *Social Policy and Administration*, vol 37, no 7, pp 709-24.

Fraser, D. (2003) *The evolution of the British welfare state* (3rd edn), Basingstoke: Palgrave.

Gregory, L. and Drakeford, M. (2006) 'Social work, asset-based welfare and the Child Trust Fund', *British Journal of Social Work*, vol 36, no 1, pp 149-57.

Handler, J. (2003) 'Social citizenship and workfare in the US and Western Europe: from status to contract', *Journal of European Social Policy*, vol 13, no 3, pp 229-43.

Harker, L. (2006) *Delivering on child poverty: What would it take?*, A report for the Department for Work and Pensions, London: The Stationery Office.

Hirsch, D. (2006) *What will it take to end child poverty? Firing on all cylinders*, York: Joseph Rowntree Foundation.

Hirsch, D. (2007) 'Where now on the long road to ending child poverty?', *Parliamentary Brief*, May.

HM Treasury (2000) *Helping people to save*, London: HM Treasury.

HM Treasury (2004) *Budget 2004, Prudence for a purpose: A Britain of stability and strength*, London: The Stationery Office.

Howard, M., Garnham, A., Finnister, G. and Veit-Wilson, J. (2001) *Poverty: The facts*, London: Child Poverty Action Group.

Kempson, E., Bryson, A. and Rowlingson, K. (1994) *Hard times? How poor families make ends meet*, London: Policy Studies Institute.

Kenway, P. and Palmer, G. (2007) *Monitoring poverty and social exclusion in Wales 2007*, York: Joseph Rowntree Foundation.

Kenway, P., MacInnes, T., Kelly, A. and Palmer, G. (2006) *Monitoring poverty and social exclusion in Northern Ireland*, York: Joseph Rowntree Foundation.

Lewis, J. (1992) *Women in Britain since 1945*, Oxford: Blackwell.

Lewis, J. (1998) '"Work", "welfare" and lone mothers', *Political Quarterly*, vol 69, no 1, pp 4-13.

Lister, R. (2004) *Poverty*, Cambridge: Polity Press.

Lødemel, I. and Trickey, H. (eds) (2000) *'An offer you can't refuse': Workfare in international perspective*, Bristol: The Policy Press.

Lowe, R. (2004) *The welfare state in Britain since 1945* (3rd edn), Basingstoke: Palgrave.

McKendrick, J., Mooney, G., Dickie, J. and Kelly, P. (eds) (2007) *Poverty in Scotland*, London: CPAG.

Millar, J. (2003) 'From wage replacement to wage supplement: benefits and tax credits', in J. Millar (ed) *Understanding social security: Issues for policy and practice*, Bristol: The Policy Press, pp 123-43.

Paxton, W. and White, S. with Maxwell, D. (eds) (2006) *The citizen's stake: Exploring the future of universal asset policies*, Bristol: The Policy Press.

Peck, J. (2001) *Workfare states*, New York: Guilford Press.

Pierson, P. (1994) *Dismantling the welfare state? Reagan, Thatcher and the politics of retrenchment*, Cambridge: Cambridge University Press.

Platt, L. (2003) 'Social security in a multi-ethnic society', in J. Millar (ed) *Understanding social security: Issues for policy and practice*, Bristol: The Policy Press, pp 255-76.

Ridge, T. (2002) *Childhood poverty and social exclusion: From a child's perspective*, Bristol: The Policy Press.

Ridge, T. (2003) 'Benefiting children? The challenge of social security support for children', in J Millar (ed) *Understanding social security: Issues for policy and practice*, Bristol: The Policy Press, pp 167-88.

Ridge, T. (2005) 'Feeling under pressure: low-income girls negotiating school life', in G. Lloyd (ed) *Problem girls: Understanding and supporting troubled and troublesome girls and young women*, London: RoutledgeFalmer, pp 23-36.

Rowe, M. (2003) 'Decision making processes', in T. Buck and R. Smith (eds) *Poor relief or poor deal?: The Social Fund, safety nets and social security*, Aldershot: Ashgate, pp 102-17.

Rowntree, B.S. (2000, originally 1901) *Poverty: A study of town life*, Bristol: The Policy Press.

Sainsbury, D. and Morissens, A. (2002) 'Poverty in Europe in the mid-1990s: the effectiveness of means-tested benefits', *Journal of European Social Policy*, vol 12, no 4, pp 307-27.

Sodha, S. and Lister, R. (2006) *The Saving Gateway: From principles to practice*, London: Institute for Public Policy Research.

Tanner, E., Bennett, F., Churchill, H., Ferres, G., Tanner, S. and Wright, S. (2003) *The costs of education*, London: CPAG.

Thane, P. (1996) *Foundations of the welfare state* (2nd edn), London: Longman.

Timmins, N. (2001) *The five giants: A biography of the welfare state* (2nd edn), London: HarperCollins.

Tomlinson, J. (1998) 'Why so austere? The British welfare state of the 1940s', *Journal of Social Policy*, vol 27, no 1, pp 63-77.

Tonge, J. (1999) 'New packaging, old deal?: New Labour and employment policy innovation', *Critical Social Policy*, vol 19, no 2, pp 217-32.

Townsend, P. (1979) *Poverty in the United Kingdom*, Harmondsworth: Penguin Books.

UNICEF (2007) *Child poverty in perspective: An overview of child well-being in rich countries*, Report Card 7, Florence: UNICEF Innocenti Research Centre.

Whiteside, N. (1991) *Bad times: Unemployment in British social and political history*, London: Faber and Faber.

Williams, F. (1989) *Social policy: A critical introduction*, Oxford: Polity Press.

Wright, S. (2003) 'The street-level implementation of unemployment policy', in J. Millar (ed) *Understanding social security: Issues for policy and practice*, Bristol: The Policy Press, pp 235-53.

Part Four

Prospects

fourteen

Conclusion

Tess Ridge and Sharon Wright

Introduction

> I am standing by the shore of a swiftly flowing river and I hear
> the cry of a drowning man. So I jump into the river, put my arms
> around him, pull him to shore and apply artificial respiration. Just
> when he begins to breathe, there is another cry for help. So I
> jump into the river, reach him, pull him to shore, apply artificial
> respiration, and then just as he begins to breathe, another cry
> for help. So back in the river again, reaching, pulling, applying,
> breathing and then another yell. Again and again, without end,
> goes the sequence. You know, I am so busy jumping in, pulling
> them to shore, applying artificial respiration, that I have no time
> to see who the hell is upstream pushing them all in. (McKinlay,
> 1975, cited in Sinfield, 2004)

We start this final concluding chapter with a quote from John McKinlay
(also alluded to in Chapter Four, this volume) about the importance of
looking 'upstream' for an understanding of what is happening 'downstream'.
McKinlay's analogy was originally applied to healthcare in the US, but it has
a strong resonance with the situation of poverty and inequality in the UK and
it highlights the need to focus 'upstream' on the 'root causes' of inequality and
poverty, if we are to gain a more sophisticated understanding of the underlying
factors that drive and shape unequal social and economic relationships in the
UK today. This book, by focusing 'upstream', where poverty and inequality and
wealth are generated, as well as 'downstream', where poverty and inequality are
experienced, gives us an opportunity to understand how wealth and riches can

be enhanced and privileged through relationships of power and advantageous social and economic policies. It reveals how poverty and inequality can be generated and exacerbated by unequal and exploitative social, economic and structural relationships. In this concluding chapter we review the key points made in each chapter of the book and conclude with a reflection on current social welfare policies and future prospects. The chapter begins with a summary of the main findings.

Main findings

In the first section of the book, Karen Rowlingson, Pete Alcock and Gerry Mooney set out to establish the key concepts used in the study of poverty, wealth and inequality. In Chapter Two, Karen Rowlingson explored the nature and manifestations of wealth and riches in UK society. Drawing out the distinctions between income wealth and asset wealth she highlighted the hidden nature of asset accumulation and wealth in our society, and revealed that while there had been considerable *measurement* of incomes in the UK, there was no clear *conceptualisation or definition* of 'the rich' or 'riches'. Rowlingson drew out a key distinction between income (a flow of money) and assets (a stock of money), and highlighted the difficulties of measuring riches in the form of income and assets accurately. However, what is clear is that the rich have very high levels of assets as well as high incomes. Examining the UK in the context of global inequalities, she highlighted the widening inequality gap between the rich and wealthy and those experiencing poverty and disadvantage. Outlining the rapid growth of income and asset inequality over the past 30 years, she revealed the rise of income inequalities in the 1980s and the growth, for the first time in a century, of asset inequality in the 1990s.

Unlike the difficulties apparent in the conception and measurement of wealth, the definition and measurement of poverty presents fewer fundamental problems as poverty has long been the subject of investigation, measurement and public scrutiny. Pete Alcock's chapter (Chapter Three) highlighted the contested nature of poverty and the challenge it presents. He distinguished poverty from wider inequality as the problem of 'being without'. Unlike wealth, poverty is seen as an unacceptable state of affairs and engenders a moral imperative to act. Inequality in society has less social and moral power, although trends in inequality tell us much about the social order and are closely linked to rises in both poverty and excessive wealth. Due to the contested nature of poverty, measurement and definition is complex. Poverty changes over time and a new focus on social exclusion has drawn attention to the importance of social relationships, and restricted access to resources, opportunities and participation. Social exclusion has not replaced poverty as a focus of concern but rather revealed further dimensions of disadvantage. This has resulted in the development of multidimensional poverty measures to capture the complexities and interrelationships between inadequate incomes, poor access to resources and reduced social, economic and political participation.

Alcock pointed to the dramatic increases in poverty that occurred in the UK in the 1980s, and highlighted the disproportionate risk of poverty experienced by children and families, people with disabilities and some minority ethnic groups. Both Alcock and Mooney highlighted the ways in which poverty was an experience of powerlessness and exclusion. People experiencing poverty have little say in how poverty is defined or addressed and this serves to construct people in poverty as the 'other', a group separated out from society.

Current government policy is focused towards addressing poverty, particularly child poverty; however, as Gerry Mooney's chapter (Chapter Four) has shown, different explanations of poverty influence different policy approaches. In the 1980s and 1990s, Conservative policy pursued a 'strategy of inequality' as a means of controlling the labour force and restructuring the welfare state through free market economics. These policies resulted in a dramatic rise in inequality and the number of people living in poverty. Mooney's chapter reminds us that the condition of poverty is not a natural or inevitable facet of society but rather a product of human social relations. Drawing on a structural approach to poverty he argued that poverty, wealth and inequality were related through unequal social and economic relations. He pointed to a range of factors including the organisation of the economy, labour market conditions, and access to education, health and housing, as structural forces that influenced life chances and opportunities. In his final section Mooney drew on a Marxist analysis to explore the role of social class relations in capitalist societies, concluding that exploitative social relationships inevitably result in inequality and poverty. These unequal class relationships, he argued, are fundamental to capitalism and cannot easily be addressed, diluted or managed through social policy alone.

The second part of the book examined the main divisions in the experience of inequalities in poverty and wealth. Each chapter addressed the dynamics and experiences of poverty and wealth in the context of different groups and situations. Nicola Yeates started this part of the book (Chapter Five) with an important examination of poverty and wealth as transnational and global processes. Yeates argued that structures of economic and political power shape nations' access to and control over resources. In this context wealth, poverty and inequality in the UK are a product of global as well as local relationships. In particular Yeates pointed to the disproportionate share of global wealth held by the UK in relation to its share of world population. These excesses of wealth highlight the importance of global economic relationships and the significance of wider relationships of power, institutional structures, and policies and practices that maintain unjust global distributions of economic resources. Yeates presented compelling evidence of extreme disparities between the richest and the poorest in the world, and highlighted the concentration of economic power and resources in the top tenth (especially the top one tenth of 1%) of the world's population. Yeates reminded us that addressing global inequalities was not about what 'other countries do', but, critically, about what happens in our own country and our relationships with others in the world.

In Chapter Six, Danny Dorling and Dimitris Ballas continued the focus on global as well as national and local inequalities by providing a valuable historical and geographical insight into the development of current divisions of wealth in society. Mapping and analysing social and economic change they revealed that socioeconomic and spatial polarisation is increasing locally, nationally and globally. At a national level the wealthy are becoming disproportionately wealthy, increasingly polarised and spatially segregated. As Dorling and Ballas pointed out, poverty and wealth are not opposite sides of the same coin, but rather extreme ends of a continuum, best seen as a very different sized, multifaceted, many-sided die. Each is related to the other, both entailed social exclusion from the norms of society. The 'exclusively wealthy' mainly lived in a ring of areas to the west of London in the south of England. For those in poverty, spatial concentrations of poverty meant that in some city areas over half of all households were living below the breadline. A 'pear-shaped' picture of economic development was revealed as 'productive' winners moved away from the majority of the population who lived in an underperforming bulge of regions. At a global level, Dorling and Ballas challenged the World Bank myth, generated by richer 'donor countries', that there was a convergence in world living standards. They showed instead a severe worldwide divergence in health, wealth and learning. Their analysis revealed a devastating picture of accelerating and deepening divisions of poverty and inequality across the world.

In addition to spatial distributions of wealth and poverty, there are further divisions of inequality, and the next five chapters explored the role of the deep social cleavages of gender, ethnicity, age and health in access to socioeconomic resources. These are not discrete categories and there is considerable interaction between them. Gill Scott's chapter (Chapter Seven) focused on gender issues and revealed important differences between men and women in their access to assets and economic resources. Both men and women are at risk of poverty although the risks, causes and consequences differ. Men's risk of poverty relates to unemployment, geographic location, ethnicity and lack of qualifications. Women have a much higher general risk of poverty and their position as the main carers of children can result in financial dependence on men. Labour market inequalities, poor childcare provision, unequal pay and interrupted employment histories lead to further disadvantage for women in older age, as they suffer from inadequate pension provision. However, Scott pointed to a growing trend for some women to have a stronger engagement with the labour market, considerably increasing their chances of accumulating wealth and assets. Inequalities between men and women can obscure the importance of inequalities between different groups of women in relation to class, health, family structure and ethnicity. Labour's anti-poverty policies have important gender implications and Scott highlighted some of the key provisions in relation to increased financial support for children, and additional support for lone parents to encourage them into employment. However, the government's strong emphasis on the economic welfare of children is not always in the best interests of women. Scott argued that there had been little attempt to address the costs of a lifetime of caring or gendered inequalities in the accumulation of wealth and assets.

Akwugo Emejulu's chapter (Chapter Eight) explored some of the explanations for the variation in levels of poverty and inequality of wealth and income between minority ethnic groups and between minority ethnic groups and the rest of the population. Emejulu's chapter reminds us that 'wealth' – as an accumulation of savings, investments and pensions – is a social construction, and that some minority ethnic groups may interpret and accrue wealth very differently. Emejulu's analysis revealed a highly diverse and complex picture of minority ethnic inequalities. Not all minority ethnic groups are disadvantaged or discriminated against in the same way; there is diversity and difference within groups and between groups. Whereas some Indian and Chinese men and women are managing to gain access to higher-paid employment and to accumulate wealth, other groups such as Bangladeshi, Pakistani, Black African, Black Caribbean and Other Black background groups experienced extreme labour market disadvantage and discrimination, which served to keep them concentrated in low-paid, low-skilled employment, where there was little opportunity to accumulate wealth. Emejulu argued that any understanding of the complex economic circumstances of minority ethnic groups and individuals must also be situated within the wider socioeconomic contexts of class and gender. For Pakistani and Bangladeshi women, traditional gender roles, parenting and elder care affect their participation in the labour market, while minority women who are in employment tend to be concentrated in low-paid, low-status work. Emejulu argued that the current policy focus on employment-led anti-poverty policies does little to address entrenched labour market discrimination or respond to the diversity of family structures and practices evident in minority ethnic households.

Chapters by Petra Hölscher and Jay Ginn both addressed the issue of age. Hölscher (Chapter Nine) looked at childhood and revealed the considerable depth of socioeconomic inequalities experienced by children. The eradication of childhood poverty by 2020 is a key policy aim of the current UK Labour administration, and Hölscher revealed that although child poverty rates have fallen, there were still substantial numbers of children living below the poverty line. Hölscher's chapter revealed the multidimensional impact of poverty and social exclusion on children's lives. Exploring poverty from a rights-based approach she highlighted children's legitimate claims on society for a secure and enriching childhood. The importance of children's economic well-being is often couched in terms of their future outcomes as adults and workers, the 'social investment approach'; however, as Hölscher pointed out, the impact of poverty on children's current situation in childhood was also a critical issue that needed to be addressed. Labour's policies to eradicate child poverty focused strongly on welfare-to-work measures, new services for children and young people and increased cash benefit provision for children; however, to continue to reduce child poverty and to meet the government's target for a 50% reduction by 2010 there had to be increased investment in benefits and tax credits as well as in education.

Jay Ginn's chapter (Chapter Ten) examined the financial circumstances of older people, and the variation of income and material assets among different age groups. Poverty in old age has severe consequences for people who are unable to improve their financial circumstances through labour market participation and they are reliant on pensions and means-tested state benefits for their incomes. As in previous chapters a lack of financial and material resources reflected gender, class and ethnic inequalities generated during working life. Poverty affects at least one fifth of older people, and single older women are disproportionately likely to be reliant on inadequate, means-tested state benefits. The pension system perpetuates inequality between older people, in particular differences between public and private pensions. Means-tested benefits are delivered through the Pension Credit system, which has been instrumental in stabilising pensioner poverty. However, Ginn argued that the delivery of support for older people through complex and stigmatised means-tested benefits rather than through National Insurance pension entitlements resulted in poor take-up rates as older people experienced claiming benefits as confusing, intrusive and demeaning. The need for the Pension Credit arose from the meanness and inadequacy of British state pensions, and Ginn's chapter reminds us of the critical role played by government policy in mediating the risks of poverty, particularly for groups such as older people who are at an especially high risk.

The chapter on health by Mary Shaw, Ben Wheeler, Richard Mitchell and Danny Dorling (Chapter Eleven) tackled the long-standing link between poverty, inequality and ill-health. It revealed that, despite overall improvements in general health and life expectancy, income-based health inequalities still persisted. A wealthy lifestyle brought good health and longevity, while people experiencing poverty were more likely to suffer poor health, increased risks of disability and chronic illness and die early. Chronic ill-health and disability could be both a cause and a consequence of poverty and Shaw et al pointed to the damaging interaction between exclusion from the labour market through ill-health and the disadvantages of long-term reliance on inadequate levels of means-tested benefits, which fail to cover both everyday needs and the additional costs related to disability. In contrast, wealth and affluence could buy a range of social and material advantages that had an impact on health, including better housing, clean and healthy environments, good nutrition and the time and money to participate fully if desired in social and cultural life. Wealth and affluence could also purchase the advantages of private screening and healthcare. Shaw et al's analysis of inequalities in access to healthcare revealed how health inequalities were further exacerbated by inequities in healthcare access and provision.

The final part of the book examined the role of the state in mediating inequalities in income, poverty and wealth. In Chapter Twelve, Michael Orton focused on state approaches to wealth and revealed that there was considerable scope across a range of policy areas for the government to influence wealth accumulation and inequality. He focused on two key areas: taxation and the provision of public services. Orton showed how different taxes, and forms of taxation, impacted differently on affluent and low-income households. In particular 'tax breaks' and 'legal' tax avoidance acted to preserve wealth and protect assets. These fiscal advantages were only part of the 'hidden welfare state', which disproportionately favours the wealthy. Orton looked critically at the assumption that 'the rich pay taxes and the poor receive the benefits', and argued that the considerable fiscal advantages accruing to the wealthy through 'tax loopholes' and 'allowances' and the extra benefits that the middle classes gained from universal public-funded services like health and education, were largely hidden and went unremarked on. The voluntary self-exclusion of the richest, serviced by private education and healthcare and living in gated communities, was also a significant concern. Contrasting this trend with the enforced social exclusion of those in need, Orton argued that this voluntary exclusion could have powerful repercussions for society and social cohesion.

In Chapter Thirteen, Tess Ridge and Sharon Wright explored state approaches to dealing with poverty, social exclusion and inequalities. This chapter focused on two key areas of policy: social security through the tax and benefits system and employment policy including welfare-to-work policies. The chapter began with a historical overview of the role of the state in alleviating poverty, and revealed how social, political and ideological constructions of poverty played a fundamental role in determining political commitment to respond to poverty, the types of policies that were proposed and how they were implemented. The enduring legacy of the Poor Laws, including the principle of 'less eligibility' and pernicious and persistent assumptions about the 'deserving' and 'undeserving poor', are still present in some form in today's policy climate. The historical overview ended with Labour's pledge to end child poverty and a policy agenda that was underpinned by a strong welfare-to-work agenda. Social security benefits and tax credits play a key role in addressing poverty and social exclusion and Labour have used this system to increase support for children and families and to try and make work pay through tax credits. However, Ridge and Wright revealed persistent tensions within the social security system about the role of social security, entitlement, generosity of payments and delivery mechanisms. Increased means testing, stigma and inadequate provision undermined social security as a safety net and led to a two-tier system of support which privileged employment and penalised people who were not in paid employment. Labour's welfare-to-work policies are based on an individualised citizenship responsibility to work and have served to reinforce the stigmatisation of benefit recipients as 'welfare dependent', with 'independence' being constructed as possible only through paid employment. This has devalued the role of unpaid carers and delegitimised absence from the labour market. This form of welfare-to-work policy is limited in its capacity to tackle poverty, not least of all because of the low levels of minimum wages. Policy dilemmas exist for those who are unable to work, through ill-health, disability or caring responsibilities (for example, lone parents). Eradicating poverty for these groups will have to involve an approach beyond paid employment.

Final reflections

The main purpose of this book has been to develop a conceptual understanding of wealth, inequality and poverty. Its central premise is that poverty and inequality cannot be understood or adequately addressed without an equally clear critical understanding of richness and wealth and its role in society. Throughout the book we examined inequalities in the distribution of resources (income and assets) between different social groups in the UK, and we considered them in relation to key policy interventions. It is evident from the contributions of authors who are experts in their field that the UK is in the grip of an extremely powerful and damaging trend towards growing social inequality, with entrenched poverty and disadvantage at one end of the socioeconomic spectrum and excessive accumulation of riches concentrated in the hands of a privileged minority at the other.

The study of richness and wealth is a relatively new field of research and it is apparent that much of the dynamic processes of wealth creation and asset accumulation lie hidden from view. There are no clear indicators or measures of wealth and assets and no real public or political scrutiny of the amassment of riches on a national or international scale. The economic and political means by which privilege and economic status are preserved and enhanced are also obscured. It is clear from Orton's chapter (Chapter Twelve) that government policies can play a key role in the preservation of privilege and the accumulation of wealth and assets. Yet there is a 'natural' assumption that wealth creation is necessarily a good thing and that there is no role for the government to play in managing or moderating excessive wealth and asset accumulation. A lack of critical and political will to acknowledge and address the intimate links between richness, poverty and inequality have stifled public awareness of the damaging socioeconomic impact of largely unfettered opulence and privilege.

In stark contrast to the hidden and mainly untempered world of privilege, the harsh realities of poverty and disadvantage have always been the subject of public scrutiny, policy intervention and control. The role of policy is critical; however, as we have seen, social welfare policies to address poverty and disadvantage are generated by different political regimes and informed by diverse understandings and explanations of the underpinning causes and consequences of poverty. At the time of writing there is a Labour administration with a strong commitment to eradicate child poverty. This is in stark contrast to the Thatcher administration of the 1980s, which pursued a 'strategy of inequality' as part of a policy drive to roll back state provision and allow free market competition. This resulted in a devastating increase in the number of people living below the poverty line. Even so, under Labour, inequality is continuing to rise and what Dorling and Ballas have called a 'pear-shaped' Britain has emerged (see Chapter Six). Although current policies to address poverty across a range of areas, including health and education, have an important role to play in reducing child poverty, there has been a general lack of political will to intervene in adult poverty – other than through welfare-to-work programmes – and little or no policy impetus to address wealth, or rising socioeconomic inequality.

The main policy thrust at this time has been towards eradicating child poverty, with children an appropriate focus for intervention given the disproportionate numbers who are living below the poverty line. However, children (although not their parents) are seen as safe political subjects for welfare interventions and Labour's child-poverty policies are heavily informed by a 'social investment' approach that focuses on children's future worth as workers. Labour's child poverty strategy depends very heavily on welfare-to-work policies, with support for low-income workers, but a reluctance to raise the incomes of parents who are out of work, in line with enduring principles of 'less eligibility'. The dangers of relying heavily on work-led policies have been exposed throughout the book, especially in relation to long-term gender discrimination and caring issues for women, insecure employment conditions, low pay and entrenched racial discrimination in the labour market. Several of the chapters have argued that welfare-to-work is not a sufficient answer to the unequal distribution of wealth in the UK (and globally), which results in millions of people experiencing poverty. Poverty for older people has also been targeted with the introduction of the Pension Credit. However, current pension policy on both sides of the political spectrum favours encouraging private pension provision and limiting public pensions and this is likely to result in the perpetuation of inequality, stigma and means testing in older age.

Prospects

What does the future hold? We have seen that poverty cannot be tackled without addressing wider inequalities and wealth, yet there appears to be no political will to do so. It is clear that anti-poverty policies still have strong elements of control and, despite a political climate that is more conducive to social justice, enduring notions of the 'deserving' and 'undeserving poor' can still be detected in government discourse and policy formulations.

The Labour government has set itself challenging targets and child poverty is proving difficult to reduce. There are already key tensions in the welfare-to-work approach and unless adequacy of benefits for parents out of work is addressed Labour's deadlines are unlikely to be reached. There is an underlying ambivalence in Labour's policy design and eradicating child poverty is at present based on a structural understanding of poverty, in sharp contrast to the more individualistic diagnosis of poverty within welfare-to-work programmes. A change of government is possible and could signal a change of direction. There are also significant changes in policy directions emerging in the new devolved administrations. At the time of writing, Labour's commitment to eradicate child poverty still remains strong; however, a change to focus on children and families in the 'severest' poverty may signal a move towards different, more individualistic explanations of poverty, and associated policy prescriptions concerned more with 'sticks' than 'carrots' around encouraging people into work or around lifestyles or parenting.

We have seen the dominance of the employment agenda and the tensions within it, but there is also a clear limit to labour market policies that cannot and do not adequately address caring responsibilities (children and elder care), or the financial security of those who cannot work. Without policies to address caring responsibilities, especially given the policy push towards more private pension provision that makes no allowance for periods of unpaid caring work, women will continue to be pension-poor, perpetuating their predominance among those who need to claim means-tested benefits in later life. The issue of income adequacy in social security benefits remains fundamental to any prospect of reducing poverty and inequality and delivering secure safety net provision for those who cannot work and are forced to rely on social welfare.

Finally, there is an urgent need for UK governments to find the political will to address processes of wealth and asset accumulation, and to respond to the concentration of wealth among the privileged elite. Rising trends in socioeconomic inequality threaten the stability and fabric of our society.

Extreme wealth and privilege in the UK is also disproportionate to an equitable distribution of the world's wealth, and it is essential that there is recognition that processes of power and the control of economic resources play a significant role in the generation and perpetuation of poverty and inequality at a global as well as a national level.

References

McKinlay, J.B. (1975) 'A case for refocusing upstream: the political economy of sickness', in A. Enelow (ed) *Behavioral aspects of prevention*, Houston: American Heart Association.

Sinfield, A. (2004) 'Preventing poverty in market societies', Paper presented at 'European Social Policy: Meeting the Needs of a New Europe', ESPAnet Conference, Oxford, 9–11 September.

Index